EXPLORING LAW'S EMI
THE JURISPRUDENCE
RONALD DWORKIN

Exploring Law's Empire:

The Jurisprudence of Ronald Dworkin

Edited by
SCOTT HERSHOVITZ

OXFORD
UNIVERSITY PRESS

*This book has been printed digitally and produced in a standard specification
in order to ensure its continuing availability*

OXFORD
UNIVERSITY PRESS

Great Clarendon Street, Oxford OX2 6DP
United Kingdom

Oxford University Press is a department of the University of Oxford.
It furthers the University's objective of excellence in research, scholarship,
and education by publishing worldwide. Oxford is a registered trade mark of
Oxford University Press in the UK and in certain other countries

© the several contributors 2006

The moral rights of the author have been asserted

Reprinted 2012

Crown copyright material is reproduced under Class Licence
Number C01P0000148 with the permission of OPSI
and the Queen's Printer for Scotland

British Library Cataloguing in Publication Data
Data available

Library of Congress Cataloging in Publication Data
Data available

ISBN 978-0-19-954614-5

Preface

The plan for this book was simple: ask leading scholars in jurisprudence and constitutional law who are sympathetic to Ronald Dworkin's work to write essays about it. The invitation was open-ended. Authors were asked to contribute to Dworkin's project by offering new arguments for old conclusions, by offering new arguments for new conclusions consistent with Dworkin's project, by filling gaps, or by criticizing Dworkin's work to show how it could be improved. We hoped that in putting together a collection of such essays, and by asking Dworkin to respond to them, we would enrich the discourse to which Dworkin has contributed so much.

With such an open-ended invitation, we were bound to get an eclectic mix of essays, and that was the point. The scope of Dworkin's contributions to our understanding of law is vast. He has made seminal contributions to debates over doctrinal and theoretical issues in American constitutional law, to debates over topics such as civil disobedience and the obligation to obey the law, and, of course, to our understanding of the nature of law and its relationship to morality. And this list leaves unmentioned much of Dworkin's groundbreaking work in political and moral philosophy, which has had a significant impact on legal discourse. We therefore set authors loose with the charge that they should engage with whatever aspect of Dworkin's work they saw fit, not simply to honor it, but to increase our understanding of it and push it forward. In that way, we hoped to produce a book that would explore the full richness of Dworkin's contributions to our understanding of law's empire.

While there is no overall theme to the book that resulted, a number of themes recur throughout. Justice Breyer's introductory essay recounts a discussion Dworkin led at a conference of international judges. Justice Breyer goes on to describe how Dworkin's work has influenced the way judges on constitutional courts around the world conceive of their role in democratic societies.

Dworkin's constitutional theory is further examined in essays by Chris Eisgruber, Jim Fleming, and Rebecca Brown. Eisgruber and Fleming address the role of history in Dworkin's moral reading. Eisgruber argues that history has a more significant role in Dworkin's account than many recognize. But he argues that the moral reading as Dworkin presents it does not provide a fully satisfactory account of constitutional interpretation because it does not adequately explain how American-style constitutionalism, which requires a legislative supermajority to overrule a constitutional decision, facilitates government based on principles of justice. Fleming's essay examines the relationship between Dworkin's moral reading and both process-oriented and originalist approaches to constitutional interpretation. Brown's essay explores the influence that Dworkin has had on the development of constitutional law in the United States. She focuses on the ways in which Dworkin's constitutional theory helped scholars come to terms with *Brown v. Board of Education*, and she traces Dworkin's influence on contemporary constitutional law.

Essays by Susan Hurley and Scott Hershovitz transition the book from explorations of Dworkin's constitutional theory to explorations of his legal theory more generally. Hurley argues for the somewhat counterintuitive view that the content of the law is not simply a function of actual cases which courts have decided, but is also a function of hypothetical cases which courts have not and may never be called upon to decide.[1] She develops a coherence account of legal reasoning similar to Dworkin's, and she addresses objections Kenneth Kress has raised to such accounts. Hershovitz's essay tackles a different aspect of legal reasoning—stare decisis. He argues that accounts of stare decisis that justify the practice of following precedent by appealing to the values of efficiency and fairness are unsuccessful. Stare decisis, he urges, is best understood as a practice which promotes integrity in adjudication.

Integrity is also a subject of investigation in three further essays. Dale Smith considers problems in Dworkin's account of checkerboard solutions, policies that Dworkin claims are defective due to a lack of integrity. Smith aims to clarify the ways in which checkerboard solutions are defective. Jeremy Waldron considers objections the Critical Legal Studies movement raised to Dworkin's theory of law as integrity and the adequacy of Dworkin's response. Waldron suggests that there is a tension between the role of integrity in Dworkin's account of legal practice and his constructivist approach to legal interpretation. Finally, Stephen Perry considers integrity as it relates to the problem of political obligation. His essay clarifies the relationship between Dworkin's account of political obligation and his account of the nature of law.

This volume ends where Dworkin's career began—with questions about the nature of law. John Gardner's essay considers whether law has a distinctive purpose, and the role that such a purpose plays in Dworkin's account of law. Gardner argues that some of Dworkin's commitments in this regard push him towards legal positivism. Mark Greenberg, on the other hand, argues for a broadly Dworkinian view of the nature of law, on which value facts are among the determinants of the content of the law. Greenberg's approach is novel because it focuses on law's metaphysics—on, as he puts it, "how facts make law"—rather than on how judges and lawyers come to know what the law is. Greenberg's argument extends across two essays. The first essay was originally published in *Legal Theory*;[2] the second essay,

---

[1] Hurley's essay was previously published as *Coherence, Hypothetical Cases, and Precedent*, 10(2) OXFORD JOURNAL OF LEGAL STUDIES 221 (1990). It is reprinted here by kind permission of Oxford University Press.

[2] Greenberg's essay was previously published as *How Facts Make Law*, 10 LEGAL THEORY 157 (2004). It is reprinted here with permission.

which is published here for the first time, responds to a family of objections to the argument of the first essay and further develops that argument in the course of criticizing positivist theories commonly associated with H. L. A. Hart.

The volume concludes with responses from Ronald Dworkin. Dworkin comments on each essay, but focuses his attention on those that challenge views he has defended. His responses are in each instance illuminating and they contain valuable statements of his views across a range of topics.

Each of the contributors to this book played an important role in its production, and I am grateful to all of them for the work they took on. Three deserve special thanks: Chris Eisgruber, John Gardner, and Mark Greenberg. Chris hosted a conference at Princeton University in September 2004, at which many of the essays in this book were presented. Mark and John have been incredibly generous with their support and encouragement. This project would not have come to fruition without their help, and I appreciate all that they did. I also appreciate the support—and patience—of John Louth and Gwen Booth, our editors at Oxford University Press.

Collectively, our deepest gratitude is reserved for Ronnie. All of us know that our work would be less insightful and less exciting had he not taught us so much. We appreciate his willingness to join our project and engage with our essays. We didn't set out to write a conventional *festschrift*, but we hope that in developing and criticizing Ronnie's work, we have honored him nonetheless.

SAH
Washington, D.C.
January 2006

Contents

List of Contributors

Stephen Breyer is an Associate Justice of the United States Supreme Court.

Rebecca L. Brown is the Allen Professor of Law at Vanderbilt Law School.

Ronald Dworkin is the Frank Henry Sommer Professor of Law at New York University School of Law and the Bentham Professor of Jurisprudence at University College London.

Christopher L. Eisgruber is the Provost of Princeton University and the Laurance S. Rockefeller Professor of Public Affairs in the Woodrow Wilson School and the University Center for Human Values.

James E. Fleming is the Leonard F. Manning Distinguished Professor of Law at Fordham University School of Law.

John Gardner is the Professor of Jurisprudence at the University of Oxford.

Mark Greenberg is Acting Professor of Law and Assistant Professor of Philosophy at the University of California, Los Angeles.

Scott Hershovitz is a faculty-designate at the University of Michigan Law School. He currently practices law in Washington, D.C.

S. L. Hurley is Professor of Philosophy at the University of Bristol and a Fellow of All Souls College, Oxford.

Stephen Perry is the John J. O'Brien Professor of Law and Professor of Philosophy at the University of Pennsylvania Law School.

Dale Smith is a lecturer in the Faculty of Law at Monash University, Australia.

Jeremy Waldron is University Professor at New York University Law School.

Introduction: The "International" Constitutional Judge

Stephen Breyer

In July 2000 a small group of jurists from several western nations, mostly judges, met for a week in Southern France to discuss the judge's role in our increasingly similar, interdependent societies. Our focus was upon constitutional judges, including judges of international courts. We did not try to reach conclusions. We hoped to learn through conversation.[1]

Professor Dworkin led a discussion about the judge's moral authority, a matter we had entitled, with some irony, "the secular papacy." His paper tied the discussion to a more basic view of constitutional law, which he set forth in three theses.[2] First, law, particularly constitutional law, inevitably embodies standards that require a judge to make moral decisions. Administrative law, for example, sets aside agency actions that are "unreasonable," "disproportionate," or an "abuse of power." Constitutional law protects "liberty," including "freedom of speech," "freedom of the press," and "freedom from unreasonable searches and seizures." Judges cannot apply these standards in difficult cases without revealing their own moral views, at least those that concern proper political structure (itself a matter of political morality). The thought that judges must rely upon their own "political convictions"[3] makes judges uncomfortable. But there is no satisfactory alternative.

Secondly, it is not "undemocratic"[4] for unelected officials such as judges to possess the power to enforce these standards. This is not because "the people . . . do not object to" the judicial practice "and, from time to time in different ways endorse it."[5] Nor is it because "democracy compromised" is a "better form of government" (say, because it produces "a more just community by protecting the rights of minorities").[6] Rather, it is because the best "conception" of "democracy"[7] is a conception under which "majority rule is fair;" and majority rule is "fair" only when certain conditions are met. Where these conditions are realized, then democracy in its best sense is realized. Insofar as the judge helps to assure that those conditions are met, the judge's work helps to support democracy itself.

---

[1] *See generally*, JUDGES IN CONTEMPORARY DEMOCRACY: AN INTERNATIONAL CONVERSATION (R. Badinter & S. Breyer eds., 2004). [2] *Id*. at 67–79.
[3] *Id*. at 71. [4] *Id*. at 73. [5] *Id*. [6] *Id*. at 73–74. [7] *Id*. at 74.

Thirdly, societies increasingly have turned to judges to assure that these conditions are met because they are increasingly uncertain that parliaments or "the people themselves"[8] will do so unaided. Before the "short and terrible Twentieth Century"[9] many thought that parliaments alone might do so by properly balancing the "general interest" with "fairness to individuals."[10] That is to say, legislatures might "at once" be "the voice and the conscience of the people," pursuing "the general interest, but subject to ancient constraints of fairness and decency to individual citizens." Some thought this because they held the aristocratic notion that parliament embodied the wisdom of a "political elite"[11] with the best interests of the nation at heart. Others thought this because they held the romantic notion that parliament embodied the majority's "decent and honorable general will."[12] But given a Twentieth Century history that discredited both notions, societies now seek institutionally to separate the "social accelerator" from the "moral brake."[13] And they have given judges ever greater authority to operate the latter.

What controls the judge when he or she exercises this increased authority? The control lies not only in the general ends they pursue—assuring the conditions of a democracy in its best sense, namely, fair majority rule—but also in the specific means they employ, in particular the process of judicial reasoning. This process encompasses the judicial "responsibility for articulation," which constrains judges to "do nothing that they cannot justify in principle, and to appeal only to principles that they thereby undertake to respect in other contexts as well."[14]

These three theses require elaboration, a matter that I leave to Professor Dworkin and to others to pursue elsewhere. Here, I shall simply note that the judges at the conference found that the theses, though set forth in summary form, usefully informed a wide-ranging discussion, touching upon subjects as disparate as judicial activism, court/media relations, and international human rights tribunals. I shall also point to several aspects of Dworkin's theses that may help to explain their broad appeal to practical judges, not themselves legal philosophers, at work in different national and international settings.

For one thing, Dworkin accurately described the role that reason plays in the judicial process. He said that judges "owe us . . . an argument that meets two conditions. First they have to believe it; they must offer it in good faith *as* an argument. Second, it has to connect what they do in a particular case with something more general and basic."[15] He added that "in the end, what argument a judge finds convincing will depend on that judge's more general attitude and convictions, and no one can demonstrate to those who do not share these attitudes and convictions that they are inescapably right. But they must seem right, after open argument and serious reflection, to those who rely on them."[16] As a judge, I would say that that is how it seems to us. And I would add that in a modern era where we must apply old values

8 *Id.* at 75.   9 *Id.* at 77.   10 *Id.*   11 *Id.* at 76.   12 *Id.*
13 *Id.* at 70.   14 *Id.* at 78.   15 *Id.* at 250.   16 *Id.* at 250–251.

to new, highly complex, technically-shaped circumstances, the need to base judicial decisions upon clear reasoning seems more important than ever.

Others at the conference elaborated upon this basic idea. Some pointed out that the judicial process also provides a forum for serious reasoned argument, not only in the special judicial sense just mentioned, but also as providing "a place of debate, of public discussion and decision." Unlike a modern legislature the members of which do not usually "debate" each other (but rather often speak to show their own side, via media reports, how strongly they support its views), a "judicial forum" helps to organize "differing fluctuating opinions for and against a particular matter. It is a place where lawyers representing differing interests publicly have to confront contrary opinions."[17] It permits "a continuous exchange of opinions," thereby helping "the public debate along."[18]

For another thing, Dworkin's definition of judges' constitutional objectives, namely the identification of conditions essential to a fair democratic process, imposes a significant constraint upon the constitutional judge's exercise of lawful authority. Applying this basic principle, judges should not interpret highly general constitutional language, such as the word "liberty" in a Constitution, so broadly that it encompasses "all the values that a decent society should permit"[19] or answers all the complex questions that society confronts (say, whether nuclear power is too dangerous to permit a legislature to adopt it). Democracy demands that legislatures, not courts, make the trade-offs among such conflicting, desirable objectives as "security and efficiency or environmental amenities."[20] Legislators, not judges, will ordinarily decide how to rank both desirable objectives and undesirable behaviors.

The discussion also showed how these two elements of Dworkin's theses—his substantive description of what constitutional judges at a basic level are seeking to do and his procedural insistence upon the use of reason—could inform the debate about new "international" or "trans-national" tribunals. Can citizens of different nations reach agreement about which conditions are necessary for modern democracy to flourish, or are there too many culturally based disagreements to maintain confidence in a court with jurisdiction over such matters? To what extent should we circumscribe jurisdiction to produce agreement, say limiting the jurisdiction of international human rights courts to the most serious kinds of violations? Is there an inverse relation between agreement about basic democratic conditions and insistence upon political control? Where jurisdiction is broad, will citizens of different nations increasingly insist upon control over the nomination of some, or all, of the individual judges? How detailed should we make the definitions of individual "international" human rights crimes? Should it be up to legislatures or to courts to decide, for example, whether rape is "torture" or simply a serious crime? Dworkin's theses do not answer these questions, but they do provide a framework that helps to guide us towards proper answers.

---

[17] *Id.* at 97.   [18] *Id.* at 96–97.   [19] *Id.* at 49–50.   [20] *Id.* at 50.

The most important characteristic of Dworkin's theses and their related philosophy, however, concerns their relation to the matter of the approach a judge should take to interpreting the highly general language of the Constitution. American judges must apply the Constitution in ways that vindicate, in today's highly complex society, the basic values that the Founders enunciated more than 200 years ago. To treat the Constitution as if it contains a laundry list of the Founders' *specific* detailed expectations is to doom to extinction its more basic and general democratic objectives. But to do the contrary, to read the scope and content of that eighteenth-century language as evolving in light of modern circumstances risks the judges' assumption of the legal authority to impose their own subjective views of what is "good" upon the Nation. Some judges and scholars believe that, to avoid the latter, judges should approach the Constitution with what one might call "literalist," "traditionalist," or "originalist" attitudes. Are such approaches necessary to keep subjective judicial decision-making in check?

Dworkin's views suggest they are not. His theses point to standards, based upon important general values embodied in a Constitution that establishes, if not the "best" form, at least a very good form, of democracy. Defining judges' constitutional objectives as identifying the conditions necessary for a workable democracy limits the judicial role and guides judges' discretion. Dworkin's views also suggest that through the use of reason a constitutional judge can produce an opinion that is transparent, permitting an informed reader to criticize the opinion in light of substantive standards. The result is a system that allows the public, and the judge, to know when an opinion goes too far, thereby keeping judicial subjectivity in check. The standards are not totally objective. Indeed, they permit, perhaps sometimes require, judges to invoke their own notions of political morality. But even then they permit informed public criticism. And that is the point. Criticism is perhaps the best way to keep subjective judicial decision-making in check. I doubt that those who advocate literal or "traditionalist" or "originalist" theories can do any better.

In this sense Dworkin's theses are highly practical. They cast light on a question that divides the American judiciary as never before. They, like the bulk of his constitutional thought, have had considerable impact upon American constitutional law. And I am not surprised they generated stimulating and helpful discussion in an international forum as well.

1

Should Constitutional Judges be Philosophers?

Christopher L. Eisgruber[*]

I. Introduction

Ronald Dworkin has urged American judges and lawyers to embrace the "moral reading of the [United States] Constitution." The moral reading insists that the Bill of Rights and the Fourteenth Amendment "invoke moral principles about political decency and justice."[1] Some critics worry that the moral reading emphasizes morality too much. They believe that it gives short shrift to text and history and that it calls upon judges to become philosophers instead of lawyers.[2] Dworkin, in return, has contended that his theory allows ample room for historical reasoning. Yet, when Dworkin interprets the Constitution, the principles that he finds in it are very abstract ones—such as the principle that "government must treat everyone as of equal status and with equal concern"—and his analysis of them is thoroughly philosophical. Historical concerns rarely figure in his arguments.

Why is Dworkin's "moral reading of the Constitution" so moral—that is, why is it concerned so much with moral issues and so little with other considerations, including historical ones? Can Dworkin's "moral reading" in fact accommodate historical argument and other traditional forms of legal reasoning, or does it require constitutional judges to become philosophers? If the latter, is that requirement defensible? This essay examines these questions. It concludes that the abstract, philosophical character of Dworkin's constitutional interpretation is partly—but only partly—a matter of Dworkin's intellectual style. The general theoretical parameters of his

* For helpful comments on earlier drafts, I would like to thank Ronald Dworkin, Mark Greenberg, Lewis Kornhauser, Liam Murphy, Larry Sager, the Faculty and Fellows of Princeton's University Center for Human Values, and the NYU Colloquia in Constitutional Theory and in Law, Philosophy, and Social Theory. The Filomen D'Agostino and Max E. Greenberg Faculty Research Fund at the New York University School of Law and the Woodrow Wilson School at Princeton University provided financial support for this research.

[1] R. M. Dworkin, Freedom's Law: The Moral Reading of the Constitution 2 (1996).

[2] An example of such criticism is M. McConnell, *The Importance of Humility in Judicial Review: A Comment on Dworkin's Moral Reading of the Constitution*, 65 Ford. L. Rev. 1269 (1997).

"moral reading" permit interpreters with different styles to invoke history more often than Dworkin himself does. This preliminary conclusion is consistent with Dworkin's claim that lawyers who want to make historical arguments should do so within the umbrella of the moral reading rather than in opposition to it.

Dworkin's emphasis upon abstract moral principle is not, however, wholly attributable to his intellectual style. This essay's second conclusion, and its most important claim, is that Dworkin's arguments about moral principle and the Constitution presuppose an unarticulated, controversial theory about the purpose of written constitutions and super-majoritarian amendment procedures. They pre-suppose, in particular, a theory that explains why people might adopt a constitu-tion with super-majoritarian amendment procedures if they aim to accommodate evolving judgments about abstract standards of justice. Some of Dworkin's critics deny that such an explanation is possible. They believe that the Constitution is hard to amend because its purpose is to entrench past practices against revision on the basis of subsequent judgments by later generations. Lawyers and judges who hold this view about the Constitution sometimes assume that they should interpret ambiguous constitutional provisions in ways that increase the influence of the past upon the present. They believe that they are thereby faithful to what they take to be the Constitution's chief purpose—namely, preventing change. As it turns out, there exist reasons to reject this past-oriented view of the Constitution's purpose. These reasons, however, are not yet part of the case that Dworkin has offered on behalf of his position, and they depend on considerations different in kind from those upon which he typically relies (they depend, in particular, upon pragmatic judgments about political institutions). Unless supplemented by such reasons (or some comparable theory of the Constitution's purpose), Dworkin's theory of constitutional interpretation is significantly incomplete.

II. History Within the Moral Reading

Almost three decades ago, Dworkin called for "a fusion of constitutional law and moral philosophy."[3] His subsequent work has carried out that project. When Dworkin offers views about specific constitutional issues, moral philosophy takes center stage. For example, when Dworkin analyzes the Equal Protection Clause, he says that there are only two possible interpretations of it. One possibility is that the Clause merely requires government to honor the terms of its laws, whatever those laws may say. If the law prohibits theft, then the police must enforce that law against anybody who steals, without regard to the race of the culprit or victim. This princi-ple is a very weak one. It does not preclude the government from writing racially dis-criminatory terms straight into its laws; it merely prohibits the executive and judicial branches from discriminating when the legislature has not authorized them to do so.

---

[3] R. M. DWORKIN, TAKING RIGHTS SERIOUSLY 149 (1977).

Dworkin says that precedent forecloses this minimialist interpretation of the Equal Protection Clause. I doubt that anybody would disagree. But, according to Dworkin, "[o]nce that much is conceded, . . . then the principle must be something *much* more robust, because the only alternative, as a translation of what the framers actually *said* in the equal protection clause, is that they declared a principle of quite breathtaking scope and power: the principle that government must treat everyone as of equal status and with equal concern."[4] And just like that we are off to the philosophical races, free (if not compelled) to consult liberal political theory in order to determine the meaning of "equal status and concern."

Indeed, Dworkin says that, on his approach to the Constitution, it "seems unlikely that anyone who believes that free and equal citizens would be guaranteed a particular individual right will not also think that our Constitution already contains that right, unless constitutional history has decisively rejected it."[5] Moreover, "since liberty and equality overlap in large part," the Equal Protection Clause and the Due Process Clause will "each be comprehensive in that same way"—comprehensive enough, that is, to embrace every right appropriate to free and equal citizens. One clause—or indeed, either of two clauses—will suffice to answer every civil liberties need! Dworkin's argument seems to make not only history, but much of the constitutional text (including the Bill of Rights, which singles out specific liberties for constitutional protection), superfluous.

It is thus easy to see why critics accuse Dworkin of eliding the distinction between constitutional law and moral philosophy. Nevertheless, as James E. Fleming has correctly argued, Dworkin's approach to constitutional interpretation can accommodate a great deal of historical argument.[6] To begin with, Dworkin does not claim that *every* constitutional provision articulates a moral principle. On the contrary, he points out that some provisions (he mentions the Third Amendment, which prohibits the government from quartering troops in homes during peacetime, and the Presidential Qualifications Clause, which requires that the President be thirty-five or older) do not.[7] Moreover, even with regard to provisions that do state moral principles, Dworkin permits interpreters to use history when deciding *which* principle is named by the provision. For example, Dworkin says that when construing the Equal Protection Clause, judges should remember that "Congressmen of the victorious nation" were "trying to capture the achievements and lessons of a terrible war" and so likely enacted an expansive moral principle rather than a limited one.[8]

In addition, Dworkin maintains that judges owe allegiance to precedent as well as to constitutional principle. The obligation to fit past decisions limits the ability of judges to honor their moral convictions about, for example, the principle embodied in the Equal Protection Clause. Thus, as we have seen, Dworkin contends that precedent prevents judges from reading the Clause so narrowly that it

---

[4] DWORKIN, FREEDOM'S LAW, *supra* note 1, at 10.   [5] *Id.* at 73.
[6] J. E. Fleming, *Fidelity to Our Imperfect Constitution*, 65 FORD. L. REV. 1335 (1997).
[7] DWORKIN, FREEDOM'S LAW, *supra* note 1, at 8.   [8] *Id.* at 9.

would stipulate "only the relatively weak principle that laws must be enforced in accordance with their terms, so that legal benefits conferred on everyone . . . must not be denied, in practice, to anyone."[9] He also maintains that precedent prevents judges from reading the Clause so broadly that it would require equality of wealth.[10]

Finally, Dworkin's theory permits history to play a role internal to moral and political argument. History might enrich political theory in at least three ways: with examples that stimulate reflection; with data about institutional performance and human behavior; and with rhetorical resources that enhance the persuasive power of moral argument. Dworkin does not discuss connections of this kind; perhaps he believes that political theorists have little to learn from history. Yet, that belief, if indeed Dworkin holds it, is not a necessary part of his view of the Constitution. If we believe that moral principles are best identified and applied through historical reflection or argument, then Dworkin's moral reading of the Constitution will compel us to consult history.

This last possibility bears emphasis. Some influential defenses of historical argument about the Constitution depend on claims about policy-making in general, not about constitutional law in particular.[11] These claims, which sometimes operate under the banner of "pragmatism," suggest that we should rely on contextual arguments about institutions and history whenever we make policy decisions, not just when we are interpreting a written Constitution. Dworkin has argued vigorously on behalf of abstract moral theory and against pragmatism and its cousins.[12] Nevertheless, those arguments are distinct from his defense of the moral reading. If one believes that historical reasoning of some sort is in general the best way to make practical moral judgments, then one will also believe that historical reasoning is the key to applying the moral principles identified by Dworkin's "moral reading."

III. What the Moral Reading Entails

If the moral reading can in principle accommodate historical and structural argument, why is Dworkin's own application of the theory so heavily dependent upon moral philosophy? Critics might suppose that, whatever the capacity of the moral reading to accommodate historical argument, it must somehow stack the deck against historical and other non-philosophical forms of reasoning. Dworkin, after all, names the conception "the moral reading," not "the historical reading" or "the pragmatic reading." It appears no accident that, in practice, the reading recommends something like moral philosophy. Dworkin acknowledges that many constitutional scholars would prefer a middle ground between his philosophical approach to the Constitution and the rigid historicism of strictly

---

[9] DWORKIN, FREEDOM'S LAW, *supra* note 1, at 9.   [10] *Id.* at 11.

[11] *See, e.g.*, L. Kramer, *Fidelity to History—and Through It*, 65 FORD. L. REV. 1627 (1997).

[12] See especially R. M. Dworkin, *In Praise of Theory*, 29 ARIZ. ST. L.J. 353 (1997).

originalist interpretive protocols.[13] Dworkin, however, has taken a strong line against such approaches, claiming that a third way between the moral reading and strict originalism is not only unattractive, but entirely unavailable.[14]

This surprising claim turns out to be correct, but only because the moral reading's entailments are more modest than its provocative name would suggest. Dworkin's moral reading of the Constitution boils down to two propositions: (1) the Constitution's meaning depends upon what the framers intended to say, not upon how they expected the Constitution to be applied;[15] and (2) when the framers invoked abstract moral language, they used it in its ordinary sense, as referring to abstract moral principles.[16] These propositions yield an important result: as we shall see, they rule out a common form of originalist argument. But the moral reading makes the Constitution less thoroughly moral than one might suppose, because it tells us little, if anything, about which moral principles the framers invoked.

The moral reading's first proposition depends upon the idea that there is a difference between the meaning of a concept and our views about how best to apply the concept.[17] It is easy to construct examples that exhibit the validity of this distinction. Suppose somebody tells you, "You should respect equality—by which I mean you should respect equality itself, not just my theory about it. My theory of equality suggests that affirmative action policies are wholly consistent with the ideal of equality, but I might be mistaken about that view, and, if so, then you should oppose affirmative action."[18] You might find it implausible that anybody would utter such a speech (or you may think the speech unbearably pompous). But the speech is not unintelligible: it is perfectly possible for a speaker to distinguish between equality itself and her view of equality. She can do so because there is a difference between what "equality" means and her view (or anybody else's view) of how equality applies in particular cases.

The speaker's views about equality thus do not define the meaning of the concept she invokes. Her intentions nevertheless matter to the content of her instructions. In particular, it matters that she intended to invoke the concept we commonly call "equality" and not some other concept. We would not disrespect her instructions if we rejected her views about whether affirmative action is

---

[13] DWORKIN, FREEDOM'S LAW, *supra* note 1, at 14–15.   [14] *Id.*

[15] *Id.* at 13 ("The moral reading insists that the Constitution means what the framers intended to say").

[16] *Id.* at 7 ("Many . . . clauses are drafted in exceedingly abstract moral language. . . . According to the moral reading, these clauses must be understood in the way their language naturally suggests: they refer to abstract moral principles and incorporate these by reference, as limits on government's power"). *Id.* at 2 ("Most contemporary constitutions declare individual rights in very broad and abstract language. . . . The moral reading proposes that we all . . . interpret and apply these abstract clauses on the understanding that they invoke moral principles about political decency and justice").

[17] On the distinction between the "meaning" and "application" of concepts, *see* M. D. Greenberg and H. Litman, *The Meaning of Original Meaning*, 86 GEO. L.J. 569, 586–591 (1998).

[18] This example, of course, tracks Dworkin's famous example from TAKING RIGHTS SERIOUSLY, where he discusses a father who wants his children to honor the best conception of fairness, which might differ from his own conception. DWORKIN, TAKING RIGHTS SERIOUSLY, *supra* note 3, at 134.

consistent with equality, but we would indeed do so if we simply substituted some other concept—such as "color-blindness" or "libertarianism" or "good health"— for "equality." In Dworkin's terminology, we would then be ignoring what the speaker intended to say, rather than merely her intentions, hopes, or expectations about the consequences her instructions would have.

Once we understand the distinction between the meaning of a concept and our views about how it should be applied, the moral reading's first proposition quickly follows. The proposition states that if the framers intended to incorporate a particular concept in the Constitution (such as "equality"), then the Constitution requires us to respect that concept, not the framers' expectations about how the concept would be applied. It is hard to see why anybody would take the opposite view. Certainly respect for the framers would not recommend doing so—the framers, by hypothesis, intended to refer to the concept, not their expectations, in the Constitution. Nor is there any apparent reason of political justice, unrelated to respect for the framers, that would justify allowing their expectations to govern at the expense of the concept that they intended to incorporate into the Constitution.[19] Indeed, originalists generally concede this point. For example, Justice Antonin Scalia writes that "it is simply incompatible with democratic government, or indeed, even with fair government, to have the meaning of a law determined by what the lawgiver meant, rather than by what the lawgiver promulgated."[20]

The moral reading's first proposition tells us nothing, however, about whether the framers actually intended to invoke "equality" or any other moral concept in the Constitution (it tells us only that if they did so, then the Constitution's meaning depends upon the meaning of that concept, not upon the framers' expectations about how it would be applied). The second proposition, by contrast, addresses what the framers said. It maintains that they sometimes used abstract moral concepts in the Constitution, and it insists that they used those concepts in their ordinary sense—which is to say, they used them to refer to abstract moral ideas. Dworkin's argument for this point is simple. He says, "The Framers were careful statesmen who knew how to use the language they spoke. We cannot make good sense of their behavior unless we assume that they meant to say what people who use the words they used would normally mean to say."[21]

Is that simple argument sufficient to establish Dworkin's claim? Keith Whittington contends that it is not. Whittington points out that people sometimes

---

[19] Professor Michael Moore has argued that neither the framers' intended meaning *nor* their expectations should determine what the Constitution means. M. S. Moore, *Justifying the Natural Law Theory of Constitutional Interpretation*, 69 FORD. L. REV. 2087, 2096–2099 (2001). On Moore's view, Dworkin is too much concerned with history and framers' intention. I will put this interesting view to one side for purposes of this essay, where my project is to assess the charge that Dworkin has been *too little* interested in history.

[20] A. SCALIA, A MATTER OF INTERPRETATION: FEDERAL COURTS AND THE LAW 17 (A. Guttman, ed., 1997).

[21] R. M. Dworkin, *The Arduous Virtue of Fidelity: Originalism, Scalia, Tribe, and Nerve*, 65 FORD. L. REV. 1249, 1253 (1997); *see also* DWORKIN, FREEDOM'S LAW, *supra* note 1, at 8–9, 76.

use words in unconventional ways, so that meaning depends upon "context."[22] He suggests, by way of example, that a boss might speak in a shorthand that is understood by his subordinates.[23] Whittington concludes that it is at least partly an "empirical question" whether the framers used words in their ordinary sense, and that Dworkin's theory is unconvincing because it fails to adduce any relevant historical evidence.[24]

Whittington is half right: the question whether the framers used words in their ordinary sense is indeed partly "empirical" and dependent upon "context."[25] But to characterize the question as empirical is not to say that it depends upon a detailed excavation of the legislative record or the framers' expectations. The decisive piece of evidence about the "context" (to use the term Whittington favors) of the framers' words is the uncontested fact that the framers were engaged in a national constitution-making project. That project is different from a conversation between a boss and his employees, or between other people who know one another personally and so have developed communicative shorthands. Except in very rare circumstances, it would be both impractical and unattractive for constitution-makers to use words in any but their ordinary sense. The framers of the American constitution were a large group—at a minimum, they included all the ratifiers as well as all the drafters. It is hard to imagine how so many people in so many places could have communicated effectively if they were not using words in their ordinary sense. Even aside from this practical problem, principles of fair notice require that laws either use words in their ordinary sense or at least clearly indicate departures from it. It would be possible, in principle, to take the latter route: the framers might have stipulated that they were using certain words in a special way—as "terms of art," for example. But we would expect that declaration to be very prominent, not just in the drafting process, but also in the ratifying conventions, and perhaps in the text of the Constitution itself.

Perhaps Whittington, or somebody else, will be able to find widespread statements of this kind, in which the framers explicitly note that they are assigning exceptional meanings to words used in the Constitution. But until somebody comes forward with such statements, the available empirical evidence cuts overwhelmingly in Dworkin's favor. There is, as he says, no way to "make good sense of [the framers'] behavior unless we assume that they meant to say what people who use the words they used would normally mean to say."[26] Not surprisingly, many originalists have endorsed something very much like the moral reading's second proposition. For example, Judge Robert Bork has written that "[w]hen lawmakers use words, the law that results is what those words ordinarily mean."[27]

---

[22] K. Whittington, *Dworkin's "originalism": The Role of Intentions in Constitutional Interpretation*, 62 REVIEW OF POLITICS 197, 213–214 (2000).   [23] *Id.* at 215–216.

[24] *Id.* at 214, 216.

[25] Dworkin takes the same view. "[W]e must know something about the circumstances in which a person spoke to have any good idea of what he meant to say in speaking as he did." DWORKIN, FREEDOM'S LAW, *supra* note 1, at 8.

[26] Dworkin, *Arduous Virtue of Fidelity*, *supra* note 21, at 1253.

[27] R. H. Bork, THE TEMPTING OF AMERICA 144 (1997).

The two propositions of the moral reading are thus relatively modest. They not only *might* be endorsed, but in fact *have been* endorsed, by prominent originalists such as Scalia and Bork. They more or less echo views articulated almost two centuries ago by John Marshall, who wrote that the drafters and ratifiers of the Constitution "must be understood to have employed words in their natural sense, and to have intended what they have said."[28] Yet, despite its relatively uncontroversial premises, the moral reading has an important consequence for the status of practices that existed when the Constitution was written. The moral reading's first proposition says that if the framers invoked moral principles, then the Constitution's meaning is determined by the meaning of those principles, not by the framers' views about how they would apply to contemporary practices. The moral reading's second proposition says that the framers did in fact invoke moral principles. It follows that, in the words of Mark Greenberg and Harry Litman, "original meaning, properly understood, must [allow for] the possibility that a traditional practice is unconstitutional."[29]

The moral reading thus rules out a popular form of originalist argument which supposes that "[w]hen a practice not expressly prohibited by the Bill of Rights bears the endorsement of a long tradition of open, widespread, and unchallenged use that dates back to the beginning of the Republic, we have no proper basis for [holding it unconstitutional]."[30] Originalists must argue by reference to the principles the framers invoked in the Constitution; they are not entitled to assume that the framers' practices were consistent with those principles.[31] If the moral reading were to succeed in disciplining originalist argument in this way, it would greatly improve constitutional argument.

The moral reading does not, however, say anything about *which* principles the framers invoked. One might (correctly) suppose that history is relevant to answering that important question. We have therefore not yet identified the features of Dworkin's interpretive method that render it so thoroughly moral. To do so, we must proceed beyond the moral reading and investigate how Dworkin determines which principles the American framers invoked.

IV. Ambiguous Text, Good Framers, and Moral Principles

Dworkin provides a general prescription about how to determine which moral principles the Constitution invokes. He says that we must construct "different elaborations" of constitutional phrases, "each of which we can recognize as a principle of political morality that might have won [the framers'] respect," and then we must ask "which of these it makes most sense to attribute to [the framers], *given*

---

[28] *Gibbons v. Ogden*, 22 U.S. (9 Wheat.) 1, 188 (1824).

[29] Greenberg and Litman, *supra* note 17, at 571.

[30] *Rutan v. Republican Party of Ill.*, 497 U.S. 62, 95–96 (Scalia, J., dissenting). For more extensive discussion of this view, *see* Greenberg and Litman, *supra* note 17, at 574–582.

[31] *Id.* at 597–617.

everything else we know."[32] What else we know may include facts about constitutional history; thus, as we have already noticed, Dworkin says that the principles we attribute to the framers of the Fourteenth Amendment must fit the mindset of a Congress trying to "capture the achievements and lessons of a terrible war."[33]

Yet, as we have already seen, the principles that Dworkin ultimately identifies are exceedingly abstract. What leads Dworkin to those principles? He claims that the constitutional text itself is responsible for his conclusions. According to Dworkin, the Constitution's "key clauses are drafted in the most abstract possible terms of political morality."[34] He supports this claim by pointing out that the Fourteenth Amendment "commands 'equal' protection of the laws, and also commands that neither life nor liberty nor property be taken without 'due' process of law."[35] That is true, of course. We can easily add other provisions to Dworkin's list.[36]

Dworkin's argument, however, glosses over the complexity of constitutional language. None of the Constitution's expansive phrases sound unambiguously in moral principle. On the contrary, all of them mix justice with positive law in mysterious proportion. The Constitution demands not "equality" but "the equal protection of the laws;" it protects not against "deprivations of liberty" but against "deprivations of liberty without due process of law;" and it guarantees not "the privileges and immunities of free citizens" but the "privileges [and] immunities" attendant upon a particular legal status, that of "citizens of the United States." The Constitution's sonorous phrases are hard to interpret because they couple diverse terms without explaining the relationship among them. What does it mean to guarantee the "equal protection of the laws"? Does it mean that law must live up to the standards of equality? Or does it mean that equality must be toned down to accommodate the practical, political functions of the law?

Dworkin's construction of the Due Process Clauses is especially vulnerable. Other interpreters have thought that those Clauses by their terms impose only procedural restrictions upon the government. John Hart Ely, for example, said that "there is simply no avoiding the fact that the word that follows 'due' is 'process.'" In Ely's view, "substantive due process" is an oxymoron akin to "green pastel redness."[37] Ely's "process-means-process" argument would be stronger if the Clauses said "without fair process" or "without legal process" or simply "without due process," rather than without "due process of law," a combination that beefs up "process" in a way that common sense cannot easily decode. Does it matter that the Constitution adds "of law" to "due process"? Perhaps not to positivist legal theorists, who believe that the meaning of legal rules depends entirely upon the processes through which they were enacted. For these theorists, the reference to law merely compounds the reference to process. But Americans have never understood

---

[32] DWORKIN, FREEDOM'S LAW, *supra* note 1, at 9 (Author's emphasis).   [33] *Id.*

[34] *Id.* at 72.   [35] *Id.*

[36] *E.g.*, the Fourteenth Amendment also prohibits the states from abridging "the privileges or immunities of citizens of the United States."

[37] J. H. ELY, DEMOCRACY AND DISTRUST: A THEORY OF JUDICIAL REVIEW 18 (1980).

the concept of law in purely positivist ways. The American legal tradition has consistently recognized a connection between law and justice. That connection is written into the text of the Constitution, which declares itself to be "supreme Law" and which lists among its purposes "to establish justice."[38]

So Dworkin might well be right about the meaning of the Due Process Clauses. Nevertheless, the Constitution never quite articulates explicitly the grand moral principles that Dworkin attributes to it. Moreover, his interpretation renders much of the text redundant. On his view, for example, the Fourteenth Amendment contains two consecutive clauses—the Due Process Clause and the Equal Protection Clause—each of which protects all the rights appropriate to a free government. The Fifth Amendment's Due Process Clause does likewise, so that the other eight amendments in the Bill of Rights appear superfluous. Of course, it is entirely possible that the framers repeated themselves—perhaps they took several stabs at expressing a difficult idea. Still, the apparent repetition fits awkwardly with Dworkin's highly textual form of argument. Unfortunately for him, the constitutional text says both less and more than his philosophical approach to the Constitution requires: less, because it never states a pure, comprehensive moral principle clearly; more, because it uses many duplicative phrases where, according to Dworkin, one would suffice.

I do not believe that the constitutional text can, without more, bear the weight that Dworkin puts upon it. There is, however, a (nontextual) reason why we might interpret the Equal Protection Clause and the Due Process Clauses in the expansive way that Dworkin recommends. The reason invokes a kind of interpretive charity: all other things being equal, it will always make sense to attribute the most noble principles and purposes to the framers.[39] We might rephrase our interpretive task in this way: "The framers who drafted the Due Process Clauses and the Equal Protection Clauses were not content to itemize specific instances of government misbehavior; instead, they drafted general principles to govern the nation in the future. Which principles did they choose?" Why would we want to say the framers did less than the best they could have done? Once we agree that the framers might have put aside their prejudices to endorse justice and equality in general, it seems insulting to assume they did anything less.

Given an ambiguous and potentially sweeping moral principle, we will face a strong tug to read the best into that principle. Historical circumstances are unlikely to provide much of a barrier. Suppose, for example, that we discover that the framers of the Fourteenth Amendment all shared some ugly prejudice that would have kept them from respecting equality in full measure.[40] Perhaps this prejudice led them to enact unjust statutes in the course of their political careers. Could we say that, in light of this prejudice, it "makes sense to attribute" to the

---

[38] For further discussion, *see* C. L. Eisgruber, *Justice and the Text: Rethinking the Constitutional Connection Between Principle and Prudence*, 43 Duke L. J. 1, 48–53 (1993).

[39] On the inherent optimism of interpretation, *see* Dworkin, Freedom's Law, *supra* note 1, at 38.

[40] It does not matter that the prejudice be very ugly. The argument would go through equally well if we substituted "second-best view" for "ugly prejudice."

framers some dilute or truncated principle of equality consistent with their prejudices? No, for we will then be confronted with the fact that the framers could have
made their prejudices explicit, but chose not to. It is possible that the principle
they enacted embodied their prejudices, but it is also possible that the framers
enacted a broader principle which—while they might have hoped and believed it
to be consistent with their prejudices—transcended their prejudices. All other
things being equal, why not select the more flattering characterization?

For practical purposes, the only way to avoid associating an exceptionally broad
moral principle with the sweeping, enigmatic phrases of the Fourteenth
Amendment is to identify some reason which would lead the framers, at their very
best, to refrain from writing full, robust principles of equality and liberty into the
Constitution. Here lies the true engine that drives Dworkin's philosophical treatment of the Constitution. It is a powerful motor indeed. The logic that got us to
this stage in the argument is simple. The Constitution includes ambiguous phrases
that might refer to sweeping principles of political morality. The Constitution is
the standard against which Americans judge their government. Those two propositions, virtually uncontestable, create a strong presumption in favor of using moral
and political philosophy to interpret the Constitution's abstract phrases: standards
for judging government ought to be good ones rather than bad ones. Dworkin has
seen these points clearly and exploited them powerfully.

The moral ambition of Dworkin's constitutional method is thus not merely the
product of his intellectual taste. Nor, however, does it derive directly from the surprisingly modest entailments of the "moral reading" of the Constitution. Instead,
Dworkin's philosophical approach to adjudication results from a particular view of
constitutionalism: Dworkin tacitly assumes that the best framers would write
abstract, sweeping moral principles into their constitutions. This assumption has
considerable appeal. The best constitution-maker might well be the one who drafts
the most clarion and expansive statements of political morality. On the other hand,
American constitutional processes permit, and have in fact sponsored, the writing of
different kinds of provisions, some of which are detailed and others of which
(including the Equal Protection and Due Process Clauses) are murky. Is that because
Americans have been second-rate constitution-makers? Or might they reasonably
have aspired to do something besides stating principles of political morality?

V. Integrity and the Constitution

Dworkin's own political theory suggests one reason why good constitution-
makers might aim at entrenching principles different from those recommended
by pure moral theory. Dworkin insists upon the existence of a value that he calls
"integrity."[41] Integrity demands that a nation's political decisions manifest principled consistency over time. According to Dworkin, integrity ranks with equality

---

[41] Dworkin, Law's Empire 166 (1986).

and fairness as a political value. He tells us that integrity constrains what real, historical polities can do. Utopian theorists may describe what political arrangements best satisfy the demands of equality and fairness, but leaders of an ongoing political enterprise must also concern themselves with the relation between their present policies and earlier ones.[42]

If there exists a value such as integrity, then surely it should matter to constitution-makers, who aspire to design real governments, not utopian theories. Dworkin discusses integrity mainly in connection with the obligation of judges to respect past precedents, and so one might suppose that constitution-makers need take it into account only when fashioning judicial institutions. Yet, Dworkin's theory does not explain why integrity should be uniquely applicable to adjudication.[43] We might conclude that it applies to government action more generally. If so, integrity could give good constitution-makers a reason to choose principles that incorporated the requirements of integrity along with those of equality and fairness. For example, they might entrench a commitment to "traditional American principles of equality and fairness" rather than simply to "equality and fairness." And that, in turn, would give us reason to interpret ambiguous constitutional language (such as "no state shall deprive any person of life, liberty or property without due process of law") to include a reference to American tradition—because, on the assumptions just stated, that would be the most charitable interpretation of what the framers said.

This line of argument discloses an irony in Dworkin's defense of the moral reading. Dworkin launched his extraordinary work in legal philosophy three decades ago by observing that judges scrutinize precedent more intently in the hardest cases, cases that cannot be resolved on the basis of precedent alone and so force judges to draw visibly upon political and moral values. Dworkin refused to dismiss the judicial fascination with precedent as mere delusion or smokescreen; he devoted his jurisprudential career to identifying a conceptually rigorous middle ground between deferring to past decisions and making fresh judgments of political morality.[44] That is what led him to discover the value of integrity.[45] Now Dworkin protests when constitutional scholars insist upon doing in the domain of constitutional interpretation what he himself did when analyzing *stare decisis*.

That is, of course, merely ironic, not contradictory. Adjudication and constitutional interpretation are different practices, and a solution appropriate to one might fail with respect to the other. Nevertheless, Dworkin's position ought to make him mildly uncomfortable, for he argues not merely that some third position between originalism and the moral reading is *wrong* but that none exists.

---

[42] DWORKIN, LAW'S EMPIRE, *supra* note 41, at 164–165.

[43] I owe this observation to Lewis Kornhauser. Dworkin does in fact recognize a principle that he calls "integrity in legislation," but it is the different principle of "integrity in adjudication" that "explains how and why the past must be allowed some special power of its own in court." DWORKIN, LAW'S EMPIRE, *supra* note 41, at 167.

[44] *See, e.g.*, DWORKIN, TAKING RIGHTS SERIOUSLY, *supra* note 3, at 81, 87, 112. *See also* R. M. DWORKIN, A MATTER OF PRINCIPLE 147 (1985); DWORKIN, LAW'S EMPIRE, *supra* note 41, at 15, 20, 130–131, 228.

[45] DWORKIN, LAW'S EMPIRE, *supra* note 41, at 166.

One has to wonder why there is a middle ground when reading precedent but not when reading the Constitution.

In fact, I think the two practices too similar to justify the different conclusions Dworkin reaches about them. If adjudicators have principled reasons to temper moral demands (and constitutional principles) by reference to past practice, than so too might constitution-makers and constitutional interpreters. That does not count as a reason for rejecting the moral reading; the argument I have offered about integrity accepts the two propositions discussed earlier (namely, that the Constitution means what the framers intended to say, and that they intended to state moral principles). The argument, in other words, is consistent with Dworkin's claim that there is no middle ground between the moral reading and strict versions of originalism. The argument does show, however, that there exists a conceptually coherent middle ground between strict originalism and Dworkin's own *application* of the moral reading—that is, between fidelity to highly specific historical practices on the one hand and to the most abstract possible moral principles on the other.

VI. The Importance of Constitutional Purposes

The argument of the preceding section depended upon a particular conception of integrity. Many people might reject that conception, either because they do not recognize integrity as an independent value, or because they do not believe it should be extended from adjudication to constitution-making. In this section I describe other, more widely shared premises that, if accepted, might cause good constitution-makers to refrain from constitutionalizing abstract moral principles.

The argument begins from the observation that the analysis of constitution-making is itself an interpretive inquiry. In other words, our account of constitution-making must both *fit* and *justify* it.[46] When we ask what good constitution-makers would do, we must remember that they are making a constitution (rather than designing the ideal political system, constitutional or not), and we must describe their role in a way consistent with that ambition. We must accordingly ask what purposes are served by constitutions like the American one. Many popular theories about the United States Constitution pay special attention to one fact about it: the Constitution permits super-majorities to entrench specific judgments against later change. Two hundred years ago, for example, many people apparently thought that no foreign-born person should hold the office of President; that no Senator should be younger than thirty; and that a jury trial should be available in all federal torts cases in which the plaintiff sought more than twenty dollars. Americans must abide by those judgments even if they now appear silly. Americans may, of course, amend the Constitution, but Article V of the Constitution

---

[46] On "fit" and "justification" as dimensions of interpretation, *see* Dworkin, A Matter of Principle, *supra* note 44, at 160; Dworkin, Law's Empire, *supra* note 41, at 52–53, 239.

makes amendment extremely difficult. The Constitution's obduracy (that is, its barriers against amendment) and its specificity are striking, and any good theory about the Constitution's role in the American political system must explain them.

People have used these features of the Constitution to argue that the point of the Constitution is to strip present-day Americans of the ability to govern themselves and compel them to honor instead the specific judgments of earlier generations. Put more floridly, these theories maintain that the Constitution's purpose is to empower "the dead hand of the past." For example, Supreme Court Justice Antonin Scalia says that the Constitution's "whole purpose is to prevent change— to embed certain rights in such a manner that future generations cannot take them away."[47] In Scalia's view, the decision to establish a written, obdurate constitution reflects a lack of confidence in future generations. "A society that adopts a bill of rights is skeptical that 'evolving standards of decency' always 'mark progress,' and that societies always 'mature,' as opposed to rot."[48]

Scalia's theory supplies a reason why later generations should refrain from using their own, best moral judgment to interpret the Constitution's abstract phrases; indeed, on Scalia's account, the whole point of constitutionalism is to avert the exercise of judgment by later generations, whose judgment (it is feared) might be rotten. Scalia's theory belongs to a larger family of constitutional theories all of which assert that the purpose of written constitutions is, for one reason or another, to preclude Americans from engaging in open-ended moral argument. For example, Walter Berns maintains that the purpose of the American Constitution was to "negate and minimize" moral controversies which might disrupt the peace that is an essential pre-condition of liberty and democracy.[49] He argues that the exercise of "lawyer[s'] . . . private [moral] judgment" in constitutional adjudication is inconsistent with that goal.[50]

Dworkin, by contrast, does not offer any theory to justify the extraordinary rigidity of the American Constitution. As a result, his expansive view of constitutional rights appears to be the product of historical and textual accidents. The Framers of the Constitution entrenched specific and now obsolete judgments about (among other things) contractual liberty, guns, and juries. Nevertheless, the Constitution came to include certain clauses which (according to Dworkin) protect every right we should demand from a government. America's hard-to-amend Constitution seems calculated to favor stability and conserve past practices, but it turns out to contain sweeping moral principles which demand potentially radical reforms. What stunning good fortune!

---

[47] Scalia, A Matter of Interpretation, *supra* note 20, at 40–41.

[48] *Id.* Many other lawyers and scholars, with viewpoints quite different from Scalia's, also build their constitutional theories around the fact that Article V permits super-majorities to entrench specific judgments against later revision. *See, e.g.,* B. Ackerman, We the People: Foundations 14 (1991).

[49] W. Berns, *Taking Rights Frivolously,* in Liberalism Reconsidered 51, 59 (D. MacLean & C. Mills, eds., 1983).   [50] *Id.* at 64.

Dworkin's theory of constitutional interpretation is thus incomplete. To answer arguments like those made by Scalia, Berns, and others, Dworkin must offer an alternative account of American constitutional institutions and super-majoritarian amendment procedures.

VII. The Pragmatic Virtues of Super-majoritarian Amendment Rules

To rebut "dead hand" theories of constitutionalism, we must explain why reasonable constitution-makers might create super-majoritarian amendment procedures if they aim to establish government on the basis of evolving standards of justice. That project turns out to be easier than one might first suppose. The key idea is this: we can regard super-majoritarian amendment procedures as mechanisms to discipline and structure, rather than abrogate, the exercise of independent judgment about political justice by subsequent generations.

I will briefly sketch one such account of super-majoritarian amendment procedures, an account that I elaborate at greater length in my book, *Constitutional Self-Government.*[51] There, I contend that super-majoritarian amendment procedures can serve at least three pro-democratic purposes. First, they prevent majorities from consolidating power at the expense of minorities. Various constitutional institutions may protect the rights and interests of minorities. Federalism and localism are examples: they permit national minorities to exercise power as local majorities. Judicial review is another institution that might protect the rights of minorities and individuals. If amendment procedures were thoroughly majoritarian, national majorities might use them to consolidate their power. Super-majoritarian amendment procedures make it more difficult for majorities to do so. This justification for super-majoritarian procedures does not depend on the idea that there is anything especially good about past practices or that the political judgment of future generations is "rotten." Instead, the idea is that super-majoritarian amendment procedures safeguard political institutions that discipline current-day judgment to take into account the interests of minorities as well as majorities.

Secondly, super-majoritarian amendment procedures help to establish stable political institutions. Stable institutions are indispensable to effective government. If people argue too much about how to count the votes or when to hold an election, they will not be able to select and implement policies regarding national security, social welfare, or civil rights. Under some circumstances, especially when polities are young, flexible amendment procedures may destabilize institutions. Political parties and interest groups may find it tempting to open and reopen questions about institutional design either because of a public-regarding impulse

---

[51] C. L. EISGRUBER, CONSTITUTIONAL SELF-GOVERNMENT 12–20 (2001).

to perfect their institutions, or because they want to increase their own power. Of course, the opposite problem also exists: if amendment procedures are too demanding, people may find it impossible to make needed reforms. Nevertheless, it is at least possible that super-majoritarian amendment procedures may help people to establish and maintain effective political institutions. Once again, this rationale for super-majoritarian procedures does not depend upon the idea that it is desirable to preserve past practices or avoid the exercise of present-day judgments about justice: on the contrary, it rests upon a recognition that people must have stable political institutions in order to make and implement such judgments.

Thirdly, super-majoritarian amendment procedures create incentives that may improve the quality of institutional reform. As Lawrence G. Sager has pointed out, the American Constitution's demanding amendment procedures encourage constitution-makers and constitution-amenders to think about the longterm consequences of reform.[52] Because the Constitution is hard to change, constitution-makers are reminded that their children and grandchildren must live with the consequences of their decisions. If the Constitution were easier to amend, framers and ratifiers might instead focus on short-term objectives, assuming that future majorities were free to undo their work if it proved uncongenial to later circumstances. That would be a mistake: institutional reforms have lasting consequences even when they are not constitutionally entrenched. For example, there is no constitutional provision that protects the Department of Energy, but that does not mean that the Department is easily abolished once it is created. On Sager's account, the point of super-majoritarian amendment procedures is not to preserve past practices, but rather to discipline reforms so they do not favor short-term, specific practices and judgments at the expense of evolving views about justice and the common good.

In *Constitutional Self-Government*, I argue that all three of these functions, including the first one, should be understood as pro-democratic. More specifically, I argue that democracy differs from pure majoritarianism, so that democracy requires solicitude for the rights and interests of minorities as well as majorities.[53] For present purposes, we need not concern ourselves with these claims about democracy. We can reject the "dead hand" theory, and accept Dworkin's approach to constitutional language, so long as we can regard the Constitution's super-majoritarian amendment procedures as serving purposes consistent with the goal of creating a government that respects very abstract standards of justice. It is then a separate question whether we should conceive of that government as democratic, or whether we should instead regard it as another form of government— say, "constitutional democracy"—that limits democracy in order to promote liberty or some other aspect of constitutional justice.

---

[52] L. G. Sager, *The Incorrigible Constitution*, 65 N.Y.U. L. Rev. 893, 951–953 (1990).

[53] Eisgruber, Constitutional Self-Government, *supra* note 51, at 18–20, 52–56. *See also* C. L. Eisgruber, *Constitutional Self-Government and Judicial Review: A Reply to Five Critics*, 37 U. S. F. L. Rev. 115, 120–128 (2002); C. L. Eisgruber, *Dimensions of Democracy*, 71 Ford. L. Rev. 1723, 1725–1738 (2003).

Nor need we conclude that Article V is perfect, or optimal, in order to conclude that its purpose is consistent with the goal of honoring abstract standards of justice. It is entirely possible that Article V is too demanding, so that its net *effect* is to "empower the dead hand of the past."[54] But that conclusion, if we endorsed it, would not give us any reason to accept Scalia's view, which is that a constitution's "whole purpose is to prevent change." We have identified reasons why good constitution-makers might make amendment difficult even if the goal of constitution-making is to create a government that honors evolving judgments about abstract standards of justice. Those reasons remain valid even if America's framers miscalculated and made the American Constitution too hard to amend. It would be perverse to assume that, if the framers designed suboptimal amendment procedures, we should interpret their more abstract constitutional provisions in a way that magnifies, rather than ameliorates, their error.

If Dworkin endorsed a theory of super-majoritarian amendment procedures akin to the one that I have proposed, he could easily employ that theory to buttress his expansive readings of the Constitution's liberty-bearing clauses. Perhaps Dworkin has in mind another, quite different theory of constitutionalism. But in any event Dworkin owes us some theory of constitutionalism.[55] For the moment, Dworkin's presentation of his theory relies too heavily upon claims about hermeneutics—claims about the interpretation of language and law in general (as opposed to claims about American constitutional procedures and institutions in particular). As a result, there is a conceptual gap between his "moral reading of the Constitution" and his broad reading of the Due Process and Equal Protection Clauses. The "moral reading" entails only that those clauses state abstract moral principles; the moral reading tells us nothing about *which* principles they state. In particular, it does not tell us whether those Clauses state that "the government must treat everyone as of equal status and with equal concern."[56] Dworkin cannot remedy this deficiency by appealing to the text of the Clauses; they speak with Delphic obscurity. Dworkin's own theory suggests that we should interpret those terms in a way that would make them consistent with the provisions that a good drafter of the American Constitution would have enacted. But to know what provisions a good drafter would enact, we must know what it means to do a good job drafting an American-style constitution (that is, a constitution which is written and hard to amend). In other words, we must know what purposes are served by having an American-style constitution. And to know that, we must have Dworkin's theory of constitutional institutions, a theory he has not yet given us.

---

[54] For discussion of this possibility, *see* EISGRUBER, CONSTITUTIONAL SELF-GOVERNMENT, *supra* note 51, at 20–25.

[55] As Jed Rubenfeld has said, Dworkin must pay more attention to "what kind of text the Constitution is and who its interpreters are." J. Rubenfeld, *On Fidelity in Constitutional Law*, 65 FORD. L. REV. 1469, 1477 (1997). Unfortunately, Rubenfeld understands this inquiry as pertaining to the Constitution's legitimacy and authority, rather than its purposes or function. The demands of political legitimacy are too weak to be helpful; many varieties of constitutionalism (and, for that matter, non-constitutional government) will qualify as legitimate.

[56] DWORKIN, FREEDOM'S LAW, *supra* note 41, at 10.

VIII. Conclusion

In my view, Ronald Dworkin has analyzed the structure of judicial reasoning in American constitutional law more perspicuously than has any other commentator. My aim here has been not to contest his position, but rather to clarify some of its presuppositions. My interpretation of Dworkin's "moral reading" has two important consequences, both of which I hope that Dworkin might accept. First, although Dworkin long ago called for a "fusion of constitutional law and moral philosophy," the moral reading does not require that result. The moral reading requires judges who decide constitutional cases to focus on moral principle, but they might do so without engaging in philosophical analysis. What matters most is not whether judges view the Constitution through the lens of history or philosophy or something else, but whether they aim at moral principle. There is a great difference between consulting history at the expense of our judgments about justice (as Scalia purports to do)[57] and consulting history to discipline and improve our judgments about justice. That difference, I believe, swamps the significance of methodological differences among judges who agree that the Constitution demands judgments about moral principle, but who disagree about whether those judgments should take the form of philosophical analysis or interpretations of American history. My argument thus permits a negative answer to the question that forms the title of this essay: it is at least possible that judges have no cause to study moral philosophy, and should continue, as lawyers have traditionally done, to steep themselves in the lessons of political history instead.

Secondly, if judges fail to approach the Constitution in the proper spirit, they are likely to do so because they subscribe to a mistaken view about the Constitution's purpose. Many people believe, as Scalia apparently does, that the point of constitutionalism is to empower the "dead hand of the past" and so to deny the ability of later generations to govern themselves on the basis of their own best judgments about justice and the common good. It is easy to see why people reach that mistaken conclusion, and once they are in its grip, they believe themselves duty-bound to vindicate historical opinion even at the expense of justice. To correct this mistake, one needs a persuasive account of how constitutionalism facilitates government on the basis of abstract standards of justice. One must explain, in particular, why the Constitution quite reasonably prescribes specific, obdurate rules with respect to some issues, but leaves other issues open to vigorous and heated debate. Dworkin's argument for the "moral reading of the Constitution," with its almost exclusive emphasis upon what the Constitution says, does not address the purpose of constitutionalism.

---

[57] Larry Kramer has described Scalia as embracing a kind of "judicial asceticism" under which "it literally becomes necessary [for Scalia] to reach some results that [he] knows are unjust." L. Kramer, *Judicial Asceticism*, 12 CARDOZO L. REV. 1789, 1795 (1991).

2

The Place of History and Philosophy in the Moral Reading of the American Constitution

*James E. Fleming**

I. Introduction

Ronald Dworkin has long recognized that the fundamental questions of "What is the Constitution?" and "How should it be interpreted?" are the central questions of fidelity in constitutional interpretation.[1] From his first book, *Taking Rights Seriously*,[2] to his book, *Freedom's Law*,[3] Dworkin has argued that commitment to interpretive fidelity requires that we recognize that the Constitution embodies abstract moral principles rather than laying down particular historical conceptions and that interpreting and applying those principles require fresh judgments of political theory about how they are best understood. He now calls this interpretive strategy the "moral reading" of the Constitution. Yet, narrow originalists such as Robert H. Bork and Justice Antonin Scalia have asserted a monopoly on concern for fidelity in constitutional interpretation, claiming that fidelity requires following the rules laid down by, or giving effect to the relatively specific original understanding of, the framers and ratifiers of the Constitution.[4] They have

---

* I prepared this essay for the conference, "Exploring Law's Empire: The Jurisprudence of Ronald Dworkin," held at Princeton University on September 18, 2004. The essay is largely drawn from my article, *Fidelity to Our Imperfect Constitution*, 65 FORDHAM L. REV. 1335 (1997), which I prepared for a symposium, *Fidelity in Constitutional Theory*, 65 FORDHAM L. REV. 1247–1818 (1997), for which Ronald Dworkin gave the keynote address.
[1] These questions of "What?" and "How?," along with the question of "Who is to interpret?," are the basic interrogatives of constitutional interpretation. *See* W. F. MURPHY ET AL., AMERICAN CONSTITUTIONAL INTERPRETATION 17–20 (3d ed. 2003).
[2] R. DWORKIN, TAKING RIGHTS SERIOUSLY 131–149 (1977) [hereinafter DWORKIN, TAKING RIGHTS SERIOUSLY].
[3] R. DWORKIN, FREEDOM'S LAW: THE MORAL READING OF THE AMERICAN CONSTITUTION 1–38, 72–83 (1996) [hereinafter DWORKIN, FREEDOM'S LAW]; *see also* R. Dworkin, *The Arduous Virtue of Fidelity: Originalism, Scalia, Tribe, and Nerve*, 65 FORDHAM L. REV. 1249 (1997), reprinted in R. DWORKIN, JUSTICE IN ROBES 117 (2006).
[4] *See* R. H. BORK, THE TEMPTING OF AMERICA: THE POLITICAL SEDUCTION OF THE LAW (1990); A. SCALIA, A MATTER OF INTERPRETATION (1997); A. Scalia, *Originalism: The Lesser Evil*, 57 U. CIN. L. REV. 849 (1989).

charged that constitutional theorists who reject these claims are "revisionists" who disregard fidelity, thereby subverting the Constitution. Dworkin has vigorously and cogently punctured the narrow originalists' pretensions to a monopoly on fidelity, arguing that commitment to fidelity entails that we pursue integrity with the moral reading of the Constitution and that they, the narrow originalists, are the real "revisionists."[5]

I shall analyze two strategies for responding to the narrow originalists' claim to a monopoly on fidelity. Dworkin takes the first: Turn the tables on the narrow originalists. He argues that commitment to fidelity entails the very approach that they are at pains to insist it forbids, and prohibits the very approach that they imperiously maintain it mandates. The second is taken by Bruce Ackerman and Lawrence Lessig, to say nothing of Lessig's sometime co-author, Cass R. Sunstein: Beat the narrow originalists at their own game.[6] Ackerman, Lessig, and Sunstein advance fidelity as synthesis and fidelity as translation as "broad" or "soft" forms of originalism that are superior, as conceptions of originalism, to narrow originalism. What is "broad" or "soft" about their forms of originalism is that these theorists conceive original understanding at a considerably higher level of abstraction than do the narrow originalists.[7] At the same time, they argue that the quest for fidelity requires that we reject Dworkin's moral reading.[8] Indeed, Lessig and Sunstein

---

[5] DWORKIN, FREEDOM'S LAW, *supra* note 3, at 74–76; R. DWORKIN, LIFE'S DOMINION: AN ARGUMENT ABOUT ABORTION, EUTHANASIA, AND INDIVIDUAL FREEDOM 125–129 (1993) [hereinafter DWORKIN, LIFE'S DOMINION]. I take the term "integrity" from Dworkin's conception of "law as integrity." *See* R. DWORKIN, LAW'S EMPIRE 176–275 (1986) [hereinafter DWORKIN, LAW'S EMPIRE]. For an insightful analysis of Dworkin's general conception of legal reasoning in relation to fidelity, *see* G. C. Keating, *Fidelity to Pre-Existing Law and the Legitimacy of Legal Decision*, 69 NOTRE DAME L. REV. 1 (1993).

[6] *See* B. ACKERMAN, WE THE PEOPLE: FOUNDATIONS (1991) [hereinafter ACKERMAN, WE THE PEOPLE]; B. Ackerman, *A Generation of Betrayal?*, 65 FORDHAM L. REV. 1519 (1997); L. Lessig, *Fidelity and Constraint*, 65 FORDHAM L. REV. 1365 (1997) [hereinafter Lessig, *Constraint*]; L. Lessig, *Understanding Changed Readings: Fidelity and Theory*, 47 STAN. L. REV. 395 (1995); L. Lessig, *Fidelity in Translation*, 71 TEX. L. REV. 1165 (1993) [hereinafter Lessig, *Fidelity*]; L. Lessig & C. R. Sunstein, *The President and the Administration*, 94 COLUM. L. REV. 1 (1994); C. R. SUNSTEIN, LEGAL REASONING AND POLITICAL CONFLICT (1996) [hereinafter SUNSTEIN, LEGAL REASONING]. Other works illustrating the emergence of a form of broad originalism include M. J. PERRY, THE CONSTITUTION IN THE COURTS: LAW OR POLITICS? (1994); M. S. Flaherty, *History "Lite" in Modern American Constitutionalism*, 95 COLUM. L. REV. 523 (1995); W. M. Treanor, *The Original Understanding of the Takings Clause and the Political Process*, 95 COLUM. L. REV. 782 (1995).

[7] *See* SUNSTEIN, LEGAL REASONING, *supra* note 6, at 171–182; B. Ackerman, *Liberating Abstraction*, 59 U. CHI. L. REV. 317 (1992).

[8] For an example of Lessig's rejection of Dworkin's moral reading, *see* Lessig, *Fidelity, supra* note 6, at 1259–1261. For an example of Sunstein's rejection of Dworkin's moral reading in favor of an alternative moral reading, *see* C. R. Sunstein, *Earl Warren Is Dead*, NEW REPUBLIC, May 13, 1996, at 35 (reviewing DWORKIN, FREEDOM'S LAW, *supra* note 3). For Ackerman's rejection of Dworkin's "rights foundationalism" in favor of his own conception of "dualist democracy," *see* ACKERMAN, WE THE PEOPLE, *supra* note 6, at 6–16. For examples of interpretations of Ackerman's work as an attempt to develop a broad form of originalism, *see* Flaherty, *supra* note 6, at 579–590; J. E. Fleming, *We the Exceptional American People*, 11 CONST. COMMENTARY 355, 369–370 (1994); F. Michelman, *Law's Republic*, 97 YALE L.J. 1493, 1521–1523 (1988); S. Sherry, *The Ghost of Liberalism Past*, 105 HARV. L. REV. 918, 933–934 (1992) (reviewing ACKERMAN, WE THE PEOPLE, *supra* note 6).

make the Borkish suggestion that Dworkin's project is not one of fidelity, but one of improvement.[9] Thus, the broad originalists attempt to develop an intermediate theory between narrow originalism and the moral reading.

Dworkin argues that the search for an intermediate theory is pointless and that the moral reading is the only coherent strategy for interpreting the Constitution.[10] I shall explore the reasons for constitutional theorists' resistance to the moral reading, and for their persistence in searching for an intermediate theory in the form of a broad originalism. Dworkin offers one reason: They are in the grip of an unfounded assumption, the "majoritarian premise," which leads them to reject the moral reading on democratic grounds. In Part II, I critique his analysis and, more generally, assess his constitutional conception of democracy and his moral reading as a substantive theory of the Constitution. Then, in Part III, I put forward a second reason, which centers on the idea of fidelity: They are in the hold of another problematic assumption, the "originalist premise," which causes them to reject the moral reading on "fidelist" grounds. There I assess Dworkin's moral reading as a theory of constitutional interpretation. I contend that the broad originalists, like the narrow originalists, fundamentally misconceive fidelity. The commitment to fidelity to the Constitution entails, as Dworkin argues, that we should interpret it so as to make it the best it can be.[11] But broad originalists such as Lessig mistake this commitment to fidelity as proof that Dworkin is an "infidel."[12] Ironically, in the name of interpretive fidelity, the broad originalists, like the narrow originalists, would enshrine an imperfect Constitution that does not deserve our fidelity. Only under the moral reading do we have much hope of interpreting our imperfect Constitution in a manner that might deserve our fidelity.[13] Finally, in Part IV, I suggest that the moral reading is a big tent, and urge liberal and progressive theorists who have resisted the moral reading in favor of questing for a broad originalism to reconceive their work as coming within it: in particular, as being in service of the moral reading by providing a firmer grounding for the moral reading in fit with historical materials than Dworkin has offered.

---

[9] Lessig & Sunstein, *supra* note 6, at 11 n.35, 85 n.336.

[10] DWORKIN, FREEDOM'S LAW, *supra* note 3, at 14, 18.

[11] DWORKIN, LAW'S EMPIRE, *supra* note 5, at 176–275; R. DWORKIN, A MATTER OF PRINCIPLE 146–166 (1985) [hereinafter DWORKIN, A MATTER OF PRINCIPLE].

[12] Lessig, *Fidelity, supra* note 6, at 1260.

[13] Elsewhere, I have characterized the constitutional theory that I develop, constitutional constructivism, as a "Constitution-perfecting theory," as distinguished from a "process-perfecting theory." *See* J. E. FLEMING, SECURING CONSTITUTIONAL DEMOCRACY: THE CASE OF AUTONOMY 4–5, 226–227 (2006). I mean "perfecting" in the sense of interpreting the Constitution with integrity so as to render it a coherent whole, not in Monaghan's caricatured sense of "Our perfect Constitution" as a perfect liberal utopia. *See* H. P. Monaghan, *Our Perfect Constitution*, 56 N.Y.U. L. REV. 353, 356 (1981). Dworkin addresses the "perfect Constitution" objection, which is that his interpretations of the Constitution always seem to have "happy endings" or "liberal endings." DWORKIN, FREEDOM'S LAW, *supra* note 3, at 36. He concedes that the Constitution is not perfect, for it does not protect "all the important principles of political liberalism." *Id.* Nonetheless, he argues that "[i]t is in the nature of legal interpretation—not just but particularly constitutional interpretation—to aim at happy endings." *Id.* at 38. In that sense, Dworkin's moral reading is also a Constitution-perfecting theory.

II. The Moral Reading and the Majoritarian Premise: or, The Moral Reading as a Substantive Theory of the Constitution

In *Freedom's Law*, Dworkin argues that the moral reading of the Constitution is more faithful than the originalist strategy is to the text of the Constitution and the conception of democracy it presupposes. He contends that "the only substantial objection to the moral reading, which takes the text seriously, is that it offends democracy."[14] Moreover, he argues that constitutional lawyers and scholars who make this objection are in the grip of an unfounded assumption, the "majoritarian premise."[15] This is the assumption that the fundamental value or point of democracy is commitment to the goal of majority will. This premise undergirds a majoritarian conception of democracy that is not true to our scheme of government and that indeed obscures the true character and importance of our system.[16] As an alternative, Dworkin offers a constitutional conception of democracy which conceives the fundamental point or value of democracy to be concern for the equal status of citizens.[17] He then considers and rejects three arguments for the majoritarian premise, which are rooted in liberty, equality, and community.[18] I believe that Dworkin's arguments for the moral reading and against democratic objections rooted in the majoritarian premise are sound. But I shall criticize his formulation of a constitutional conception of democracy—or constitutional democracy—and his own moral reading as a substantive theory of the Constitution.

First, Dworkin is right to lay bare and criticize the majoritarian premise and the majoritarian conception of democracy that stems from it. For too long, that premise and conception have hobbled constitutional theory by providing a misguided and misleading account of our constitutional scheme. They have driven constitutional theorists to regard as deviant or anomalous certain integral features of that scheme. Most famously, that premise and conception underlie Alexander M. Bickel's anxious claim that judicial review is a "deviant institution" that poses a "counter-majoritarian difficulty" in our democracy.[19] Dworkin in effect turns Bickel on his head,[20] for Dworkin's formulation of the "majoritarian premise" as an unfounded assumption is the inverted mirror image of Bickel's formulation of the "counter-majoritarian difficulty" as the root problem. On Dworkin's view, the fact that many constitutional theorists are obsessed with the "counter-majoritarian difficulty" presents a serious problem, because it obscures from them the true character of our system and prevents them from embracing the moral reading.

---

[14] DWORKIN, FREEDOM'S LAW, *supra* note 3, at 15.   [15] *Id.* at 16.   [16] *Id.* at 15–17.
[17] *Id.* at 17–18.   [18] *Id.* at 21–31.
[19] A. M. BICKEL, THE LEAST DANGEROUS BRANCH: THE SUPREME COURT AT THE BAR OF POLITICS 16, 18 (2d ed. 1986).
[20] Similarly, Sunstein has suggested that Dworkin has stood Judge Learned Hand on his head. *See* SUNSTEIN, *supra* note 8, at 36.

But Dworkin would be wrong to suggest—and I do not believe that he does so—that all democratic objections to the moral reading, in particular those advanced by the broad originalists, are rooted in the majoritarian premise and the majoritarian conception of democracy. For example, Sunstein makes democratic objections to Dworkin's moral reading from the standpoint of his own non-majoritarian conception of democracy—deliberative democracy—and of his less abstract, more pragmatic conception of legal reasoning.[21] Moreover, Sunstein advances these objections through developing an alternative moral reading of the Constitution, rather than rejecting completely the idea of a moral reading. This form of criticism is presumably the type that Dworkin would welcome, for it engages the idea of a moral reading rather than wholly rejecting it.[22]

Secondly, Dworkin is correct in arguing that a constitutional conception of democracy—or a conception of constitutional democracy—better fits and justifies our constitutional text and practice than does a majoritarian conception of democracy. He is persuasive in contending that protection of, and respect for, rights that are the conditions for moral membership in our political community are themselves preconditions for the legitimacy of the outcomes of majoritarian political processes.[23] Here Dworkin appears to have taken a page out of John Hart Ely's book, *Democracy and Distrust*,[24] in arguing for conceiving our rights as preconditions for the legitimacy or trustworthiness of democracy. But unlike Ely, Dworkin would include, among the conditions of democracy, certain "substantive" rights such as moral independence, in addition to "procedural" rights like the right to vote.[25]

Dworkin is mostly right about what the conditions of moral membership in our political community are. But the architecture of his constitutional theory is problematic. I fear that Dworkin's characterization of all of these substantive and procedural rights as "democratic conditions" may lead to unnecessary trouble and resistance. Many readers may resist his argument that substantive rights like moral independence are "democratic conditions." Even if they grant that both substantive and procedural rights must be protected for the outcomes of the majoritarian political processes to be legitimate or trustworthy, they may suspect that he is pulling a fast one, or making it too easy, or being too clever by packing all of the rights that constrain majoritarian political processes into the "democratic conditions."[26] To observe, as Dworkin might, that such readers' objections seem to

21 *See* C. R. SUNSTEIN, THE PARTIAL CONSTITUTION (1993) [hereinafter SUNSTEIN, PARTIAL CONSTITUTION]; SUNSTEIN, LEGAL REASONING, *supra* note 6.

22 DWORKIN, FREEDOM'S LAW, *supra* note 3, at 38.

23 *Id.* at 24; *see* DWORKIN, LIFE'S DOMINION, *supra* note 5, at 123.

24 J. H. ELY, DEMOCRACY AND DISTRUST (1980).

25 DWORKIN, FREEDOM'S LAW, *supra* note 3, at 24–26, 349 n.5. For Dworkin's earlier critique of Ely, *see* R. Dworkin, *The Forum of Principle*, 56 N.Y.U. L. REV. 469 (1981), reprinted in DWORKIN, A MATTER OF PRINCIPLE, *supra* note 11, at 33 [hereinafter Dworkin, *The Forum of Principle*].

26 L. G. Sager has made a similar critique of the architecture of Dworkin's theory, although his primary focus was on the theories of Ely, Ackerman, and Frank Michelman. *See* L. G. Sager, *The Incorrigible Constitution*, 65 N.Y.U. L. REV. 893, 942–948 (1990) (criticizing Dworkin's

presuppose the unfounded majoritarian premise may be true, but unhelpful if the aim is to persuade them to abandon it.

I believe that there is a more straightforward and plausible theoretical structure through which to present conceptions of constitutional democracy like Dworkin's. Elsewhere, I criticize the architecture of constitutional theories such as those of Ely and Sunstein, which attempt to frame or recast all of our basic liberties, both substantive and procedural, as preconditions for representative or deliberative democracy.[27] I argue instead for a constitutional constructivism,[28] a conception of constitutional democracy with two fundamental themes: first, securing the basic liberties that are preconditions for *deliberative democracy*, to enable citizens to apply their capacity for a conception of justice to deliberating about the justice of basic institutions and social policies, and secondly, securing the basic liberties that are preconditions for *deliberative autonomy*, to enable citizens to apply their capacity for a conception of the good to deliberating about and deciding how to live their own lives. Together, these themes for securing constitutional democracy afford everyone the common and guaranteed status of free and equal citizenship in our morally pluralistic constitutional democracy.[29] (This conception has affinities to Dworkin's view that the fundamental point or value of our scheme of government is concern for the equal status of citizens.)[30] I offer my account, constitutional constructivism, as the guiding framework that best fits and justifies our constitutional text and underlying constitutional order.[31]

Moreover, I contend elsewhere that there are good reasons for conceiving our basic liberties in terms of securing the preconditions for deliberative democracy and deliberative autonomy instead of framing them as, or reducing them into, preconditions for democracy.[32] The first reason is prophylactic: Articulating a constitutional constructivism with these two themes protects us against taking

"constitutive account"). In his recent book, Sager analyzes and criticizes Dworkin's theory as being, like Ely's and Michelman's theories, a "democratarian account." L. G. SAGER, JUSTICE IN PLAINCLOTHES: A THEORY OF AMERICAN CONSTITUTIONAL PRACTICE 132–137 (2004) [hereinafter SAGER, JUSTICE IN PLAINCLOTHES].

[27] FLEMING, *supra* note 13, at 4–5, 29–34, 43–51.

[28] I mean constitutional constructivism in two senses. First, I intend a general methodological sense of constructivism, illustrated by Dworkin's conception of constitutional interpretation as constructing schemes of principles that best fit and justify our constitutional document and underlying constitutional order as a whole. Dworkin originally put forth this conception by analogy to Rawls's conception of justification in political philosophy as a quest for reflective equilibrium. DWORKIN, TAKING RIGHTS SERIOUSLY, *supra* note 2, at 159–168. Secondly, I intend a specific substantive sense of constructivism, exemplified by John Rawls's conception of the equal basic liberties in a constitutional democracy such as our own as being grounded on a conception of citizens as free and equal persons, together with a conception of society as a fair system of social cooperation. J. RAWLS, POLITICAL LIBERALISM (1993).

[29] FLEMING, *supra* note 13, at 3–6, 61–74. I develop this theory by analogy to Rawls's political constructivism. See RAWLS, *supra* note 28.

[30] *See* DWORKIN, FREEDOM'S LAW, *supra* note 3, at 17.

[31] For examples of Dworkin's formulations of the two dimensions of best interpretation, fit and justification, *see* DWORKIN, LAW'S EMPIRE, *supra* note 5, at 239; DWORKIN, A MATTER OF PRINCIPLE, *supra* note 11, at 143–145; DWORKIN, TAKING RIGHTS SERIOUSLY, *supra* note 2, at 107.

[32] FLEMING, *supra* note 13, at 78–79.

flights from substance to process by recasting substantive liberties as procedural liberties or neglecting them. The second, related reason is architectonic: Presenting our basic liberties in these terms illustrates that the two fundamental themes of deliberative democracy and deliberative autonomy are co-original and of equal weight. The third, more general reason is heuristic: Articulating our basic liberties through these two themes keeps in view that our constitutional scheme is a dualist constitutional democracy, not a monist or majoritarian representative democracy. A final reason is elegance: the importance of being elegant (though not too reductive) in constructing a constitutional theory. I originally advanced these reasons for adopting the architecture of a constitutional constructivism with the foregoing two themes as part of a critique of the architecture of process-perfecting theories such as Ely's and Sunstein's, which recast our basic liberties, substantive and procedural, as preconditions for representative democracy or deliberative democracy, but they also apply with some force to the architecture of Dworkin's conception of such basic liberties as preconditions for democracy. That is, the architecture of a constitutional theory with these two themes, which together secure the preconditions for constitutional democracy, has these advantages over the architecture of Dworkin's theory.

Thirdly, and most importantly—to make explicit what has been implicit in my critique of the structure of Dworkin's constitutional theory—Dworkin never has developed a moral reading as a general substantive liberal theory of our Constitution and underlying constitutional democracy. To be sure, he has written powerfully and cogently about the major constitutional issues of the day, and has done so from a coherent and consistent viewpoint. Indeed, no one has made greater contributions to constitutional theory than Dworkin has. But Dworkin has not worked up a comprehensive yet elegant account of our basic liberties and constitutional essentials as a substantive theory to beat Ely's and Sunstein's process-perfecting theories.

That has been my project over the past decade or so. I have sought to develop a *Constitution-perfecting theory* as an alternative to the *process-perfecting theories* advanced by Ely and Sunstein.[33] According to the latter theories, the Constitution's core commitment is democracy, and judicial review is justified principally when the processes of democracy, and thus the political decisions resulting from them, are undeserving of trust. Process-perfecting theories are vulnerable to the criticism that they reject certain substantive liberties (such as privacy, autonomy, liberty of conscience, and freedom of association) as anomalous in our scheme, except insofar as such liberties can be recast as procedural preconditions for democracy. Yet process-perfecting theories persist, notwithstanding such criticisms, because no one has done for "substance" what Ely has done for "process." That is, no one has developed an alternative substantive Constitution-perfecting theory—a theory that would reinforce not only the procedural liberties (those related to deliberative democracy) but also the substantive

---

[33] *See id.* at 4–5.

liberties (those related to deliberative autonomy) embodied in our Constitution and presupposed by our constitutional democracy—with the elegance and power of Ely's process-perfecting theory.

That is what my book, *Securing Constitutional Democracy*, aspires to do. I develop a Constitution-perfecting theory that secures both the substantive liberties associated with *deliberative autonomy* and the procedural liberties associated with *deliberative democracy* as fundamental, without deriving the former from the latter or, worse, failing to account for substantive liberties altogether. Unlike process theories, it provides a firm grounding for rights of privacy and autonomy, along with liberty of conscience and freedom of association, as necessary to secure individual freedom and to promote a diverse and vigorous civil society. My theory also shows how basic liberties associated with personal autonomy, along with those related to democratic participation, fit together into a coherent scheme of basic liberties and constitutional essentials that are integral to our constitutional democracy.

Finally, Dworkin is right to conceive courts as a "forum of principle,"[34] while recognizing that legislatures and executives are also "guardians of principle."[35] Some liberals and progressives, emphasizing Dworkin's conception of courts as "the forum of principle," have criticized his theory for being too court-centered and for ignoring "the Constitution outside the courts."[36] That criticism, although understandable, is plainly overstated. Dworkin has always made clear that legislatures, executives, and citizens also have responsibilities to interpret the Constitution.[37] Sanford Levinson recognized this early on, and appropriately interpreted Dworkin as a constitutional "protestant" instead of a court-centered "catholic" on the question, "Who is to interpret the Constitution?"[38]

Dworkin makes a nod in the direction of endorsing Lawrence G. Sager's well-known view that certain constitutional principles required by political justice are judicially underenforced, yet nonetheless may impose affirmative obligations outside the courts on legislatures, executives, and citizens generally to realize them more fully.[39] Sager's view is an important component of a full moral reading or justice-seeking account of the Constitution. For it helps make sense of the evident "thinness" or "moral shortfall" of constitutional law, while still offering a moral

[34] Dworkin, *The Forum of Principle*, supra note 25.

[35] DWORKIN, FREEDOM'S LAW, *supra* note 3, at 31.

[36] *See* SUNSTEIN, LEGAL REASONING, *supra* note 6, at 59–60; SUNSTEIN, PARTIAL CONSTITUTION, *supra* note 21, at 9, 145–146, 374 n.35.

[37] *See* DWORKIN, FREEDOM'S LAW, *supra* note 3, at 31.

[38] S. Levinson, *"The Constitution" in American Civil Religion*, 1979 SUP. CT. REV. 123, 141 (interpreting Dworkin as a constitutional "protestant" on the question "Who is to interpret the Constitution?"); *see* S. LEVINSON, CONSTITUTIONAL FAITH 42–44 (1988). Dworkin has also referred to his approach on this question as a "protestant" approach. *See* DWORKIN, LAW'S EMPIRE, *supra* note 5, at 190, 413.

[39] DWORKIN, FREEDOM'S LAW, *supra* note 3, at 33–34. For Sager's view, see SAGER, JUSTICE IN PLAINCLOTHES, *supra* note 26; L. G. Sager, *Justice in Plain Clothes: Reflections on the Thinness of Constitutional Law*, 88 NW. U. L. REV. 410 (1993); L. G. Sager, *Fair Measure: The Legal Status of Underenforced Constitutional Norms*, 91 HARV. L. REV. 1212 (1978).

reading or justice-seeking account.[40] I would urge Dworkin to consider adopting such a view. (Of course, many questions would remain concerning what is and what is not judicially enforceable.) I believe that he could do so without undermining his arguments against the majoritarian premise.

III. The Moral Reading and the Originalist Premise: or, The Moral Reading as a Theory of Constitutional Interpretation

Next, I shall consider another reason why the broad originalists have resisted the moral reading, which centers on the idea of fidelity: They are in the grip of what I shall call the "originalist premise." This is the assumption that originalism, rightly conceived, is the best, or indeed the only, conception of fidelity in constitutional interpretation. On this view, fidelity by definition, or at least as practiced in our constitutional culture, must be concerned with following the original meaning of the text, the original understanding of the framers and ratifiers, or the like. The originalist premise leads to objections to the moral reading on the ground that it is "nonoriginalist," "revisionist," or not "fidelist."

The originalist premise is expressed in its most extreme form by Bork, who asserts that originalism is the only possible approach to constitutional interpretation that is faithful to the historic Constitution and consonant with the constitutional design. He rejects all other approaches, most especially those like Dworkin's, as "revisionist."[41] In recent years, the originalist premise has also been manifested in the emerging strain of broad originalism in liberal and progressive constitutional theory. For example, Lessig evidently takes the view that originalism, by definition, is the only method of fidelity. Most strikingly, he has made the Borkish assertion that Dworkin is an "infidel," and he and Sunstein have suggested that Dworkin does not even have a method of fidelity.[42] I believe that the originalist premise, as much as the majoritarian premise, drives the broad originalists' resistance to Dworkin's moral reading.

In unpacking what I have loosely called the originalist premise, I shall examine several reasons why some liberal and progressive constitutional theorists have resisted Dworkin's moral reading in favor of searching for an intermediate theory in

[40] For a justice-seeking account or moral reading of the Constitution that is thicker, or countenances less moral shortfall through judicial underenforcement than does Sager's view, *see* S. A. BARBER, WELFARE AND THE CONSTITUTION (2003); S. A. BARBER, THE CONSTITUTION OF JUDICIAL POWER (1993) [hereinafter BARBER, POWER]; S. A. BARBER, ON WHAT THE CONSTITUTION MEANS (1984) [hereinafter BARBER, CONSTITUTION]; S. A. Barber, *Justice-Seeking Constitutionalism and Its Critics*, paper presented at the New York University School of Law Colloquium on Constitutional Theory (Apr. 20, 1995) (unpublished manuscript on file with the author).

[41] BORK, *supra* note 4, at 187–240. This is the obligatory footnote where I must acknowledge that Raoul Berger is more extreme than Bork (or, for that matter, Scalia). *See* R. BERGER, GOVERNMENT BY JUDICIARY: THE TRANSFORMATION OF THE FOURTEENTH AMENDMENT (1977).

[42] Lessig, *Fidelity*, *supra* note 6, at 1260; Lessig & Sunstein, *supra* note 6, at 11 n.35, 85 n.336.

the form of a broad originalism. More generally, I discuss the reasons for the emergence of this strain of broad originalism. I contend that none of these reasons is a good reason for the broad originalists not to endorse the moral reading, properly conceived. My general stance is to support broad originalism to the extent that its proponents undertake it in service of the moral reading, but to criticize it to the extent that they believe it is sustainable as an alternative to the moral reading.

A. The Turns to History and to Text, History, and Structure

First, the broad originalists seek to reclaim history, and indeed the aspiration to fidelity, from the narrow originalists. They believe that liberals and progressives ignored or neglected history for so long that they practically ceded it to conservatives.[43] The broad originalists undertook the "turn to history" to show that their constitutional theories, aspirations, and ideals are firmly rooted in our constitutional history and practice, and indeed provide a better account of our constitutional text and tradition than do those of the conservative narrow originalists.

The liberal and progressive project of reclaiming history and fidelity from the narrow originalists is understandable and laudable. But it is understandable and laudable if undertaken in service of the moral reading, not as an alternative to it. This project would explain a turn to history, but not necessarily a turn to originalism. They are not the same thing.[44] And it would explain a turn to history in order to pursue an historically grounded moral reading. But it would not necessarily explain a turn to history that turns away from the moral reading. The turn to history should not become an escape into history.[45] Why not conceive the turn to history as doing "fit" work in support of a liberal or progressive moral reading rather than as a broad form of originalism that rejects the moral reading?

Secondly, more generally, these liberals and progressives aim to ground their arguments in the text, history, and structure of the Constitution, and they believe that a broad originalism is more promising along these lines than is the moral reading.[46] Some recite this trilogy of sources of constitutional meaning as if it were a litany. Like the turn to history, the turn to text, history, and structure is an understandable and worthy project. Liberals and progressives should firmly ground their

---

[43] *See* L. KALMAN, THE STRANGE CAREER OF LEGAL LIBERALISM 132–163 (1996).

[44] The major criticism I have of Kalman's fine book is that she seems to treat the turn to history and the turn to originalism as if they were the same thing.

[45] *See* C. Woodard, *Escape into History*, N.Y. TIMES (Sept. 15, 1996), §7 (Book Review), at 33 (reviewing KALMAN, *supra* note 43).

[46] Among the enthusiasts of text, history, and structure are Sunstein, Akhil Amar, and Jeffrey Rosen. *See* SUNSTEIN, PARTIAL CONSTITUTION, *supra* note 21, at 119–122; A. R. Amar, *Intratextualism*, 112 HARV. L. REV. 747 (1999); A. R. Amar & V. D. Amar, *Is the Presidential Succession Law Constitutional?*, 48 STAN. L. REV. 113 (1995); J. Rosen, *A Womb with a View*, NEW REPUBLIC (June 14, 1993), at 35 (reviewing DWORKIN, LIFE'S DOMINION, *supra* note 5); *"Life's Dominion": An Exchange*, NEW REPUBLIC (Sept. 6, 1993), at 43 (exchange between Dworkin and Rosen concerning Rosen's book review, *supra*).

arguments in text, history, and structure, not to mention practice, tradition, and culture. But this turn is not necessarily a turn to originalism and against the moral reading. Indeed, recourse to structure in constitutional interpretation typically involves drawing inferences from political theory, not merely recovering, translating, or extrapolating from the original meaning of the text.[47] The turn to text, history, and structure becomes a turn against the moral reading only if its proponents claim to be elaborating text, history, and structure without making recourse to political theory. Such a claim would be problematic and implausible. Why, then, do the liberal and progressive enthusiasts of text, history, and structure cast their arguments as broad originalist arguments rather than as arguments in support of better grounding the moral reading?

Thirdly, I suggest that the answer to the question—Why have the turns to history and to text, history, and structure become turns to broad originalism and against the moral reading?—is to be found in considerations of litigation strategy or judgments about the types of arguments that are appropriate in our constitutional culture. The thought seems to be that our constitutional culture is largely originalist (or positivist), and therefore that arguments in constitutional law, to be successful, simply must be framed in an originalist mold. A view of this sort seems to animate the work of broad originalists such as Ackerman, Lessig, and Akhil Amar. I have heard a strong version of this view articulated roughly as follows: The only way that liberals and progressives have any hope of persuading Justice Scalia to accept their interpretations of the Constitution is to make originalist arguments.

To this view I have four responses. (1) The attempt to persuade Scalia that fidelity to the Constitution leads to any liberal or progressive conclusions is a fool's errand. There can be no serious doubt that Scalia's mind is ideologically impervious to liberal or progressive constitutional arguments.[48] Worse yet, this attempt disfigures and debases constitutional theory by causing theorists to recast their arguments in a narrow originalist mold dictated by Scalia.

(2) It is telling that the greatest liberal constitutional theorist-litigator of our time, Laurence H. Tribe, has not adapted his constitutional theory to such an originalist litigation strategy. To be sure, he has eschewed grand theory, as if to say, "no theorists here, just us common lawyers." But his conception of constitutional interpretation in his academic writing is much closer to Dworkin's theory than to the broad originalist views of Ackerman, Lessig, and Amar.[49]

---

[47] For examples of accounts of inferences from structure that recognize this, *see* C. L. BLACK, JR., STRUCTURE AND RELATIONSHIP IN CONSTITUTIONAL LAW (1969); W. F. HARRIS, II, THE INTERPRETABLE CONSTITUTION 144–158 (1993); FLEMING, *supra* note 13, at 90–91 (furthering the "unfinished business of Charles Black").

[48] Notwithstanding possible appearances to the contrary, *Texas v. Johnson*, 491 U.S. 397 (1989), and *R.A.V. v. City of St. Paul*, 505 U.S. 377 (1992), cases in which Scalia supported stringent judicial protection of freedom of speech, are not counterexamples. For instructive analyses of Scalia's First Amendment jurisprudence, as manifested in such decisions, *see* M. TUSHNET, A COURT DIVIDED: THE REHNQUIST COURT AND THE FUTURE OF CONSTITUTIONAL LAW 130–155 (2005).

[49] *See* L. H. TRIBE & M. C. DORF, ON READING THE CONSTITUTION 17, 81–87 (1991); L. H. Tribe, *Taking Text and Structure Seriously: Reflections on Free-Form Method in Constitutional Interpretation*,

(3) Our constitutional culture is not as originalist as the broad originalists seem to assume. It certainly requires constitutional lawyers and scholars to pay homage to history and to fit with historical materials, but that is not to say that it is originalist.[50] Originalism is an *ism*, a conservative ideology that emerged in reaction against the Warren Court. Before Richard Nixon and Robert Bork launched their attacks on the Warren Court, originalism as we know it did not exist.[51] Constitutional interpretation in light of original understanding did exist, but original understanding was regarded as merely one source of constitutional meaning among several, not a general theory of constitutional interpretation, much less the exclusive legitimate theory. Indeed, history was regarded as secondary to, and merely as extrinsic evidence of, the meaning of text and structure.[52] Scholars wrote about the "uses of history" in constitutional interpretation rather than contending that enforcing original understanding was the only defensible conception of fidelity.[53] Moreover, original understanding, especially at a relatively specific level, understood to be largely indeterminate and inconclusive. As Justice Jackson famously put it in concurrence in *Youngstown Sheet & Tube Co. v. Sawyer*:[54]

Just what our forefathers did envision, or would have envisioned had they foreseen modern conditions, must be divined from materials almost as enigmatic as the dreams Joseph was called upon to interpret for Pharaoh. A century and a half of partisan debate and scholarly speculation yields no net result but only supplies more or less apt quotations from respected sources on each side of any question. They largely cancel each other. And court decisions are indecisive because of the judicial practice of dealing with the largest questions in the most narrow way.[55]

Regrettably, many constitutional lawyers and scholars in recent years seem to have lost sight of this great wisdom. It is important to note that Laura Kalman, in her fine intellectual history of recent constitutional theory, has practically suggested that

108 HARV. L. REV. 1223 (1995) (criticizing the (broad originalist) theories of Ackerman and Amar); L. H. Tribe, *The Puzzling Persistence of Process-Based Constitutional Theories*, 89 YALE L.J. 1063, 1072–1077 (1980), reprinted in L. H. TRIBE, CONSTITUTIONAL CHOICES 9 (1985) (retitled *The Pointless Flight from Substance*) (criticizing Ely's theory for taking a "pointless flight from substance," just as Dworkin critiqued Ely's theory for doing so, *see* Dworkin, *The Forum of Principle, supra* note 25). For a critique of the broad originalist theories of Ackerman and Lessig from a theoretical perspective similar to Tribe's, *see* M. C. Dorf, *Integrating Normative and Descriptive Constitutional Theory: The Case of Original Meaning*, 85 GEO. L.J. 1765 (1997).

⁵⁰ The Senate's rejection of the Bork nomination was at least in part a rejection of Bork's narrow originalism. *See* DWORKIN, FREEDOM'S LAW, *supra* note 3, at 276–286, 287–305.

⁵¹ W. W. Crosskey may be an exception, but he was roundly criticized as exceptional. *See, e.g.,* H. M. Hart, Jr., *Professor Crosskey and Judicial Review*, 67 HARV. L. REV. 1456 (1954) (reviewing W. W. CROSSKEY, POLITICS AND THE CONSTITUTION IN THE HISTORY OF THE UNITED STATES (1953)).

⁵² *See* J. tenBroek, *Admissibility and Use by the United States Supreme Court of Extrinsic Aids in Constitutional Construction*, 26 CAL. L. REV. 287 (1938).

⁵³ *See* C. A. MILLER, THE SUPREME COURT AND THE USES OF HISTORY (1969); J. G. Wofford, *The Blinding Light: The Uses of History in Constitutional Interpretation*, 31 U. CHI. L. REV. 502 (1964).

⁵⁴ 343 U.S. 579 (1952).   ⁵⁵ *Id.* at 634–635 (Jackson, J., concurring).

the best professional historians know better than to be originalists, but that some constitutional lawyers and scholars who have taken the turn to history do not.[56]

(4) Finally, we should put the following question to the broad originalists: If our constitutional culture is so originalist, why do so many originalists complain that so many constitutional law cases and so many features of our constitutional practice cannot be justified on the basis of originalism?[57] The answer is that our constitutional culture is not as originalist as the broad originalists have supposed. Or that its commitment to originalism is more honored in the breach than in the observance. Or that Dworkin is right in arguing that "[s]o far as American lawyers and judges follow any coherent strategy of interpreting the Constitution at all, they already use the moral reading," but that there is a confused "mismatch" between the role of the moral reading, which is embedded in our constitutional practice, and its reputation, which is that it is illegitimate.[58]

B. The Celebration of "Fit" to the Exclusion of "Justification"

Another reason why some liberal and progressive constitutional theorists resist the moral reading and attempt to develop a broad originalism is that they believe that Dworkin's theory does not take history and "fit" seriously enough, or that it suffers from a "problem of fit."[59] Their objection has two aspects. In the first place, they claim, Dworkin does not do the concrete groundwork necessary to show that his interpretations of the Constitution adequately fit the historical materials including original understanding and precedents. In the final analysis, they claim, he will too readily reject as mistakes any historical materials that do not fit his political theory. For both reasons, they are dubious about whether Dworkin's theory, as Dworkin himself practices it, actually constrains constitutional interpretation to be faithful to anything other than his own liberal political theory.

In response, I would distinguish between Dworkin's theory of fidelity as integrity with the moral reading and Dworkin's own application of it, and urge: "Do as Dworkin says, not as he does." That is, I would argue that Dworkin's theory of fidelity as integrity is the best conception of fidelity, but would concede that Dworkin himself may not always satisfactorily do the fit work that his own theory

---

[56] KALMAN, *supra* note 43, at 167–190; *see* J. N. RAKOVE, ORIGINAL MEANINGS 3–22 (1996); J. Appleby, *Constitutional Conventions*, N.Y. TIMES (July 21, 1996), §7 (Book Review), at 20 (reviewing RAKOVE, *supra*). *But see* RAKOVE, *supra* at 7 (criticizing Jackson for overstating the point in the passage from *Youngstown* quoted in text).

[57] *See* BORK, *supra* note 4; H. P. Monaghan, *Stare Decisis and Constitutional Adjudication*, 88 COLUM. L. REV. 723 (1988). For a highly instructive analysis of the gap between originalist theory and our constitutional practice, *see* Dorf, *supra* note 49.

[58] DWORKIN, FREEDOM'S LAW, *supra* note 3, at 2, 4.

[59] For a broad originalist claim that Dworkin does not take fit seriously enough, *see* Flaherty, *supra* note 6. For a positivist claim that Dworkin's theory suffers from a "problem of fit," *see* A. J. Sebok, *The Insatiable Constitution*, 70 S. CAL. L. REV. 417 (1997). For a narrow originalist critique along these lines, *see* M. W. McConnell, *The Importance of Humility in Judicial Review: A Comment on Ronald Dworkin's "Moral Reading" of the Constitution*, 65 FORDHAM L. REV. 1269 (1997).

calls for, or that he may do it too abstractly to satisfy these critics that he takes fit as seriously as he should. Dworkin's splendid essays in constitutional theory in the *New York Review of Books* may aggravate such concerns. He writes these essays in a style designed to reach and persuade a larger audience of citizens, not in a technical style to demonstrate to constitutional lawyers and scholars that he has done his historical homework. Ironically, to the extent that Dworkin has indeed become, in T.M. Scanlon's estimation, "our leading public philosopher,"[60] he may have diminished the appeal of his theory and his work to some constitutional lawyers and scholars. For in their view, his "public philosophy" may not provide a good model for the kind of scholarship that shows the proper regard for the aspiration to fidelity, and that gives fit as well as justification its due.

Furthermore, some broad originalists evidently resist Dworkin's moral reading because they believe, as Bruce Ackerman once put it, that "fit is everything."[61] To state the matter in terms of Dworkin's well-known argument that the best interpretation has two dimensions—fit and justification—they seem to believe that fidelity is purely a matter of fit with historical materials, rather than also a matter of justification in political theory.[62] Fit and history do have a role in the quest for fidelity to the Constitution, but a limited one. We should acknowledge the place of history in constitutional interpretation—as a constraint that comes into play in the dimension of fit—but should keep it in its place. Broad originalists tend to exaggerate the place of history and to give it a greater role than it deserves and than it is capable of playing.

History is, can only be, and should only be a starting point in constitutional interpretation. It has a threshold role, which is often not dispositive. In the dimension of fit, history helps (or should help) screen out "off-the-wall" interpretations or purely utopian interpretations, but often does not lead conclusively to any interpretation, let alone the best interpretation. History usually provides a foothold for competing interpretations or competing theories. It alone cannot resolve the clash among these competing interpretations or competing theories. Deciding which theory provides the best interpretation is not an historical matter of reading more cases, tracts, or speeches or more scrupulously doing good professional history. To resolve the clash among competing interpretations or competing theories, we must move beyond the threshold dimension of fit to the dimension of justification. History rarely has anything useful, much less dispositive, to say at that point.[63] In deciding which interpretation among competing acceptably fitting interpretations is most faithful to the Constitution, we must ask further questions: Which interpretation provides the best justification, which makes our

[60] T. M. Scanlon, *Partisan for Life*, N.Y. Rev. Books (July 15, 1993), at 45, 45 (reviewing Dworkin, Life's Dominion, *supra* note 5).

[61] *See* Bruce Ackerman, Remarks at the New York University School of Law Colloquium on Constitutional Theory, Nov. 16, 1993 (colloquy between Ackerman and Dworkin).

[62] For Dworkin's formulations of the two dimensions of best interpretation, fit and justification, see sources cited *supra* in note 31.

[63] Indeed, as stated above, the best professional historians know better than to be originalists; unfortunately, some constitutional lawyers and scholars do not. *See supra* text accompanying note 56.

constitutional scheme the best it can be, which does it more credit, or which answers better to our best aspirations as a people?[64] These questions are not those of an "infidel," Lessig notwithstanding.[65] They are required by the quest for fidelity in the sense of *honoring* our aspirational principles, not merely *following* our historical practices or the original meaning of the text.[66] And the commitment to fidelity is an aspiration to the best interpretation of the Constitution, not merely to best fit with the historical materials or original meaning (or best translation of them). The view that fidelity is merely a matter of fit—or that "fit is everything"—mistakenly assumes that the Constitution is defined, and exhausted, by the historical materials.

More generally, some broad originalists may resist the moral reading because they believe that fidelity requires following historical materials and eschewing political theory. But broad originalists understand constitutional interpretation in terms of "liberating abstraction," or conceive original understanding at a relatively high level of abstraction.[67] When they elaborate abstract original understanding, they will find that they are not able to do so purely as a matter of historical research, translation, or extrapolation. Instead, they will have to do so as a matter of—and through recourse to—bounded political theory.

IV. Reconceiving the Moral Reading as a Big Tent

The upshot of my analysis of the reasons why the broad originalists have resisted the moral reading in favor of trying to develop an intermediate theory is that we should conceive the moral reading as a big tent that can encompass broad originalist conceptions such as those of Ackerman, Sunstein, and perhaps even that of Lessig. Broad originalists have employed the argumentative strategy of using Bork and Scalia, on the one hand, and Dworkin, on the other, as rhetorical foils or extremes against which to set up their arguments.[68] This strategy leads to the unfortunate results of caricaturing Dworkin's arguments and, worse yet, obscuring similarities and common ground between the moral reading and broad originalism.

---

[64] *See* DWORKIN, FREEDOM'S LAW, *supra* note 3, at 8–11; DWORKIN, LAW'S EMPIRE, *supra* note 5, at 176–275.   [65] Lessig, *Fidelity*, *supra* note 6, at 1260.

[66] For development of the idea that the Constitution embodies aspirational principles rather than merely codifying historical practices, *see* FLEMING, *supra* note 13, at 112–116, 226–227. For similar ideas, *see* BARBER, POWER, *supra* note 40, at 60–61; BARBER, CONSTITUTION, *supra* note 40, at 84–85; F. I. Michelman, *Super Liberal: Romance, Community, and Tradition in William J. Brennan, Jr.'s Constitutional Thought*, 77 VA. L. REV. 1261, 1312–1320 (1991); Michelman, *supra* note 8, at 1496, 1514.

[67] *See* SUNSTEIN, LEGAL REASONING, *supra* note 6, at 171–182; Ackerman, *Liberating Abstraction*, *supra* note 7.

[68] *Compare* ACKERMAN, WE THE PEOPLE, *supra* note 6, at 10–16 (criticizing Dworkin) *with* B. Ackerman, *Robert Bork's Grand Inquisition*, 99 YALE L.J. 1419 (1990) (reviewing and criticizing BORK, *supra* note 4); *compare* SUNSTEIN, LEGAL REASONING, *supra* note 6, at 48–53 (criticizing Dworkin) *with* SUNSTEIN, PARTIAL CONSTITUTION, *supra* note 21, at 96–110 (criticizing Bork); *see also* Lessig, *Fidelity*, *supra* note 6, at 1260 ("From the perspective of the two-step fidelitist, both the originalist [such as Scalia] and the Dworkinian are infidels").

Again, I would urge the broad originalists to reconceive their projects as being in support of the moral reading, not as offering alternatives to it. They can help by providing firmer grounding than Dworkin has offered for the moral reading in fit with historical materials. (I do not mean to suggest that their own moral readings are the same as Dworkin's particular moral reading.) I shall close by giving three reasons for embracing the moral reading, conceived as a big tent.

The first reason is hortatory: The moral reading exhorts judges, elected officials, and citizens to reflect upon and deliberate about our deepest principles and highest aspirations as a people.[69] It does not command them to follow the authority of the past. In a word, it rejects the authoritarianism of originalism, narrow or broad, as inappropriate and unjustifiable in a constitutional democracy. As Christopher L. Eisgruber points out, it is ironic if not absurd that originalists would impose the "dead hand" of the past upon us in the name of popular sovereignty.[70] The moral reading exhorts us to conceive fidelity in terms of honoring our aspirational principles rather than merely following our historical practices and concrete original understanding, which no doubt have fallen short of those principles. On this view, fidelity is not subservient fealty.

The second, related reason is critical: The moral reading encourages, indeed requires, a reflective, critical attitude toward our history and practices rather than enshrining them. It recognizes that our principles may fit and justify most of our practices or precedents but that they will criticize some of them for failing to live up to our constitutional commitments to principles such as liberty and equality.[71] Put another way, the moral reading does not confuse or conflate our principles and traditions with our history, our aspirational principles with our historical practices.[72] Again, it recognizes that fidelity to the Constitution requires honoring our aspirational principles, not following our historical practices and concrete original understanding. That is, fidelity to the Constitution requires that we disregard or criticize certain aspects of our history and practices in order to be faithful to the principles embodied in the Constitution.

The final reason is justificatory: The moral reading, because it understands that the quest for fidelity in interpreting our imperfect Constitution exhorts us to interpret it so as to make it the best it can be, offers hope that the Constitution may deserve our fidelity, or at least may be able to earn it. Ironically, despite their pretensions to a monopoly on concern for fidelity, the originalists would enshrine an imperfect Constitution that does not deserve our fidelity.[73]

[69] I do not mean to imply that the moral reading necessarily requires completely theorized agreements. *But see* SUNSTEIN, LEGAL REASONING, *supra* note 6, at 48–53 (criticizing Dworkin's grand, abstract theorizing and calling instead for "incompletely theorized agreements").

[70] C. L. Eisgruber, *The Living Hand of the Past: History and Constitutional Justice*, 65 FORDHAM L. REV. 1611, 1613–1617 (1997). *See also* C. L. EISGRUBER, CONSTITUTIONAL SELF-GOVERNMENT (2001).

[71] *See* FLEMING, *supra* note 13, at 6, 98.   [72] *See id.* at 227.

[73] Originalism, as an *ism*, has no firm footing in our constitutional culture, and it has no place there. It is a species of authoritarianism that is antithetical to a free and equal citizenry. A regime of purportedly dispositive original meanings is, at best, beside the point of constitutional interpretation and, at worst, an authoritarian regime that is unfit to rule a free and equal people. For a similar view, *see* S. Freeman, *Original Meaning, Democratic Interpretation, and the Constitution*, 21 PHIL. & PUB. AFF. 3 (1992).

The moral reading frames questions of constitutional interpretation as matters of principle, to be decided by reflection upon, and deliberation about, basic principles and constitutional essentials, not mainly as matters of history that have largely been decided (at least abstractly) for us by our forebears who are long dead and gone. It underwrites a constitutional discourse that makes recourse to questions of principle themselves rather than primarily to other people's views on other subjects in other contexts. And the moral reading makes for a better constitutional citizenry, not to mention better interpretations of the Constitution. It does not reduce us to poring over other people's opinions concerning these questions, nor does it require us to put our arguments in the mouths of people long dead and gone or to dress up our arguments in their antiquated garb. In other words, it underwrites a deliberative citizenry, not an authoritarian one.

Thanks to Ronald Dworkin's monumental contributions to constitutional theory, we can see this clearly.

3

How Constitutional Theory Found its Soul: The Contributions of Ronald Dworkin

Rebecca L. Brown *

Like rain falling to a parched earth, Ronald Dworkin's early work lighted upon a field of constitutional thought desiccated by embarrassment over *Brown v. Board of Education*.[1] From a distance of a half century, it is difficult to appreciate the profound chagrin that had arisen from what now seems a simple judicial declaration of equality. Yet the decision had hurled the world of constitutional theory into decades of existential angst, leading it, temporarily, to lose a grasp on its soul.

Taking Rights Seriously came on the scene in the 1970s and quickly began to enrich the impoverished debate. Subsequent writings, culminating with *Freedom's Law* and its moral reading of the Constitution, increasingly refined Dworkin's ideas about law to apply more specifically to the interpretation of constitutional text.[2] Ironically, while the academy had nearly imploded over the issue of how to understand the Constitution's promise of equality, it was Dworkin's exposition of a deep and foundational notion of equality that helped direct constitutional theory toward recapturing its animating spirit. That rehabilitative effect, I suggest, is at the heart of Dworkin's contribution to constitutional theory.

 * The author gratefully acknowledges the helpful contributions of Lisa Bressman, John Goldberg, Bob Rasmussen, Christopher Yoo, and the participants in the Georgetown University Law Center Constitutional Law Colloquium and University of Colorado School of Law faculty workshop.
   [1] 347 U.S. 483 (1954).
   [2] In this essay I have taken the liberty of seeking to present intellectual, rather than chronological, sequences in Dworkin's work. This undoubtedly does some violence to the chronology of his corpus as it actually unfolded. The Dworkin works on which I am primarily relying in this essay are TAKING RIGHTS SERIOUSLY (1977); A MATTER OF PRINCIPLE (1985); LAW'S EMPIRE (1986); LIFE'S DOMINION: AN ARGUMENT ABOUT ABORTION, EUTHANASIA, AND INDIVIDUAL FREEDOM (1994); FREEDOM'S LAW: THE MORAL READING OF THE AMERICAN CONSTITUTION (1996) [hereinafter FREEDOM'S LAW]; SOVEREIGN VIRTUE: THE THEORY AND PRACTICE OF EQUALITY (2000) [hereinafter SOVEREIGN VIRTUE].

I. How Constitutional Theory Lost its Soul

Dworkin's work, with its claim that there are "right answers" to hard cases,[3] had the misfortune, perhaps, to bear some resemblance—superficial, really—to an old constitutional order that had come to be rejected with the New Deal. That old order had permitted judges to defend their decisions from criticism by claiming a passive role in interpretation that relieved them of responsibility for the jurisprudential choices they were making. In *Lochner v. New York*,[4] for example, many perceived that the Supreme Court had made special efforts "to insist the rule of law 'forced' them to reject social welfare legislation."[5] This unattractive confluence of lack of candor and anti-progressive social ends fostered eventual revolt against the notions of both an activist Supreme Court and a determinate Constitution (both of which later had associations with Dworkin, although not altogether accurately). Unsurprisingly, this revolt stoked a smoldering skepticism begun by the realists early in the twentieth century, ultimately conscripting, in some form, much of mainstream academia by the century's midpoint.

The early realist-progressives were not averse to the existence or importance of individual rights or the advancement of social ideals such as justice and liberty.[6] Quite the contrary, the writers of this period evoked a genuine sense of societal aspiration, including the betterment of the lot of the least well off.[7] But the many disappointments with what they saw as incorrect decisions from an intransigent Supreme Court had stripped them of any trust in the judiciary as the guardian of these rights.[8] Indeed, opposition to judicial review in the pre-*Brown* period was often explained by the rather pragmatic argument that judicial inquiry suffered from a backward-looking perspective and excessively limited scope, making it ill-suited to contribute to the evolution of the public good.[9]

To the extent there was constitutional theory at this time, its animating spirit committed theorists to resisting any reading of the Constitution as an impediment to badly needed social change. The Constitution was a backdrop for political institutions, enabling them to do what they deemed necessary to improve society, rather

---

[3] *See* B. Bix, Jurisprudence: Theory and Context 94–97 (1996) (discussing the nature of Dworkin's "right answer thesis").   [4] 198 U.S. 45 (1905).

[5] L. Kalman, The Strange Career of Legal Liberalism 18 (1996). The famous quote from Justice Roberts in *United States v. Butler* captures the objectionably parsimonious description of the Court's task: "to lay the article of the Constitution which is invoked beside the statute which is challenged and to decide whether the latter squares with the former." 297 U.S. 1, 62 (1936).

[6] *See, e.g.*, H. S. Commager, Majority Rule and Minority Rights 62 (1943) (arguing that "majority will does not imperil minority rights" because "the people can be trusted" to protect minority interests).

[7] Kalman, *supra* note 5, at 17–18 (describing the devotion of the realists to the regulatory state, seeking to advance the public interest through administrative programs).

[8] E. S. Corwin, Constitutional Revolution 89–90 (1941) (arguing that rights must generally depend for their protection on legislatures).

[9] R. Pound, Contemporary Juristic Theory 83 (1940).

than constraining them from seeking societal change. Thus, constitutional theorists were willing to accept the administrative state without serious constitutional objection because of its potential to expand the opportunity for good government.[10]

The Supreme Court's approach to liberty claims during this period is quite consistent with the view that the Constitution is best interpreted as imposing the fewest obstacles on the political branches in the achievement of needed reforms. The constitutional standard for assessing liberty claims held that individual liberties would prevail unless restrictions were necessary in the common good. The *Lochner* case, conceiving of the police power and the common good narrowly, struck down regulatory measures in 1905. By 1937, however, the Court was ready to understand the police power more broadly, with the common good reconceived to include regulatory interference with private economic relations where necessary to respond to the changing social and economic order.[11] Still purporting to adhere to the balance of ordered liberty, the Court's assessments of the relative weights in the pans of the scale had altered considerably for the avowed purpose of facilitating progressive legislative programs.

The ideals of democracy and rights shared a delicate coexistence as long as legislatures could plausibly be considered the most trustworthy repositories of the rights of the people. Justice Frankfurter's ode to populism spoke a powerful message. He wrote that "[t]o fight out the wise use of legislative authority in the forum of public opinion and before legislative assemblies rather than to transfer such a contest to the judicial arena, serves to vindicate the self-confidence of a free people."[12] At a time when democracy was struggling for world opinion against, first dictatorship and then communism, it is no wonder the prevailing commitment was a belief that giving the people their voice would be a better source of freedom. This vesting of public policy decisions in a holistic entity thought of as "the people," through their elected representatives, was hailed as the hallmark of democracy. The people would enact and live under law, understood to be a system of rules, authoritative by virtue of their source in the political branches of government.

This belief system proved fragile, unable to withstand the frontal assault created by the forced acknowledgement of racial segregation.[13] Such segregation, of course, was nothing new, but (much as did slavery for the founders) it seemed to have existed, for most of the century, by the side of the Constitution and its accompanying promises of liberty and equality, without forcing anyone to notice that perhaps rhetoric and reality did not square. The New Deal, with its emphasis on addressing severe social and economic problems that united the country, took

---

[10] *See* J. M. LANDIS, THE ADMINISTRATIVE PROCESS 2 (1938) ("Without too much political theory but with a keen sense of the practicalities of the situation, agencies were created whose functions embraced the three aspects of government").

[11] R. L. Brown, *Activism is not a Four-Letter Word*, 73 U. COLO. L. REV. 1257 (2002) (arguing that the mistake of *Lochner* was not an activist protection of liberty, but in artificially constrained notion of "common good").   [12] *Minersville Sch. Dist. v. Gobitis*, 310 U.S. 586, 600 (1940).

[13] *See* R. G. McCLOSKEY, THE AMERICAN SUPREME COURT 193 (1960) (racism of Adolf Hitler contributed to a "feeling of dissatisfaction and guilt over America's own patterns of race discrimination").

the spotlight away from those even uglier problems that divided it. *Brown v. Board of Education*, to put it mildly, raised such a problem.

The blow to constitutional theory as a discipline was not a single *coup de grace*, but rather a series of inner conflicts experienced and expressed in different, but related, ways by several leading scholars of the time. Many have described this period of intellectual history with depth and perspicacity;[14] I wish only to highlight some of the significant themes in order to lay the broad-based groundwork for the symbolic role that I suggest Ronald Dworkin later came to play.

Learned Hand's 1958 Holmes Lecture is widely viewed as the focal point of debate. In that speech, he called into question the legitimacy of judicial review itself,[15] and challenged *Brown* as legislation from the bench.[16] In a somewhat more limited way, Herbert Wechsler also criticized *Brown* as unprincipled in its unjustified preference of one group's freedom of association over another's.[17] After those two very public attacks on the legitimacy of the Supreme Court's decision, as one commentator describes it, "the dam of academic criticism of the Court burst wide-open."[18] While many academics spoke in support of the outcome of the *Brown* decision, they seemed apologetic for a possible appearance of lack of principle, uncomfortable with any assertion of a necessary correlation between segregation and inequality. Academics increasingly leveled criticism at other activist decisions of the Court, consistently questioning the Court's commitment to principle and institutional integrity.[19] Charles Black, departing from this trend, courageously stepped forward and challenged the charade that allowed people to doubt that segregation caused inequality: "How long must we keep a straight face?"[20] he demanded, in reference to the claims that segregation had no connotation of oppression or inferiority. He took on the unusual role of reassuring his colleagues about the legitimacy of both the outcome as a social policy and the role of the Court in mandating it. "We as lawyers can without fake or apology present to the lay community, and to ourselves, a rationale of the segregation decisions that rises to the height of a great argument."[21]

The words "fake or apology" seem particularly apt. They describe an academy deeply unsure of itself, prone to taking different positions publicly and privately. Most constitutional scholars recognized the moral wrong of segregation at some level, but were highly uncertain of the legitimacy of enlisting the Constitution to

[14] *E.g.*, L. M. Seidman, *Brown and Miranda*, 80 CAL. L. REV. 673 (1992); M. TUSHNET, ED., THE WARREN COURT IN HISTORICAL AND POLITICAL PERSPECTIVE (1993); B. Friedman, *The Birth of an Academic Obsession: The History of the Countermajoritarian Difficulty, Part Five*, 112 YALE L.J. 153 (2002); KALMAN, *supra* note 5.

[15] LEARNED HAND, THE BILL OF RIGHTS 10, 28–29 (1958) (suggesting that the inference of judicial review from the Constitution was "not a lawless act" as long as it was limited to instances necessary to prevent the collapse of constitutional government).   [16] *Id.* at 54–55.

[17] H. Wechsler, *Toward Neutral Principles of Constitutional Law*, 73 HARV. L. REV. 1, 31–35 (1959).

[18] Friedman, *supra* note 14, at 198.

[19] *See id.* at 199–200 (discussing news reports regarding the increase in criticism of the Court from recognized authorities on jurisprudence).

[20] C. Black, Jr., *The Lawfulness of the Segregation Decisions*, 60 YALE L.J. 421, 425 (1960).

[21] *Id.* at 429.

put an end to the practice. Their understanding of constitutional law embraced only the thin guarantee of formally nonpreferential treatment, a facade of equality. It was not capacious enough to embrace *Brown's* jarring declaration that "separate" could be "inherently unequal" and thus inconsistent with the Constitution's textual promise of equal protection of the laws. In their personal moral codes, these scholars could recognize a role for principle and could apply it to conclude that racial segregation was a bad thing, causing injustice. But their commitment to law as a system of rules, with no place for morality or principle, led them to argue that the power of judges recedes when the law runs out, leaving them no authority to resolve a constitutional issue by resort to principle.

One fascinating historical account of this period illustrates the schizophrenic condition of the academy with its frequent use, in describing the views of the various theorists, of the qualifiers, "publicly" and "privately." Publicly the theorists would take one position, while privately, in correspondence, for example, they would hedge or qualify.[22] Henry Hart, for one, a principal proponent of the Legal Process school and its advocacy of judicial restraint and fidelity to legal rules, nevertheless privately raged at Hand's critique of *Brown*, which he felt would rob the polity of "any principles of social order which are independent of the appetites and wills of the contending groups."[23] Wechsler, too, despite having devoted his Holmes Lecture to the absence of principle underlying the *Brown* decision, acknowledged deep personal conflict about his attack.[24] Another account describes deep ambivalence, too, in Alexander Bickel and Philip Kurland, who "advanced withering attacks on the Court, all the while approving" many of its rights-protecting decisions.[25] The overall image portrays a Janus-faced academy, plagued by self-doubt and inner conflict.[26]

The culmination of this challenge to constitutional theory came with the early work of Alexander Bickel.[27] Perhaps the reason that he came to be described later as "the most influential scholar of his generation in the field of constitutional law,"[28] is that he had the acumen to pinpoint the precise locus of the epidemic malaise and to ease it with a palliative, if ultimately unsuccessful,[29] therapy. What

[22] KALMAN, *supra* note 5, at 33–37. See also Friedman, *supra* note 14, at 198 (suggesting Wechsler "stumbled over the decision, unable to justify it, but all the while claiming agreement").

[23] KALMAN, *supra* note 5, at 35 and n.39 (quoting Hand's papers).

[24] Wechsler, *supra* note 17, at 43.

[25] Friedman, *supra* note 14, at 251; *see also* M. Tushnet and T. Lynch, *The Project of the Harvard Forewords: A Social and Intellectual Inquiry*, 11 CONST. COMM. 463, 482 (1994) (describing Kurland's "self-doubt," Archibald Cox's slightly later "inner struggle," and general difficulty among legal process scholars to reconcile *Brown* with their school of thought).

[26] *See also* C. BLACK, JR., THE PEOPLE AND THE COURT 191 (1960) ("The greatest threat [to judicial review] is a quieter one, working within the legal profession, in the pages of the law reviews, in those self-doubts which the judges, like all other honest men in power, must recurrently feel").

[27] *See* A. BICKEL, THE LEAST DANGEROUS BRANCH: THE SUPREME COURT AT THE BAR OF POLITICS (1962).

[28] A. KRONMAN, THE LOST LAWYER: FAILING IDEALS OF THE LEGAL PROFESSION 24 (1993) (cited in KALMAN, *supra* note 5, at 37 n.42).

[29] *See* Friedman, *supra* note 14, at 219–221 & nn.286–299 (describing critiques of Bickel's model of judicial review, and Bickel's own subsequent disavowal of much of the "counter-majoritarian difficulty").

his vision enabled him to see was that the underlying conflict about *Brown* was really an identity crisis about democracy itself. In *The Least Dangerous Branch*, he chose to press a highly simple resolution.[30] Democracy was easy to understand as long as the important decisions were being made by the Congress or state legislatures.[31] Indeed, Bickel declared confidently that "the policy-making power of representative institutions, born of the electoral process, is the distinguishing characteristic of the system."[32] His emphasis on elections, along with his choice of the word "distinguishing," suggests that perhaps he was tacitly seeking to articulate democracy's distinction from Communism, a salient competitor during this Cold War period. On the matter of electoral accountability, clearly America's system of government had a strong claim to superiority, while on a metric of individual rights or entitlements, perhaps—unmentioned in Bickel's definition of democracy—the competitive advantage might be less clear.

Whatever Bickel's motivation, his simplification of the concept of democracy, reducing it to its most elemental populist foundations, captured a powerful and widely felt sentiment. But if this was democracy, then the concept of individual rights was in trouble. If democracy means the enactment into law of policies that a majority of the people favor, and that preference is, by definition, reflected in the decisions of representative institutions, then it follows that any effort to thwart or overturn legislative decisions is anti-democratic. Indeed, that was precisely Bickel's conclusion about judicial review: he chose the words "undemocratic"[33] and "deviant,"[34] in addition to the perhaps less pejorative, and more famous, "counter-majoritarian difficulty."[35] Courts would be the last-resort guardians of the most "clear cut" constitutional values, but would restrain themselves from involvement in controversial political matters best left to the politically accountable branches. "The more fundamental the issue," Bickel wrote, "the nearer it is to principle, the more important it is that it be decided in the first instance by the legislature."[36]

The Least Dangerous Branch served to facilitate a seductive forgetfulness about what a constitutional democracy is. It would not be understood as the "inarticulate and complex"[37] idea encompassing a collection of interacting mechanisms working in different directions to ensure a combination of procedurally sound representative political government, along with "insight and wisdom and justice."[38]

---

[30] This book was not by any means the end of Bickel's thinking on the subject, and in later works he revised and, to some extent, complicated his views about democracy. See A. BICKEL, THE SUPREME COURT AND THE IDEA OF PROGRESS 175–181 (1970); A. BICKEL, THE MORALITY OF CONSENT (1975). My focus here is on the impact of the 1962 book.

[31] Bickel paid little heed to the growing insights about the inexact correspondence between legislative decisions and majority will, propounded by such theorists as Robert Dahl and David Truman. See KALMAN, *supra* note 5, at 38–39 (describing Bickel's apparent rejection of pluralism) *See also* BICKEL, THE SUPREME COURT AND THE IDEA OF PROGRESS, *supra* note 30, at 84–86 (later recognizing some basic interest group role, but still emphasizing the preeminence of the vote as the sole concern of the Court).   [32] Bickel, *supra* note 27, at 19.

[33] *Id.* at 17.   [34] *Id.* at 18.   [35] *Id.* at 16.   [36] *Id.* 161.

[37] BLACK, *supra* note 26, at 179.   [38] *Id.* at 182.

Instead, the new understanding of democracy was much easier to comprehend: it was majority rule.

But this was a loss for constitutional theory, as majority rule is flat and self-contained; it looks neither backward for wisdom nor forward for aspiration. The argument could no longer be (as it had been in the New Deal period) that the popularly elected branches of government are most trusted to produce the best social ends, and that, accordingly, they should be given as free a rein as possible in the formulation of public policy. *De jure* segregation and its accompanying unjust treatment of individuals, as well as the persecutions of the McCarthy era, had foreclosed trust of that sort. If that were the argument that constitutional theory propounded, it would have had to concede that there were no rights to begin with—a thin disguise for the fundamentally skeptical point that there are, in fact, no rights against the state.[39] Most were not willing to go that far. All that was left for constitutional theory, then, was the argument that majority rule was an end in itself, that whatever most of the people wanted they should have, in the name of democracy. This exclusive focus on the process of government decision-making suggested that courts should be careful, apologetic, humble, and concerned about their own legitimacy.[40] Bickel's grudging account gave no guidance as to *how* the constitutional issues of the day should be decided, as long as they were resolved by the right political body, which was, nearly always, the legislature or executive, responding to majoritarian preference. This is a theory of constitutional law, but it is a cynical theory, without a sense of overarching purpose of advancement toward any substantive societal ideal. In short, his theory captured the sense of ambivalence and self-doubt of constitutional theory generally. It took the last step toward sapping the discipline of its soul.

Literature teaches us that people who lose their souls tend to vacillate in schizophrenic torment between what they sense to be their true spirits and the temptations that draw them away. They are denied the luxury of inner peace and self-knowledge. Dr. Faustus, who traded his soul to the devil in exchange for fabulous magical power, is portrayed as frequently subjected to the opposing enticements of the good angel, urging him to repent and serve God, and the evil angel, exhorting him to follow his lust for power.[41] Dorian Gray, too, having pledged his soul in exchange for ageless beauty, is racked by a duality that is reconciled only in his death.[42] These figures sought the simplicity of an unmitigated good—for them, power or youth—and sought, to their own doom, to reject the possibility of balance among complex and competing human faculties.

And so it was, in less poetic form, for constitutional theory. Even if with the best of intentions, the discipline succumbed to the enticement of simplicity over

[39] Taking Rights Seriously, *supra* note 2, at 146.

[40] *See* C. R. Sunstein, One Case at a Time: Judicial Minimalism on the Supreme Court (1999) (carrying forward this theme in later work).

[41] C. Marlowe, Doctor Faustus (Roma Gill ed. 1990).

[42] O. Wilde, The Picture of Dorian Gray (Wordsworth ed. 1992).

complexity, concrete answers over abstract ideals, losing track of what the American Constitution had been since its inception. The academy's schizophrenic reaction to *Brown*—recognizing the necessity of its outcome, while still resisting the institutional muscle that permitted the judiciary to reach it legitimately—is symptomatic of this loss of core mission. Scholarship argued back and forth about how best to hold the Court back, how to restrain it, from overstepping the narrow bounds permitted it by a system conceived in majoritarian supremacy.[43] Judicial review, and, with it, the enforcement of individual rights, was an embarrassment to the Constitution rather than its highest calling. What served instead, as a final cause, was elusive. The candor and commitment necessary to face up to a banishment of rights from the democracy were lacking, yet the preservation of a shell with no defining contours left a vacuum of direction and purpose. Thus, it plausibly could be said in these times that "the institution of judicial review has somehow faded out of the picture—or, what is far worse, has been converted into a mere ritual of acquiescence, or in plainer terms a solemn if not particularly pious fraud."[44]

It was not appropriate to talk too much about rights, or even justice.[45] Anyone who presumed to do so ran the risk of being accused of offending democracy or favoring "judicial tyranny."[46] Political rhetoric, following the lead of the academy, spoke of aspirations of "strict construction" and "judicial restraint,"[47] both of which were code words for reading rights in the Constitution as parsimoniously as possible.[48] Anything else, it was claimed, was "making" law rather than "interpreting" it.[49]

With Ronald Dworkin came the restorative balm of candor and the frank commitment to constitutional ideals. He was not literally alone, of course, in his aggressive program of taking rights seriously. But his work stands out for its relentless challenge to the false dichotomies that had become commonplace in constitutional thinking: between making and interpreting law, between rank rights skepticism

---

[43] *See* E. Chemerinsky, *The Supreme Court, 1988 Term—Foreword: The Vanishing Constitution*, 103 HARV. L. REV. 43, 73 (1989) (documenting the widespread adoption of the "majoritarian paradigm", "the idea that judicial review . . . is in tension with American democracy").

[44] BLACK, *supra* note 26, at 191.

[45] *See* M. Horwitz, *The Warren Court and the Pursuit of Justice*, 50 WM. & MARY L. REV. 5, 11 (1993) (describing how Chief Justice Warren was ridiculed for asking attorneys whether their position was just: "Sophisticated legal scholars did not speak that way").

[46] *See, e.g.*, R. H. Bork, *Neutral Principles and some First Amendment Problems*, 47 IND. L. J. 2–3 (1971) (arguing that judges necessarily abet "tyranny" if they exceed their proper sphere).

[47] *See* TAKING RIGHTS SERIOUSLY, *supra* note 2, at 31–37.

[48] *See* J. F. SIMON, IN HIS OWN IMAGE: THE SUPREME COURT IN RICHARD NIXON'S AMERICA 8–9 (1973) (by "strict constructionists," President Nixon "meant that he would appoint judges who took less active and reform-minded views").

[49] *See Changes Nixon May Make in Federal Courts*, U.S. NEWS & WORLD REP., Dec. 2, 1968, at 42 (quoting President Nixon as stating, "In my view, the duty of a Justice of the Supreme Court is to interpret the law, not to make law, and the men I appoint will share that view"). The alleged dichotomy has persisted. See President's Remarks Announcing the Nomination of Clarence Thomas to Be an Associate Justice of the Supreme Court of the United States and a News Conference in Kennebunkport, Maine, 27 WEEKLY COMP. PRES. DOC. 868 871 (July 1, 1991) (then-President George H. W. Bush's suggestion that the nominee would "faithfully interpret the Constitution and avoid the tendency to legislate from the bench").

and deference to political institutions, between self-government and judicial activism. "Why has a sophisticated and learned profession," he mused, "posed a complex issue in this simple and misleading way?"[50] In restoring complexity to constitutional democracy, his work both reinvigorated prior commitments and brought new focus to the value so critical to the latter part of the twentieth century, at the heart of the disagreement about judicial power, and foundational to American democracy—the value of equality.

II. The Moral Reading of the Constitution

Ronald Dworkin set a place for principle at the table of constitutional theory. He argued that the moral skeptics of the 1930s and 1940s were impoverished in their rejection of morality as part of law. The positivist emphasis on law as command, with authority commensurate to its source in the people, erroneously limited law to a formal set of rules that had no use for morality in its enforcement and application. To Dworkin, this was an unacceptable mask to impose on law of any kind, but his attacks on positivism and utilitarianism had particular resonance for constitutional law. Because Dworkin saw all law as a system of rights recognition and protection, his vision readily lent itself to employment in the development of constitutional law and theory. His understanding of law as comprising not just legal rules, but also principles, provided an apt foundation from which to construct an interpretative edifice for the Constitution itself, for Dworkin a rich source of such principle.

Dworkin's method calls upon the judge faced with an adjudicative issue to discover principles by looking backward in time to the practices and traditions in the nation's history.[51] Evolving from common law to constitutional law, the "moral reading" of the Constitution asks judges to find what Dworkin calls the "best" conception of constitutional moral principles that would fit the historical record, which includes constitutional text, evidence of contemporaneous understanding, precedent, and societal experience over time. These principles, in turn, inform the resolution of current issues of the day, without necessarily determining outcomes.

For the first time, the idea of balancing individual liberty against the community's needs came under critical scrutiny. Dworkin argued for recognition of moral rights against the government—those that it would be wrong for a government to transgress even for the best of reasons rooted in the common good.[52] These moral claims that all individuals hold against their government are determined by a political judgment regarding the limits of government power in the free society that our Constitution establishes and maintains. This is an appropriate task for a

---

[50] TAKING RIGHTS SERIOUSLY, *supra* note 2, at 148.

[51] *See* LAW'S EMPIRE, *supra* note 2, at 228–229; see also BIX, *supra* note 3, at 91 (explaining Dworkin's interpretative method).

[52] *See* TAKING RIGHTS SERIOUSLY, *supra* note 2, at 139.

judge who is not second-guessing the underlying choices regarding policy or personal moral commitment that underlie the law, but rather is testing that enactment against a constitutional principle such as justice or equality.[53]

In seeking the principles to guide this exercise of political judgment, Dworkin borrows a basic technique from his arch-opponents, the originalists. Like them, he asks the judge to consider the textual provision at issue in its historical setting, as well as whatever meaning can be derived. What he prescribes next, however, expands the interpretative endeavor beyond what the originalist would do. His investigation of the original intent is important in the search for the guiding principles that were intended to guide society through time. How those principles will be applied, however, is not governed by the original understanding, but rather by the moral judgment of the present-day judge. That approach facilitates consistency and fidelity to constitutional ideals such as liberty and equality, without straitjacketing society with outgrown conceptions of what those concepts actually require in specific cases. This effort to reach across temporal and ideological canyons is the hermeneutical device that Dworkin offers in the quest for coherence and integrity in constitutional interpretation. He anticipates moral progress.

This search for principle in our collective past supplies one defense against the common charge that Dworkin gives judges too much power to inject personal preference into constitutional meaning.[54] While Dworkin does not deny the inevitable element of personal judgment in the Herculean job of identifying and

[53] I have struggled with the terminology before, in commenting upon Christopher L. Eisgruber's CONSTITUTIONAL SELF-GOVERNMENT (2001), which shares some common ground with Dworkin. *See* R. L. Brown, *A Government For the People*, 37 U.S.F. L. REV. 5 (2002). One thing the two share is the use of the word "moral" to describe the constitutional questions that courts are charged with resolving. I continue to believe that the debate about principled judicial review would be edified if we made a clearer distinction between personal-moral questions, such as whether it is morally acceptable to terminate a pregnancy, and political-moral questions, such as whether it is morally permissible for a government to dictate matters involving deep personal conscience and bodily integrity. Although both types of issue may be presented in a single case, they are distinguishable, and importantly so, in my view. The use of the word "moral" to describe both has led some to argue with Dworkin, I believe, at cross-purposes. Richard Posner, for example, argued, in connection with his attack on Dworkin and what he terms moral theory, that the Court in *Roe v. Wade* "ducked the moral question." *See* R. A. Posner, *Problematics of Moral and Legal Theory*, 111 HARV. L. REV. 1637, 1703 (1998). I take it that he meant that the Court avoided the question whether a fetus is a person—what I would call the *personal*-moral question, or first-order moral question. But the Court in *Roe* did indeed answer the *political*-moral question, or second-order moral question (what I believe Dworkin would view as the principal moral question presented in the case), by resolving whether the government may regulate this particular aspect of private decision-making. If we could substitute something like the words "political judgment" for "moral judgment," I believe some of the rabid objection to Dworkin's work (as substituting judicial morality for personal, and the like) could be calmed, or at least cabined to areas of genuine disagreement. This does not go to the substance of Dworkin's theory, but is rather an effort to stave off one type of mischaracterization thereof.

[54] A related charge accuses Dworkin of bringing back the ghosts of natural law into constitutional interpretation. Dworkin has vigorously defended his distinction between natural law and moral principle, the latter being accessible through history and reason, tethered to societal values and traditions, while the former is not. *See* S. GUEST, RONALD DWORKIN 84 (1991) (explaining that Dworkin does not claim that "there is a 'natural' answer 'out there', which supplies an 'objectivity' to moral and legal argument").

applying principle, he does deserve credit for seeking mightily to frame the inquiry so as to avoid the appeal to the personal. He charges the judge with asking questions about the Constitution and the constitutional structure that we have, and grounding the answer to that inquiry in reason brought to bear on *shared* experience and value, rather than *personal* experience and value.[55] His steadfast insistence on the existence of accessible moral truth, while subjecting him to ridicule,[56] enriched the project of ascertaining appropriate limits on government power.

While the source of principle is in the past and present, its trajectory points toward the future by relying on a judgment of how best to reconcile past practice with the aspirations of the polity. What could be more inspiring to a discipline struggling to find itself than a plea for "moral progress, and though history may show how difficult it is to decide where moral progress lies, and how difficult to persuade others once one has decided, it cannot follow from this that those who govern us have no responsibility to face that decision or to attempt that persuasion."[57]

Dworkin's method does not abandon law; but rather redefines what counts as law. Unlike Hart, he does not ask the judge to step beyond the law and decide hard cases on the basis of something other than law, like policy. Instead, he endows law with a key component, principle, that prevents it from ever running out. The moral reading of the Constitution, in particular, claims an authority deriving from the Framers of the Constitution themselves, boasting not only consistency with their original intent, but also fidelity to the text that they adopted as fundamental law. This claim attaches to every significant stage of constitutional drafting: the original document, the Bill of Rights, and the Civil War Amendments. The language of these rights-protecting provisions of the Constitution, phrased as they are in "exceedingly abstract moral language"[58] such as the "right" of free speech, "due" process, and "equal" protection, incorporates a set of abstract moral principles as limits on governmental power.[59] He can thus accommodate principle in the interpretative process without compromising the authority many claim is vital to judicial legitimacy. If these constitutional principles seem, too coincidentally, to correspond to basic tenets of liberal political thought, it is the result, not of Dworkin's preferences, but of the Framers'. They constructed our nation's basic commitments, after all, "in the bright morning of liberal thought."[60]

Central to the moral reading is the decision to conceive this set of constitutional principles at its most general and aggregate level so as to establish an overarching guide for specific interpretations of the document. Dworkin has read the principles set out in the Constitution, taken together, to commit the United States to the proposition that "the government must treat all those subject to its dominion as having equal moral and political status; it must attempt, in good faith, to

---

[55] *See* FREEDOM'S LAW, *supra* note 2, at 10–11.

[56] *See* R. A. POSNER, THE PROBLEMATICS OF MORAL AND LEGAL THEORY at 3 (1999) (calling the idea of an accessible, objective moral order "spurious").

[57] TAKING RIGHTS SERIOUSLY, *supra* note 2, at 147.   [58] FREEDOM'S LAW, *supra* note 2, at 7.

[59] *Id.*   [60] *Id.* at 38.

treat them all with equal concern; and it must respect whatever individual free-doms are indispensable to those ends . . . ."[61] This foundational insight has come to be known as Dworkin's notion of "equal concern and respect," which he has developed throughout his work, and has been, to some degree, the trademark of his approach to constitutional interpretation. Although he initially attributed the principle to Rawls,[62] it is Dworkin who gave that principle life as a foundation for constitutional theory.

It is the principle of equal concern and respect, enshrined into positive law in the Constitution, that provides the starting place for analysis of all individual rights. It is a principle much deeper and more substantive than a mere formal equality. It contemplates real limits on government's use of its powers in its treat-ment of people: "Government must treat those whom it governs with concern, that is, as human beings who are capable of suffering and frustration, and with respect, that is, as human beings who are capable of forming and acting on intelli-gent conceptions of how their lives should be lived."[63] It thus embraces more than mere equality of treatment, including also the rights we generally think of as autonomy and liberty rights. These concepts of individual liberty are implicit in the equality-based proposition that government can never constrain one person's pursuit of the good life on the rationale that another's conception of a life well led is superior.[64] This proposition helps to suggest both the contours of what kinds of particular liberties must be respected and what kinds of reasons governments must (or may not) offer in support of any state effort to curtail them. Both this identification of protected liberty rights and the inquiry into state reasons are evident in the Supreme Court jurisprudence under the Due Process Clause. Sounding in liberty, these inquiries are latent in that thick conception of equality—"the most radical conception of equality there is."[65]

Dworkin's reliance on the text of the Bill of Rights and the Fourteenth Amendment to supply the pedigree for the principle of equal concern and respect, although apparently genuine, should not be overstated.[66] It is quite evident that

---

[61] *Id.* at 8.

[62] TAKING RIGHTS SERIOUSLY, *supra* note 2, at 181. Indeed, Dworkin devoted considerable atten-tion to arguing that Rawls can be explained only by attributing to him a deep recognition of equal concern and respect as a natural entitlement with which all persons are endowed, rather than as a product of contract. *Id.* at 178–183. Whether or not this is the correct reading of Rawls, Dworkin made clear that it is the correct reading of Dworkin. *See id.* at 272–273 (explaining the concept of equal concern and respect as a "postulate[] of political morality").   [63] *Id.* at 272.

[64] Dworkin has articulated the relationship between liberty and equality in different ways. At times, he has seemed to suggest that equality may be viewed as prior to liberty because a just govern-ment could not recognize a right to liberty that would conflict with a proper understanding of equality. *See* R. Dworkin, *What is Equality? Part 3: The Place of Liberty*, 73 IOWA L. REV. 1, 10 (1987). Yet he has always resisted the idea that either liberty or equality is instrumental to the other, arguing that the two are reconcilable ideals that merge into a fuller account of treating all persons with equal concern. *See* SOVEREIGN VIRTUE, *supra* note 2, at 123.   [65] TAKING RIGHTS SERIOUSLY, *supra* note 2, at 182.

[66] *See* E. B. Foley, *Interpretation and Philosophy: Dworkin's Constitution*, 14 CONST. COMMENT. 151, 154 (1997) (reviewing FREEDOM'S LAW) (questioning the candor of Dworkin's reliance on text).

Dworkin's commitment to the authority of the principle as intrinsic to our Constitution derives from other sources, in addition to the collective decision by politicians of prior centuries to concur in the use of a few fortuitous adjectives. Although the abstract quality of the selected words does indeed support the intuition, the principle of equal concern and respect is probably more accurately understood, at least in part, as an inference from the fact and existence of the constitutional democracy itself.

Like Bickel, Dworkin had the political acumen to recognize that the battle over judicial review involved the very definition of democracy, and he addressed that issue head on. He rejected all efforts to frame the question as how far democracy can properly be *compromised* for the sake of rights—an apologetic Constitution. Dworkin's critics seemed to suggest that democracy should be understood as falling at one end of a continuum, with justice in opposition at the other end, and rights just trade-offs in between. Under this view, the difference between Dworkin and Bickel would be simply where they would draw the line of acceptable trading off. But Dworkin conceived the question quite differently.[67]

For Dworkin, democracy is a means to attain justice, not its polar opposite. In contrast to Bickel, who identified democracy with majoritarianism, Dworkin saw democracy as instrumental to the achievement of equal status for all citizens.[68] Under this view of democracy, the legitimacy of government institutions is measured, not by the degree to which they respond to popular will, but by the degree to which they provide the conditions necessary to achieve the moral objective. Accordingly, the criticism of any institution as democratically "deviant" (Bickel's word for the unelected judiciary), would apply only if government failed to respect and promote the goal of equal status for all.

This conception of the American democracy has two tremendous assets. First, it does a much better job than does Bickel of explaining the Constitution that we have. Those who seek to equate our democracy with majoritarianism have a difficult time explaining the various structures established in the Constitution for tempering, buffering, and constraining the power of majority rule.[69] Under Dworkin's view, however, the Constitution's structuring of the three branches with different means and kinds of political accountability and diverse kinds of institutional checks is entirely consistent with the end of equal concern and respect. It portrays a robust and holistic organism whose parts work in interdependent ways toward a common objective. Secondly, Dworkin eliminates the need for the "moral regret" that is inevitable if one sets up a dichotomy in which legitimate government is poised in potential opposition to the project of doing what is right (essentially, the *Brown* dilemma). This view entails a moral cost to be borne whenever a court must overturn a legislative act that undermines the rights of

---

[67] FREEDOM'S LAW, *supra* note 2, at 15.   [68] *Id.* at 17.

[69] *See* R. L. Brown, *Accountability, Liberty, and the Constitution*, 98 COLUM. L. REV. 531, 552–558 (1998) (arguing that if our Constitution was intended to establish a majoritarian government, it is a failure).

citizens.[70] In contrast, Dworkin sees the invalidation of unjust laws as the fulfillment of the very end of legitimate government. When injustices are overturned or avoided, government has achieved its highest aspiration, which is a cause for moral celebration, not moral regret. Accordingly, his view makes possible an energetic, rather than an apologetic, Constitution.

At the same time that Dworkin cut the constricting bonds of Bickelian restraint and allowed the circulation to flow into the judiciary by charging it with an active role in the protection of individual rights, he also exercised care to preserve his interpretations of the Constitution as interpretations, not rewritings, of that document. He has consistently refuted the critics' attribution to him of a claim to untether the judiciary from all constraint. The caricature of Dworkin's view has him arguing that only the judge's opinion about objective moral reality is pertinent to his or her decision on a matter of constitutional interpretation. Dworkin, however, has steadfastly persisted in his commitment to the "integrity" of the law, by which he means that judges "must not deploy moral principles, no matter how much they are personally committed to such principles, that cannot be defended as consistent with the general history of past Supreme Court decisions and the general structure of American political practice."[71] The task, as Dworkin has consistently defined it, is the daunting job of gleaning both principles and their appropriate application from the Constitution and society that we, at the present time, have, recognizing that these are the product of influences bearing on the present from many forces in our past.

This is a job that requires honest acknowledgment of not only the principles that provide the ideals of a free society, but also the instances in our past that may not represent our highest attainment of those ideals. This opportunity for judges to be realistic and use what they know makes possible the open use of judgment and the critique thereof, actually facilitating public debate about our societal ideals. It is a dynamic approach to constitutional theory that restores to the Constitution a sense of purpose and grants to the society that it enables the opportunity to evolve.

Where the prior constitutional theory had struggled with "fake and apology,"[72] Dworkin's was candid. Where prior theory was schizophrenic, Dworkin's was single-minded. Where prior theory had sunk to "despair,"[73] Dworkin's was optimistic. Where prior theory accorded no affirmative role to the Constitution in contributing to the aspirations of society, Dworkin's expressly sought out the "best" of

---

[70] Some go so far as to suggest that invalidation of a law on constitutional grounds violates the rights of those who supported it. *See, e.g.*, R. H. BORK, THE TEMPTING OF AMERICA: THE POLITICAL SEDUCTION OF THE LAW 147 (1990) (when a judge recognizes new constitutional rights, "he violates not only the limits to his own authority but, and for that reason, also violates the rights of the legislature and the people.").

[71] FREEDOM'S LAW, *supra* note 2, at 319. The fuller concept of law as integrity is explored in LAW'S EMPIRE, *supra* note 2.   [72] *See supra* note 21, and accompanying text.

[73] *See* Black, *supra* note 20, at 428 (suggesting that "legal acumen has only one proper task—that of developing ways to make it permissible for the Court to use what it knows; any other counsel is of despair").

our traditions as part of the project of constitutional interpretation. And he reconciled the two faces of academic thought about *Brown*.

While most of academia acknowledged that *Brown* had to be right, they appeared to treat it as some sort of special case that, although inconsistent with their overall theory of judicial review, could be justified by some special dispensation. Even Robert Bork, one of the most committed originalists and rights skeptics of all, later conceded that *Brown* was right even though it did not square with either originalism or rights skepticism.[74] Bickel seemed to think that *Brown* was right, even though it did not square with any application of his prescription of passive virtues as guides to judicial behavior. Wechsler thought *Brown* was right even though he could not find a "neutral principle" to justify it. The list could go on. But how strange it is that none of these scholars appeared to take the admitted rightness of *Brown*, coupled with the inability of their own theories to justify it, as evidence that their theories should be reexamined.

Dworkin's theory not only tolerates *Brown*, but requires it.[75] The moral principle emanating from the Constitution and its history commits the government to treatment of all its citizens as equals, with equal political status. It was quite obvious by 1954 that official school segregation was not consistent with such equal status, even if one chose to believe that in 1866 it had been.[76] Thus the Supreme Court had no choice, if acting on the moral reading, but to hold the practice unconstitutional. No beating of the breast was necessary, nor would the decision be a cause for ambivalence and angst. Moral intuition and law had found reconciliation.

This accession to moral decision-making fit well in what was, after all, a historical period in which explicitly moral issues held an unusually salient place in public debate. Martin Luther King, Jr. was making his mark on history by leveling an explicitly moral challenge to segregation in public facilities.[77] Other civil rights leaders called attention, in various ways, to the injustice of race discrimination, often framing the arguments as a moral imperative for civil rights reform. The Cold War engaged Americans in explicitly moral comparisons between democracy and socialism. The controversy over the war in Vietnam, too, was expressed often in overtly moral terms, on the issue of the justice, both of the war itself and of the government's treatment of its citizens in connection with the war. The feminist movement, also framing much of its message in moral terms, added more voices to the cacophony of public moral argument that characterized the times.[78]

Considering the overall tenor of this political climate, it seems all the stranger that, until Ronald Dworkin came along, most prominent constitutional theorists

---

[74] *See* BORK, *supra* note 70, at 81–84.

[75] *See* LAW'S EMPIRE, *supra* note 2, at 387–389 (discussing how Hercules would resolve *Brown*).

[76] FREEDOM'S LAW, *supra* note 2, at 13.

[77] *See* M. Luther King, Jr., *Letter from the Birmingham Jail, in* WHY WE CAN'T WAIT (1964) (asserting that "segregation is . . . morally wrong" and exhorting victims of injustice to exercise their "moral responsibility to disobey unjust laws").

[78] *See* G. Steinem, Wisdom Quotes, <www.wisdomrevjone.com> ("Law and justice are not always the same").

of the time had found no place for moral argument in their thinking about society's constitutive commitments.[79] Dworkin's conception of democracy, by contrast, was deeply responsive to the moral demands of society at that time, and since.

III. Contributions

For some critics, Dworkin's insistence upon the existence of right answers stirs echoes in their minds of the formalists of the early twentieth century.[80] But the ears of those who hear that echo deceive them. Dworkin does not claim that the Constitution determinately answers all questions. To the contrary, he calls constantly for human judgment to be interposed between the issue and the Constitution for identification of the relevant principle. He explicitly recognizes that the process of identifying principle "will leave many possibilities open."[81] "[T]houghtful judges must then decide on their own which conception does most credit to the nation."[82] Right answers do exist, but no one necessarily has a way to know what they are.[83] Their existence provides the aspiration for judges acting in good faith.

While this may seem superficially detached, it is in fact grounded in American identity and values. The people who constitute this democracy are given a voice in constitutional discourse in at least two important ways. First, judges are charged with finding "our" principles when they seek to apply a constitutional provision to a case. Remaining faithful to constitutional practice by supplying a filtering function, the theory finds constitutional principle, not by direct appeal to people's preferences, but by interposing the judgment of a judge who is charged with taking the longer view, to locate principle in whatever evidence is available.

A second way Dworkin draws popular political views into the dynamic reading of constitutional text is through a vigorous confirmation process. By offering a robust and complex job description for those appointed to the bench, he provides much opportunity for discussion of substantive issues and qualifications related to

[79] This is not to deny the significant contributions, of course, of fellow travelers in the journey toward more robust recognition of individual rights under the Constitution. Any list of important theorists who sought to advance the cause of rights during this time must include, among others, T. Grey, *Do We Have an Unwritten Constitution?*, 27 STAN. L. REV. 703 (1975); J. Skelly Wright, *Professor Bickel, the Scholarly Tradition, and the Supreme Court*, 85 HARV. L. REV. 769 (1971); L. Tribe, *Structural Due Process*, 10 HARV. CIV. RTS-CIV. LIB. L. REV. 269 (1975); F. Michelman, *The Supreme Court, 1968 Term—Foreword: On Protecting the Poor Through the Fourteenth Amendment*, 83 HARV. L. REV. 7 (1969); C. BLACK, STRUCTURE AND RELATIONSHIP IN CONSTITUTIONAL LAW (1965); Wellington, *Common Law Rules and Constitutional Double Standards: Some Notes on Adjudication*, 83 YALE L.J. 221 (1973).

[80] *E.g.*, M. McConnell, *The Importance of Humility in Judicial Review: A Comment on Ronald Dworkin's "Moral Reading" of the Constitution*, 65 FORDHAM L. REV. 1269, 1278 (1997).

[81] FREEDOM'S LAW, *supra* note 2, at 9.   [82] *Id.* at 11.

[83] *See* LAW'S EMPIRE, *supra* note 2, at ix (explaining that "whether we have reason to think an answer is right is different from the question whether it can be demonstrated to be right").

that job description. If a judge is expected to use judgment rather than eschew it, his or her competence for that position should be tested by inquiries into all the facets of human judgment that could be expected to influence the judge's identification and application of principle.

The strongest evidence that Dworkin's is a theory about our Constitution and our society, rather than some "Utopia" of his own fabrication,[84] is that he has made a difference in the law of the land. It seems clear, at the least, that his energetic defense of the role of rights in the constitutional scheme has changed the terms of the theoretical and doctrinal debates to focus more on which rights to protect, and how, rather than whether to protect them.

Chronologically, the first major sign that Dworkin was on to something important in constitutional theory came in a somewhat hostile setting, John Hart Ely's extremely influential *Democracy and Distrust*. This is a book conspicuously and explicitly committed to rejecting the attribution of substantive values to the Constitution. Thus, one might not expect to find there a reliance on a core idea of the one theorist perhaps most closely associated with a substantive reading of the Constitution.[85] Yet in an unadorned footnote, the simple citation speaks volumes: "34. R. Dworkin, Taking Rights Seriously 180 (1977)."[86] As the following discussion shows, this indispensable citation, no mere flourish, supports the pivot upon which turns Ely's argument for a representation-reinforcing understanding of judicial review. In order to show the (unacknowledged) significance of the role of Dworkin's idea to Ely's work, it will be necessary to sketch out a short description of the intellectual moves that contribute to the thesis of *Democracy and Distrust*.

Ely's argument began with the observation that the concept of representation, as understood by those who founded the American nation, was richer and more complex than simply a structure of rulers and ruled. Indeed, as he recognized, it embraced a unique amalgam of the two interests.[87] The idea was that the legislators "would live under the regime of the laws they passed and not exempt themselves from their operation: this obligation to include themselves among the ruled would ensure a community of interest and guard against oppressive legislation."[88]

---

[84] Among those who have leveled this argument is J. C. Harrison, *Utopia's Law, Politics' Constitution* (Reviewing FREEDOM'S LAW), 19 HARV. J.L. & PUB. POL'Y 917 (1995–1996).

[85] *See* J. HART ELY, DEMOCRACY AND DISTRUST 56–57 (1980) (discussing and rejecting the three-part proposition that "moral philosophy is what constitutional law is properly about, that there exists a correct way of doing such philosophy, and that judges are better than others at identifying and engaging in it.").   [86] *Id.*, at 82 n.34.

[87] Ely's book is notoriously short on historical support, but on this point it turns out that there is good evidence of the claim that the American notion of representation was new and unique in ways critical to the argument Ely was constructing. *See* R. L. Brown, *Liberty, the New Equality*, 77 NYU L. REV. 1491, 1512–1520 (2002) (exploring the historical foundations and implications of the representation argument).

[88] ELY, *supra* note 85, at 78 & n.16; see Brown, *supra* note 87, at 1520–1528 (explaining the community of interests idea and arguing for its extension to support judicial review of modern-day liberty claims).

The principal enforcement mechanism for this obligation of governors to governed was the possibility of being turned out of office on election day.

What was missing from this "insurance policy," quite effective at protecting the interests of most of the people through political accountability, was any protection for those whose interests might differ from those of most of the people. The opportunity for electoral correction of unreasonable treatment of those minorities is not readily apparent in this representative structure.[89] Ely's explanation for this omission was that, for our forebears, the people were an essentially homogeneous group whose interests did not vary significantly.[90] The importance of this claimed homogeneity, of course, is that it would, if true, largely take care of the minority problem because "legislation in the interest of most would necessarily be legislation in the interest of all".[91] Whatever incidental problems of this sort that might arise would be taken care of either by the Bill of Rights or by the institutional structures of the federal government.

Ely suggested that, as time went on in the nation's early years and vital differences within the population increased, these structural strategies became more and more clearly insufficient to protect against the abuse of minorities by majorities. This is the point at which Ely propounded the central claim of his book: that the traditional American theory of representation, requiring representatives to honor the interests of a majority of their constituents and be bound by the laws that bound them, had to be *and was* extended so as to ensure that the representatives would, somehow, keep faith with the interests of various minorities as well. The obvious question was how this faith would be manifested in a system in which the majority has the power to make policy and pass laws. It was clear that there would have to be losers in the democratic process, and that the Constitution could not possibly be offended every time some law was passed that an outvoted group disliked. Yet if Ely was going to argue that courts may legitimately (which meant, for him, without evaluating the merits of government policies or their justifications) police the representative process for "malfunctions" of that process, then it was critical that he identify what type of breach, of what obligation on representatives, would indeed constitute such a malfunction. If the only obligation on representatives was faithfully to carry out the wishes of the majority of their constituents, assuming all citizens had the opportunity to vote, then there would be no ground for judges to intervene when the majority chose to burden groups of smaller numbers.

This presented a cavernous gap for Ely. He had argued, to this point, that it is not the courts' job to subject legislation to substantive screening. In this regard he carried forward the thinking of many of the post-*Brown* advocates of judicial restraint. Yet, unlike many of those earlier scholars, he was determined to justify

---

[89] Ely, *supra* note 85, at 78.

[90] *Id.* at 79. The accuracy of this statement is subject to some dispute, and Ely acknowledged that homogeneity of the population was more a republican ideal than a reality, even in the 18th century.

[91] *Id.*

both *Brown* and much of the other judicial activism practiced by the Warren Court. What the theory needed was a way to understand the process of "representation" as encompassing an obligation to engage in some basic substantive consideration of the interests of those who may be on the losing side of policy decisions. Without that more capacious definition of representation, it would seem that a court limited to representation reinforcement would strike down no law unless someone were excluded from the process altogether. The biggest challenge to construction of this new understanding of representation was to anchor it in the Constitution by showing where such an obligation on legislators to minority constituents might reside.

Yet Ely took care of the problem in one bizarre sentence making no direct reference to the Constitution. The sentence addressed this very issue, the need to maintain a community of interests between the representative and his or her minority constituents in the quest to avoid majority tyranny. "Naturally," wrote Ely, "that cannot mean that groups that constitute minorities of the population can never be treated less favorably than the rest, but it does preclude a refusal to *represent* them, the denial to minorities of what Professor Dworkin has called 'equal concern and respect in the design and administration of the political institutions that bind them.'"[92]

And so it was that representation-reinforcement theory's chasm, the need for a new understanding of representation that could be policed by self-restrained courts, was bridged by Dworkin's idea of equal concern and respect. The critical new definition of "representation"—which, in turn, would supply the boundaries of legitimate judicial review—was built upon this core insight.

Once across this bridge, Ely was then free to proceed with a theory of representation reinforcement. If the notion of a democratic government imposes on representatives an obligation to accord equal concern and respect to all their constituents, then any legislation passed out of either disregard for, or intentional malice toward, any group fails the test for "procedural" integrity and justifies judicial intervention.

In pressing the importance of Dworkin to Ely, my purpose is not to join those who have criticized Ely for claiming the impossible when he purported to liberate the Constitution from substantive commitments.[93] I seek only to suggest that Dworkin's insight as to equal concern and respect is virtually indispensable to the construction of any kind of theory that seeks to reconcile democracy and constitutionalism, as Ely's did. Even a constitutional theory that struggles mightily to

---

[92] ELY, *supra* note 85, at 82 (citing R. DWORKIN, TAKING RIGHTS SERIOUSLY 180 (1977)) (emphasis in original). An omitted internal footnote mentioned that, for persons to be "represented," "their interests are not to be left out of account or valued negatively in the lawmaking process." *Id.* at 82 n.33.

[93] *See* L. H. Tribe, *The Puzzling Persistence of Process-Based Constitutional Theories*, 89 YALE L.J. 1063, 1077 (1980); M. Tushnet, *Darkness on the Edge of Town: The Contributions of John Hart Ely to Constitutional Theory*, 89 YALE L.J. 1037 (1980).

eschew Dworkin finds him pivotal to its effort to escape the leveling crush of pure majoritarianism—a formidable tribute to a core idea.

But Dworkin's conquest of Ely, and with him, much of the Legal Process school of thought, is not the end of the story. As the agony over *Brown* slowly faded into the distant past, the would-be heirs to the Legal Process school have undergone fertilization, infancy and development into distinct, but identifiable, offspring. In 1996, Dworkin wrote *Freedom's Law*, dedicated to attacking the "majoritarian premise," just as *Taking Rights Seriously* had styled itself, nearly twenty years earlier, as an attack on positivism and utilitarianism. In many respects, little had changed other than the names of the antagonists. The majoritarian premise, which had led to the call for "strict construction" during the Nixon years, has supported development or cultivation of such repackaged schools of thought as judicial minimalism, originalism, pragmatism and the new institutionalism of administrative law.

Just as Bickel called for judges to exercise their "passive virtues" to keep themselves out of societal contests, judicial minimalism calls for courts to leave as much as possible undecided, leaving room for moral issues to be resolved through the political processes.[94] This approach, I have suggested, is not respectful of the equal status of all citizens, but rather entrenches enacted law without regard to the strength or validity of the interests of those burdened by the codification of majority preferences.[95] Despite protestations to the contrary, its failure to require judicially evaluated reasons for divisive legislation renders it strongly majoritarian in its effect. It is the heir to the "Passive Virtues" name.

The majoritarian premise has infected much of structural constitutional theory as well.[96] Administrative law scholarship seeks to justify decisions based on who makes them, and how accountable the decision-maker is to popular control, rather than judging them on how well they are protecting the rights of individuals and achieving good government. Calls for the President to have more control of administrative agencies, based on an accountability argument, have become a familiar part of the constitutional separation-of-powers literature.[97] The administrative issues involving deference to agency interpretations of statutes reflect the same trend, both in the *Chevron* case itself and in the many scholarly paeans to it.[98]

---

[94] SUNSTEIN, *supra* note 40, at 3–6.   [95] *See* Brown, *supra* note 87, at 1538.

[96] *See* L. Schultz Bressman, *Beyond Accountability: Arbitrariness and Legitimacy in the Administrative State*, 78 NYU L. Rev. 461 (2003) (describing the new views of the administrative state as profoundly majoritarian).

[97] *See, e.g.*, L. Lessig & C. R. Sunstein, *The President and the Administration*, 94 COLUM. L. REV. 1, 94 (1994) (the President must have control over agencies to preserve accountability, one of two "central values of the framers' original executive"); S. G. Calabresi & S. B. Prakash, *The President's Power to Execute the Laws*, 104 YALE L.J. 541 (1994) (arguing for a unitary theory of the executive branch, based largely on accountability arguments); E. Kagan, *Presidential Administration*, 114 HARV. L. REV. 2245 (2001) (arguing that increased presidential involvement in agency decisions can increase the legitimacy of agencies by increasing majoritarian control of administrative lawmaking).

[98] *See Chevron v. NRDC*, 467 U.S. 837 (1984); A. Scalia, *Judicial Deference to Administrative Interpretations of Law*, DUKE L.J. 511, 518 (1989); L. H. Silberman, *Chevron—The Intersection of Law and Policy*, 58 GEO. WASH. L. REV. 821 (1990).

Another reincarnation of vanquished opponents is the form of pragmatism that is wholly consequentialist in its aspirations, which elicits the same responses from Dworkin that the utilitarian approaches elicited in decades past.[99] Ultimately, this approach revives the proposition that individual liberty can and should be sacrificed to strong or powerful claims of the common good, a proposition that Dworkin continues to refute. And, of course, the originalist/textualist school is still alive and well, with Justice Scalia at the forefront of those urging those techniques as means to constrain judges from judging.[100] To all these returning opponents, Dworkin has refined and targeted his responses, but has not wavered from his basic insights and commitments. He has forced contender after contender to take him on, but still plausibly can claim that they have repeatedly failed to justify any alternative to the moral reading.[101]

Thus Dworkin is not the St. George who valiantly slays the dragon. He is more the Great Wall that steadfastly keeps the threatening hordes from storming the city, age after age. His theories are as sound and important in responding to the modern skeptics as they were nearly four decades ago. His ideas have been developed and refined over the years, and his practice of discussing real cases in publicly accessible lay publications has remained testament to his abiding commitment to the Constitution as a means to facilitate the self-government that is our constitutional birthright.

In the Supreme Court, the influence of Dworkin's work can be detected in several places. One is the retreat from the representation-reinforcing approach to judicial review of equal protection claims. That theory had been evident in the Court's equal protection jurisprudence, both before and after Ely's book.[102] The development of suspect-class doctrine, the tiers of scrutiny, and the concept of motivation as the touchstone of equal protection all reflect the sense that the goal of judicial review of equality claims is to ensure that legislative classifications have not arisen out of malice. But, facing different kinds of claims, the Court and several of its members individually have retreated from that more process-based approach to equal protection and displayed a greater willingness to engage in some version of a moral reading of the Constitution. Whether one can lay credit—or blame—for this development at Dworkin's feet is hard to say, but clearly his work contributed to an intellectual atmosphere in which this elevation of principle over mere representational regularity could be put forward with a straight face.

---

[99] *See* R. Dworkin, *Darwin's New Bulldog*, 111 HARV. L. REV. 1718, 1719 (1998) (in challenge to the claims of Richard Posner, lamenting uncertainty about "when the antitheory episode in our intellectual history will have run its course."). There are other forms of pragmatism that may be less squarely in conflict with Dworkin, such as certain forms of practical reasoning which seek to identify moral norms for use in the resolution of statutory issues. *See* W. N. Eskridge & P. P. Frickey, *Statutory Interpretation as Practical Reasoning*, 42 STAN. L. REV. 321 (1990).

[100] *See* A. Scalia, *Originalism, The Lesser Evil*, 57 U. CINN. L. REV. 849 (1989); A. Scalia, *The Rule of Law is the Law of Rules*, 56 U. CHI. L. REV. 1175 (1989).

[101] *See* FREEDOM'S LAW, *supra* note 2, at 14.

[102] *See, e.g., U S v. Carolene Prods.*, 304 U.S. 144, 152–153 n.4 (1938); *City of Cleburne v. Cleburne Living Center*, 473 U.S. 432 (1985) (applying Ely's factors to deny heightened scrutiny).

The case I have in mind most conspicuously is *Adarand v. Pena*,[103] in which the Supreme Court held that any government use of race in decision-making must be subjected to strict scrutiny, regardless of motivation. Significant there was the heedlessness of the Supreme Court of the circumstance that the individuals claiming to be burdened by the minority set-aside provision at issue possessed none of the classic "suspect" features that would ordinarily lead a Court to fear that their interests might not get adequate representation in the political process, features that had once been a pre-condition to a heightened degree of judicial intervention. That would have been the traditional analysis of such a case under a Bickelian or Elysian legislative-supremacy, representation-reinforcing view. Yet the Court took an entirely different approach. Instead it identified a moral principle, color-blindness, sought (unsuccessfully, in Dworkin's view) to ground it in constitutional text and precedent, and determined that any compromise of that principle was deserving of the most intrusive level of judicial scrutiny. This case is difficult to explain except on a moral reading of the Constitution, even if the justices in the case may be criticized for selecting a principle that is not well defended by reference to our nation's history and practices.

Fingerprints of the moral reading can be detected in the joint opinion in *Planned Parenthood v. Casey* as well.[104] That opinion reflects a significant departure both from the earlier case that it purported to affirm (*Roe v. Wade*,[105] 1973) and from other fundamental rights precedent. It acknowledged for the first time "a realm of personal liberty which the government may not enter," grounded in American law by some authority other than a strictly textual application of the Bill of Rights, an authority bearing many indicia of a Dworkinian principle.[106]

Dworkin's thick portrayal of equality continues to exert an important influence today. The use of a principle of equal concern and respect, as a foundation for implementing democracy, is as sound and robust today as it was thirty years ago. Perhaps it is even more important than ever, as the society becomes increasingly heterogeneous (the reason Ely was forced to make use of the principle), the legislative and electoral processes increasingly inaccessible, and the challenge of securing good and fair laws through representative democracy increasingly daunting.

Perhaps most valuable to current constitutional law is the use of equality commitments to give life to the protection of fundamental liberties. A recent Term of the United States Supreme Court brought a stunning example of the importance of Dworkin's substratum of equal concern and respect to one of the divisive issues

---

[103] 515 U.S. 200 (1995).

[104] 505 U.S. 833 (1992).   [105] 410 U.S. 113 (1973).

[106] *Compare Casey*, 505 U.S. at 846 ("neither the bill of Rights nor the practices of States at the time of the adoption of the Fourteenth Amendment marks the outer limits of the substantive sphere of liberty which the Fourteenth Amendment protects") *with Griswold v. Connecticut*, 381 U.S. 479 (1965) (seeking to ground right to marital privacy in penumbras emanating from textually enumerated rights).

of the twenty-first century.[107] In *Lawrence v. Texas*,[108] in which the Court invalidated the Texas law prohibiting same-sex sodomy, the Court relied on the protection of liberty under the Due Process Clause, and expressly declined, indeed, to resolve the case under the Equal Protection Clause. But Dworkin's principle of equal concern and respect was in evidence nonetheless.

The *Lawrence* Court made a significant departure from the rhetoric and doctrine of prior cases raising liberty claims. In times past, it had been common for the Court to make sharp distinctions between claims based in liberty and those sounding in equality. Indeed, it was Justice Robert Jackson who, in 1949, warned that the court should be wary of striking down state laws under the Due Process Clause, but should be less reluctant to ensure equality.[109] More recently, Justice Scalia expressed a similar instinct in the *Cruzan* case, when he rejected the use of the Due Process Clause as a source of protection for liberty, arguing that it is the Equal Protection Clause— "which requires the democratic majority to accept for themselves and their loved ones what they impose on you and me"—that is "our salvation."[110] For those uncomfortable with judicial review, equality was a more palatable value than liberty, because it was ostensibly not substantive.

It was this mode of thinking that was responsible for the development of different doctrinal frameworks for constitutional claims brought to protect liberty and those seeking equal protection of the laws. Some cases confounded the distinction: is a law banning interracial marriage an affront to equality or to liberty? In those cases, the Court muddled through, adhering as best it could, imperfectly at times, to its distinct lines of analysis.[111] These lines had their roots in different clauses of the Constitution and continued to reflect different intuitions about judicial review and democratic process.[112]

But Dworkin supplies a different way to think about liberty and equality claims. Starting from a notion of equal concern derived from the concept of democracy itself, he leads us to an obligation of respect for whatever individual freedoms are indispensable to the achievement of equal status. Thus, some

---

[107] A second case in the same Term, *Grutter v. Bollinger*, 539 U.S. 306 (2003), fulfilled a prediction made by Dworkin in his discussion of whether racial diversity in a university setting would give rise to a compelling state interest sufficient to justify race-conscious admissions policies. *See* SOVEREIGN VIRTUE, *supra* note 2, at 420–426 (accurately suggesting that the *Bakke* principle remains good law, and recommending an emphasis, borne out in the case, on diversity as the predominant state interest supporting such programs). I do not take the Court's opinion in *Grutter*, however, to be an application of his moral reading, particularly since it applies strict scrutiny as a result of *Adarand v. Pena*, a precedent that Dworkin would not endorse (even if it does employ a moral reasoning of its own). *See id.* at 417.   [108] 539 U.S. 558 (2003).

[109] *Railway Express Agency, Inc. v. New York*, 336 U.S. 106, 112 (1949) (Jackson, J., concurring).

[110] *Cruzan v. Director, Mo. Dep't of Health*, 497 U.S. 261, 300 (1990) (Scalia, J., concurring).

[111] *See Loving v. Virginia*, 388 U.S. 1 (1967) (deciding liberty claim with reference to the miscegenation law's affront to equality).

[112] *See* Brown, *supra* note 87, at 1491–1500 (discussing inter-relations between liberty and equality, the traditional judicial preference for equality, and the need for a more satisfactory merging of the two ideals).

substantive freedoms are derivative of one's entitlement to be treated by one's government with equal respect.

The Supreme Court's opinion in *Lawrence* appeared to approach its "liberty" question with the principle of equal respect in mind. The Court found that the particular non-public, non-commercial, consensual, private "common" sexual practices engaged in by the two adult petitioners were "entitled to respect." Eschewing the more formalistic inquiry that had been the hallmark of the prior liberty cases, which asked whether a particular claimed liberty is "fundamental" under societal traditions and judicial precedent,[113] this Court engaged in the more substantive inquiry whether the state had "demean[ed] their existence or control[led] their destiny." This novel inquiry—and even the language in which it is expressed, it seems to me—can be traced directly to Dworkin and the principle of equal concern and respect.

A second way in which the *Lawrence* opinion both departed from prior case law and appeared to embrace Dworkin was in its consideration of the state's proffered justifications for its law. A reading of prior liberty cases would have led one to predict that the asserted interests of the state in the case would provide a significant focus of discussion in the opinion. Accordingly, much speculation had been voiced on whether the state of Texas would be able, if required, to assert a "compelling interest" in support of its law. Even taking into account a prior holding that the moral beliefs of a community could supply a *rational basis* for a law restricting *non*-fundamental liberties,[114] it seemed unlikely that such a rationale could be considered compelling if the Court were to find the right to be, in fact, fundamental.

But the Court never got to that issue, any more than it had gotten to the "fundamental rights" determination itself. Having found that the law was demeaning and that it failed to accord the necessary respect to its citizens, the Court went on, simply, to hold that the state had proffered "no legitimate state interest which can justify its intrusion into the personal and private life of the individual."[115] The state had argued in this case that it was entitled to support its law solely by asserting "the State's long-standing moral disapproval of homosexual conduct."[116] The Court, therefore, had an opportunity to discuss the sufficiency of moral beliefs to meet doctrinal standards; or, in effect, to balance the strength of the liberty of the petitioners against the community's contrary interest, as precedent had suggested it should do. But, departing from decades of jurisprudence taking this more utilitarian approach, the Court declined to engage in the

---

[113] *See, e.g., Washington v. Glucksberg*, 521 U.S. 707 (1997) (holding right of terminally ill to assisted suicide not fundamental because not deeply rooted in tradition); *Bowers v. Hardwick*, 478 U.S. 186 (1986) (holding right to engage in homosexual conduct not fundamental because not deeply rooted in tradition); *Michael H. v. Gerald D.*, 491 U.S. 505 (1989) (plurality finding right of biological father to relationship with child conceived in adultery not fundamental because not deeply rooted in tradition).

[114] This was the then-novel position taken in *Bowers v. Hardwick*, 478 U.S. 186 (1986).

[115] 539 U.S. at 526.

[116] *Lawrence v. Texas*, No. 02–102, Respondent's Brief, Feb. 17, 2003, at 41.

balancing. In the Court's written opinion, one could almost detect the whisper of Dworkin's 1977 warning that government "must not constrain liberty on the ground that one citizen's conception of the good life . . . is nobler or superior to another's." This postulate, he had emphasized, "is a conception of equality, not of liberty . . . ."[117] It appears that a quarter-century later, these insights have found expression in the law of the land.

This aspect of Dworkin's work shows great promise for addressing one of the most difficult contemporary constitutional issues arising under the Due Process Clause, the problem of evaluating the relative strengths of, on the one hand, a claim to liberty, and, on the other, a state assertion of the need to restrict it. The Court has been unable to ground this inquiry, on either side of the balance, in any teleological commitments that would help frame the determination of a statute's validity. Wanting to avoid the charge that it is legislating from the bench, it has struggled to identify some metric against which a claimed liberty right could be evaluated, but has been unable to settle on one because it has articulated no over-arching theory of what it is protecting or why. This noncommittal protection of liberty rights has resulted in an often formalistic fragmentation of liberty into two categories, some being "fundamental" and others "ordinary."[118] The conse-quences of attaching one of these labels are huge, yet the normative impulses underlying the dichotomy are elusive. This leads the Court more and more to relegate claims to the default category of "ordinary" liberties, leaving them to the mercies of legislative grace.

When the Court has attempted qualitative evaluation of liberties, its analysis has been unsatisfying. For example, while acknowledging that some of the liberties it has recognized as fundamental in the past have had something to do with auton-omy, the Court, in the assisted suicide case, explicitly rejected autonomy as a defin-ing feature of a fundamental right.[119] The Court has buffeted around the idea of societal tradition as a way to identify protected interests, but that has caused more problems than it has solved. This approach to identifying fundamental rights has persistently sparked the still unresolved controversy about the level of generality at which to search for societal traditions, as well as the thorny question of which history to select in cases of conflicting evidence.[120] Moreover, the tradition method has never adequately responded to the more normative question why the backward-looking reliance on past societal practice *should* provide the limits of

---

[117] TAKING RIGHTS SERIOUSLY, *supra* note 2, at 273.

[118] *See* R. L. Brown, *The Fragmented Liberty Clause*, 41 WM. & MARY L. REV. 65 (1999) (arguing that this fragmentation inappropriately impedes the protection of liberty).

[119] *See Glucksberg*, 521 U.S. at 727–728; ("That many of the rights and liberties protected by the Due Process Clause sound in personal autonomy does not warrant the sweeping conclusion that any and all important, intimate, and personal decisions are so protected.").

[120] *See* G. R. STONE, L. M. SEIDMAN, C. R. SUNSTEIN, and M. V. TUSHNET, CONSTITUTIONAL LAW 890–891 (4th ed. 2001) (describing dispute between Justice Scalia and Justice Brennan on the appropriate level of abstraction at which to search for traditions).

protected liberty going forward in an evolving society.[121] Thus, the Court has not succeeded in ordering different liberties into an intelligible hierarchy.

On the state's side of the ledger, the doctrinal picture has been equally dim. The cases have supplied no framework within which to measure the strength or validity of state interests offered in support of regulatory restrictions on liberty. Moral arguments, such as that made by Texas in support of its sodomy statute, are especially difficult to quantify as "rational" or "compelling," in the absence of some broader theory addressing the appropriate use of state power in a free society. This lack of guidance for evaluating the limits of regulatory authority has enabled those on the side of regulating states to launch a liberty claim of their own. The claim is that the citizens who support a statutory restriction on liberty have a "right" to enact their beliefs into law without interference from the Constitution. According to this view, it is a violation of *their* liberty to strike down laws they have passed to constrain the objectionable behavior of others.[122] The "freedom of association" claim, raised in opposition to the *Brown* decision,[123] is one version of this argument. The Court, having constructed no theory of how our Constitution protects liberty, has been without the means to repudiate the devastating implications of this argument.

Dworkin's work gives courts the tools with which to begin addressing both types of deficit in the case law. On the liberty side, the principle of equal concern and respect suggests some contours for a method of discerning which types of liberty must be specially guarded in a constitutional democracy. Dworkin has constructed arguments along these lines in addressing several of the major liberty issues to arise in recent years; the analysis that these arguments share is the normative vision of liberty protection as a way to secure a certain minimal degree of dignity and equal moral status for all citizens, a value traceable to both liberty and equality ideals.[124] This anchoring of liberty to political theory provides guidance in the understanding of why some claims might be more compelling than others. Dworkin solves the problems of level of generality and conflicting traditions, so irksome to court precedent, with his elements of fit and integrity in the interpretation of the Constitution.

Dworkin's approach also provides a start for developing a principled way of evaluating asserted state interests. His response, in particular, to those who make the claim described above—that collective self-determination is compromised by enforcement of individual rights—suggests contours for a method of evaluating state justifications for laws generally. He does not reject the community self-determination argument on its face. After all, its claim, that a majority of a

---

[121] *See* R. L. Brown, *Tradition and Insight*, 103 YALE L.J. 177, 200–205 (1993) (discussing several theoretical objections to use of tradition as defining point for individual rights).

[122] FREEDOM'S LAW, *supra* note 2, at 21. Bork, for one, has explicitly made this claim. *See supra* note 70.

[123] *See* Wechsler, *supra* note 17, at 35 (characterizing the "heart of the issue" in *Brown* as the choice by a state between denying association to those who wish it and imposing it on those who would avoid it).   [124] *See* FREEDOM'S LAW, *supra* note 2, at 111.

community has the right to determine the nature of the entire community through law, is an essentially moral argument and, as such, must be taken seriously. In order for the claim to succeed, however, the underlying interest in collective self-government must itself meet moral standards. Thus, the community seeking to determine its own values through legal restrictions on liberty must meet the minimal obligation to respect the needs and prospects of all members of the affected community. Accordingly, just as a community would obviously not have a moral entitlement to employ its right to self-government so as to enslave some members of the community for the benefit of the others (even if 99 per cent voted to enslave the remaining 1 per cent), it would also be precluded, more generally, from dictating what its citizens think about matters of political, moral or ethical judgment, no matter how many members might share one view.

This recognition of a basic moral obligation on government provides a way of beginning to distinguish and evaluate asserted government interests. A requirement that all laws accord equal concern and respect to all members of a community can begin the process of distinguishing laws that legitimately seek to protect the public good from those that simply impose contested visions of the good life on an unwilling minority. Although admittedly difficult, this inquiry is far more substantive and meaningful than the apparently *ad hoc* jurisprudence that led the Supreme Court, without elaboration, to pronounce one day that a community's moral preferences are sufficient to support restraints on individual liberty (in *Bowers v. Hardwick*), and then another day that they are not sufficient (in *Lawrence v. Texas*). Dworkin's work makes possible a meaningful, normative inquiry, and thus holds the key to a coherent liberty jurisprudence for the twenty-first century.

IV. Conclusion

In the end, it is a question of optimism or pessimism. The schools of constitutional thought to which Dworkin has sworn eternal opposition are characterized by skepticism, cynicism, distrust, and pessimism. Dworkin's works, by contrast, have fought valiantly for the proposition that the American people can do better, that our form of government was conceived under the sun of enlightenment, that it committed us to the ideals expressed in the Preamble of the Constitution.[125] The hope of true equality, so far elusive to our society, is within our grasp, he assures us: "we must hold to the courage of the conviction . . . that we can all be equal citizens of a moral republic." [126] With his enduring faith, Ronald Dworkin helped to reclaim for constitutional theory its itinerant soul.

---

[125] *See* E. J. McCaffery, *Ronald Dworkin, Inside-Out* (reviewing FREEDOM'S LAW), 85 CAL. L. REV. 1043, 1058 (1997) (describing Dworkin's resolute nonskepticism and belief in moral and social improvement). [126] FREEDOM'S LAW, *supra* note 2, at 38.

4

Coherence, Hypothetical Cases, and Precedent

*S. L. Hurley**

Coherence accounts of practical reasoning in general, of which legal reasoning is a particular case, postulate the existence of a theory, sought in deliberation, which best displays as coherent the relationships among specific reasons for action that conflict in application to the case to be decided. These relationships are discovered in part by considering how the same conflicting reasons apply in other cases, the resolution of which is settled. Ronald Dworkin's account of legal reasoning in *Law's Empire* is an example of a coherence account. Coherence accounts provide elements of various familiar conceptions of practical reasoning, such as the Rawlsian conception of reflective equilibrium as the outcome of a process of mutual adjustment between theory and intuition, and the decision-theoretic conception of rationality in terms of adjustment between data about preferences, criteria of choice, and principles of consistency.[1] I have elsewhere discussed the general rationale and motivation for coherence accounts of practical reasoning, illustrated the process of seeking coherence through deliberation with both legal and ethical examples, abstractly characterized the search for coherence, and considered various problems to which the abstract characterization gives rise.[2] In this paper I shall:

First, briefly set out my abstract characterization of deliberation as a search for coherence;

* For helpful suggestions and comments on earlier drafts that saved me from various errors and unclarities, I am grateful to Ronald Dworkin, Mark Greenberg, and Joseph Raz: needless to say, responsibility for all remaining errors is entirely my own. This paper was originally published in 10 (2) OXFORD J. LEGAL STUD. 221–251 (1990) and is reproduced here with permission.
    [1] *See* J. RAWLS, A THEORY OF JUSTICE (1971); and R. L. KEENEY AND H. RAIFFA, DECISIONS WITH MULTIPLE OBJECTIVES: PREFERENCES AND VALUE TRADEOFFS (1976).
    [2] *See* my NATURAL REASONS (1989), chapters 4, 10, 11, 12, etc. Many background issues about the nature and objectivity of coherentist practical reasoning are raised by the argument of this article which I cannot here address at length in NATURAL REASONS. They include: the need for substantive constraints on the description of the problem in terms of conflicting reasons, the relationships of these constraints to the structure and process of coherentist deliberation and the explanatory character of the resulting theories, the nature and limitations of the authority of theories about conflicting reasons, and many others.

Secondly, consider various further examples of legal and ethical reasoning and indicate briefly the way in which they provide instances of my general coherentist characterization of deliberation;

Thirdly, point out the generally similar roles within coherentist accounts of practical reasoning of settled actual cases and settled hypothetical cases as data to be accounted for the sought-after theory or principles;

Fourthly, present an objection to coherence accounts of legal reasoning in particular discussed by Kenneth Kress, who argues that they may give rise to retroactive application of legal principles when new cases are decided between the occurrence of the events litigated and litigation of them (the problem of intervening cases); and

Finally, consider various possible responses to Kress's argument. I shall briefly evaluate and put aside the possible responses of giving intervening cases prospective effect only, and of accepting intervening case retroactivity as not so bad. I shall then go on to diagnose the source of the problem by evaluating the relationships among concept of coherence, hypothetical cases, and the doctrine of precedent. I will show that the weaker coherentist requirement of treating like cases alike within practical reasoning in general is not sufficient to give rise to the problem of intervening cases, but that the stronger requirement imposed by the doctrine of precedent within legal reasoning in particular is necessary for the problem to arise. The distinction between the weaker and stronger requirements turns on the asymmetrical treatment of actual and hypothetical cases by the doctrine of precedent, by contrast with their symmetrical treatment in coherentist practical reasoning in general. However, I shall then argue that, when this asymmetry is properly understood, neither is the doctrine of precedent by itself sufficient to give rise to the problem of intervening cases, but only does so when the intervening legal decision is not *ex ante* correct, and that the role of hypothetical cases in coherentist practical reasoning in fact limits the problem of intervening case retroactivity. I shall conclude, following suggestions made by Dworkin, that intervening case retroactivity does not present a problem for coherence accounts such as his in particular.

I. An Abstract Characterization of Deliberation, and Coherence Functions

Our subject matter is deliberation about what to do when the reasons that apply to the alternatives conflict. The alternatives may be possible individual actions (e.g. keeping one's promise and risking someone's life, or breaking it and avoiding risk to life), or possible judicial actions (e.g. holding that a statute violates the Equal Protection Clause, or that it does not). The reasons that apply to the alternatives may be of various kinds, depending on the context of deliberation.

An individual may deliberate about his own conflicting self-interested reasons, when no one else is significantly affected by the alternatives, or about a conflict involving the interests of others; the applicable reasons may be ethical, aesthetic, etc. A judge deliberates about conflicting legal reasons: legal doctrines, precedents, rights, principles, policies, as expressed within various legal practices and institutions, by cases, statutes, a constitution, legal scholarship, etc.

Coherence accounts claim that to say a certain alternative ought to be done is to say that it is favoured by the theory, whichever it may be, that gives the best account of the relationships among the various specific reasons that apply to the alternatives in question. Which theory is in fact the best theory, which best displays the applicable reasons as coherently related, is not specified by a coherence account *per se*. Rather, it is left to deliberation to discover what the best theory is. A coherence account merely claims that what ought to be done is whatever alternative the best theory, whatever that is, favours. Thus the deliberator's task is to discover the theory that best displays coherence. Deliberation involves a process of constructing hypotheses about the content of what I call a "coherence function'," which represents the theory sought and which takes us from alternatives ranked by specific reasons to all-things-considered rankings of alternatives. Of course the coherence function must meet certain conditions, and the all-things-considered ranking must meet certain conditions. For example, the latter ranking should not be intransitive. However, I shall not be considering the full range of these conditions in this article, but only those embodied in the requirements of treating like cases alike and of the doctrine of precedent.[3]

The process of deliberation can be analysed into five stages. At the *first* stage, we specify the problem. We try to arrive at a characterization of the alternatives at issue, and to determine what various specific reasons apply and how they rank the alternatives. We here exercise our abilities to perceive the world in terms of ethical, or legal, or other reason-giving concepts. (This is the issue spotting stage familiar to law students; however, there is much more to legal deliberation than issue spotting.) Assuming the reasons that apply conflict, that is, rank the alternatives at issue differently, we proceed to the *second* stage, and examine more carefully the various specific reasons that apply. Perhaps when we consider the purpose of one reason, it will turn out to have a rather different import than we originally thought in this particular case. At any rate, at this stage we develop and firm up our local conceptions of the various specific reasons that apply, without yet trying to arrive at a global conception of their relations to one another.

At the *third* stage we begin gathering data, by looking for other issues to which the conflicting reasons examined at stage two apply. In particular we are looking

---

[3] For discussion of such conditions, *see* my NATURAL REASONS, *supra* note 2, chapter 12.

for settled cases. They may have actually been decided, or may be posed as hypothetical issues, the resolution of which can be taken as evident. By a "settled" case, I mean a case which, if actual, is such that its resolution is clear to the relevant decision-maker or decision-makers, and which, if hypothetical, is such that its resolution would be clear to the relevant decision-maker or decision-makers were the case to be considered. (That a resolution of a particular case is or would be clear does not mean that it cannot be mistaken; settledness in particular cases is a matter of what is or would be believed to be correct, not necessarily of what is correct. However, it is of the nature of a coherentist account of what should be done, in terms of coherence with settled cases in general, that not all settled cases can be mistaken. I will return to this point below.) Thus, at least as a conceptual matter, not all actually decided cases are settled, and some settled cases are hypothetical, not actual (see Section VIII below for more on this use of "settled"). We may give settled actual cases more weight than settled hypothetical cases, or we may give them equal weight. The doctrine of precedent in law gives settled actual cases more weight than settled hypothetical cases, though usually only when the settled cases are those of the same court or higher courts of the same jurisdiction; actual cases of lower courts or courts of other jurisdictions may be treated on a par with settled hypothetical cases. However, as we shall see, this difference in weight may only be significant under certain circumstances.

The *fourth* stage is the heart of the deliberative process. At this stage we engage in all-out theorizing, looking for hypotheses which account for the resolutions of issues we found at stage three. That is, we are trying to formulate hypotheses about the relationships between the conflicting reasons under various different circumstances present in the stage three cases, which account for those resolutions. To this end we examine the stage three cases for distinctive circumstances or dimensions which seem to enhance or diminish the weight of one of the conflicting reasons in relation to the other. When we have formulated such an hypothesis, we try to test it, by going back to stage three and looking for further settled cases in which the same reasons apply and in which the circumstances identified by the hypothesis are present. We thus go back and forth between stages three and four, looking for settled actual and hypothetical cases that help us to refine our hypotheses about the relationships between the conflicting reasons in various circumstances.

Finally, at the *fifth* stage, we work out the consequences of the best hypothesis we have arrived at for the original case at issue. That is, we apply that hypothesis about the relationships between the applicable reasons to the circumstances present in the case at issue. This hypothesis is a partial specification of a coherence function, which takes us from the rankings of alternatives involving various circumstances or dimensions by the conflicting reasons to an all-things-considered ranking.

This characterization of deliberation can be pictured in terms of a *deliberative matrix*. The data gathered at stage three can be represented as follows, where in each row, alternatives are ranked above or below one another by the applicable reasons.

Table 4.1.: The deliberative matrix

	Reason X	Reason Y	Resolution, all-things-considered
case at issue:	alt a	alt b	?
	alt b	alt a	
settled actual cases:	alt d	alt c	alt c
	alt c	alt d	alt d
	alt e	alt f	alt e
	alt f	alt e	alt f
settled hypothetical cases:	alt g	alt h	alt h
	alt h	alt g	alt g
	alt j	alt i	alt j
	alt i	alt j	alt i
	etc.	etc.	etc.

I present the matrix with only two conflicting reasons, X and Y, merely for convenience; there is no restriction on the number of reasons that may be represented. (Indeed, multi-dimensional conflicts give rise to interesting theoretical questions.)[4] During stage four the alternatives are analysed and more fully characterized in terms of various circumstances and dimensions of the cases which may help to explain their resolution. These circumstances may be represented by adding propositions, p, q, etc, to the alternatives in each row. The content of such a proposition may be quantitative or non-quantitative. A hypothesis would then take the form: "Reason X tends to outweigh Reason Y when it is the case that p, while Reason Y tends to outweigh Reason X when it is the case that q; when it is the case that both p and q, but not r, Reason X has more weight, but when r is present as well, Reason Y has more weight," and so on.[5]

[4] Which I pursue in NATIONAL REASONS, *supra* note 2, chapters 12 and 13.

[5] This schematization, applied to legal deliberation, may be compared to that employed by the programme HYPO, developed by Edwina Rissland and her student Kevin Ashley, and discussed in a Harvard Law School seminar on artificial intelligence and legal reasoning, conducted by Rissland Autumn Term 1987. *See* K. D. Ashley, *Modelling Legal Argument: Reasoning with Cases and Hypotheticals*, PhD dissertation, 1987, University of Massachusetts, Dept of Computer and Information Science. While there are many differences in detail between the two approaches, I do not believe there is any incompatibility in principle between them. The role of HYPO's "dimensions" is similar to the role of my propositions p, q, etc in the analysis of actual and hypothetical settled cases at stage four. Perhaps I try to say a bit more than Rissland and Ashley do about the role of hypotheticals in reaching legal conclusions, in that the answers to hypothetical questions feed back into the resolution of the case at issue via the coherence function, but again I do not believe that what I say is incompatible with their approach. Perhaps the most striking difference is that over whether to use favourableness to conflicting legal doctrines or favourableness to plaintiff as opposed to defendant, as the basic means of organizing the data. Often, within a narrowly limited area of the law, such as trade secrets law, plaintiffs will typically represent one legal doctrine, and defendants another, so that the two approaches are in principle quite similar. However, the doctrine-oriented rather than party-oriented method of organization may have advantages when one comes to generalize beyond a narrow limited area of the law, so that plaintiff and defendant no longer typically

Two points of clarification may be helpful. First, I do not in this paper aim to give a full account of what is distinctive about legal reasoning in particular, but rather to consider what follows about legal reasoning from the fact that it has the general features of practical reasoning, understood along coherentist lines. My examples in the next section are intended to illustrate the application of the coherentist account of practical reasoning in general to legal problems, rather than to illuminate what is distinctive about legal reasoning in particular. I will go on to consider the distinctively legal doctrine of precedent in the context set by a view of legal reasoning as having the general features of coherentist practical reasoning. This is important to understand for purposes of my discussion below of the problem of intervening cases, since my eventual response to Kress in Sections VII and VIII turns on the features that legal reasoning shares with practical reason in general, on a coherentist view of it, with respect to the role of hypothetical cases. Such general features of coherentist practical reasoning limit the effects of the distinctively legal doctrine of precedent in giving rise to intervening case retroactivity, and thus illuminate the source of the problem. But I would certainly not claim that the generally coherentist character of legal reasoning as a kind of practical reasoning plus the features of precedent I consider provide a full account of what is distinctive about legal reasoning in particular; this is not my purpose. Secondly, I would expect the account and illustrations of practical reasoning to be controversial to the extent they represent a kind of deliberative rationality with respect to conflicting ends, values or reasons, the possibility of which has often been denied, for example, in favour of a view of practical reasoning as exclusively instrumental, or in favour of more radically sceptical or nihilistic views about practical rationality (in the legal context, consider certain views associated with the critical legal studies movement, or parodies thereof). However, I cannot join these issues here.

II. Some Examples of Legal and Ethical Deliberation Analysed

I have elsewhere considered in detail and at length a legal illustration of this general account of practical reasoning, the stages of deliberation, and the deliberative matrix. That discussion involved deliberation about the relationships between the conflicting legal doctrines of estoppel and of consideration in cases now usually

represent particular legal doctrines. By organizing the cases according to legal doctrines directly rather than by plaintiffs' and defendants' positions, one may hope to keep theoretical score as one moves from one area of law to another in which the same doctrines apply, and to bring insights about the relationships between legal doctrines from one area to the next.

Of course, different ways of perceiving what legal doctrines apply will yield different analyses, but that is the way the law is, and an analysis which reflects this relativity of conclusion to starting point may be illuminating. Moreover, we can in principle start with as many different legal doctrines as we think may be relevant; again, there is no need to restrict the number of reasons weighed against one another by the coherence function to two.

covered by the doctrine of promissory estoppel.[6] I will not here give another lengthy and detailed illustration, but rather will give several sketchy illustrations. I hope in the former discussion to have persuaded readers that my account can be made to work in detail. In this discussion I rather aim to persuade readers that the account applies readily and intuitively in a wide range of cases. Accordingly I shall not work out the details of my applications here, but shall merely briefly indicate how the framework of my account would fit the examples.

Let us begin with the case of *California v. Carney*.[7] In *Carney*, Fourth Amendment issues were raised by a warrantless police search of a motor home, parked in a downtown San Diego parking lot. The police had reason to believe that Carney, the owner of the motor home, was exchanging marijuana for sex acts. They observed a young boy enter the motor home and leave again an hour and a quarter later. On questioning by the police, the boy said that such an exchange had just occurred. The police then knocked on the door, and when Carney came out they entered the motor home without a warrant and found marijuana. A further search of the vehicle at the police station revealed more marijuana, in cupboards and in the refrigerator. The parking lot where the warrantless search occurred was a short distance from a courthouse where a warrant could easily have been obtained.

The case and its oral argument, rich in hypothetical cases, have been analysed by Edwina Rissland to illustrate the idea of a "dimension," which is used by the case-based reasoning programme HYPO to generate hypothetical cases.[8] My treatment of the case essentially adapts her analysis to my framework, and illustrates, I believe, the compatibility of my framework and the notions of a deliberate matrix and a coherence function, with Rissland's dimension-based analysis. As she points out, *Carney* is a case in which there is a conflict between a citizen's expectations of privacy, protected by the Fourth Amendment's prohibition of unreasonable searches and seizures, and the responsibilities and desires of the police to investigate and control drug use and other prohibited activities. Thus, the first row of our matrix for the case at issue involves at least two kinds of legal reasons: I shall refer to them as reasons of Privacy, and reasons of the Police Power. The alternatives in the case at issue are to allow or to disallow the warrantless search of the motor home in *Carney* under the Fourth Amendment. Reasons of Privacy would favour disallowing the search, while reasons of the Police Power would favour allowing it. We want to discover how reasons of Privacy and reasons of the Police Power are related to one another with respect to warrantless searches. Settled actual cases at the next several rows of the matrix tell us that reasons of Privacy are augmented relative to those of the Police Power in circumstances in which the warrantless search at issue is of someone's home; if we sum

---

[6] *See* NATURAL REASONS, *supra* note 2, chapter 11.
[7] *California v. Carney*, 471 U.S. 386 (1985).   [8] *See supra* note 3.

up these circumstances in proposition p, we can hypothesize that Privacy is augmented relative to the Police Power when it is the case that p. By contrast, settled cases tell us, the Police Power is augmented relative to Privacy when the warrantless search at issue is of a vehicle; if we sum up the latter circumstances in proposition q, we can hypothesize that Privacy is diminished relative to the Police Power when it is the case that q. We have thus begun to specify a coherence function which weighs Privacy against the Police Power in various circumstances.

While these hypotheses about the relations between Privacy and the Police Power are well supported by settled cases, they really only set the stage for the *Carney* problem, since the motor home in *Carney* is both a home and a vehicle. We need a finer analysis of relevant circumstances in order to resolve the conflict in this case. Thus we look for other settled cases, actual or hypothetical, in which these two reasons come into conflict, in circumstances in which the home-vehicle distinction is difficult to draw. On the basis of such cases, we try to arrive at a hypothesis that will help police to draw the home-vehicle distinction in a reliable and straightforward way in cases in which aspects of both home and vehicle are present; that is, we would like to find a "bright-line" distinction, which will not require police officers to make excessively subtle or difficult determinations. We will try various hypotheses about the relevant circumstances, or dimensions of cases, and will test them against various actual and hypothetical cases.

The fact that the thing to be searched is a vehicle seems to augment the Police Power reason relative to those of Privacy in part because it is inherently mobile, such that requiring a warrant would leave it time to "get away" and would greatly frustrate legitimate exercises of the Police Power, and also because vehicles are not usually used as homes, and thus not the objects of normal expectations of privacy. These hypotheses are developed and tested in oral argument by reference to hypo-thetical cases in which vehicles are also homes, but some of which are more inher-ently mobile, or more home-like than others, owing to varying circumstances and dimensions. The presence of wheels is obviously dispensable to inherent mobility in the case of most boats, with respect to which presumably reasons of the Police Power predominate. Nor is the presence of wheels decisive in the case of motor homes with wheels but which are not self-propelling and which are permanently connected to utilities supplies, with respect to which presumably reasons of Privacy predominate. Location in a temporary parking lot as opposed to a perma-nent motor home park strengthens the case with respect to inherent mobility and hence with respect to the weight of Police Power reasons. But a counter-example to that hypothesis would seem to be the case of someone very poor who cannot afford a permanent spot for his vehicle but lives in it behind curtains, on the move from day to day. The presence of the normal accoutrements of a home, such as a refrigerator, in a vehicle, may strengthen reasons of Privacy; but again we would seem to have a counter-example when the refrigerator is used solely to store marijuana, as seemed to be the case in *Carney*, and not for home-like purposes.

From among these various circumstances and dimensions of hypothetical cases, the best hypothesis will focus on objective factors that are straightforward for the police to ascertain before deciding whether to search without a warrant or not (as the contents of a refrigerator are not), so as to provide police with "bright-line" guidance. This is because the investigation needed to apply an excessively subtle distinction will make for a prior, unprincipled defeat of reasons of Privacy, while a strong presumption in favour of home-likeness to accommodate all unusual uses of vehicles as homes would in effect eliminate the vehicle exception to the warrant requirement and would thus excessively compromise the Police Power. Thus the need for bright-line guidance in effect provides a way for the theory to get around the apparent counter-example to inherent mobility hypothesis provided by the poor person who lives in his car. The case does not really provide a counter-example, after all, since the police cannot tell that such unusual vehicles are homes without privacy-infringing investigation; and it is already settled by the vehicle exception that the alternative of disallowing searches of *any* vehicles which might possibly be homes has been ruled out. The majority opinion in *Carney* indicates in effect that the best hypothesis makes the relation between reasons of Privacy and those of the Police Power in cases involving vehicles that may be homes turn on objective indications of mobility and use for transportation, rather than on the more difficult-to-ascertain home-like uses of the vehicle. If the presence of the former characteristics is expressed by proposition r, the majority's hypothesis is that when it is the case that r, as it was in *Carney*, reasons of the Police Power outweigh reasons of Privacy, and thus support the warrantless search at issue. The majority implicitly regard this hypothesis as supported by the hypothetical cases considered, given the need for bright-line guidance. By contrast, the dissenting opinions seem to prefer a hypothesis which gives more of a role to the home-like character of the place in strengthening reasons of Privacy.

Equal Protection cases raised under the US Constitution are a fertile source of illustrations of the coherentist framework, as the jurisprudence of varying degrees of relationship to various state interests served by challenged classifications lends itself immediately to representation within a deliberative matrix. In discussing several such cases I shall not stop to assign labels, p, q, etc., to the propositions employed in hypotheses about the relations among the conflicting reasons in various circumstances. I shall merely identify the general categories of reasons in play, and try to draw out the hypotheses about the relations between the reasons in play that are implicitly tested by appeal to various settled cases. It should be evident, however, how labels could be assigned and hypotheses located within a deliberative matrix. In Equal Protection cases one category of legal reasons is provided by the Equal Protection Clause itself: reasons of Nondiscrimination, which oppose legal classifications which fail to treat similarly situated citizens in similar ways. Further categories of reasons are provided by whatever state interests are supposed to be served by the challenged classification.

In *Parham v. Hughes*,[9] for example, the father of an illegitimate child challenged a law which prevented him from recovering for the wrongful death of his child, where an unmarried father who had filed papers to legitimize the child, or the mother of the illegitimate child, would have been allowed to recover. If he could be regarded as similarly situated with other parents of illegitimate children who were allowed to recover for wrongful death, then reasons of Nondiscrimination would favour striking the statute down. However, the state considered that it had an interest in promoting the integrity of the legitimate family unit, and that reasons of Legitimacy favoured restricting recovery for wrongful death to unmarried fathers who had filed to legitimize their children and unmarried mothers. The implication seems to be that such a restriction would provide incentives to unmarried fathers to file to legitimize their children. Moreover, the state also claimed to have an interest in avoiding difficult problems of proof of paternity, and that reasons of Provability favoured the restriction of wrongful death suits for the death of children born illegitimate to fathers who had filed to legitimize and mothers, whose identity would rarely be in doubt. Thus we seem to have a conflict between reasons of Nondiscrimination, on the one hand, and reasons of Legitimacy and of Provability, on the other.

The court held that this state scheme did not violate Equal Protection or Due Process by discriminating against unmarried fathers relative to unmarried mothers, because fathers and mothers of illegitimate children are not similarly situated since, under Georgia law, only fathers *can* by voluntary unilateral action make an illegitimate child legitimate. That is, the plurality opinion seems implicitly to support the hypothesis that when it is the case that men and women are not similarly situated *owing to a difference in their legally imposed abilities and status*, that difference may provide a basis for a statutory classification which does not constitute invidious discrimination, such that, when such a classification is related in the right way to the right kinds of state interests, the latter outweigh reasons of Nondiscrimination.

The dissent appeals to a hypothetical case to refute the plurality's hypothesis. Justice White writes:

There is a startling circularity in this argument. The issue before the Court is whether Georgia may require unmarried fathers, but not unmarried mothers, to have pursued the statutory legitimization procedure in order to bring suit for the wrongful death of their children. Seemingly, it is irrelevant that as a matter of state law mothers may not legitimate their children, for they are not required to do so in order to maintain a wrongful-death action. That only fathers *may* resort to the legitimization process cannot dissolve the sex-discrimination in *requiring* them to. Under the plurality's bootstrap rationale, a State could require that women, but not men, pass a course in order to receive a taxi license, simply by limiting admission to the course to women.

[9] 441 U.S. 347 (1979).

In the taxi licence hypothetical, men and women would not be similarly situated, owing to their differing legally imposed abilities, i.e. their differing abilities to enrol in the course. But here it is clearly absurd to suppose that this prior discrimination, unscrutinized, could provide a justification for further discrimination in the form of a statutory classification requiring only women to pass the course in order to get a licence. Thus the hypothetical case provides a counter-example to the plurality's hypothesis. The implication of the dissenting opinion is that the embedded distinction must itself be scrutinized, and not merely taken as given. In *Parham*, the embedded distinction was one with respect to the ability to file papers to legitimize: only men were able to do so. It is hard to see how a rule making it impossible for women to file papers to legitimize children serves either the state interest in promoting the legitimate family unit or in avoiding proof of paternity issues. Permitting women to file as well as men would have no adverse effects whatsoever on either of these state interests.

The dissent goes on to appeal to another counter-example, this time a type of actual rather than hypothetical case, to the hypothesis that reasons of Legitimacy outweigh those of Nondiscrimination if allowing members of one class but not another to sue for wrongful death serves the state interest in promoting the integrity of the legitimate family unit. The dissent points out that unmarried mothers and fathers who file to legitimize but remain unmarried defy the integrity of the legitimate family unit, just as do fathers who fail to file, but the former are allowed to sue for wrongful death while the latter are not.

In *Craig v. Boren*, the question was whether a statute prohibiting the sale of weakly alcoholic beer to males under 21 and females under 18 constituted denial to males aged 18 to 21 of equal protection of the law. On behalf of the statute it was urged that statistical evidence about the relative tendencies of males and females aged 18 to 21 to drink and drive supported the gender line. Thus we have a conflict between reasons of Nondiscrimination and the state interest in Preventing Drunk Driving. The Court rejects the hypothesis that reasons of Nondiscrimination can be overcome by the interest in Preventing Drunk Driving when the latter is served by "statistically measured but loose-fitting generalities concerning the drinking tendencies of aggregate groups." In doing so it appeals to hypothetical variations on the *Craig v. Boren* statute involving statistically supported ethnic or racial lines instead of gender lines aimed at alcohol regulation. The assumption made is that such ethnic or racial lines would not be acceptable, despite statistical support, and that reasons of Nondiscrimination would predominate in such cases: "In fact, social science studies that have uncovered quantifiable differences in drinking tendencies dividing along both racial and ethnic lines strongly suggest the need for application of the Equal Protection Clause in preventing discriminatory treatment that almost certainly would be perceived as invidious." The Court illustrates its comments with reference to statistical evidence to the effect that Jews, Italian Catholics, and black teenagers tend not to be problem drinkers, in contrast to whites and North American Indians.

Finally, consider the uses of hypothetical and actual cases in ethical argument, as illustrated by the debate between Stephen Pepper and David Luban over whether lawyers in an adversary system should help their clients to do legal but unethical acts. Pepper argues that under many circumstances the answer is "yes." He argues roughly as follows. We hold the value of individual autonomy to be more important than getting people to do the ethically right act in a wide range of cases; for example, we allow that people should have the legal power to disinherit a child for marrying outside the faith, even though we may agree that it would be wrong to do so. Individual autonomy in our complex society requires, in many cases, legal assistance; only with the help of lawyers can people, in many circumstances, be "first class citizens." Therefore lawyers should give their clients the legal help required for individual autonomy even when it permits them to do unethical acts.

Luban replies by arguing that, while it is true that, since exercising autonomy is good, helping people exercise autonomy is good, this is only half the story. "The other half is that since doing bad things is bad, helping people do bad things is bad. The two factors must be weighed against each other, and this Pepper does not do." That is, Pepper's general hypothesis that when helping someone to do a legal but unethical act is favoured by reasons of autonomy, reasons of autonomy prevail, is too crude. Luban appeals to an analogous hypothetical case to defeat the unqualified hypothesis:

Compare this case: The automobile, by making it easier to get around, increases human autonomy; hence, other things equal, it is morally good to repair the car of someone who is unable by himself to get it to run. But such considerations can hardly be invoked to defend the morality of fixing the getaway car of an armed robber, assuming that you know in advance what the purpose of the car is. The moral wrong of assisting the robber outweighs the abstract moral goodness of augmenting the robber's autonomy.[10]

Not only may reasons of autonomy sometimes be outweighed by the wrongness of the act in question, but even if the balance of reasons favours allowing the agent to do the unethical act himself, it does not necessarily follow that it will also favour helping him to do it. The balance between autonomy and conflicting reasons may be struck differently in different circumstances, i.e. with respect to omitting to prevent as opposed to positively aiding.

Another argument Pepper makes is that allowing lawyers to weigh the wrongness of acts and thus act as screens to filter out certain legally permissible acts is to submit individuals to "rule by an oligarchy of lawyers."[11] The implication of the term "oligarchy" is that such weighing and screening by lawyers would constitute an elitist centralization of ethical decision-making highly threatening to the

---

[10] D. Luban, *The Lysistratian Prerogative: A Response to Stephen Pepper*, AMERICAN BAR FOUNDATION RESEARCH JOURNAL 639 (1986).

[11] S. Pepper, *The Lawyer's Amoral Ethical Role: A Defense, A Problem, and Some Possibilities*, AMERICAN BAR FOUNDATION RESEARCH JOURNAL 617 (1986).

value of individual autonomy, and that, when this would be the result, reasons of autonomy should prevail. Luban offers a counter-example to this implied hypothesis:

> . . . there is no oligarchy of lawyers, actual or potential, to worry about. An oligarchy is a group of people ruling *in concert*, whereas lawyers who refuse to execute projects to which they object on moral grounds will do so as individuals, without deliberating collectively with other lawyers. The worry about a hidden Central Committee of lawyers evaporates when we realize that the committee will never hold a meeting, and that its members don't even know they are on it. An analogy will clarify this. No doubt throughout history people have often been dissuaded from undertaking immoral projects by the anger, threats, and uncooperativeness of their spouses. It would scarcely make sense, however, to worry that this amounts to subjecting autonomous action "to rule by an oligarchy of spouses." There *is* no oligarchy of spouses.

Luban seems to accept for the sake of argument that screening by a true Central Committee might well be intolerable. But if weighing and screening by spouses does not constitute an elitist centralization of ethical decision-making highly threatening to the value of individual autonomy, it is not clear how this can be regarded as the result when we substitute "lawyers" for "spouses." Indeed, Luban suggests that informal social pressures are an essential complement to legal rules in regulating harmful behaviour. (Note that I am not here endorsing Luban's conclusions, but only using his arguments to illustrate certain characteristic features of deliberation.)

III. Hypothetical Cases as Thought Experiments

The role of the settled cases appealed to in the above examples of deliberation is analogous in some respects to the role of data in scientific theorizing. In both areas, that is, one looks both for relevant data, or clear cases, and for generalizations that account for what seems to be clearly the case (though of course such apparent clarity is not infallible in either area), and uses the latter generalizations to make determinations about further cases. In neither area is the best account of the data deductively entailed by the data. Nevertheless, in both areas the data in some sense determines the best theory (or theories, in the case of a tie or moderate degree of underdetermination of theory by data). The best theory (or theories— I will hereafter omit the qualification, but it continues to apply) is some function of the data, in the sense that if the best theory were other than what it is, the data would have to be different in some way. This is just another way of saying that situations that are relevantly similar in respect of data must be treated consistently in theoretical respects, or, more briefly, that like cases should be treated alike. With respect to legal deliberation, this general consistency requirement is that cases relevantly similar, in respect of applicable legal doctrines and distinguishing circumstances, should be similarly resolved.

Of course, the analogy should not be strained; some of the general roles of ethical and legal deliberation and theorizing are very different from those of scientific theorizing. Scientific theories are used to predict what will happen on the basis of causal theories that account for what has happened in well-designed experiments, and sometimes also for what it is thought would have happened under significant counterfactual circumstances. The basis for scientific hypotheses are thus experimental data and sometimes intuitions gathered in "thought experiments," such as Einstein's famous thought experiments about flashlights emitting beams of light in trains travelling at close to the speed of light. Scientific hypotheses generate predictions which are then tested against the results of further experiments.

By contrast, ethical and legal deliberation can hardly be described as having the role of predicting what will be done on the basis of causal theories. Rather, it has a normative role: to give guidance in extending consistently to the case at issue a series of settled ethical or legal judgments about what should be done when the applicable ethical or legal reasons conflict. Its normative hypotheses thus aim to account for clear resolutions of past cases in which the relevant reasons stood in conflict, and also for clear resolutions of significant hypothetical cases, designed to test the relationships between the conflicting reasons. Deliberative hypotheses are used to generate not mere predictions of decisions and actions, but decisions and actions themselves; hypotheses cannot be tested against the very decisions and actions they generate. Rather, they are tested against cases, both actual and hypothetical, in which the right answer about how a conflict of reasons should be resolved is settled.[12]

Despite the differences between scientific, causal theorizing, and deliberative, normative theorizing, it is important to recognize the way in which both kinds of theorizing are responsible to the data to be explained. The requirement that the sought-after hypothesis explains the data can be seen as the source of the deliberative requirement of consistency, the general requirement that like cases be treated alike. Some philosophers have regarded it as puzzling how one could hold that both:

(1) the right answer about which alternative should be done is not entailed by the nonevaluative facts about the alternatives (*nonreductionism*: what should be done does not reduce to nonevaluative facts about the alternatives)

and:

(2) one must treat alike cases that are alike in respect of nonevaluative facts, so that if there is a difference between two cases in respect of what should be done,

---

[12] I do not suggest that scientific, ethical or legal deliberation are to be understood instrumentally rather than realistically; it is common ground between instrumentalism and realism that theoretical propositions should be able to be used in practical roles, e.g. to predict, explain or guide. I am concerned here to avoid overstating the analogy between the practical roles of scientific and deliberative theorizing rather than to take a position on the further issues that divide instrumental and realistic views of theories.

there must be some difference between them with respect to the nonevaluative facts about the alternatives as well (*supervenience*: what should be done supervenes on nonevaluative facts about the alternatives).

While there is no logical incompatibility between (1) and (2), the puzzlement about how they can both hold can be expressed by asking: If the right answer is not entailed by the nonevaluative facts, then what is the source of the requirement that cases alike in nonevaluative respects be treated alike?[13] However, recognition of the way in which right answers to questions about what should be done reflects hypotheses that are required to explain the data about settled cases provides a response to this puzzlement. The best theory about the data is not entailed by—cannot be deduced from—the data. Nevertheless, it is essential to the notion of a theory responsible to data that the best theory, whatever it may be, treats like cases alike. The source of this requirement is the essential explanatory aspirations of theories: a theory the content of which varies independently of the data it purports to account for to that extent does no explanatory work. This remains true even though the best theory is not entailed by the data.[14]

Thus, the requirement that like cases be treated alike has its source in the theoretical nature of judgments about what should be done when reasons conflict, which is highlighted by coherence accounts. Moreover, the data to which theories about what should be done are responsible are settled cases, both actual and hypothetical. If in general the role of settled cases in deliberation is somewhat analogous to that of experimental data in scientific theorizing, then the role of hypothetical cases in particular may be regarded as somewhat analogous to that of thought experiments.[15] It is important for our understanding of the requirement that like cases be treated alike that we include settled hypothetical cases, cases the answer to which would be clear were they to arise, as well as settled actual cases among the data to be explained. For reasons that will emerge in what follows, this is particularly important in the case of legal deliberation, where the general requirement that like cases be treated alike must be distinguished from the further specific requirement imposed by the doctrine of precedent. My examples in the previous section make clear that, since legal deliberation and argument often turn not merely on settled actual cases but also on settled hypothetical cases, effective legal reasoning often requires one to discover or construct revealing hypothetical cases;[16] a coherence account provides a framework for understanding the function

---

[13] *See, e.g.*, S. BLACKBURN, SPREADING THE WORD (1984), chapter 6.

[14] For further discussion of supervenience, irreducibility and explanation, *see* NATURAL REASONS, *supra* note 2, chapter 14.

[15] The effective postulation of hypothetical cases thus has something in common with effective experimental design.

[16] I do not suggest the existence of a positive professional obligation imposed on court or counsel to discover or construct hypothetical cases, but of a normative requirement that arises from characteristic features of legal reasoning as a species of practical reasoning. It may be that my account of the

of hypothetical cases in legal reasoning. Hypothetical cases are not merely *posed* by lawyers and judges, but *answers* to questions about how they should be resolved are often taken for granted in a way which the argument of the case at issue depends on. The answers to hypothetical cases may be implicitly assumed rather than explicitly stated, but nevertheless they are often depended on in the reasoning of opinions, in a way that may be explicitly represented within a deliberative matrix. This is to say that legal hypotheses are responsible to data about settled hypothetical cases as well as settled actual cases; both are among the cases with respect to which the requirement that like cases be treated alike must be understood. Nevertheless, as we shall see, the doctrine of precedent imposes a further constraint on legal deliberation in giving actual settled cases *more weight* than that of hypothetical settled cases for purposes of determining what counts as treating like cases alike.

IV. Kress on Coherence Accounts and Retroactivity: The Problem of Intervening Cases

In an interesting article entitled "Legal Reasoning and Coherence Theories: Dworkin's Rights Thesis, Retroactivity, and the Linear Order of Decision," Kenneth Kress argues that the role within coherence theories such as Dworkin's of coherence with past decisions and deference to precedent makes for retroactive applications of the law. In Kress's view, retroactivity may occur if settled law changes between the occurrence of the events being litigated and the adjudication of them, since at adjudication the most coherent account of settled cases will be responsible to actual cases decided after the occurrence of the events litigated. What Kress calls the "ripple effect":

. . . depends upon legal rights being a function of settled law and upon the temporal gap between events being litigated and their eventual adjudication. Judicial decisions often change the settled law. Often, if not always, the settled law will be changed between the occurrence of events being litigated and their eventual adjudication. In consequence, a litigant's rights will sometimes also be changed. If changes in the settled law change the dispositive legal right, a litigant who would have prevailed given the legal rights existing at the time of the occurrence will lose because he no longer has that right at the time of adjudication. The opposite is true of the opposing litigant.

This is retroactive application of the law.[17]

---

latter is particularly influenced by characteristic features of the legal system in the United States, such as the prominent role of the posing of "hypos" in Supreme Court oral argument, in legal education, etc.

[17] K. J. Kress, *Legal Reasoning and Coherence Theories: Dworkin's Rights Thesis, Retroactivity, and the Linear Order of Decisions*, 72 CAL L.R. 369, 380 (1984).

I shall refer to the problem Kress identifies as *the problem of intervening cases*. Kress regards this as a particularly serious problem for Dworkin's rights-oriented version of a coherence account of legal reasoning, since Dworkin works his account up in the course of criticizing Hart's account for the scope it gives to judicial discretion and for the retroactive applications of the law which judicial discretion involves.

However, Kress regards the problem as generalizable: it applies to any coherence account which is conservative in the sense that it adheres to the dominant conception of precedent. According to the latter, legal truths depend in part on prior legal decisions. The general form of the problem is that the best theory about settled law may change between the time the events occurred and the time they are litigated, owing to intervening legal decisions. "The mere historical fact of a prior decision influences the decisions in later cases, and thus the law, because it enlarges the settled law with which later decisions must cohere."[18] This is in effect just to say that the prevalent conception of precedent gives more weight to settled actual cases than to settled hypothetical cases for purposes of determining what counts as treating like cases alike.

V. A First Response: Prospective Application

What is the correct response to or diagnosis of the problem of intervening cases? Let us first briefly consider and dismiss, with Kress, the possibility that present legal practice should be changed so as to base legal decisions on law settled at the time the events adjudicated occurred rather than at the time of adjudication. Kress suggests that to give decisions only prospective effect in this way is particularly appropriate when decisions are legislative in character; as he puts it: "The doctrine of prospective overruling is the legacy of legal realism, the doctrine that maintains that judges legislate." However, Kress considers and rejects this possible response to his problem, on theoretical grounds and on pragmatic grounds (such as the difficulties of determining which events are relevant for purposes of dating the law to be applied). I find his pragmatic arguments against this line of response fairly persuasive.[19]

---

[18] *Id*. at 400.

[19] *Id*. at 386–387: "It is unlikely that the revised . . . theory could be developed in detail, or utilized by judges if it could, for several reasons. First, the possibility of temporally extended events and transactions raises difficult problems in determining the date of the law to be applied. These problems are compounded if several related but separable transactions are being litigated and there are multiple issues. The prospect of applying the law at different times to different but related aspects of a complicated transaction raises unappealing complexity. Further and perhaps insuperable complexity arises if it is possible to analyze the overall transaction in multiple ways into different temporal components. Unless we can be sure that one temporal analysis will be superior to all others, we will need rules to choose among the various analyses. More important, it is unclear what precedential effect should be given to a decision that applies law from many time periods, law that by definition differs from the law that would be applied to an event that occurred at that time of adjudication if litigated at that time."

However, if Kress's own objections to giving intervening cases prospective effect only are persuasive, his problem is not just a problem for coherentists; it cannot be avoided by "frank" assimilation of adjudication to legislation. Moreover, even if we assume for the sake of argument that the correct response to the problem of intervening cases is to give them prospective effect only, I am not persuaded that this response would be inconsistent with a coherence account. To the extent that retroactivity is the concomitant of a conception of precedent that gives more weight to actual than hypothetical cases, a coherentist could argue that it is the fact that actual decisions may change the law, through the operation of precedent, that makes prospective application appropriate. But this law-changing effect of precedent should not be confused with "legislative" discretion to make law for the case at hand; these are two logically distinct issues. That is, the occurrence of a judicial decision may change what the law requires from that point on, through the operation of precedent, even though the judge had no antecedent discretion as to how that case should be decided.[20] Even if only mistaken intervening decisions can change the law, as Dworkin urges (see Section VIII) below, nevertheless a mistaken decision that changes the law through the operation of precedent is logically distinct from quasi-legislative discretion to make new law.

See especially Kress's note 77, commenting on the line of criminal procedure cases involving prospective-only application. Kress distinguishes the "more common form" of prospective-only application, which nevertheless applies intervening decisions to pending cases, from the more extreme form that would be necessary to avoid ripple effect retroactivity, which would deny the "new" rule to pending cases as well. For the "more common form," *see Linkletter v. Walker*, 381 U.S. 618 (1965), which did apply the intervening decision to pending cases.

It may be objected to that Kress has not addressed the line of criminal procedure cases subsequent to *Linkletter* which explicitly discuss the application of intervening decisions to pending cases. *See Stovall v. Denno*, 388 U.S. 293 (1967); *Desist v. United States*, 394 U.S. 244 (1969), especially Justice Harlan's dissent; *Shea v. Lousianna*, 470 U.S. 51 (1985), especially Justice White's dissent. The Court divides over the problem of intervening cases, and moreover, seems to change its own position. *Stovall* and *Desist* come down in favour of nonretroactivity by refusing to apply the intervening decisions to pending cases in which the relevant events of police conduct occurred prior to the intervening decisions. However, Justice Harlan's dissent in *Desist*, favouring precedent over nonretroactivity, becomes the Court's position in *Shea*, where Justice White dissents, arguing on nonretroactivity grounds. A nice self-referential problem of intervening cases about the problem of intervening cases, the logic of which I will not even attempt to untangle!

In reply, it should be kept in mind that the degree to which the Court is willing to consider and countenance intervening case retroactivity in the criminal procedure context, where police reliance on earlier cases is in question, may well not generalize. Thus, an acceptable degree of retroactivity with respect to police reliance, which cuts in *favour* of criminal defendants, may not be acceptable in general, that is, where the intervening case might cut *against* criminal defendants and undermine *their* reliance rather than police reliance, or where it might change the positions of civil litigants. It would be interesting to develop an integrated view of retroactivity doctrine within and without the criminal procedure context, and to try to isolate the special effects of the criminal procedure context on retroactivity doctrine, but I cannot do so here.

[20] Kress does allow for this type of view. Kress, *supra* note 17, at 386; he does, at 382, distinguish judicial discretion from judicial creation of law.

So, if the correct response to the problem of intervening cases is prospective-only application, a coherence account is not thereby defeated, since there is no inconsistency between a coherence account and this response. On the other hand, Kress's pragmatic reasons against this response to the problem are equally valid given legislative accounts of judicial reasoning. So if this response is ruled out, it is not only coherence accounts that are left with a problem. Let us thus suppose, for the sake of argument, that the prospective-only response to the problem of intervening cases is to be ruled out (but for a qualification relating to changes in settled cases with extra-judicial sources, see the end of Section VII below).

VI. A Second Response: It's Not So Bad

Consider a second possible response envisaged by Kress to the problem of intervening cases, namely, that of accepting the retroactivity in question as, for one reason or another, not all that bad. And at any rate, a coherentist might add, the problem of intervening cases is not a problem for coherence accounts in particular, since they will still involve less retroactivity than accounts of adjudication as *ex ante* discretionary do.[21]

Just how objectionable would intervening case retroactivity be? Perhaps coherentists should not regard it as a matter for particular concern. Kress offers Dworkin something like this possible position in a footnote (though in fact this is not Dworkin's response to the problem):

> Dworkin believes that the unfairness of retroactive application of law is not fully explained by the rule of law requirements to give prior notice, satisfy justified expectations, and the like. . . . Dworkin must take this position because the controversial nature of right answers even when they exist means, as Dworkin admits, that right answers often cannot be demonstrated and therefore often are not known in advance . . . Dworkin's objection to retroactivity appears to focus on the importance of giving a principled justification for enforcing judicial decisions. Dworkin's concern with retroactivity derives from the belief that creating and applying new rights at the time of adjudication cannot be given a principled justification . . . Arguably, therefore, ripple effect retroactivity with its consequential disruption of expectations and failure to provide notice is not the kind of retroactivity that would concern Dworkin.[22]

Though Kress's article was published before *Law's Empire*, this suggestion seems reasonably consistent with Dworkin's views in *Law's Empire* about respect for precedent and coherence as expressing the integrity and personification of the

---

[21] This *tu quoque* on behalf of coherence accounts seems to be borne out by the Court's oscillation between precedent and nonretroactivity in *Stovall, Desist* and *Shea, supra* note 19, where the issues do not arise as a consequence of any particular theory of adjudication.

[22] Kress, *supra* note 17, at 384.

community. On the above suggestion, people would simply be on notice that their claims were subject to requirements of coherence with possible intervening precedents. Perhaps one could justify the retroactivity to people on the grounds of their membership in a community with the virtues of integrity, which unfortunately entail such retroactivity. People could of course try, perhaps through their lawyers, to anticipate intervening precedents as best they could, by identifying any relevant settled hypothetical cases. But the possibility would remain that an unsettled hypothetical case might become a decided actual case and thus create an unanticipated intervening precedent.

We might fill out this possible line of response further. I claimed there is no inconsistency between admitting that the mere fact that a judge has decided a case may change the law and claiming that in deciding it he has no discretion. Perhaps the mere fact that the judge has decided the case changes the law, not through an exercise of discretion, but as a result of his efforts to discover the right answer. The retroactivity problem may arise because in law, as is not the case in science, the mere fact of theorizing by a judge itself counts as a further piece of data for later theorizing. But perhaps so long as the judge can give a principled justification for his decision, even if it was not reliably predictable, the change to the law represented by his decision is not arbitrary. Recognizing such changes, it might be argued, is itself supported by the considerations of coherence and community integrity that support respect for precedent. People know that the legal system gives weight, in this timeless sense, to intervening precedents, even if they do not know that they are ahead of time. Is this really any more objectionable than not knowing the right answer itself ahead of time?

Of course, we accept that it may be hard to determine what the best account of settled cases would say about the case at issue, before it is decided. What the best theory really is, and how it bears on the case at issue, may be quite controversial.[23] But these are epistemological problems, not problems of true retroactivity; changes in our knowledge of the law should be distinguished from changes in the law. It simply is often extremely difficult to know what the law requires; perhaps only the best lawyers know for sure, and we cannot afford them. But nevertheless we are held to the law, and we must do the best we can to understand what it is. It is unfortunate, and gives rise to unfairness, that the law is so complex and difficult, and that access to it so expensive and restricted; but again these are not problems of true retroactivity. It might be objected to that if from a litigant's practical point of view the effects of the "mere" epistemological problem and those of "true" retroactivity are much the same, and we can live with the former, then the latter cannot be so bad. But the stubborn intuition remains that true retroactivity is somehow more profoundly unfair than are the effects of the

---

[23] This paper is not intended to address the problem of whether systematically wicked law is really law; on this *see, e.g.,* R. DWORKIN, LAW'S EMPIRE 102–108 (1986).

epistemological problem. Let us therefore, for the sake of argument, also put the "not-so-bad" response aside.

VII. The Source of the Problem: Coherentism as Opposed to Precedent

Consider what features of a system of decision-making are necessary or sufficient to give rise to the problem of intervening cases. As we have seen, coherence accounts of practical reasoning give settled cases an important role as the data, so to speak, to which the theories or principles sought in deliberation are responsible. Moreover, coherence accounts impose a general requirement with respect to settled law of treating like cases alike (which I will sometimes refer to as "the weaker requirement"). That is, legal truths are a function of, among other things, settled law;[24] resolution of the actual case at hand must be consistent with the resolution of comparable settled cases. While, concerning any particular settled case, it is possible that the best theory of settled cases may show that it is mistaken, if theoretical coherence overall with settled cases is the standard, then it is not possible for all settled cases to be mistaken; hence coherentist consistency involves a certain element of conservatism. However, while these elements are present in coherence accounts of legal reasoning in particular, they are not sufficient to give rise to the problem of intervening cases or any distinctive issues about retroactivity. The latter only arise in virtue of a further requirement (that I will sometimes refer to as "the stronger requirement," since it is not entailed by the weaker requirement), imposed by the doctrine of precedent in the legal context in particular, namely, that actual settled cases are to be given more weight, in virtue of having actually been decided by a court, than hypothetical settled cases, or, in Kress's words, that "prior decisions are to be accorded weight which may influence the outcomes in later cases merely by virtue of the fact that the decisions have occurred."[25] Since the stronger requirement *imposed* by the doctrine of precedent is not a necessary feature of all coherence theories, Kress is wrong to the extent that he suggests that the prospect of intervening case retroactivity arises for all coherence theories.[26]

---

[24] Kress, *supra* note 17, at 380.   [25] *Id.* at 400.

[26] *Id.* at 398 (" . . . since nothing in the argument has relied on the details of any coherence theory, it should be clear that ripple effects will occur in all coherence theories . . . "). *See also id.* at 371 ("The ripple effect will occur in any coherence theory with a principle of conservation. In adjudication, precedent provides the conservative element"). However, *compare* his concessions to the distinction between coherence theories in general and the legal doctrine of precedent in particular at the very end of the article. *Id.* at 401–402. It is possible that, despite the way Kress introduces his problem by reference to coherence theories in general, not just in law, *id.* at 369–370, the remarks quoted above should be interpreted as restricted to legal contexts, which involve the doctrine of precedent in particular. But my primary purpose is to address Kress's interesting problem on the merits, and the substantive issues I consider arise however Kress's remarks are interpreted.

Decision theory provides one illustration of coherentist reasoning minus the stronger requirement of precedent; within decision theory, coherence with settled preferences provides a standard for the determination of problematic preferences, but settled preferences about actual alternatives that have issued in actual decisions are not given greater weight in principle than settled preferences about hypothetical cases. Consideration of decision theory, in which no problem of intervening cases arises, will thus help to bring into focus the way in which the problem depends on the stronger requirement of precedent.

Suppose a decision theorist is trying to help a decision-maker arrive at decisions about certain difficult issues where his criteria of choice or goals conflict. The decision theorist aims to discover the decision-maker's indifference curves with respect to those conflicting criteria or goals in order to help him to make the decision among the actual alternatives that places him on his highest indifference curve. To do this the decision theorist must depend on data provided by the decision-maker about what his preferences clearly are or would be in various cases which are easier for him to decide about than is the case at issue. These cases need not all involve feasible alternatives; some may be purely hypothetical. The exercise is one of extrapolating consistently from the set of settled preferences to a determination of the case at issue. Perhaps some of the settled preferences of the decision-maker are outliers and cannot be regarded as consistent with the rest within any theoretically acceptable representation of the decision-maker's preference space; such settled preferences may be disregarded as "mistakes." But it is of the nature of this exercise that there cannot be too many such mistakes. Settled preferences are here the data for which the decision theorist's representation of the decision-maker's preference space must account. Theories may tell us that some of the data they aim to account for is suspect or corrupt, and must be disregarded, but ultimately theories are supported by data. The basis for regarding some settled preferences as mistaken is their failure to cohere with the rest; thus there cannot be a basis for regarding too many of them as mistaken (though, of course, just what counts as "too many" is difficult to specify).

The conservatism of this interpretative exercise is also attributed by a coherence account to legal reasoning: not too many settled cases can be regarded as mistakes, or the basis for regarding them as mistaken is itself undermined. However, these elements of conservatism do not entail that settled actual cases should be given more weight than settled hypothetical cases, and hence they are not sufficient to give rise to the problem of intervening cases. The mere fact that a decision-maker actually makes an intervening decision between the time at which certain events occur and the time at which he must face a further problematic decision about those events does not alter the set of settled cases with which his second problematic decision must cohere. (Of course, a change of mind does alter the set of settled cases; but this is a different matter.) A settled case may be equally settled, whether actual or hypothetical. More generally, the set of settled cases does not coincide with the set of actual cases. Not all actual cases are settled (some are problematic), and not all settled cases are actual (some are hypothetical).[27]

If the stronger requirement of adherence to precedent were not imposed on legal reasoning in addition to the weaker elements of conservatism imposed by a coherence account and shared with decision theory, no problem of intervening cases would arise in law either. To see this, consider a revisionary conception of the law as equally responsible in principle to both settled actual and settled hypothetical cases, so that the change of a settled case's status from hypothetical to actual between occurrence of the events litigated and their adjudication cannot via precedent change the law about the later case. Such a revisionary conception of the law is compatible with a generally coherentist approach to practical reasoning, but it omits the distinctively legal doctrine of precedent. Now, whether a case is settled or not does not depend on whether it has actually been decided; a settled case is equally settled whether its current status is actual or hypothetical, and retroactivity does not arise in the way Kress envisages.

Kress considers the possibility that the law does not change purely in consequence of legal decisions, but points out that this would be to purchase unchanging right answers at the cost of dispensing with the doctrine of precedent. He writes: "Judicial decisions change the settled law" and: "To deny that law and legal rights change at all in response to new decisions is to deny that legal rights are, at least in part, determined by settled law."[28] While I think he is correct to regard the denial of any change of law in response to new actual decisions as giving up the doctrine of precedent, nevertheless, it is logically possible to hold that legal rights are, at least in part, determined by settled law, without holding that a change in a case's status from hypothetical to actual is *per se* a change from unsettled to settled. It is just this logical space that is occupied by the revisionary conception of law we are now considering, which in effect does not incorporate the doctrine of precedent as we know it. Of course, new legal decisions may reflect extra-judicial changes in the settled law. But absent extra-judicial changes, under the revisionary conception new legal decisions would not change settled law, though they might change our awareness of it.

Kress further points out that, within Dworkin's theory at least, "While at each point in time, there are right answers to all or nearly all legal issues, the right answer that is given may not be the same as that which would be given at another point in time, in consequence of changes in institutional history." However, giving hypothetical and actual settled cases equal weight would *not* mean that the law cannot develop and change, but merely that such developments and changes,

---

[27] *Cf.* Kress on the analogy between legal and scientific theorizing, *id.* at 392n, and on the character of settled law, *id.* at 278. My use of the term "settled" here does not coincide with his, but I believe that something like my use is essential to convey what is distinctive about coherentist views of practical reasoning, and of legal reasoning in so far as it is a species of practical reasoning.

[28] *Id.* at 380, 393.

in *both* actual and hypothetical cases, would reflect *extra-judicial* developments and changes in institutional history, social practices, etc.[29] Cases that were unsettled might become settled as the law develops, in response to extra-judicial developments. But under the revisionary conception a case would not change from unsettled to settled *merely* by becoming the subject of a judicial decision and changing status from hypothetical to actual.

I emphasize that I have invoked this revisionary conception of law not in order to endorse it, of course, but merely to illustrate my claim that the problem of intervening cases does not arise from the coherentist character of legal reasoning *per se*, but rather from the further distinctive asymmetrical treatment of actual and hypothetical cases by the doctrine of precedent in particular. The point of the distinction between coherentist practical reasoning absent the doctrine of precedent and legal reasoning with the doctrine of precedent is not to suggest we should respond to Kress's problem by doing away with precedent, but rather to contribute to diagnosing the source of the problem. This distinction is important because it is the general character of consistency and conservatism with respect to hypothetical as well as actual cases in coherentist practical reasoning, which legal reasoning shares and which the doctrine of precedent does not eliminate but rather supplements, that supports the view I go on to assert in Section VIII below, namely, that the special role of precedent in legal reasoning only makes a difference when the decided cases appealed to as precedent were not *ex ante* correct.

It may be objected that intervening case retroactivity would occur even under the revisionary conception of law, so long as the law is subject to change such that coherence with intervening, newly settled cases may be invoked to justify legal decisions about events that occurred before the change. Perhaps the objector will admit at this point that it would not matter whether the change in settled cases occurs within the category of actual or hypothetical cases; it need not be the result of a change in status from hypothetical to actual. But so long as the possibility of change in the set of settled cases is admitted, even though the initiation of change is distributed across actual and hypothetical cases, it may be claimed that the problem of intervening cases would remain.

Advocates of coherence accounts are not committed to denying that the law may change. However, they may wish, as Dworkin does, to deny that judges should initiate such changes, as opposed to trying to discover what the best theory of settled law requires. (There is nothing analogous to this division of labour between the judiciary and other, law-making, branches of government, in the ethical and decision-theoretic versions of the pursuit of coherence. In these latter cases, the deliberator plays the legislative as well as the judicial role; his decisions may reflect changes of mind that originate changes in the set of settled cases. At the same time, there is no problem of retroactivity, although if someone changes his mind about what he should have done after doing it, he may well regret having done it.) On the view that

---

[29] *See and compare id.* at 392–394.

the judicial role is to discover the law, not to make it, changes in judicial perception of the content of settled cases, whether actual or hypothetical, *ought* to reflect extra-judicial legal developments, such as changes in social practices and customs with constitutive bearing on the law,[30] or in legislative or administrative background. Such extra-judicial developments put members of society on fair notice, and changes in legal theory which reflect such intervening changes should in principle be applied prospectively only.[31] However, legislative and administrative changes usually *are* applied prospectively only. Moreover, changes in social practices usually occur gradually enough that worry about such a change intervening between the time of the events litigated and their adjudication may often seem contrived and artificial. Perhaps there are occasionally abrupt, revolutionary changes in social practices, but they are surely unusual. Perhaps in these unusual cases changes in settled hypothetical cases which reflect the change in social practice should in theory be given effect prospectively only (although there may be practical difficulties in identifying such cases and the time of the change of social practice involved). Such exceptions would have a rationale in the extra-judicial source of the change, and could be admitted without threatening the normal judicial practice to the contrary. Thus, extra-judicial changes in law do not threaten my claim that the problem of intervening cases does not arise from the coherentist character of legal reasoning *per se*, but rather from the distinctive asymmetrical treatment of actual and hypothetical cases by the doctrine of precedent in particular.

In summary, the purely coherentist revisionary conception of law as lacking the stronger requirement, imposed by the doctrine of precedent, would support the following argument. Either cases intervening between the occurrence of events and

---

[30] *See* R. DWORKIN, TAKING RIGHTS SERIOUSLY 40–42 (1977).

[31] An example would be given by a slight variation of the sequence of events in *California Federal Savings and Loan Association v. Guerra*, 107 SCt 683, 479 U.S. 272 (1987). In *Cal Fed*, a pregnant worker's employer brought suit seeking a declaration that a California statute requiring employers to provide leave and reinstatement to employees disabled by pregnancy was pre-empted by the federal statute, Title VII, which prohibited sex discrimination. The court upheld the California Statute, although in the 1976 case of *General Electric Co v. Gilbert*, 429 U.S. 125 (1976), it had interpreted Title VII in a different manner, reasoning that discrimination against pregnant persons was not sex discrimination because many non-pregnant persons are female. In 1978 Congress expressed its disapproval of the *Gilbert* reasoning by amending Title VII to make clear that it intended sex discrimination to include discrimination against pregnant persons. The disputed events in the *Cal Fed* case occurred in 1982: the employee took a pregnancy leave, and when she informed her employer she was ready to return to work she was told her job had been filled and there were no available positions. She filed a complaint under the California statute and her employer brought a suit seeking a declaration that the statute was pre-empted by Title VII's ban on sex discrimination. The case was decided in 1987.

Now suppose that between the *Gilbert* decision in 1976 and the 1978 amendment to Title VII events like those disputed in *Cal Fed* occurred, but only came to trial after the *Cal Fed* decision. Then *Cal Fed* would have the status of an intervening case. However, it would have been following an extra-judicial initiation of an addition to the settled law, namely, the amendment of Title VII in 1978. Under these circumstances it would seem that the legislative change should be given prospective effect only.

their adjudication reflect intervening extra-judicial changes in settled law or they do not. If they do, the prospective-only application of the new legal hypotheses supported by the newly settled law is appropriate for the same reason that prospective-only application is appropriate for legislative decision-making, namely to avoid the unfairness of retroactivity. In such circumstances, we have judicial reflections of extra-judicial legal developments, not judicial law-making.[32] Cases that articulate such developments and incorporate them within a coherent legal theory may change what we believe the law to be, but they do not in themselves change the law, any more than an illuminating new scientific theory changes the truth about what the best theory is merely by changing our beliefs about what it is. On the other hand, if the intervening cases do not reflect extra-judicial changes, then either they are settled or they are not. The mere fact that they have been actually decided does not resolve this question. If an intervening case is not settled, the fact that it has been decided between the occurrence of events and their adjudication does not change the settled law. The fact that the case has been explicitly considered and decided *per se* does not make it a case that is clear to the relevant decision-makers. Moreover, it may have been a settled case before it was decided, if its resolution would have been clear had it been considered. That is, either the intervening case is not settled, despite being actual, or is settled, and was before it was decided. Either way, there is no retroactivity. Thus the coherentist character of the revisionary conception of law as merely requiring that like cases be treated alike and that hence not too many settled cases be regarded as mistaken is not sufficient to give rise to the problem of intervening cases; in addition, the doctrine of precedent is necessary.[33]

VIII. The Source of the Problem: Precedent as Opposed to Mistake or Underdetermination

There thus seems to be a—perhaps surprising—tension between the doctrine of precedent, on the one hand, and the requirements of fairness which make retroactivity objectionable, on the other. But perhaps the doctrine of precedent is not sufficient to give rise to the problem of intervening cases either, though necessary. It seems clear that the revisionary coherentist conception of law I sketched in the last section, under which no distinction of weight at all is drawn between settled actual and settled hypothetical cases, involves a substantial departure from the doctrine of precedent as we know it. Nevertheless, the doctrine of precedent as we know it is compatible with the significant influence of settled hypothetical cases; it does not require that status as actual and status as settled coincide. Because of this, the argument that applied to the revisionary conception of law to show that intervening case retroactivity would not arise may be available, at least under certain circumstances, in a legal system that does incorporate the doctrine of

---

[32] As in the variation on *Cal Fed, supra* note 31.   [33] *Cf.* Kress, *supra* note 17, at 401–402.

precedent. I will briefly consider some cases to illustrate the point that status as actual and status as settled do not in fact coincide. I will then go on to try to sharpen the diagnosis of the intervening case retroactivity. I shall argue, largely following suggestions made by Dworkin, that only actual intervening decisions that are *ex ante* mistaken, or at least not uniquely correct (in cases of underdetermination), but which the doctrine of precedent nevertheless presumptively constitutes as judicially-initiated changes in the law, give rise to retroactivity.

Not all actually decided cases are settled; indeed, some actual cases, even some that are settled, may be mistaken,[34] in virtue of their failure to cohere with other settled, including actual, cases. Dependence on some actual cases is avoided, even if they have not been explicitly overruled as mistaken, because they are highly controversial, and/or considered uncertain, dubious, or poor authority. Moreover, the doctrine of precedent may not treat actual cases of courts of other jurisdictions as settled. An example of an intervening actual case which was nevertheless not settled is that of *Brown v. Porcher*.[35] In *Brown*, the US Court of Appeals held that the construal of a South Carolina statute to disqualify any claimant who voluntarily left her most recent employment because of pregnancy violated a federal statute providing that no person shall be denied unemployment compensation under state law solely on the basis of pregnancy. *Brown* was decided in 1981; the US Supreme Court denied certiorari in 1983. In 1980, however, events had already occurred which gave rise to the closely related case on the same issue of *Wimberly v. Labor and Industrial Relations Commission*, which went up on appeal through the Missouri court system to the Missouri Supreme Court (in 1985), and eventually reached the US Supreme Court (in 1987).[36] The Missouri Court of Appeals had followed *Brown*, despite reservations concerning the soundness of its reasoning; but the Missouri Supreme Court reversed, declaring that it had never subscribed to the notion that Missouri state courts were bound to follow the decisions of lower federal courts in construing federal statutes.[37] The Missouri Supreme Court declined to follow *Brown*. "We do not mean to suggest that a lower federal court's construction of a federal statute is wholly irrelevant. The courts of this state should 'look respectfully to such opinions for such aid and guidance as may be found therein' . . . In some circumstances it may be appropriate for a state court to defer to long established and widely accepted federal court interpretations of federal statutes." But it evidently felt that *Brown* was not a settled case in this sense. The US Supreme Court eventually resolved *Wimberly* in favour of the Missouri view and against *Brown*. But the point to be made here is not that *Brown* was mistaken; perhaps it was correct. It is rather that *Brown*, the intervening case, did not change the settled law because it was not a settled case,

---

[34] As Kress admits, *id.* at 378.

[35] 660 F.2d 100 (1981), *cert denied*, 459 U.S. 1150 (1983). Perhaps various abortion cases provide other current examples.   [36] 107 SCt 821 (1987), 479 U.S. 511 (1987).

[37] Justice Donnelly, concurring in the result, denied that US Supreme Court decisions interpreting the US Constitution are binding on the states.

from the perspective of the Missouri Supreme Court. Thus, whether or not *Brown* was correct, the best theory about settled law, which should determine the outcome in the similar case which comes to trial after *Brown*, was not altered by the intervening case. If the result in *Brown* were to have been upheld as the correct result, there would nevertheless have been no retroactive application of the decision in the intervening case, since, as the Missouri Supreme Court implied, it was not a settled case. Continuing uncertainty about the right answer is just that, not retroactivity.

Furthermore, there are many settled hypothetical cases which are more deeply entrenched and would be more difficult to justify regarding as mistaken than many actual cases: we are lucky that such cases have remained hypothetical rather than actual. They have not become actual, in some cases, because the flagrant violations of rights they would involve luckily have not occurred in our communities. But they are nonetheless clearly settled for being hypothetical. A good example is found in Justice Marshall's eloquent dissent in the recent case of *United States v. Salerno and Cafaro*. The majority had upheld a statute permitting the denial of bail altogether in certain cases against Due Process and Excessive Bail Clause challenges, on the grounds in part that the statute is a regulatory rather than a punitive measure. Justice Marshall writes:

The ease with which the conclusion is reached suggests the worthlessness of the achievement. The major premise is that "[u]nless Congress expressly intended to impose punitive restrictions, the punitive/regulatory distinction turns on 'whether an alternative purpose to which [the restriction] may rationally be connected is assignable for it, and whether it appears excessive in relation to the alternative purpose assigned [to it].'" The majority finds that "Congress did not formulate the pretrial detention provisions as punishment for dangerous individuals", but instead was pursuing the "legitimate regulatory goal" of "preventing danger to the community" . . . Concluding that pretrial detention is not an excessive solution to the problem of preventing danger to the community, the majority thus finds that no substantive element of the guarantee of due process invalidates the statute.

Justice Marshall produces a settled hypothetical case as a counter-example to the majority's hypothesis about the punitive/regulatory distinction. He goes on:

This argument does not demonstrate the conclusion it purports to justify. Let us apply the majority's reasoning to a similar, hypothetical case. After investigation, Congress determines (not unrealistically) that a large proportion of violent crime is perpetrated by persons who are unemployed. It also determines, equally realistically, that much violent crime is committed at night. From amongst the panoply of "potential solutions", Congress chooses a statute which permits, after judicial proceedings, the imposition of a dusk-to-dawn curfew on anyone who is unemployed. Since this is not a measure enacted for the purpose of punishing the unemployed, and since the majority finds that preventing danger to the community is a legitimate regulatory goal, the curfew statute would, according to the majority's analysis, be a mere "regulatory" detention statute, entirely compatible with the substantive components of the Due Process Clause.[38]

He regards the absurdity of this conclusion as a settled aspect of the law, and nonetheless settled for the fact that the case envisaged is merely hypothetical. Here is a settled hypothetical case that is more entrenched, and less likely to be regarded as mistaken by the best legal theory, than many actual cases.

We have considered two cases in which the dissenting opinions appeal persuasively to hypothetical cases to defeat hypotheses on which the majority opinion seems to turn, *Parham* and *Salerno*. Suppose for the sake of argument that these decisions were mistaken up to the time of the decision, or *ex ante* mistaken. Nevertheless the doctrine of precedent tells us we cannot assume them to be *ex post* mistaken; we cannot infer an *ex post* mistake from an *ex ante* mistake because the fact of the actual decision may change the law. It is possible that an *ex ante* mistake is so serious that the enormity of the mistake outweighs its precedential force, and it remains a mistake even *ex post*; but the mere fact of the decision has loaded the balance against this possibility. A mistake must be more serious, must be more deeply incoherent with the settled law, including hypothetical as well as actual cases, to be an *ex post* mistake than to be an *ex ante* mistake; the difference is a matter of degree, a matter of how much must be uprooted to accommodate the law to the mistake.

We see then that the doctrine of precedent permits determinately *ex ante* mistaken decisions to change the law;[39] such decisions, as intervening cases, may give rise to retroactivity. Of course, the doctrine of precedent is not addressed to mistakes in particular; it does not perversely dignify *ex ante* mistaken actual decisions as opposed to *ex ante* correct actual decisions by presumptively constituting only the former as law henceforward. But precedential force is not needed to constitute an *ex ante* correct decision as correct *ex post*; in this respect it is redundant (though of course it may feature non-redundantly in the reasoning from previous precedents that makes the decision *ex ante* correct). No special method of transition between *ex ante* standing and *ex post* standing is needed in the case of correct decisions; precedent has no law-changing work to do in these cases. Since resolutions that are *ex ante* correct all things considered do not conflict with one another to begin with, increasing the weight of a correct settled case as it changes from hypothetical to actual makes no difference. Of course, courts may not *know* whether the actual cases they defer to as having precedential force were *ex ante* mistaken or not. Nevertheless, we may issue a challenge: how, on coherentist assumptions,

---

[38] *U S v. Salerno*, 107 SCt 2095, 2107–2108 (1987), 481 U.S. 739, 758–759 (1987).

[39] *Cf.* Kress's claim, *supra* note 17, at 394, that "wholesale and final determination of the truth or falsity of all possible legal propositions leaves no room for the operation of the dominant notion of precedent."

could the precedential force of a decision, other than one reflecting extra-judicial legal developments, change the *law* itself, as opposed to our *beliefs* about it, if that decision were *ex ante* correct?

This in effect is Dworkin's response to the problem of intervening cases. He argues as follows.[40] He does consider that integrity requires us to give weight to the fact that a case was actually decided so, even if it was decided wrongly. Either an intervening case is wrongly or rightly decided. Suppose it is wrongly decided. Then it will indeed change the law retroactively, and for the worse, since it was wrongly decided. That is one reason it is so important for judges to reach the right answer! We can accept that there is objectionable retroactivity in this case, but that is not a consequence of the coherentist account of adjudication, or of the doctrine of precedent, but rather of the fact that the wrong answer was reached. Suppose, on the other hand, that the intervening case was rightly decided; then we are presented with a challenge. How could a correct decision in an intervening case make for retroactive change of the law?[41] How could the affirmation of a correct hypothesis itself change hypotheses in subsequent cases from right to wrong or vice versa? It might make the correct answers to later cases more evident or predictable, but this is not what Kress needs for his claim; retroactivity involves a change in the law, not merely a change in our beliefs about the law.

For the moment put aside the possibility, which I will return to, that the correct decision (not merely our beliefs about it) was *ex ante* underdetermined, rather

---

[40] In discussion.

[41] Kress gives an example, in which the force of precedent is conceived in a mechanical way to involve counting the number of steps required for privity of contract, which he claims is a paradigm case of coherentist reasoning. *See id.* at 382–383. However, it can be dismissed as not an example of Dworkinian, or more generally, coherentist reasoning at all since it does not involve consideration of the reasons or principles that support particular results.

Some implicit support is founded in Supreme Court cases for Dworkin's view that a correct decision in an intervening case does not change the law. In the criminal procedure context, see in particular the dissents by Justice Harland and Justice Fortas in *Desist, supra* note 19, Justice Harlan writes: " . . . If a 'new' constitutional doctrine is truly right, we should not reverse lower courts which have accepted it; nor should we affirm those which have rejected the very arguments we have embraced. Anything else would belie the truism that it is the task of this Court, like that of any other, to do justice to each litigant on the merits of his own case. It is only if each of our decisions can be justified in terms of this fundamental premise that they may properly be considered the legitimate products of a court of law, rather than the commands of a super-legislature." *See also* H. Schwartz, *Retroactivity, Reliability and Due Process,* 33 U. CHI. L. REV. 719, 748–749 (1966). In *Hanover Shoe v. United Shoe Machinery Corp,* 392 U.S. 481 (1968), an antitrust case, the US Supreme Court discussed the intervening case issue explicitly writing: "The theory of the Court of Appeals seems to have been that when a party has significantly relied upon a clear and established doctrine, and the retrospective application of a newly declared doctrine would upset that justifiable reliance to his substantial injury, considerations of justice and fairness require that the new rule apply prospectively only." The Supreme Court, however, did not find before it a situation in which there was a clearly declared judicial doctrine upon which a party had relied and which was overruled in favour of a new rule. The intervening cases in question did not indicate that the issues they decided were novel, or that they involved a departure from an earlier line of case or the need for innovative principles. "Whatever development in antitrust law was brought about was based to a great extent on existing authorities and was an extension of doctrines which had been growing and developing over the years." *Id.* at 496–499.

than mistaken. To claim, following Dworkin, that precedent only makes a difference given an *ex ante* mistake does not amount to saying that precedent does not make any difference to the way people *should* reason about the law. One can hold that decided cases do and should make a difference to the way people should reason, via the doctrine of precedent, *though they are ex ante mistaken*— even if one also holds that they make a difference only when they are *ex ante* mistaken, since they must be either correct or mistaken, and if they are correct their actually being decided makes no difference. The argument for the latter qualification derives from the role of hypothetical cases in coherentist practical reasoning in general; precedent is an additional special feature of legal reasoning, but it does not eliminate the general role of hypothetical cases in legal reasoning as a special case of practical reasoning. Precedent does and should make a difference to correct reasoning about what the law is, and this is why, in part, the problem of retroactivity does arise. Reasoning from an *ex ante* mistaken precedent is not itself mistaken simply because of the *ex ante* mistake.

The argument as to under what circumstances an intervening precedent can change the law may be elaborated as follows. Either the intervening decided case was *ex ante* correct or *ex ante* mistaken; moreover, either the corresponding hypothetical case was settled in the same way as the actual case was decided, or it was not so settled. Then there are four cases to consider. Suppose first that the decision was *ex ante* (but not *ex post*) mistaken in fact, but nevertheless settled, i.e. it was, or would have been, wrongly believed of the corresponding hypothetical case that the (in fact) mistaken decision would be the correct decision for such a case. False beliefs about the *ex ante* law have been replaced by true beliefs about the *ex post* law, made true because the law has changed, in virtue of an *ex ante* mistaken precedent that is good *ex post* law. The retroactivity problem arises with respect to what the law is (though not with respect to beliefs about the law), but that is due to the *ex ante* mistaken decision. Secondly, suppose that the decision was *ex ante* (but not *ex post*) mistaken, though not settled as a hypothetical case. In this case the law and beliefs about it may change as a result of the decision, but again retroactivity is associated with an *ex ante* mistaken decision. Thirdly, suppose the decision was *ex ante* correct and settled. In this case there is change neither in the law nor beliefs about it, so no retroactivity problem can arise.

The fourth case is the interesting case: here the decision was *ex ante* correct, but the corresponding hypothetical case was not settled in accord with the correct decision. The truth about the law has not changed as a result of the correct decision, though what is believed about it *may* have changed (again, the change from hypothetical to actual does not *necessarily* entail a change from unsettled to settled, since a decided case may remain unsettled). If beliefs about the law do not change as a result of the correct decision, neither the law nor beliefs about it have changed, so it is hard to see how the correct decision in a subsequent case could change. If beliefs about the law do change, it may be in one of (at least) two ways. On the one hand, they may have been undetermined before, and may now be settled in accord with the correct decision. Could this change in belief, absent a change in the law, be sufficient to change what the law is in a subsequent case? Whatever considerations they were in virtue of which the intervening decision was correct still obtain, and, to the extent they ever applied to the subsequent case, apply equally after the intervening case is decided. How could the mere addition of true beliefs about these unchanged considerations change the correct decision in the subsequent case, as opposed to making it more evident? On the other hand, beliefs about the law may have been mistaken before the intervening case, and they may have changed to accord with the correct decision in the case. How could this change from false to true beliefs about the intervening case change the law, as opposed to beliefs about it, in the subsequent case? It does not help to point out that according to a coherence account not too many settled cases can be mistaken, because we are now supposing the prior beliefs were false; if they were true, we are back to case three above, and there is no retroactivity. Whatever considerations they were in virtue of which the prior beliefs about the hypothetical version of the intervening case were false would apply also to the subsequent case, to the extent relevant. If we continue to assume that the law in the subsequent case was either determinately one thing or another at each point, and no change of law with respect to the intervening case was brought about by its correct decision, the challenge on coherentist assumptions still stands: how could a decision in the subsequent case be changed from correct to mistaken or vice versa merely as a result of a change in beliefs about the law in the intervening case from false to true, given no change in the law itself with respect to that case? Note that it is incorrect to object here that the determinacy assumption leaves no room for the operation of precedent, since we have seen that it does leave room for it in cases of mistaken decisions. What is at issue is whether precedent can make a difference given correct intervening decisions.

At this point we should consider the consequences of suspending the assumption of determinacy. If we allow that prior to a decision the right answer (not merely beliefs about it) may be underdetermined, then precedent may make a difference not just as a result of *ex ante* mistake, but also as a result of resolving *ex ante* underdetermination. Dworkin, of course, would resist the possibility of underdetermination in arguing for his right answer thesis, so it does not, in the absence of an independent argument against the right answer determinacy thesis, help Kress make a case against Dworkin in particular. But some coherentists might accept the possibility of underdetermination, so it is relevant to the general discussion with respect to coherentism.

Thus, from a theoretical point of view at least, intervening case retroactivity can be laid at the feet, not of coherentist legal reasoning, or even of the doctrine of precedent, but rather of mistaken decisions, and perhaps also of underdetermination of the law, to the extent a given version of coherentism admits this possibility. That legal mistakes are unfair to people is hardly news; the theoretical novelty and interest of the problem of intervening cases thus looks to diminish to the extent mistakes are its source. Moreover, the use of the problem as a means of criticizing Dworkin's version of coherentism in particular is limited by his rejection of the possibility of underdetermination. The general shape of my response to Kress with respect to the problem of intervening cases has been to draw out the consequences of a coherentist view of practical reasoning in general for legal reasoning and the doctrine of precedent in particular, which consequences limit intervening case retroactivity. The argument has proceeded by presenting a challenge to show how, *given the role of hypothetical cases within coherentist views of practical reasoning*, a correct, as opposed to *ex ante* mistaken or indeterminate, intervening case could give rise to retroactivity. Of course, we may reject coherentist views and their consequences with respect to the doctrine of precedent altogether, but then we depart from Kress's subject matter. Note that my aim has not been to dispute the interest of the retroactivity problem which Kress has highlighted, but rather his conception of coherentism in general and Dworkin's version thereof in particular as the proper targets of the argument.

In pursuing my course of argument, however, I have at several points had to put considerable weight on the distinction between changes in the law and changes in our beliefs about the law in particular cases. Coherentism admits this theoretical distinction on a case-by-case basis, even though it ties the right answers and beliefs about them together globally in the way indicated in Section VII above, in that not too many settled cases can be mistaken. However, perhaps from a more pragmatic point of view, one more concerned with matters of notice and predictability, which may be closer to that of litigants and potential litigants, this distinction has been strained even so. Perhaps it is from this more pragmatic point of view that a distinctive problem about intervening cases arises.

5

Integrity and Stare Decisis

Scott Hershovitz*

Many think that stare decisis binds even the highest court in a jurisdiction to follow precedents that were decided incorrectly. Indeed, the view is commonly held by legal scholars[1] and judges[2] alike. But if that is what stare decisis really requires, it is puzzling. What could justify a principle that requires courts to make the same mistakes over and over again? Surely a better principle (one that most of us endorse) is that people should own up to their mistakes and seek *not* to repeat them. Could legal reasoning really be so different from everyday reasoning that principle requires courts to make mistakes repeatedly rather than correct them?

We need to clarify the question before we can answer it. There are two varieties of stare decisis—horizontal and vertical. Vertical stare decisis requires that lower courts follow the decisions of higher courts. Horizontal stare decisis requires that a court follow its own precedents. Vertical stare decisis is less mysterious than horizontal. The deference lower courts show to higher courts facilitates coordination among judges, and it has the potential to improve judicial decision making to the extent that higher court judges have greater expertise than lower court judges. Neither coordination nor expertise, however, can explain the practice of a court considering itself bound by its own precedents. This essay explores the mystery of horizontal stare decisis. For ease of exposition, I shall use "stare decisis" to refer to horizontal stare decisis.

The view that stare decisis condemns courts to repeat their mistakes neither fits nor justifies our legal practice. Fit is problematic because, with some regularity,

* Thanks to Jules Coleman, William Fetcher, Lewis Kornhauser, Scott Sharpiro, Seana Shiffrin, and Nicos Stavropouls for helpful comments and conversations.

[1] *See, e.g.*, L. Kornhauser, *An Economic Perspective on Stare Decisis*, 65 CHI.-KENT L.REV. 63, 65 (1989) (describing stare decisis as "a practice that, paradoxically, demands that a court adhere to a prior decision it considers wrong"); L. Alexander, *Constrained by Precedent*, 63 S. CAL. L. REV. 1, 4 (1989) ("I shall focus on those situations . . . in which a subsequent court believes that, though a previous case was decided incorrectly, it must, nevertheless . . . decide the case confronting it in a manner that it otherwise believes is incorrect").

[2] "[T]here is nothing to do except stand by the errors of our brethren of the week before, whether we relish them or not." B. CARDOZO, THE NATURE OF THE JUDICIAL PROCESS 150 (1921).

courts overrule precedents that they regard as mistaken. Justification is problematic because, as we shall see, the values most often cited in defense of stare decisis—efficiency and fairness—cannot underwrite a general practice of following incorrectly decided precedents.

The key to understanding the practice of stare decisis, I shall argue, lies elsewhere. Specifically, it lies in the virtue Ronald Dworkin calls integrity. Integrity is a value that is realized by patterns of behavior across time. The unique demand that integrity makes upon both individuals and courts is that they recognize that what they have done in the past affects what they ought to do now. Stare decisis, I aim to show, promotes integrity in judicial decision making.

I also aim to show that stare decisis is a broader practice than we traditionally conceive it. On an integrity-based view, stare decisis is the practice of engaging with history, not just by following precedents, but also by distinguishing them and, when appropriate, overruling them. Overruling a precedent, and sometimes even distinguishing one, are often thought of as acts that run counter to the demands of stare decisis. But if we think of stare decisis as a practice in which courts strive to exhibit integrity in decision making, then we can see that distinguishing and overruling precedents are ways that a court engages with its own history. As we shall see, a court with no concern for the integrity of its own decision making would not need to distinguish or overrule its precedents. It could simply ignore them.

I

Many investigations of stare decisis ask some version of the question, "What justifies adherence to a decision known to be wrong?"[3] The canonical expression of the principle—*stare decisis et not quieta movere*—does not, on its face, require following decisions known to be wrong. The Latin means "to stand by things decided, and not to disturb settled points."[4] Of course, it is reasonable to assume that some things that have been decided were decided incorrectly. So stare decisis will, on occasion, require courts to conform to incorrectly decided precedents.

This observation, however, is insufficient to motivate the idea that to justify stare decisis we need to explain why courts should adhere to precedents they regard as wrongly decided. After all, by the same implication, the canonical formulation also demands that courts follow precedents they regard as correct. Indeed, it demands that courts follow settled points of law without reference to the correctness of the decisions that settled them. So it is somewhat of a puzzle why those investigating stare decisis tend to ask what justifies following incorrectly decided precedents rather than, say, what justifies adhering to a decision irrespective of its merit.

---

[3] *See e.g.*, J. Macey, *The Internal and External Costs and Benefits of Stare Decisis*, 65 CHI.-KENT L. REV. 93, 94 (1989) ("Professor Kornhauser approaches the issue of stare decisis by pondering the question of what justifies adherence to a prior legal decision known to be wrong") (discussing Kornhauser, *supra* note 1); Alexander, *supra* note 1, at 4.

[4] BLACK'S LAW DICTIONARY (8th ed., 2004).

The answer, I think, lies in a particular view many have of stare decisis. Richard Fallon expresses the view as follows:

> Because a court that believes a prior decision to have been correct can always reaffirm the correctness of its ruling without reliance on its precedential status, the force of the doctrine of stare decisis lies in its capacity to perpetuate what was once judicial error or to forestall inquiry into the possibility of legal error.[5]

Fallon actually expresses two views of stare decisis in this passage. The first is that the force of stare decisis "lies in its capacity to perpetuate what was once judicial error." The second is that the force of stare decisis lies in its capacity to "forestall inquiry into the possibility of legal error." The first view is the one that is of immediate interest.

The view that the force of stare decisis "lies in its capacity to perpetuate what was once judicial error" is a common one. In response to a litigant who argued that a precedent should be overturned because it was incorrect, Judge Posner recently opined that stare decisis would be "out the window" if the incorrectness of a decision was a sufficient ground for overruling it.[6] According to Posner, "no doctrine of deference to precedent is needed to induce a court to follow the precedents that it agrees with; a court has no incentive to overrule them even if it is completely free to do so."[7] On this view, stare decisis has no force—does not make a difference—insofar as it requires courts to follow correctly decided precedents. It is only when stare decisis requires courts to follow incorrectly decided precedents that it makes a difference to judicial reasoning. If this is right, to justify stare decisis, we would need to justify a practice of following incorrectly decided precedents.

The structure of this argument will be familiar to students of jurisprudence. Some argue that legitimate authorities are incapable of making a difference in what their subjects ought to do. Either an authority directs a subject to do something she ought to do anyway, in which case the directive makes no difference in the subject's normative situation, or the authority directs a subject to do something she ought not to do. On the assumption that authorities that direct people to do things they ought not to do are illegitimate, it appears that legitimate authorities can make no difference in what their subjects ought to do. This claim is known as the *no difference* thesis.[8] Proponents of the no difference thesis are apt to hold the view that the normative force of an authority lies in its capacity to bind people to do things they ought not to do.

---

[5] R. H. Fallon, Jr., *Legitimacy and the Constitution*, 118 HARV. L. REV. 1787, 1823 n.3 (2005) (citing Michael Stokes Paulsen, *Abrogating Stare Decisis by Statute: May Congress Remove the Precedential Effect of Roe and Casey?*, 109 YALE L.J. 1535, 1538 n.8 (2000) ("The essence of the doctrine [of stare decisis] . . . is adherence to earlier decisions, in subsequent cases . . . even though the court in the subsequent case would be prepared to say, based on other interpretive criteria, that the precedent decision's interpretation of law is wrong")).

[6] *Tate v. Showboat Casino Marina Partnership*, 431 F.3d 580, 582 (7th Cir 2005).

[7] *Id.* at 582–583.

[8] *See* J. RAZ, THE MORALITY OF FREEDOM 48 (1986) ("The no difference thesis asserts that *the exercise of authority should make no difference to what its subjects ought to do*, for it ought to direct them to do what they ought to do in any event").

The most important problem with the no difference thesis is that sometimes what a subject ought to do is underdetermined by the reasons she has. For example, drivers have a reason to drive on the same side of the road as everyone else, but no particular reason to drive on the left or right. An authority can make a difference by giving drivers a reason to drive on the right, say, without requiring drivers to do anything they ought not to do.[9]

The argument that stare decisis only makes a difference when it requires courts to follow incorrectly decided precedents suffers from a similar defect. Stare decisis can make a difference by requiring courts to follow precedents that were neither correct nor incorrect when decided. Some dispute that there are such cases, but they are a logical possibility if not a legal one. If a particular precedent represents merely one among a number of permissible decisions that an earlier court could have selected, writing, as it were, on a blank slate, then a principle requiring a later court to follow that precedent makes a difference without demanding that the court follow a precedent that was decided incorrectly.

Another problem with the view that the force of stare decisis lies in its capacity to perpetuate judicial error is that it construes too narrowly the impact stare decisis can have on the outcome of cases. Fallon points out that a court following a precedent it regards as correctly decided can reach the same result without following the precedent. At most, this supports the view that stare decisis makes no difference in what a court *ought* to decide (though we have just seen that even this is not true). But even when a case is governed by a correctly decided precedent, stare decisis may well make a difference to what the court considering it actually decides. Stare decisis, after all, makes the later court more likely to read the earlier, correctly decided precedent, and doing so may save that court from making errors of its own.

The upshot is that the force of stare decisis does not lie in "its capacity to perpetuate what was once judicial error." Stare decisis can make a difference, even when it requires adherence to correctly decided precedent. Thus, there is no reason to think that to justify the practice of stare decisis, we need to justify the practice of following incorrectly decided precedents. We may need to justify following incorrectly decided precedents as part of justifying the broader practice of simply following precedent. However, if we start out by asking what justifies following incorrectly decided precedents, we misconstrue the import of stare decisis and cut ourselves off from the resources necessary to understand it.

II

A better question to ask is "What justifies adherence to a precedent irrespective of its merit?" Adherence to a precedent irrespective of merits would, to use Fallon's words, "forestall inquiry into the possibility of legal error." This second question is

[9] *Id.* at 30.

better than our first, but it is also misleading in that we do not actually have a practice of adhering to precedent without regard to merit. Courts in the United States and (more recently) in the United Kingdom do, from time to time, overturn even long-standing precedent. Below, I shall argue that overturning precedents is part and parcel of the practice of stare decisis, notwithstanding the fact that when a precedent is overturned we often speak as if the demands of stare decisis have been ignored or trumped. However, since much of the best work on stare decisis sets out to explain why courts ought to follow precedent irrespective of merit, we shall continue our inquiry into what might justify such a practice.

To justify adhering to judicial decisions irrespective of their merit, one needs to pull off a challenging trick. One has to show both that judicial decisions are deserving of deference as a class *and* that individual decisions deserve deference even when a subsequent court believes that the earlier, precedential court made a mistake. This is a difficult task, but it is not a task that we are unfamiliar with from other contexts. To justify obeying an authority, one must pull off a similar trick.

Authorities provide merit-independent reasons for action.[10] A mother can order her daughter to play inside or outside. Her order provides a reason for her child to act quite apart from its merit, quite apart from whether it would be better for the child to play inside or out. This general truth is not without limits, of course. A mother who orders her child to ingest arsenic greatly exceeds the scope of her legitimate authority. But within limits, the merit of the order is irrelevant to the question of whether it gives the child a reason to act. Every parent who has uttered the words, "Because I said so" implicitly endorses this view of parental authority.

To explain when and why authoritative orders are deserving of deference, Joseph Raz offers the *normal justification thesis*.[11] Roughly speaking, the normal justification thesis holds that an authority is legitimate for a person if she will do a better job of conforming to the reasons that apply to her by following the authority's orders than she would by following her own lights. Authorities can satisfy the normal justification thesis through, among other things, special expertise, or the ability to solve coordination problems. To illustrate: a doctor is an authority on medical matters in virtue of her special knowledge; the state is an authority on traffic matters in virtue of its ability to solve coordination problems.

When the normal justification thesis is satisfied, one has a reason to give an authority's orders deference as a class, as well as a reason not to deny deference when one believes there is reason to doubt the merit of a particular order. If one refused to follow the order of a legitimate authority whenever one believed that it was in error, the advantage one would get from following the orders as a class would be lost. Thus the normal justification thesis pulls off the trick when it comes to authoritative orders—it justifies deference to authoritative orders as a class, and deference to particular orders even when one has reason to believe they are mistaken.

---

[10] *See* J. Gardner, *Legal Positivism: 5½ Myths*, 46 AM. J. JURIS. 199, 208–209 (2001).

[11] Raz, *supra* note 8, at 53. For a short introduction to Raz's account of authority, *see* S. Hershovitz, *Legitimacy, Democracy, and Razian Authority*, 9 LEGAL THEORY 201 (2003).

If we were interested in justifying vertical stare decisis, we could invoke the normal justification thesis. Higher courts are authorities for lower courts. The authority is based on an ability to coordinate action, and perhaps (one might hope) on expertise as well. Each lower court judge has reason to decide cases as most other judges would decide them, and a practice of treating higher court cases as authoritative facilitates this aim. To the extent that higher court judges have superior expertise to lower court judges (or even simply more time and resources to bring to bear on a case), lower court deference to the ruling of higher courts will improve lower court decision making.

Raz's trick will not work for horizontal stare decisis, however. There is no reason for the highest court in the land to believe that it will, on the whole, decide cases better by conforming to its own previous decisions than it would by following its own current lights. The coordination justification that works so well for lower courts has no bearing.[12] Expertise cannot do the work either because later versions of a court generally have more information available to them than earlier versions, and (again, one hopes) members of roughly equal skill and knowledge.[13] Thus, if the trick can be pulled off for horizontal stare decisis, it has to be done some other way.

III

One common approach to justifying stare decisis is to argue that the practice is efficient. Justice Cardozo took this tack, suggesting that "the labor of judges would be increased almost to the breaking point if every past decision could be reopened in every case."[14] Cardozo's observation, if true, would be a premise in a narrow argument for the efficiency of stare decisis, focusing on the conservation of judicial resources.

One suspects that Cardozo is correct. If you always start with a blank canvas, you spend a lot of time painting the background. But it is not entirely obvious that Cardozo is right. Stare decisis may indeed conserve resources, but it also consumes

---

[12] When a court is composed of many members, and not all members of the court hear every case, coordination concerns may well support horizontal stare decisis. Thus, circuit courts of appeals in the United States, which typically hear cases in three-judge panels selected at random from a larger set of judges, may use horizontal stare decisis as a means of coordinating action among all the judges on the court. But such an explanation sheds no light on why the United States Supreme Court, for example, would consider itself bound to follow its own precedent, since every Justice typically hears every case. For a discussion of the impact different institutional structures have on the justification of stare decisis, *see* Kornhauser, *supra* note 1.

[13] F. H. Easterbrook, *Stability and Reliability in Judicial Decisions*, 73 CORNELL L. REV. 422, 423 (1988) ("In principle, modern judges have all the information available to their forbears, plus any discoveries in the interim, and the benefit of hindsight. Judges often decide cases on the basis of predictions about the effects of the legal rule. We can examine these effects—both for other strands of doctrine and for the world at large—and improve on the treatment of the earlier case").

[14] CARDOZO, *supra* note 2, at 149. *See also*, J. P. Stevens, *The Life Span of a Judge-Made Rule*, 58 N.Y.U. L. REV. 1, 2 ("Perhaps the doctrine is of special interest to judges because it provides special benefits for judges. It obviously makes their work easier").

them. In a system with precedent, judges (and lawyers) spend time and money researching prior cases. The revenues of Lexis and Westlaw are a cost of stare decisis, as are the salaries of judicial clerks and many law firm associates.

Precedent allows judges to rely on previous cases, but it also demands that judges distinguish cases, an occasionally laborious task. An armchair investigation suggests that opinions do not grow shorter as the volume of precedent grows larger. If anything, the trend is towards longer opinions with more citation and quotation, and this is in part a consequence of stare decisis. Of course, many controversies are settled without judicial involvement because stare decisis makes the outcome of a case virtually certain. Additionally, stare decisis allows judges to dispose of many cases (and many issues within cases) summarily. So even if published opinions grow longer as a consequence of stare decisis, it may still be that judicial resources are conserved by the practice.

Jonathan Macey has gone so far as to argue that stare decisis allows judges to maximize their own leisure time by allowing them to free-ride on the efforts of earlier jurists.[15] Whatever its effect on judicial leisure time, it seems likely that stare decisis conserves judicial resources, or at least allows those resources to be deployed more efficiently. But the question is more complex than it appears at first glance, and it would require serious empirical study to resolve. Importantly, even if it were established that stare decisis conserves judicial resources, that fact would not go very far towards justifying the practice. Judicial resources are just one kind of resource among many, and if efficiency is to justify stare decisis, we must know that the gains in conserving judicial resources are not offset by losses elsewhere. That is, stare decisis must be efficient for society, not simply efficient for judges.

In an intriguing study of the efficiency of stare decisis, Lewis Kornhauser carefully delineates the potential sources of judicial error that could lead us to regard previous decisions as mistaken (changes in values, changes in the world, improvements in information, and incompetence).[16] Kornhauser provides a nuanced analysis of the value of stare decisis in the face of different sorts of error and in different institutional contexts. Rather than recap Kornahauser's analysis, I want instead to make some general remarks about the conclusions that Kornhauser reaches and the prospects for an economic justification for the practice of following precedents irrespective of their merit.

Kornhauser says that "the desirability of stare decisis will depend on the particular 'facts' of the situation the law seeks to govern."[17] He illustrates this by considering the desirability of stare decisis applied to the liability rules governing accidents between drivers and pedestrians. Suppose that the value of walking is fixed. If the value of driving is low, then strict liability will be preferred to negligence. Conversely, if the value of driving is high, then negligence will be preferred. Suppose further that in a regime with stare decisis, courts stick to the rules they announce regardless of the actual value of driving, whereas without stare decisis,

---

[15] Macey, *supra* note 3, at 111.   [16] Kornhauser, *supra* note 1.   [17] *Id.* at 86.

in each case, courts announce the legal rule that is optimal given the value of the injurer's activity.

To know whether stare decisis is desirable in these circumstances, one must know certain facts about the relative valuations of the walking and driving. Kornhauser explains as follows:

Suppose the valuations of the activities are such that both injurer and victim should adopt moderate (or low) levels of the activity. Under stare decisis, the actor who escapes liability will always adopt a higher level of activity. Under a practice of no stare decisis, however, each actor will be uncertain whether she will bear the cost of an accident. This uncertainty will induce her to adopt an activity level intermediate to the one she would adopt if she escaped liability for certain. For certain relative values of activities, then, the uncertainty over the legal rule induces the actors to adopt activity levels closer to the social optimum.[18]

Kornhauser's illustration shows that to know whether stare decisis is an efficient practice for courts to adopt with respect to the rules governing liability for accidents between pedestrians and drivers, one must know something about walking and driving.

This is hardly surprising. One would expect that the efficiency of a rule that entrenches other rules against change would depend in part on the efficiency of the rules entrenched and the nature of the behavior the rules govern. This has important ramifications for the possibility of an economic justification of stare decisis. The principal of stare decisis applies generally. With limited exceptions, the application of stare decisis does not depend on the substantive area of law involved. Stare decisis applies in contract as well as tort, in family law as well as corporate law. It applies to the rules that govern liability between pedestrians and drivers, as well as the rules that govern liability between farmers and ranchers. Stare decisis is often said to carry less weight in the realm of constitutional law because it takes a legislative supermajority to undo a Supreme Court decision. Notwithstanding that, we do not observe the nuanced application of stare decisis to specific classes of rules that we would expect to find were the efficiency of the practice the driving force behind it. As Macey puts it:

[I]n Kornhauser's model, the adjustment costs facing the relevant parties determine whether social welfare is being maximized by a legal regime of stare decisis. But courts have exhibited little, if any, ability or inclination to delve into the adjustment costs facing the parties before them . . . .[19]

Efficiency seems a poor explanation of stare decisis as we know it in part because the practice is insensitive to the facts that determine whether or not it is efficient in any given context.

We should be skeptical of attempts to argue that a practice of following precedent regardless of merit is across-the-board efficient because whether or not such a practice is efficient depends crucially on the rules that the practice entrenches and

---

[18] *Id.*   [19] Macey, *supra* note 3, at 95.

on the particulars of the behavior those rules govern. However, one aspect of efficiency that is sometimes appealed in order to justify stare decisis deserves special attention: the value of certainty in the law. If judges were unconstrained by precedent, some say, the law might shift unpredictably and people would be unable to plan their affairs. This would have undesirable consequences (stunted markets, stunted psyches, etc.), and to the extent that stare decisis ameliorates these consequences, it may be instrumentally valuable.

No doubt, for particular areas of law, there is much to be said in favor of certainty. When it comes to the interpretation of insurance contracts, or the rules governing secured transactions, it may well be more important to have a consistently applied rule than to have a good rule. When certainty is sufficiently valuable to outweigh any loss from the entrenchment of a suboptimal rule, the need for certainty will support a practice of adhering to precedent irrespective of merit.

We should be careful not to push certainty explanations too far. As Kornhauser explains: " 'Certainty' justifications for stare decisis often include 'reliance' or 'planning' arguments, but these arguments are only as strong as the value of the planned conduct."[20] To take an extreme but illustrative example, note that *Plessy v. Ferguson*[21] allowed Southerners to plan their affairs in the certainty that the federal government would not interfere with state-created racial caste systems. The value of the activities planned in reliance on *Plessy* was hardly sufficient to warrant continued adherence to the precedent. Indeed, it seems inappropriate to weigh the "benefit" of segregation-based plans against the cost of segregation-caused harms at all. *Plessy* is, as noted, an extreme example, and it represents a paradigm of a case that ought to have been overruled. But the point is this: if one appeals to certainty to justify following precedents irrespective of merit, then one must be prepared to defend the value of the conduct planned in reliance on the rules entrenched. It is easy to defend the value of conduct planned in reliance on stable interpretations of insurance contracts, and impossible to defend the value of conduct planned in reliance on *Plessy*. In the middle lies a vast grey area in which the value of conduct planned in reliance on previously announced legal rules may or may not be sufficient to warrant a practice of deferring to those rules irrespective of their merit. Certainty arguments, like efficiency arguments more generally, may well support stare decisis for particular types of legal rules. But neither certainty nor efficiency can underwrite an across-the-board practice of deferring to precedent without regard to merit.

IV

Fairness is another value commonly thought to underwrite stare decisis. But arguments in favor of the fairness of stare decisis face an objection similar to

---

[20] Kornhauser, *supra* note 1, at 78.   [21] 163 U.S. 537 (1896).

the one that plagues arguments in favor of its efficiency. Fairness may well demand that courts treat the litigants in like cases alike, and stare decisis encourages that. But fairness also makes demands regarding the outcome of particular cases, and stare decisis can entrench unfair results. A practice that accords deference to the rules announced in *Plessy* or *Korematsu v. United States*,[22] for example, entrenches particularly pernicious forms of unfairness against legal change. Whether stare decisis is on the whole fair depends on the relative magnitude of the gains in fairness from treating litigants in different cases alike and the losses from entrenching particular unfair results. It is far from obvious that, on the whole, stare decisis promotes fairness, and the question is, in part, an empirical one.

Fairness does not hold out any more hope of justifying across-the-board stare decisis than efficiency does, even if we accept the idea that litigants in different cases ought to be treated alike. And we should have doubts about that claim, at least as it is relevant to stare decisis. Fairness may demand that we apply the same rules to litigants in neighboring courtrooms, but it does not clearly demand that we apply the same rules to litigants separated by decades. Comparative claims of fairness—claims of the form *A* deserves X because *B* received X—are only persuasive to the extent that the *A* and *B* are similarly situated. Litigants can frequently claim the benefit of stare decisis even though they are far removed in both time and place from the source of the precedent.

There are, of course, non-comparative claims of fairness that might support stare decisis. Non-comparative claims of fairness are claims about how one deserves to be treated irrespective of how others are treated. Many of the norms we associate with due process are norms of non-comparative fairness. For example, it is unfair to detain a person indefinitely without the opportunity for a hearing before an impartial fact finder, and it would not make it fair to do this as a matter of routine practice. It is also unfair to punish a person for violating a criminal statute passed after the alleged violation, and it would not improve the situation if people were commonly punished for ex post violations. More relevant to stare decisis, perhaps as a matter of non-comparative fairness, people ought to be given notice of the rules that will be applied to them, an aim stare decisis could help facilitate. Or perhaps as a matter of non-comparative fairness, courts shouldn't disturb settled expectations. These sorts of claims may well justify stare decisis in delimited areas of the law. But this is subject to the point made above. To determine whether stare decisis is fair, gains in fairness from providing notice or protecting settled expectations must be weighed against the losses from entrenching unfair rules. Because of this, fairness, like efficiency, is incapable of providing justification for an across-the-board practice of following precedent irrespective of merit.

[22] 323 U.S. 214 (1944).

V

We started our inquiry with the question, "What justifies adherence to a decision known to be wrong?" We saw that this question is misleading because it does not accurately capture what stare decisis requires. So we asked a different question: "What justifies adherence to a precedent irrespective of its merit?" This question better captures the canonical formulation of stare decisis, but it still leaves us with an intractable problem. We can explain why lower courts ought to defer to the decisions of higher courts simply by invoking Raz's normal justification thesis. But we cannot find an analogue that explains why the highest court in a land should accord its own previous decisions similar deference. Neither efficiency nor fairness does the trick.

Fortunately, to justify stare decisis, we need not justify adhering to decisions irrespective of their merits. After all, courts do not do that. With some regularity, courts overrule precedents and limit their scope by distinguishing them. We can think of overruling and distinguishing as ways of breaching stare decisis. But we can also see overruling and distinguishing as part of the practice of stare decisis. On this broader view, the central demand of stare decisis is that courts engage with the past and act with integrity.

We owe our understanding of the special connection between law and integrity to the work of Ronald Dworkin. Dworkin was the first to recognize that integrity is central to understanding our legal institutions. This was no trivial observation, because (as we shall see below) integrity may not be a value for all institutions, perhaps not even all law-like ones.

Before we can explore the connection between stare decisis and integrity, we must get a fix on what integrity is. Providing a full account is too large an endeavor to take on here, but some preliminary efforts will help us to get an alternative account of stare decisis off the ground. According to Dworkin:

> We want our neighbors to behave, in their day-to-day dealings with us, in the way we think right. But we know that people disagree to some extent about the right principles of behavior, so we distinguish that requirement from the different (and weaker) requirement that they act in important matters with integrity, that is, according to convictions that inform and shape their lives as a whole, rather than capriciously and whimsically.[23]

Acting with integrity does not require that one act correctly. Rather, it requires that one always act in accord with genuine convictions about what the right way to act is. Integrity may seem like a second-best sort of value, one to be pursued only when one cannot be confident of acting correctly. Indeed, Dworkin seems to invite this understanding of integrity by suggesting that we demand it of others

---

23 R. DWORKIN, LAW'S EMPIRE 166 (1998).

because we know that we disagree about what is right. Integrity is not a second-best value, however, and our primary reason for demanding integrity in ourselves and others is not our inability to agree about what is right. Rather, we demand integrity because, whatever doubt we have about particular moral views, we are confident that the demands of morality are coherent.[24] We are also confident that morality does not demand that we act capriciously or whimsically in matters of importance. Thus, if we are striving to act morally, we will act with integrity.

Let me put the point another way. Someone who acts with integrity may nevertheless do something she ought not to do from time to time. But someone who acts without integrity, someone who acts incoherently or capriciously in matters of importance, simply cannot be acting morally except by happenstance. A lack of integrity signifies a lack of a commitment to act morally.

An individual displays integrity when her actions taken as a whole reflect a commitment to a coherent and defensible moral view. The moral view must be coherent because the demands of morality are coherent. However, commitment to an evil moral view is no virtue simply because the view is coherent. Thus, integrity also requires that one act in accord with a defensible moral view. Otherwise, acting with integrity would not be a way of striving to act morally.

Of course, a defensible moral view is not necessarily a true one. This is why Dworkin is right when he says that the demand that we act with integrity is weaker than the demand that we act morally. However, acting with integrity is part of striving to act morally, and that is the source of its value. We respect others for their integrity even when we disagree with their actions because we recognize their genuine commitment to acting morally.

Now we get to the important part for understanding stare decisis. Acting with integrity requires recognizing that what one has done in the past is relevant to what one ought to do now. Integrity requires a commitment to a moral view, and one can only display a commitment to a moral view by a pattern of behavior across time. Constantly shifting moral views are a sign of caprice, not integrity.

Importantly, refusing to change one's moral views in the face of persuasive reason to do so is also inconsistent with integrity. Remember that integrity is valuable because it is an aspect of striving to act morally. If you are genuinely striving to act morally, you will change your beliefs and behavior in response to persuasive argument or new evidence. A rigid refusal to change one's moral convictions in the face of new information is not a sign of integrity; it is a sign of obtuseness.

There are at least two situations in which integrity requires one to repudiate one's past. The first is when one's moral convictions undergo genuine change. Integrity requires acting in accord with one's new moral convictions. If a person's moral convictions are constantly shifting, we will not say that she acts with integrity even if she always acts in accord with her genuine moral convictions. This is

---

[24] I am using "morality" in its widest sense, in which the demands of morality are coextensive with the demands of reason.

because we doubt that she has any commitment to her moral views or to acting morally. But in the normal case, revisions in one's beliefs and behaviors are not only consistent with integrity, they are required by it.

One should also repudiate one's past when one's past behavior is inconsistent with the moral commitments one has made. This is an all too common occurrence for most of us. Integrity does not require that one repeat one's mistakes; rather, it requires correcting them to bring one's behavior in accord with one's moral commitments.

These remarks are, of course, only exploratory. A full consideration of the nature of integrity demands more space and attention than available here. However, we have made enough progress in understanding what integrity demands of individuals that we can turn our attention to what integrity requires of courts.

VI

Courts are moral actors, and a court can display integrity in much the same way that an individual can. A court displays integrity when its decisions reflect a commitment to a coherent and defensible view of the rights and duties people have under the law. Such a commitment can only be displayed by a pattern of decisions across time. If a court's rulings change capriciously, if it fails to pay heed to its own pronouncements, we will doubt that it has any genuine commitment to the views it expresses. On the other hand, if the court takes seriously what it has said in the past and it displays consistency and coherence in action, we will believe that the court acts on the basis of genuine convictions about the content of the law.

Why should courts act with integrity? For insight, let us turn once again to Dworkin. He writes:

Integrity becomes a political ideal when . . . we insist that the state act on a single, coherent set of principles even when its citizens are divided about what the right principles of justice and fairness really are. We assume, in both the individual and political cases, that we can recognize other people's acts as expressing a conception of justice or decency even when we do not endorse that conception ourselves. This ability is an important part of our more general ability to treat others with respect, and it is therefore a prerequisite of civilization.[25]

We want the state (and, derivatively, its courts) to act in accord with a single, coherent set of principles for the same reason we want individuals to do so. We are confident that morality provides a coherent vision of what we owe to one another, and that that vision does not demand that the state or its agents act capriciously in matters of importance. If the state acts incoherently or capriciously in matters of importance, it cannot be acting morally except by happenstance. We may disagree

---

[25] DWORKIN, *supra* note 23, at 166.

about what morality requires of the state, but we want the state to strive to act morally. Acting with integrity is a sign that it does so.

Dworkin breaks down the demands of integrity into two principles: the principle of integrity in legislation and the principle of integrity in adjudication. The latter principle, he says, explains "why judges must conceive of the body of law they administer as a whole rather than as a set of discrete decisions they are free to make or amend one by one, with nothing but a strategic interest in the rest."[26] Stare decisis is a means by which we promote this sort of integrity in judicial decision making.

A court that considers itself bound by the principle of stare decisis recognizes that what it has done in the past affects what it ought to do now. Of course, integrity in judicial decision making is no more a matter of slavishly repeating past decisions, right or wrong, than it is for individuals. Just as individuals must sometimes repudiate their past, courts must do so as well. They must do so whenever their convictions about the content of the law undergo genuine change, and they must do so when they discover that their past decisions conflict with their genuine commitments. Of course, if a court constantly shifts its views, we will doubt that it has any genuine commitment to them, and we will not regard it as acting with integrity. But, in the normal case, a court can overturn a precedent it regards as mistaken without doing any violence to its integrity, and indeed, integrity may demand that it do so.

There is good reason to think of stare decisis as a broader practice than simply following precedent. If a court seeking to act with integrity has previously announced a rule of law, it has three options: it can follow it, it can overrule it, or it can distinguish the case. Overruling and distinguishing are as much ways of engaging with the past as following is. They are ways of saying, "we recognize that our prior decision is relevant in deciding what we ought to do now, but for these reasons we are not following it here." A court that did not consider itself bound by stare decisis would not need to overrule or distinguish cases because it would not recognize what it had done in the past as relevant to what it ought to do now.

An example of such an institution may help to make the point clear. Up until a few years ago, allegations of student conduct violations at the University of Georgia were adjudicated by an organization called the Student Judiciary.[27] The Student Judiciary heard cases running the gamut from trivial infractions like excessive noise in dorms to serious offenses such as DUI and sexual assault. Members of the Student Judiciary sat on panels as judges in what were essentially mini-trials to determine whether a student violated a rule and, if so, to impose an appropriate sanction. Sanctions ranged from reprimand to expulsion.

---

[26] DWORKIN, *supra* note 23, at 167.

[27] In the mid-1990s I was a member of the Student Judiciary at the University of Georgia, and I served for a year as its Chief Justice. The Student Judiciary has recently been replaced by the University Judiciary, a group similar in function to the Student Judiciary, but somewhat different in form.

The Student Judiciary had no system of precedent. A panel would not consider the decision of a previous panel, even if a previous decision is precisely on point. Thus, no case law grew up around the conduct rules or their implementation. Each panel treated each case as if no others had preceded it.

The Student Judiciary shunned precedent for a variety of reasons. One reason is that it was seeking to avoid some of the accoutrements of real legal systems. It did not want to require student defendants to research previous decisions, nor did it want to expend resources cataloguing them. For the Student Judiciary, efficiency counseled against stare decisis.

The most important reason for shunning precedent, however, was the way the Student Judiciary conceived of its mission. It understood itself to share the educational aims of the broader university. The organization believed that its responsibility was to provide each student who appeared before a panel with the best educational experience it could. A system of precedent might have gotten in the way of tailoring each student's hearing and sanction to their individual educational needs. Without precedent, maximum flexibility was maintained. The system's rejection of stare decisis was so complete that decisions from prior cases were not even considered relevant, let alone dispositive.

Integrity was simply not a value the adjudicative practices of the Student Judiciary recognized. This is interesting, because the Student Judiciary was as court-like as an institution can be without being part of an actual legal system. The Student Judiciary administered a system of conduct rules of general application through adjudicatory bodies with judges and lawyer-like advocates. The Student Judiciary was even an organ of the state.[28]

I suspect that the Student Judiciary was, in fact, concerned with the integrity of its decision making. Stare decisis is not the only way to promote integrity. The Student Judiciary demanded that potential members participate in lengthy training, which promoted consistency and coherence in the decisions of its panels, and members received continuing education as well. Nevertheless, in the individual case, the Student Judiciary was designed to be unresponsive to claims that a prior decision bound it to a course of action. Thus, unlike a court that adheres to stare decisis, the Student Judiciary never had the need to distinguish or overrule one of its prior decisions.

In contrast to the Student Judiciary, a court that adheres to stare decisis is different not simply because it has a commitment to following its prior decisions, but because it has committed itself to the idea that what it has done in the past is relevant to what it ought to do now. Such a court answers to its precedents, by following them, distinguishing them, and, on occasion, overruling them. Following, distinguishing, and overruling are all part of the pursuit of integrity in adjudication.

---

[28] *Red & Black Pub. Co., Inc. v. Board of Regents*, 427 S.E. 2d 257 (Ga. 1993) (holding that the Student Judiciary is subject to Georgia's Open Records Act, which applies to state agencies).

VII

This essay started with a question: could legal reasoning really be so different from everyday reasoning that principle requires courts to make mistakes repeatedly rather than correct them? Notwithstanding the traditional view of stare decisis, the answer is no. Stare decisis does not require a court to blindly follow incorrectly decided precedents. Nor does it require a court to stand by a precedent irrespective of its merit. What stare decisis does require is that courts engage with the past and act with integrity. They do this when they display a commitment to a coherent, defensible view of the content of the law.

Now that we have an expanded view of the practice of stare decisis, it is reasonable to wonder whether efficiency and fairness might not play a role in justifying it after all. Neither efficiency nor fairness seemed promising as a justification for a practice of following past decisions irrespective of their merit. But the broader practice of engaging with the past by following, overruling, and distinguishing precedent may well be both fair and efficient. Whether it is either, of course, depends on how good a job courts do of it. The efficiency and fairness of stare decisis conceived broadly still depends, in part, on the efficiency and fairness of the decisions in particular cases.

The real place for efficiency and fairness in an explanation of stare decisis is not so much in justifying the practice, but in giving it its contour. This essay has not addressed the conditions under which a court ought to overturn one of its precedents. In any given case, the question of whether a court should follow a precedent depends crucially on matters of fairness and efficiency, and on a multitude of other values as well. The fact that courts bother to engage with precedent at all, however, is best explained by judicial aspirations to act with integrity.

6

The Many Faces of Political Integrity

Dale Smith*

Crucial to a proper understanding of Ronald Dworkin's approach to law and adjudication is an understanding of what he means by "integrity." The concept of integrity is introduced in *Law's Empire*[1] via a discussion of "checkerboard solutions." However, it is far from clear what checkerboard solutions are, let alone what is wrong with them. This chapter engages in a search for an account of what is wrong with checkerboard solutions that is both a plausible interpretation of Dworkin's discussion and is defensible in its own right. In Part I, I present Dworkin's claims about checkerboard solutions. Part II then highlights an ambiguity in his discussion, before considering a number of different interpretations of his position, each of which attempts to identify a single flaw inherent in checkerboard solutions. I argue that none of these attempts succeed, before canvassing the possibility that there is more than one thing wrong with such solutions. While I suggest that this offers the most promising interpretation of Dworkin's writings on this topic, I go on (in Part III) to question whether this account of what is wrong with checkerboard solutions can provide the support for Dworkin's broader claims about integrity that he believes it can. I argue that Dworkin has failed to vindicate his claim that integrity should characteristically trump justice in cases where they conflict, and that his discussion of checkerboard solutions provides only limited support for his claim that integrity offers a good fit with our political beliefs and practices.

This chapter focuses primarily on Dworkin's discussion in *Law's Empire*, since it is there that he discusses checkerboard solutions in the greatest detail. However, since this chapter is ultimately concerned with the value of integrity, it should be acknowledged that Dworkin has developed his views about the analysis of political concepts like integrity since *Law's Empire*. In particular, he now argues that we can understand a political concept like integrity only in light of its relationship to

* I am grateful to Samantha Besson, Ronald Dworkin, Patrick Emerton, Jeff Goldsworthy, Scott Hershovitz, Lewis Kornhauser and Nicos Stavropoulos for their helpful comments on earlier drafts of this chapter.
[1] R. Dworkin, Law's Empire (1986). All references in parentheses are to this work.

other political concepts such as justice and legality.[2] On this view, we can fully understand the concept of integrity only by constructing a holistic (and interpretive) account of all our political values, at least part of which involves tracing the interrelations between integrity and other political values. As Dworkin himself points out, this is an enormous undertaking, which I cannot possibly perform in this chapter. However, I hope that this chapter could be seen to represent a modest and limited contribution towards that overarching goal, advancing to some extent our understanding of the value of integrity and its relationship to other political values such as justice and fairness.

I. What is a Checkerboard Solution?

Dworkin claims that there are two commonly accepted political values—justice and fairness.[3] However, he offers a somewhat idiosyncratic account of these two values:

Fairness in politics is a matter of finding political procedures—methods of electing officials and making their decisions responsive to the electorate—that distribute political power in the right way. That is now generally understood, in the United States and Britain at least, to mean procedures and practices that give all citizens more or less equal influence in the decisions that govern them. Justice, on the contrary, is concerned with the decisions that the standing political institutions, whether or not they have been chosen fairly, ought to make. If we accept justice as a political virtue we want our legislators and other officials to distribute material resources and protect civil liberties so as to secure a morally defensible outcome. (164–165)

Dworkin claims that there is also a *third* political ideal—the ideal of integrity. This ideal "requires government to speak with one voice, to act in a principled and coherent manner toward all its citizens, to extend to everyone the same substantive standards of justice or fairness it uses for some" (165). For example, if the government relies on majoritarian principles to justify its decisions about who may vote, it must respect the same principles when drawing electoral boundaries. Similarly, if the government appeals to the principle that people have a right to receive compensation from those who injure them carelessly as a reason why manufacturers are liable for defective cars, it must give effect to that principle in deciding whether accountants are liable for their mistakes as well (165).

---

[2] R. Dworkin, *Hart's Postscript and the Character of Political Philosophy*, 24 Oxford J. of Legal Stud. 1, 17 (2004).

[3] He mentions a further political ideal—procedural due process—but it plays no role in his argument, and so I shall leave it to one side.

Dworkin labels this ideal "political integrity" to highlight the connection with the notion of *personal* integrity, which involves acting "according to convictions that inform and shape [one's life] as a whole, rather than capriciously or whimsically" (166). Integrity becomes a political ideal when we insist that the state act on a single, coherent set of principles even though its citizens disagree about what the right principles of justice and fairness really are (166).[4]

To justify his claim that integrity is a distinct political ideal, Dworkin seeks to show that it both fits with, and provides a sound justification of, our political practices. It is in seeking to show that this ideal *fits* our political practices that he introduces the notion of a checkerboard solution. He claims that we can explain our opposition to checkerboard solutions only on the basis that we accept the ideal of integrity.

So what is a checkerboard solution? This question will occupy us for much of this chapter, but let us start with Dworkin's initial characterization of the phenomenon. He states that he is not using the word "checkerboard" to describe statutes that make distinctions that claim to be justified on the basis of a policy best served by the discriminations in question. Instead, he uses the word "to describe statutes that display incoherence in principle and that can be justified, if at all, only on grounds of a fair allocation of political power between different moral parties" (435, n. 6).

Dworkin uses the connection between fairness and checkerboard solutions alluded to in the last quotation to set up a puzzle that he believes only integrity can solve. He points out that, since we all value fairness but disagree about moral issues, it seems to follow that legislation on moral issues should be a matter "of trades and compromises so that each body of opinion is represented, to a degree that matches its numbers, in the final result" (178). For example, if people disagree about whether justice requires compensation for product defects that the manufacturer could not reasonably have prevented, why should not the legislature impose strict liability on car manufacturers but not on manufacturers of washing machines?[5] Or, if we disagree about the permissibility of abortion, why should not Parliament make abortion criminal for women who are born in even-numbered years but not for those born in odd-numbered years? (178).

Dworkin claims that this sort of solution to contested moral issues seems mandated by fairness, since it secures the kind of proportional influence of citizens over the political process that fairness (on Dworkin's definition) appears to recommend (435, n. 3). Allowing each group in society to choose some part of that society's abortion law, in proportion to their numbers, "is fairer (in our

---

[4] Several commentators have suggested that there are important disanalogies between personal integrity and what Dworkin calls "political integrity": *e.g.* J. Raz, Ethics in the Public Domain: Essays in the Morality of Law and Politics 307 (1995). However, I shall not pursue this issue here.

[5] Though I shall question whether this is really an example of a checkerboard solution: *see infra* text for note 18.

sense) than the winner-take-all scheme our instincts prefer, which denies many people any influence at all over an issue they think desperately important" (179).[6]

However, Dworkin also claims that most of us would be dismayed by checkerboard statutes that treat relevantly similar actions (for example, abortions by women born in even-numbered years and those by women born in odd-numbered years) differently on arbitrary grounds (179). This is not to say that we always oppose political compromise, or even that we always oppose *arbitrary* compromises. Dworkin allows that we tolerate arbitrary distinctions with regard to matters of policy (such as parking regulations), but claims that we do not tolerate them when matters of principle are at stake. In other words, if we are concerned only with promoting social welfare, then arbitrary distinctions are permissible, but they are unacceptable where moral issues (or someone's rights) are involved.[7] When matters of principle are at stake, we accept that each point of view should be allowed a voice in the deliberative process, but the collective decision must aim to settle on some coherent principle that is then applied in all appropriate circumstances (179).

Compromise on matters of principle is not always impermissible. Sometimes, two independent principles that we hold come into conflict, in the sense that we cannot satisfy both on this particular occasion. In such cases, we might give weight to each of those principles in a certain relation (for example, by developing a tax scheme that seeks to respect both property rights and equality of opportunity, to differing degrees). However, whatever relative weighting we give those principles must flow throughout the scheme in question, and to other decisions that involve the same two principles (435–436, n. 7). Dworkin claims that this kind of conflict differs from the contradiction contained in checkerboard statutes. In the latter case, one principle of justice is not outweighed or qualified by another in a way that expresses a ranking of the two; instead, only a single principle is involved, which is affirmed for one group and denied for another. It is this which Dworkin claims we denounce: "If there must be compromise because people are divided about justice, then the compromise . . . must be compromise about which scheme of justice to adopt rather than a compromised scheme of justice" (179).

---

[6] *See also* (435, n. 3), where Dworkin explicitly states that fairness supports checkerboard solutions. Dworkin does not specify precisely what sort of influence is required by the value of fairness, but presumably he has in mind the ability to have one's views reflected in political outcomes. On this view, one has political influence to the extent that one's favoured position is reflected in the position adopted by the political process, rather than to the extent that one participates in the political process. Whether this is an appropriate account of fairness falls outside the scope of this chapter: *see infra*, note 17.

[7] This is an over-simplification of Dworkin's views. While he claims that integrity does not require any simple form of consistency between policies (in the way that it does with regard to principles), he claims that it does have some role to play even here (221–222).

We cannot explain our opposition to checkerboard solutions by reference to the value of fairness, since we have seen that checkerboard solutions *promote* that value (by distributing political power more evenly than the alternatives). Nor, according to Dworkin, is our antipathy to internal compromise[8] based on the ideal of justice. He acknowledges that it is tempting to argue that checkerboard solutions are unjust because they treat different people differently for no good reason (whereas justice requires us to treat like cases alike). However, he claims that—while the defect in checkerboard solutions must lie in their distinctive feature (that they treat people differently when no principle can justify this distinction)—we cannot explain why this is objectionable if we focus solely on considerations of justice (180–181).

Why not? Dworkin claims that checkerboard solutions can prevent instances of injustice that would otherwise occur (181). For example, if we oppose abortion, the abortion statute described above will have the merit of at least ensuring that some foetuses (those belonging to women born on even-numbered years) are protected. Moreover, if we are a minority in society, our choice may be between supporting a checkerboard solution and allowing abortion in all cases. If so, justice seems to favour the checkerboard solution, since this would minimize instances of injustice.

Justice does not always favour checkerboard solutions. If we have majority support within society, then we may be able to achieve the optimal outcome, which will clearly not be the checkerboard solution. Nevertheless, unless we are *always* part of the majority, checkerboard solutions will sometimes be the best option available to us from the standpoint of justice. Yet, according to Dworkin, internal compromises are *always* objectionable, and we cannot explain why this is so if we focus solely on considerations of justice.[9]

A critic of Dworkin might argue that we *can* explain why checkerboard solutions are always objectionable by reference to the ideal of justice. A checkerboard solution (by definition) cannot be a fully just solution. At most, it is the least worst alternative, because it minimizes injustices that we could not otherwise prevent. Therefore, we always have reasons of justice to treat a checkerboard solution as objectionable, even if we also think that it represents the most just (or least unjust) outcome we can hope for under present circumstances.

Dworkin's response is that, not only do we reject checkerboard solutions, but many of us would prefer *either* of the alternative solutions to a checkerboard solution. For example, many opponents of abortion would (according to Dworkin) prefer that abortion *always* be available than that we adopt a checkerboard solution regarding abortion (182). This attitude cannot be explained by reference to

---

[8] Dworkin uses the phrases "checkerboard solution" and "internal compromise" interchangeably. I shall follow this practice.

[9] As we shall see, Dworkin concedes that sometimes checkerboard solutions may be acceptable, but only because our distaste for them is outweighed by other considerations.

the ideal of justice, since (from the viewpoint of an opponent of abortion) making abortion available in all cases will produce more instances of injustice than a checkerboard solution.

Dworkin recognizes that not everybody would condemn every checkerboard solution. For example, some opponents of abortion might prefer a checkerboard solution to a law that legalized abortion in all instances. However, he claims that, if they would rank a checkerboard solution below all other alternatives when considering *other* political issues, this shows that they recognize a reason not to adopt checkerboard solutions, albeit a reason that is outweighed when the substantive issue is particularly important (182–183). Alternatively, their opposition to checkerboard solutions can be seen from the fact that they would prefer a statute prohibiting abortion except for women who became pregnant as the result of being raped to a statute prohibiting abortion except for women born on odd-numbered years, even if both statutes allowed exactly the same number of abortions.[10] This preference cannot be explained by reference to the ideal of justice, since (we are assuming) there will be exactly the same number of injustices under either statute.[11] Instead, this preference reflects the fact that the former statute gives effect to principles that opponents of abortion can recognize as principles of justice (even though they reject those principles), whereas the latter statute simply affirms for some people a principle that it denies to others (183).

To summarize, Dworkin claims that we recognize at least a pro tanto reason to reject checkerboard solutions. However, he claims, fairness often supports checkerboard solutions (given that people disagree about political issues) and justice sometimes supports them (when the alternative would be even more instances of injustice). Therefore, we must look elsewhere to explain our rejection of those solutions. This suggests that there must be a third political ideal to which we attach importance, since the first two ideals do not explain our attitude towards internal compromises. Dworkin claims that this third ideal is integrity. A state that adopts a checkerboard solution lacks integrity, because it must endorse principles to justify part of what it has done that it must reject to justify the rest (183–184). It is this fact that explains our opposition to checkerboard solutions, despite the considerations of fairness that favour such solutions.

Checkerboard solutions are not the only way in which integrity can be flouted. It is also violated whenever a community adopts different laws, each of which is

[10] I shall refer to these as the rape-abortion law and the checkerboard-abortion law, respectively. Possibly to make it more plausible that the rape-abortion law would permit the same number of abortions as a checkerboard solution, Dworkin refers to a checkerboard solution whereby only women born in one specified decade each century could have an abortion (183). However, for simplicity, I shall discuss only one checkerboard solution regarding abortion—namely, the one referred to in the text.

[11] Can we explain the preference on the basis that abortions in non-rape cases are *worse* (from the viewpoint of justice) than abortions in rape cases? No, because Dworkin stipulates that, on the view under consideration, it makes no difference whether the pregnancy is a result of rape (183).

internally coherent but which cannot be defended together as expressing a coherent ranking of different principles of justice and fairness. Dworkin recognizes that our legal system "constantly" violates integrity in this way, since we cannot bring all the rules our judges enforce together under a single coherent scheme of principle, but he claims that we regard this as a flaw in our legal system (184). Of more importance for present purposes, however, is the fact that this illustrates that the adoption of checkerboard solutions is not the only way to infringe integrity, though Dworkin claims that it is a particularly flagrant and easily avoidable way of doing so (184, 217).

Finally, Dworkin acknowledges that integrity is not always more important than fairness and justice, and so law-makers should not always avoid breaches of integrity. Indeed, despite checkerboard solutions being especially egregious violations of integrity, Dworkin suggests that there may be occasions on which even a checkerboard solution may be justified. For example, a legislature that favours no-fault compensation in defective product cases might find it impossible in practice to introduce such a scheme except for car manufacturers. The introduction of such a scheme only for car manufacturers would be condemned by integrity, but favoured by justice, and this might be a case where justice is more important than integrity.[12] Nevertheless, Dworkin insists that while law-makers can occasionally favour justice over integrity, they should not "characteristically" do so (218).[13]

II. What is Wrong with Checkerboard Solutions?

It is noticeable that Dworkin describes what is wrong with checkerboard solutions in a number of different ways, not all of which are clearly synonymous. Here is a (by no means complete) sample:

- checkerboard solutions "display incoherence in principle" (435, n. 6);
- checkerboard solutions "can be justified, if at all, only on grounds of a fair allocation of political power between different moral parties" (435, n. 6);
- checkerboard solutions "treat similar [actions] differently on arbitrary grounds", in situations where matters of principle are at stake (179);
- checkerboard solutions concern a single principle "which is affirmed for one group and denied for another" (435–436, n. 7);
- checkerboard solutions "treat people differently when no principle can justify the distinction" (180); and
- checkerboard solutions do not give effect to anything that one can recognize as a principle of justice (even if one rejects that principle) (183).

[12] The example is Dworkin's (217–218).
[13] Or else their claim to legitimacy will be undermined: *see infra* text between notes 45 and 46.

Are these merely different ways of making the same point? Certainly, there are significant similarities between several of the items on this list. For example, treating similar actions differently on arbitrary grounds and treating people differently when no principle can justify the distinction may simply be two ways of describing the same thing. However, even here, much depends on what we mean by "arbitrary". If "arbitrary" means unpredictable, or without legitimate authority,[14] then it is not so clear that the two descriptions are equivalent. There may be a principle that justifies differential treatment for two people who perform similar actions, even if the decision to treat them differently is unpredictable (for example, because we were unaware of that principle before the decision) or lacks legitimate authority (for example, because the decision-maker does not have authority to deal with the relevant issues).[15]

Similarly, it is not immediately obvious that one cannot affirm a single principle for one group and deny it for another without lapsing into "incoherence in principle." For example, many countries affirm the principle of freedom of association for most of their citizens, but not for offenders who have been convicted and sentenced to jail. Do such countries lack coherence in principle? Perhaps there is more than one principle at stake in this example (and so this is not an example of affirming a *single* principle for one group and denying it for another). However, at least at first sight, more than one principle is at stake in Dworkin's examples of checkerboard solutions, as well.[16]

It is not clear what we should conclude from this. One possibility is that Dworkin equivocates as to exactly what is wrong with checkerboard solutions, switching haphazardly between different explanations. However, another possibility is that—despite appearances—these various characterizations of checkerboard solutions in fact amount to the same thing. Or perhaps there is more than one thing wrong with checkerboard solutions, reflecting the fact that there is more than one principle of integrity that they violate (just as there is more than one principle of justice or fairness).

What *is* clear, however, is that further consideration of Dworkin's account of checkerboard solutions is called for. I shall seek to provide an interpretation of Dworkin's position that both fits what he says about checkerboard solutions and is sufficiently plausible in its own right to warrant consideration. More precisely, my

[14] Both of these are possible meanings of "arbitrary" suggested by J. WALDRON, LAW AND DISAGREEMENT 167–168 (1999).

[15] Dworkin may not be using the word "arbitrary" in either of these senses. If so, however, we need to determine in what sense he *is* using the word (*see infra* Section A).

[16] In fact, it is clear that checkerboard solutions need not concern only a single principle. Imagine a variation of the checkerboard abortion law, under which abortions are permissible for women born in the first four months of the year provided the abortion is performed in the first two trimesters of the pregnancy, are never permissible for women born in the next four months of the year and are permissible for women born in the last four months of the year only if their pregnancy is the result of rape. On any reasonable way of demarcating principles, there is more than one principle at stake in this law, and yet the law is clearly a checkerboard solution, since women are treated differently depending on the month in which they were born.

aim in this Part is to find the best account of checkerboard solutions available to Dworkin, before (in Part III) considering what implications that account has for Dworkin's broader theory. To this end, I shall begin by considering whether there is a single feature of checkerboard solutions that can explain our attitude towards such solutions, before considering whether some *combination* of such features might underlie our opposition to internal compromise. However, in doing so, I shall consider only the more promising interpretations of Dworkin's views, rather than attempting a comprehensive survey of suggestions as to what is wrong with checkerboard solutions.[17]

Since I am searching for the best interpretation of Dworkin's discussion of checkerboard solutions, I shall assume that there really is something wrong with such solutions. However, even making this assumption, not all of Dworkin's examples are equally convincing. Take his example of a statute that introduces no-fault liability for car manufacturers but not for washing machine manufacturers. Might there not be a principled distinction between the two types of manufacturer? For example, defective cars might cause personal injury more often than defective washing machines, and we might consider it more important to compensate for personal injury than for other losses resulting from defective products. Rather than concluding that this represents an exception to the general rule that checkerboard solutions are unacceptable, I suggest that—if there *is* a principled distinction—this shows that Dworkin's example is not really a checkerboard solution after all.[18] Thus, I shall focus on another of Dworkin's examples, which clearly *is* a checkerboard solution—namely, a law that prohibits abortions for women born in even-numbered years but not for those born in odd-numbered years. Given the uncertainty about how to characterize checkerboard solutions, I shall seek to derive guidance from this paradigm example of an internal compromise.

A. Arbitrary Distinctions and Unreasonable Compromises

The first possibility I shall consider is that checkerboard solutions are defective because they draw arbitrary distinctions between relevantly similar people, actions

---

[17] Several commentators have argued that, contrary to Dworkin, we can explain why checkerboard solutions are undesirable by reference to the values of fairness or justice (e.g. S. Wasserstrom, *The Empire's New Clothes*, 75 GEO. L.J. 199, 249, n. 168 (1986); D. Reaume, *Is Integrity a Virtue? Dworkin's Theory of Legal Obligation*, 39 U. TORONTO L.J. 380, 391–393 (1989)). However, I am searching for the best interpretation of Dworkin's views about checkerboard solutions, and so shall leave to one side the possibility that Dworkin is wrong in claiming that the distinctive flaw of checkerboard solutions is not that they are unfair and/or unjust.

[18] A similar approach is adopted by G. C. Christie, *Dworkin's "Empire"*, DUKE L.J. 157, 185 (1987). Dworkin could argue that the proposed legislation is a checkerboard solution because—even if a principled distinction could be drawn between car and washing machine manufacturers—this was not the motivation for the distinction drawn in the legislation. Instead, that distinction was motivated by considerations of political feasibility. However, the problem with checkerboard solutions seems to lie in the nature of the distinction drawn, not in the motivation for drawing that distinction.

or situations. As we have seen, there is textual support for interpreting Dworkin in this way: he claims that checkerboard solutions treat similar actions differently on arbitrary grounds, in situations where matters of principle are at stake (179). Moreover, prima facie, this claim appears plausible. There does appear to be something arbitrary about allowing abortions for women born in even-numbered years but not for those born in odd-numbered years.

However, there are two problems with this suggestion. First, the word "arbitrary" often hides more than it illuminates. What does it mean to say that a checkerboard solution is arbitrary? Different people use the word "arbitrary" to mean different things,[19] and so being told that checkerboard solutions are arbitrary is not particularly helpful unless we are also told *in what sense* they are arbitrary. The answer to this latter question may tell us what is wrong with checkerboard solutions, but merely to claim that they are arbitrary will not further our investigation very far. In other words, our investigation may start with the proposition that checkerboard solutions are arbitrary, but it cannot stop there—it must go on to consider in what sense they are arbitrary.

A similar objection can be levelled against the suggestion that checkerboard solutions involve *unreasonable* compromises. Certainly, the checkerboard-abortion law appears unreasonable, but the purpose of our inquiry is to determine in what *way* it is unreasonable. It is not sufficient simply to note that this law appears unreasonable.

Secondly, on at least one way of giving more determinate content to the word "arbitrary," it is not clear that checkerboard solutions *are* arbitrary. Dworkin concedes that there are reasons, based on considerations of fairness, for adopting checkerboard solutions. Checkerboard solutions seem to produce a more even distribution of political influence than the alternatives, and might be championed on this basis. Presumably, this is not enough to vindicate such solutions, but—if by "arbitrary" we mean irrational or unreasoned—it may be enough to show that they are not arbitrary. There are indeed reasons (of fairness) that support checkerboard solutions, even if those reasons are outweighed by other considerations.[20]

It might be responded that there is still a sense in which checkerboard solutions are unsupported by reason, and so are arbitrary. Considerations of fairness might give us reason to compromise so that 50 per cent of women are eligible for an abortion and 50 per cent are not, but this still does not support any particular outcome. We could choose to allow abortions for those women who are born in odd-numbered years, but we could alternatively allow abortions for those women who are born in the first six months of each year. We have no reason to choose one of these outcomes over the other, and so our choice is arbitrary.[21]

---

[19] WALDRON, *supra* note 14, at 167–168 suggests three different meanings.
[20] *Cf.* A. Marmor, *The Rule of Law and Its Limits*, 23 LAW AND PHILOSOPHY 1, 29–30 (2004), though Marmor may not accept Dworkin's conception of fairness.
[21] This objection was suggested by Scott Hershovitz.

In assessing this objection, it is important to realize that we do have a reason to adopt the former option (namely, a reason of fairness). Our problem is that we also have a reason to adopt the latter option, and no reason to prefer one of these two options to the other. This sort of situation is not uncommon. For example, if we are designing traffic laws for the first time, we have a reason to require everyone to drive on the right-hand side of the road (since this would reduce collisions), but we also have a reason to require everyone to drive on the left-hand side of the road (since this would also reduce collisions), and no reason to prefer the first option to the second (or vice versa). In such situations, our decision may be arbitrary, but it is not necessarily objectionable (as the traffic example shows). Therefore, it cannot be this feature of checkerboard solutions alone that renders them objectionable.

B. Irrelevant Considerations

The most obvious explanation of what is wrong with the checkerboard-abortion law is that its application depends on an irrelevant consideration, because it makes the permissibility of abortion depend on whether one was born on an even-numbered year, a consideration that is morally irrelevant to the issue at hand. We can render this notion of "moral irrelevance" somewhat more precise by saying that a morally irrelevant consideration is one that does not provide even a pro tanto moral reason. Thus, to say that whether one was born on an even-numbered year is morally irrelevant to whether one should be permitted to have an abortion is to say that it does not provide even a pro tanto moral reason for permitting (or not permitting) one to have an abortion.[22]

It is interesting that Dworkin does not canvass this possible explanation in *Law's Empire*. Indeed, his discussion appears incompatible with it. Take his suggested alternative to the checkerboard-abortion law—namely, allowing abortions only for rape victims. Dworkin states that this alternative would be seen to be superior to the checkerboard statute even if one believes "that it makes no difference whether the pregnancy is the result of rape" (183). To believe that it makes no difference whether the pregnancy is the result of rape is to believe that whether one has been raped is irrelevant to whether one is permitted to have an abortion (that is, it does not provide even a pro tanto reason for permitting an abortion). Yet Dworkin expects someone who holds that view still to prefer the rape-abortion statute to the checkerboard-abortion statute (and he regards this preference as reflecting an opposition to checkerboard solutions that he shares).

---

[22] This may be an unduly narrow conception of moral relevance. For example, even if one does not believe that foetuses have souls, one may believe that whether they have souls is relevant to the abortion debate, since—if they *did* have souls—this would provide a pro tanto reason to oppose abortion. This suggests that a consideration may also be morally relevant if it would provide a pro tanto reason *were the non-moral facts different* (e.g. were foetuses to have souls). However, nothing in this Section (Section B) turns on this point.

Therefore, he cannot believe that the distinction between checkerboard and non-checkerboard statutes hinges on whether the statute is based on morally irrelevant considerations. He believes that we should regard the rape-abortion statute as preferable to the checkerboard-abortion statute even if we believe that both are based on morally irrelevant considerations.

Admittedly, there is another possible interpretation of Dworkin's discussion of the two abortion statutes. He may be supposing that the anti-abortionist believes that it makes no difference whether the pregnancy is the result of rape in the sense that abortion will still be impermissible, not in the sense that it does not provide even a pro tanto reason for permitting an abortion. In other words, he may be supposing that the fact that the pregnancy is the result of rape makes a difference to the pro tanto reasons that apply, but makes no difference to the overall conclusion that one should reach. If so, his discussion *is* consistent with the claim that the distinctive feature of checkerboard solutions is that they are based on irrelevant considerations, since the rape-abortion law is based on a relevant consideration (whether the pregnancy is the result of rape affects the pro tanto reasons that apply, even if it does not alter our all-things-considered conclusion).

However, if Dworkin *does* believe that the distinctive feature of checkerboard solutions is that they are based on irrelevant considerations, one might have thought that he would qualify the hypothetical anti-abortionist's view that the fact of rape makes no difference, to make it clear that she does not believe that the rape-abortion law is based on irrelevant considerations. One might also have expected him to *state* that this is what is wrong with checkerboard solutions. It is noticeable that, in the list I provided earlier of six ways in which Dworkin describes what is wrong with checkerboard solutions, none refers to "irrelevant considerations." And Dworkin does not conclude that the rape-abortion law will be treated as preferable by the anti-abortionist because it reflects a relevant consideration, but rather because it "gives effect to two recognizable principles of justice, ordered in a certain way, even though [the anti-abortionist rejects] one of the principles" (183, footnote omitted).[23]

For these reasons, the "irrelevant considerations" approach to what is wrong with checkerboard solutions does not offer a plausible interpretation of Dworkin's discussion. Moreover, leaving aside whether it reflects Dworkin's views, there are significant problems with this approach. Imagine that Anna believes that whether a pregnancy is the result of rape really is morally irrelevant, in the sense that it does not provide even a pro tanto reason for permitting abortion. She believes that a foetus is a human being, and the fact that one has been raped cannot provide even a pro tanto reason for killing a human being. (It might provide a partial *excuse* in certain circumstances, but cannot begin to *justify* such an action.)[24] Now imagine

---

[23] This explanation of what is wrong with checkerboard solutions (along with how it differs from the current explanation) is considered in Section D.

[24] It could be argued that a consideration is morally relevant if it is relevant to either the justifiability *or* excusability of a certain action (in which case, whether the pregnancy is the result of rape might

that Anna must choose between the rape-abortion law and the checkerboard-abortion law. She believes that both are based on irrelevant considerations, and so cannot distinguish between them on this basis. However, is it not likely that Anna will believe that the rape-abortion law is preferable to the checkerboard-abortion law (again, assuming that both laws allow the same number of abortions)? The former is likely to make more sense to her because she can see how someone could come to support it (even though she believes that they are wrong to do so), whereas she could not see how someone could come to support the latter.[25] This suggests that what is *distinctively* objectionable about the checkerboard-abortion law (our paradigm case of a checkerboard solution) is *not* that it is based on irrelevant considerations.

A number of objections could be offered to this argument, of which I shall consider only one.[26] This objection starts by pointing out that, according to the "irrelevant considerations" approach, something is a checkerboard solution if its application depends on considerations that are *in fact* irrelevant. Which considerations people *believe* to be irrelevant is beside the point. Therefore, it does not matter whether Anna believes that the fact that a pregnancy is the result of rape is morally irrelevant. What matters is whether that fact really is morally irrelevant. If it is, the rape-abortion law is a checkerboard solution; if it is not, the rape-abortion law is not a checkerboard solution.

There is some truth to this objection. Under the "irrelevant considerations" approach, what matters is whether a consideration is in fact irrelevant, not whether it is believed to be irrelevant. However, we need to recall the structure of Dworkin's argument. He wants to show that integrity is a genuine political value by showing that (inter alia) it fits our political practices. He tries to do this by arguing that it is the fact that we value integrity that explains why we oppose checkerboard solutions. This means that, for Dworkin's purposes, what we believe *is* pertinent. If Anna's beliefs and practices show that she does not oppose checkerboard solutions on the basis that their application depends on irrelevant considerations, then this suggests that the "irrelevant considerations" approach cannot give Dworkin what he wants. Either the "irrelevant considerations" approach is mistaken (in which case, we must look elsewhere to discover what is distinctively wrong with checkerboard solutions) or else Dworkin's argumentative strategy fails (because the correct explanation of what is wrong with checkerboard solutions does not fit with the political beliefs and practices of

be a relevant consideration). However, it is doubtful whether Dworkin can accept this argument. Of his three political values, fairness and integrity do not seem to have anything to do with excuses, and he defines justice to be concerned with the right outcome, whereas excuses are relevant to blameworthiness (not to which outcome is correct). Moreover, the "irrelevant considerations" approach would still face the further objection presented towards the end of this Section (Section B).

[25] I consider this as a possible explanation of what is wrong with checkerboard solutions in Section D.   [26] This objection was suggested by Scott Hershovitz.

people like Anna, since they distinguish between checkerboard solutions and solutions based on irrelevant factors).[27]

I am inclined to regard the first of these two possibilities as correct. If *I* believed that whether a pregnancy was the result of rape is irrelevant to the permissibility of abortion, I would still distinguish between the rape-abortion and checkerboard-abortion laws on the basis suggested above—namely, that I can see how someone could come to support the rape-abortion law, but I cannot see how someone could come to support the checkerboard-abortion law.[28] This suggests that it is not just Anna's intuitions that run contrary to the "irrelevant considerations" approach. Of course, both Anna's and my intuitions may be mistaken, but some further argument is required to show that this is in fact the case.

There is another counter-intuitive feature of the "irrelevant considerations" approach. If we focus on whether a consideration is in fact irrelevant (as opposed to whether it is believed to be irrelevant), then whether the rape-abortion law is a checkerboard solution depends on the answer to a fairly complex moral question (namely, whether the fact that a pregnancy is the result of rape provides a pro tanto reason for permitting an abortion). Similarly, whether a law permitting abortions in the first two trimesters only is a checkerboard solution depends on (inter alia) whether personhood starts from the moment of conception and whether this means that the age of the foetus is morally irrelevant. However, no such difficult moral question need be resolved to determine that the checkerboard-abortion law is a checkerboard solution—it is obvious that the permissibility of abortion should not hinge on the year in which one is born. In other words, when we look at the only clear case of a checkerboard solution that we have yet found, we can determine that it is a checkerboard solution without having to evaluate the correctness of any contested moral position. This suggests that the "irrelevant considerations" approach fails to capture what is distinctive about checkerboard solutions, since it *does* require us to evaluate the correctness of contested moral positions in order to determine whether something is a checkerboard solution.

An obvious response is that the checkerboard-abortion law is a paradigm case of a checkerboard solution precisely *because* its application clearly depends on irrelevant considerations. Whether other laws amount to checkerboard solutions will be less clear, because it will be less clear whether the considerations on which their application depends are irrelevant. However, to downplay the fact that we do not have to evaluate the correctness of any contested moral position to determine that whether a woman is born in an even-numbered year is morally irrelevant is to overlook one of the most distinctive features of the checkerboard-abortion statute

---

[27] Remember that Dworkin's discussion of the rape-abortion and checkerboard-abortion laws is meant to show that the correct explanation of what is wrong with checkerboard solutions *does* fit with the political beliefs and practices of people like Anna.

[28] Though this forms only part of the basis on which checkerboard solutions are distinguished from other solutions to political problems: *see infra* Section F.

(see Section D). To provide an account of what is *distinctively* wrong with such a statute, we need to look beyond the question of whether its application depends on an irrelevant consideration.

C. Coherence in Principle

A third possibility is that checkerboard solutions are undesirable because they lack "coherence in principle". Dworkin considers coherence in principle to be a desideratum both of single rules and of sets of rules. However, the problem with checkerboard solutions cannot be that they are inconsistent in principle with other legal rules, since they are supposed to be objectionable in their own right, without any need to consider other aspects of the legal system. Indeed, Dworkin explicitly treats incoherence in principle *between* legal rules as a way of flouting integrity that is separate from that inherent in checkerboard solutions (184). Thus, I shall focus upon coherence in principle within a single rule.[29]

Dworkin claims that legal decision-making should be a matter of principle, not of political accommodation.[30] In other words, legal decisions must be defensible by reference to a coherent set of principles. However, we have seen that (on Dworkin's account) checkerboard solutions can be defended by reference to (presumably coherent) principles of fairness. Thus, if the defect in checkerboard solutions is that they are not defensible on the basis of a coherent set of principles, it must be principles of justice that we should be considering, not principles of fairness.

With this point in mind, there is reason to ascribe to Dworkin the view that checkerboard solutions are defective because they are not defensible by reference to a coherent set of principles. Certainly, Dworkin believes that integrity involves "a commitment to consistency in principle valued for its own sake" (167). Moreover, he claims that a state that adopts a checkerboard solution lacks integrity "because it must endorse principles to justify part of what it has done that it must reject to justify the rest" (184). For example, the checkerboard-abortion law endorses the principle that women should be allowed abortions at will when explaining why women born in odd-numbered years are allowed abortions, and then rejects that principle when determining whether women born in even-numbered years are allowed abortions.[31] This suggests that Dworkin believes that checkerboard solutions lack coherence in principle, because they both uphold and reject certain principles of justice.

---

[29] Though coherence in principle *between* rules is discussed briefly *infra* in Part III, Section B.

[30] R. Dworkin, Life's Dominion: An Argument about Abortion, Euthanasia, and Individual Freedom 146 (1993). Dworkin is talking here about judicial decisions, but he demands the same of legislators (at least when moral issues are at stake).

[31] This may be what Dworkin has in mind when he says that checkerboard solutions are based on a compromised theory of justice, as opposed to a compromise regarding which theory of justice to use (179).

Let us examine this explanation of what is wrong with checkerboard solutions by considering another compromise regarding abortion, a compromise that Dworkin presumably would not regard as a checkerboard solution. This compromise involves allowing any woman to have an abortion during the first two trimesters of her pregnancy, but allowing no woman to have an abortion during the third trimester. Since this solution is (I am assuming, for the sake of the example) a compromise on a matter of justice, it must represent a middle ground between two or more principles of justice (rather than being the preferred solution in its own right). For simplicity, let us imagine that these principles are that abortion should always be permissible and that abortion should never be permissible. Yet does this not mean that this solution is objectionable on precisely the same grounds as the checkerboard-abortion law, since it endorses the principle that abortion should always be permissible when explaining why women in the first two trimesters of their pregnancy are allowed abortions, and then rejects that principle when determining whether women in their third trimester are allowed abortions? Does not this solution also lack coherence in principle because it both upholds and rejects certain principles of justice?

Surely not, one might respond. The difference is that, while this solution upholds conflicting principles of justice, it does so in a certain relation determined by a further, coherent principle of justice (namely, that—since the level of development of the foetus is relevant when determining whether an abortion is permissible—abortion should be permitted in the first two trimesters, but not in the third trimester). In other words, while our two starting principles (that abortion is always permissible and that it is never permissible) support different parts of the rule, there is a further principle of justice that supports the *whole* rule.[32] The same is not true of checkerboard solutions. For example, there is no further principle of justice that supports the whole of the rule adopted in the checkerboard-abortion law, since there is no principle of justice that supports prohibiting abortion only for women born in even-numbered years.

However, is there really no principle of justice that could support the whole of the checkerboard-abortion law? On what grounds can we dismiss someone who asserts that there *is* a principle of justice that supports this law? It is not enough that any such principle would be incorrect. The set of checkerboard solutions does not include all compromises that uphold an *incorrect* principle of justice (or else the rape-abortion law may also be a checkerboard solution, if it turns out that whether a pregnant woman has been raped should not be determinative of whether she is allowed an abortion). Nor is it enough that the application of the checkerboard-abortion law would depend upon irrelevant considerations (see *supra* Section B). A more promising suggestion is that the (purported) principle

---

[32] For the sake of the example, I am assuming that we do not regard this further principle of justice as correct, but rather regard it as an acceptable compromise between the principles of justice that different people do regard as correct.

that abortions should be prohibited only for women born in even-numbered years is not *recognizable* as a principle of justice (whereas the principle that abortions should be permitted for rape victims *is* recognizable as a principle of justice, even if it turns out to be incorrect). However, this suggestion shifts the focus from whether a solution both upholds and rejects a certain principle of justice to whether it reflects anything recognizable as a principle of justice, and so is considered in Section D.

There is a further problem with the claim that checkerboard solutions are defective because they lack coherence in principle. What motivates the requirement that legal decisions be defensible on the basis of a coherent set of principles *of justice*? It might seem obvious that no law should both uphold and reject a principle of justice in the way that the checkerboard-abortion law does. Yet (on Dworkin's account) that law can be defended by reference to a coherent set of principles *of fairness*. Is this not enough to ensure coherence in principle overall? Why do we also need coherence in terms of principles of justice? Have we not seen that fairness may require us to abandon this more narrow type of coherence, in order to ensure that everyone has an appropriate level of input into political decision-making?[33] I shall delay consideration of this issue until Part III, Section C.

D. Recognizable Principles of Justice

We have seen that a notable feature of the checkerboard-abortion law is that its application depends on a morally irrelevant consideration (namely, whether the pregnant woman was born in an even-numbered year). We have also seen that this alone is insufficient to distinguish checkerboard solutions from compromises that Dworkin considers more acceptable, such as a law restricting abortions to women who become pregnant as a result of being raped. However, even someone who considers the rape issue to be irrelevant to the permissibility of abortion can acknowledge that other people treat it as a morally relevant consideration. The same is not true of the checkerboard-abortion law—no one considers whether the pregnant woman was born in an even-numbered year to be morally relevant in the context of the abortion debate.

This suggests another way of characterizing checkerboard solutions. If a compromise upholds something that we can recognize as a moral principle (whether we accept it ourselves or not), then it is not a checkerboard solution; it is only a compromise (on a matter of principle) that does not uphold anything we can recognize as a moral principle that we condemn as an internal compromise.

---

[33] J. Waldron, *The Circumstances of Integrity*, 3 LEGAL THEORY 1, 4 (1997) points out that someone might think it is more expressive of *real* integrity for a community to acknowledge that it is torn between competing views of justice than to strive to cover up this tension by preserving coherence in principle within the law.

(In this context, "moral principle" must mean a principle of justice, since Dworkin acknowledges that checkerboard solutions can be supported by recognizable principles of fairness.)

This suggestion can be illustrated by reference to the rape-abortion law. I suggested in Section B that some people may regard the fact that a pregnancy is the result of rape as morally irrelevant, in the sense that it does not provide even a pro tanto reason for having an abortion. Nevertheless, such a person could regard the rape-abortion law as upholding a principle that is recognizably moral in nature. In other words, she could view her opponents as putting forward a genuinely moral position (albeit an incorrect one). Moreover, she could distinguish on this basis between the rape-abortion law and the checkerboard-abortion law, since the latter cannot be seen to uphold a principle that is recognizably moral in nature. Whether or not she accepts that principle herself, she can recognize that the rape-abortion law upholds a moral principle, whereas the same is not true of an abortion law based on the year in which the pregnant woman is born. The latter turns on a factor that she cannot consider to be a moral consideration even in the extended sense in which she can recognize the fact that a pregnancy is the result of rape to be a moral consideration whilst regarding it as not providing even a pro tanto reason for having an abortion. This suggests that—whether or not we agree that it is irrelevant that a pregnancy is the result of rape—we can, at least in principle, distinguish checkerboard solutions from principles that may be incorrect or based on morally irrelevant considerations but that are still recognizably moral in nature.

This reading of Dworkin is not without textual support. For example, he states that some compromises do not violate integrity "because they reflect principles of justice we recognize though we do not ourselves endorse them" (436, n.8). He gives the example of a reduction in the list of capital crimes on the basis of views about moral culpability (or some other standard generally respected in the criminal law), as opposed to allowing criminals convicted of a capital offence to escape death by drawing straws.[34] Similarly, when introducing the ideal of integrity, Dworkin states that we assume "that we can recognize other people's acts as expressing a conception of justice or fairness . . . even when we do not endorse that conception ourselves" (166). We would need to make that assumption in this context only if integrity forbids only those actions that do not express a (correct or mistaken) conception of justice or fairness.

Of course, this notion of a standard that is not recognizable as a principle of justice (or of a position that cannot be regarded as a genuinely moral position) is vague. One could try to give it more analytical rigour by suggesting that the question is whether, as a conceptual matter, a consideration can be regarded as

---

[34] Viewed in isolation, this example could be regarded as supporting either the current approach or the "irrelevant considerations" approach. However, we saw in Section B that the latter represents an implausible interpretation of Dworkin's discussion of checkerboard solutions.

moral in nature.[35] The principle underlying the rape-abortion law falls within the concept of morality, since it holds that the permissibility of abortion depends on a consideration (that a pregnancy was the result of rape) that can be treated as morally relevant by someone who is not conceptually mistaken (though she may be morally mistaken). The same is not true of conclusions drawn from the fact that a pregnant woman was born in an even-numbered year.[36] However, this can advance matters only to the extent that we have a clear understanding of what constraints are imposed by the concept of morality (or, in other words, of what can count as a *moral* reason, consideration or principle). This is itself a controversial issue.[37]

Be that as it may, there are other problems with this interpretation of Dworkin's position. Why must political compromises be based on recognizable principles *of justice*? We have seen that checkerboard solutions may be based on recognizable principles of fairness (giving everyone an input into the content of the law that is proportionate to the support they can muster within society), and why is this not enough to make a compromise recognizably moral in nature? Why should we privilege justice over fairness in the way that (this interpretation of) Dworkin requires?

One might seek to be conciliatory at this point, and suggest that whether a political compromise reflects recognizable principles of justice is one relevant consideration, though whether it reflects recognizable principles of fairness is also relevant. However, Dworkin must show more than that the former is a relevant consideration, since he claims that integrity (on this interpretation, the requirement that laws reflect recognizable principles of justice) should "characteristically" prevail over other values. He therefore needs to show that our pursuit

[35] On this view, for something to be a "recognizable principle of justice", it is not enough that one *believes* that it is a principle of justice. Instead, what counts is whether it in fact satisfies the conceptual requirements for being a principle of justice.

[36] The difference between the "irrelevant considerations" approach and the present approach could then be viewed as follows. The "irrelevant considerations" approach requires us to identify the correct *conception* of justice, since it asks whether a factor is morally relevant. Determining whether a factor is morally relevant requires us to determine what pro tanto moral reasons exist, which depends upon which conception of justice is correct. The present approach, on the other hand, requires us to consider only the *concept* of justice, since it asks whether a principle satisfies the conceptual constraints on something being a moral principle (or, more specifically, a principle of justice). It does not matter whether that principle is valid under the correct conception of justice, provided it falls within the concept of justice. *See* R. Dworkin, Taking Rights Seriously 134–135 (1977) regarding the distinction Dworkin draws between concepts and conceptions.

[37] *E.g.*, R. Hare, Sorting out Ethics (1997) claims that a strong universalizability condition is part of the very concept of morality, whereas J. Raz, Value, Respect, and Attachment 58–59 (2001) suggests that any such condition is the result of substantive moral reasoning. This means that—if the present approach is correct—a statute permitting abortion only for white women is a checkerboard solution on the former view, but not on the latter. However, presumably both views would regard the checkerboard-abortion law, along with a law that allowed abortions only for women who are more than 160 cm tall, as checkerboard solutions, since substantive moral reasoning is not needed to recognize that these factors are morally irrelevant (in the way that it is arguably needed to recognize that racial characteristics are morally irrelevant).

of fairness should, in most cases, be limited by a requirement that political decisions reflect recognizable principles of justice.

Dworkin might respond that he addresses these issues when discussing the *justification* of integrity. In discussing checkerboard solutions, he is concerned only with whether integrity fits our political practices, and so he cannot be expected to have justified that ideal at this stage. I shall consider his attempt to justify the ideal of integrity in Part III. However, even allowing that Dworkin's discussion of checkerboard solutions is meant to show only that the ideal of integrity *fits* our political practices, are those practices really best explained on the basis that we believe that compromises must reflect recognizable principles of justice? Is it really *this* that underlies our attitude towards checkerboard solutions? If not, on this interpretation the ideal of integrity cannot satisfy even the dimension of fit.

In fact, the present suggestion (that checkerboard solutions are unacceptable because they do not reflect recognizable principles of justice) does *not* fit well with the view (ascribed to us by Dworkin) that there is something distinctively wrong with checkerboard solutions. Even if the present suggestion captures some of what is wrong with checkerboard solutions, it does not expose all that is wrong with such solutions and cannot explain why we consider them to be *distinctively* flawed. To see this, imagine that a legislature passed a law requiring everybody to worship rocks (by spending a certain amount of time each week praying in front of a rock, etc). No recognizable principle of justice (I assume) could justify requiring people to worship rocks. We can imagine principles that purport to justify such a requirement (for example "rocks are sacred and deserving of supplication"),[38] but such principles would not be principles *of justice*, because they would not be concerned with achieving a morally defensible outcome (in any recognizable sense of "morally defensible").[39] Yet this law does not seem to be a checkerboard solution. It lacks one of the distinctive features of the checkerboard-abortion law, which permits some people to do X but prohibits others from doing so. The rock-worshipping statute applies to everyone, without exception, rather than treating different people differently in a way that is unjust. If this is right, the fact that a law is not based on a recognizable principle of justice cannot be a sufficient condition for it to be a checkerboard solution, since the rock-worshipping law satisfies this requirement and yet is not an internal compromise. (Indeed, some sort of differential treatment seems required by the very use of the word "checkerboard", with its connotation of dividing an area into different regions.)

Dworkin might respond that the rock-worshipping law is not a checkerboard solution because it is not supported by considerations of fairness (it is not a

---

[38] This example was suggested by Scott Hershovitz.

[39] Dworkin claims that justice is concerned with achieving morally defensible outcomes. If one instead views justice as concerned with the righting of wrongs and/or the distribution of resources, it becomes even clearer that the principle that rocks are sacred and deserving of supplication cannot be regarded as a principle of justice.

compromise between different views designed to give each side a proportionate share of their desired outcome). However, it is not clear that a law must be supported by considerations of fairness in order to be a checkerboard solution. The checkerboard-abortion law would presumably remain a checkerboard statute even if it was unsupported by any consideration of fairness (for example, because everyone agreed that abortion should always be permitted), but was instead introduced on a whim. Yet, even if this *is* a requirement for a law to be a checkerboard solution, we can imagine it being satisfied with regard to the rock-worshipping law. Imagine that society is divided about the proper relationship between Church and State. Some people desire a complete separation between the two institutions, while others want Christianity entrenched as the state religion, others desire the same of Islam, etc. The rock-worshipping law might be a (bizarre) solution to this disagreement—it gives anti-separatists some of what they want (by entrenching a religion), but also gives pro-separatists some of what they want (by refusing to entrench any religion actually endorsed within the community). Still, the rock-worshipping law differs in an important respect from the checkerboard-abortion law, in that it treats everybody according to the same principle, without exception.[40]

E. Treating People Equally

We have just seen that another noteworthy feature of checkerboard solutions is that they treat people differently in a way that cannot be justified by reference to a correct principle of justice. That is, they confer a right or benefit on one group and deny it to another group without being able to justify this differential treatment. For example, the checkerboard-abortion law denies an abortion to some women but permits it for others, and does not do so in a way that can be justified by reference to a correct principle of justice. Similarly, when Dworkin states that his "model of principle" (which is based on integrity) "commands that no one be left out . . . that no one may be sacrificed, like wounded left on the battlefield, to the crusade for justice overall" (213), the suggestion is that people should not be treated unequally even when this results in more justice overall.[41] Where the choice is between a checkerboard solution and a completely unjust solution, adopting the checkerboard solution may ensure that at least some people get treated according to just principles, but will treat people unequally (by granting benefits to some people but not to others, where this differential treatment cannot

---

[40] It also differs, in the same way, from Dworkin's other example of a checkerboard statute mentioned in Part I. Legislation that imposes no-fault liability upon car, but not washing machine, manufacturers treats victims of defective products differently depending on the sort of product that injured them.

[41] Admittedly, there is some controversy about how this metaphor should be interpreted. For a somewhat different interpretation, *see* Waldron, *supra* note 33, 19–21.

be justified by any correct principle of justice) and so should be rejected for that reason.[42]

Further support for this interpretation can be gleaned from Dworkin's statement, already noted, that checkerboard solutions involve a single principle, which is affirmed for one group and denied for another, and it is this which we denounce (436, n.7). He later states explicitly that any defect in checkerboard solutions "must lie in their distinctive feature, that they treat people differently when no principle can justify the distinction" (180).

In addition to fitting well with much of what Dworkin says about checkerboard solutions, this interpretation helps explain why the checkerboard-abortion statute is an internal compromise (because it treats people differently without any basis in justice) but the rock-worshipping law discussed in Section D is not (because it treats everyone the same). It may also help to explain why checkerboard solutions are undesirable despite being supported by considerations of fairness. It could be argued that fairness alone cannot justify treating people differently where this is unsupported by any correct principle of justice. On this view, whatever the arguments in favour of giving people equal input into their community's law-making, this cannot justify the difference in treatment inherent in checkerboard solutions. This line of thought is pursued in Part III.

However, the fact that checkerboard solutions uphold rights or benefits for some people but not others is insufficient to distinguish them from many other legal decisions. For example, the rape-abortion law permits victims of rape to have an abortion but precludes other women from having one, and so treats these two groups differently. This by itself is insufficient to render the rape-abortion law problematic, let alone to turn it into a checkerboard solution. Even more clear-cut would be a constitutional provision that confers a right to freedom of association on everyone except for criminals who are imprisoned pursuant to constitutionally valid laws. Such a provision clearly upholds a right for some people that it denies to others, yet is not a checkerboard solution.

Perhaps the distinctive feature of checkerboard solutions resides in the fact that the differential treatment they require is not justified by correct principles of justice. However, this borders on saying that a checkerboard solution is a *wrong* solution (at least as seen from the viewpoint of justice), since any law that unjustly differentiated between people would be a checkerboard solution. This would fail adequately to distinguish checkerboard solutions from any other decision that produces an unjust outcome (including the rape-abortion law, if whether a pregnant woman has been raped should not be determinative of whether abortion is permissible). There is supposed to be something *especially* wrong about checkerboard solutions, which distinguishes them from decisions that are

---

[42] This has led some people to suggest that "integrity" is simply Dworkin's name for a type of equality—namely, the equality manifested by applying the same legal principles to X that one has applied to Y: *e.g.* L. Alexander & K. Kress, *Against Legal Principles*, 82 Iowa L. Rev. 739, 755 (1997).

wrong merely because they draw distinctions that are based on incorrect principles of justice.

One alternative[43] is to ask whether the differential treatment required by a law could be justified by reference to anything *recognizable as* a principle of justice, rather than asking whether it can be justified by reference to a correct principle of justice. This would combine the present interpretation (with its focus on differential treatment) with the interpretation considered in Section D (which concentrated on whether the decision could be justified by reference to a recognizable principle of justice). As it suggests that there is more than one thing wrong with checkerboard solutions, I shall consider this possibility separately in the next section.

F. A Multitude of Sins?

So far, I have proceeded on the assumption that there is only one thing wrong with checkerboard solutions, and have sought to isolate that single flaw. Having failed to do so, I must now consider whether the reason that we reject internal compromises is because they possess *several* flaws. I shall pursue only what I consider to be the most promising line of thought in this regard—that a checkerboard solution both treats people differently in a way that is unjust and cannot be justified by reference to anything recognizable as a principle of justice.

The first advantage of this suggestion is that it recognizes that the fact that a law unjustifiably upholds a right or benefit for some people but not others is a necessary, but not sufficient, condition for something to be a checkerboard solution. As a result, this interpretation provides a basis for distinguishing between the checkerboard-abortion and rape-abortion laws. Both treat people differently, but the latter does so on the basis of a recognizable (though perhaps incorrect) principle of justice whereas the former does not. Secondly, this suggestion enables us to differentiate checkerboard solutions from laws (such as the rock-worshipping statute discussed in Section D) that are not based on recognizable principles of justice but do not treat people differently, since we have now built into our definition of checkerboard solutions a requirement of differential treatment.

Again, there is some textual support for this interpretation. Dworkin contrasts the rape-abortion statute with the checkerboard-abortion statute in the following terms:

You [i.e. an opponent of abortion] see the first of these statutes as a solution that gives effect to two recognizable principles of justice, ordered in a certain way, even though you reject one of the principles. You cannot treat the second that way; it simply affirms for some people a principle it denies to others. (183, footnote omitted)

[43] Another alternative sometimes hinted at in LAW's EMPIRE is that we should ask whether the differential treatment can be justified by any principle of justice that is consistent with the principles underlying other legal decisions. However, we saw in Section C that checkerboard solutions are meant to be problematic in their own right, not only when considered alongside other legal rules.

We see here both limbs of the current suggestion. While Dworkin does not explicitly state that both are necessary, the quotation is meant to represent the view of someone who shares Dworkin's intuitions regarding checkerboard solutions.

I believe this to be the most promising interpretation of Dworkin's discussion of checkerboard solutions. Not only does it bring together (in a coherent fashion) many of Dworkin's comments about checkerboard solutions, but it also suggests that there is something *distinctively* wrong with internal compromises (something that previous interpretations of Dworkin's position were unable to do). Moreover, it can explain our intuitive dislike of checkerboard solutions, since treating people differently in a way that cannot be defended by anything recognizable as a principle of justice appears intuitively objectionable.

III. Justifying Integrity

After considering several interpretations of Dworkin's views about checkerboard solutions, I concluded that the best interpretation is that Dworkin claims that there are two things wrong with internal compromise—it treats different people differently in a way that is unjust, and it cannot be supported by reference to anything recognizable as a principle of justice. Henceforth, I shall refer to this as the "favoured interpretation." While it is, I think, the best interpretation of Dworkin's position, it is not without its difficulties, and I shall consider two of these difficulties in Section C. First, however, I want to explore whether, if Dworkin *has* provided an acceptable account of checkerboard solutions, this account can support the various claims that he bases upon it. Thus, in Sections A and B, I shall assume that the favoured interpretation provides a satisfactory account of checkerboard solutions, and shall consider what implications that account has for the rest of Dworkin's theory of law.

A. Should Integrity Characteristically Trump Justice?

In assuming that the favoured interpretation provides a satisfactory account of checkerboard solutions, I am assuming that it explains why internal compromise is undesirable. In other words, it explains why there is always at least a pro tanto reason to reject a checkerboard solution. However, Dworkin does not claim merely that there is always a pro tanto reason to avoid internal compromises. He also claims that integrity (on the favoured interpretation, the requirement that political decisions concerning matters of principle must not treat people differently in a way that cannot be supported by any recognizable principle of justice) should characteristically trump justice in cases where these two values conflict. In particular, in cases where justice would be promoted by adopting a checkerboard solution, the pro tanto reason to reject such solutions should characteristically prevail when reaching an all-things-considered judgment about what to do. In this section, I consider whether Dworkin succeeds in establishing the truth of this further claim.

Dworkin's discussion of checkerboard solutions is meant to show only that the ideal of integrity *fits* with our political beliefs and practices (because it explains why we oppose internal compromises). His argument that integrity is indeed valuable (and should characteristically trump justice in cases of conflict) comes later in *Law's Empire*. Let us now consider that argument.

Dworkin claims that integrity has a number of benefits, but he concentrates primarily on its implications for political obligation. His argument that integrity is necessary for political obligations to arise is lengthy and subtle, and I can provide only a thumbnail sketch here.[44] Dworkin claims that political obligations are a type of "associative obligation." In other words, they are not voluntarily incurred, but rather arise simply through one's membership of a political community. However, the political community must satisfy certain criteria if political obligations are to arise. In particular, the community must display pervasive and equal concern for all its members. Dworkin claims that this requirement can be satisfied only if our political obligations are not exhausted by explicit rules. If our obligations *were* exhausted by explicit rules, then our political system could not display *pervasive* concern, because those rules would inevitably contain gaps where we would be left to our own devices. (In particular, when deciding what *new* rules to introduce, we would be free to act in our own self-interest, without concern for other people.) However, non-explicit obligations can be inferred from the explicit rules only if those rules are coherent.[45] Moreover, the coherence between the society's rules must extend to the principles underlying those rules, since the non-explicit obligations will be drawn largely from those principles. Therefore, coherence in principle (which Dworkin often equates with integrity) is a necessary condition of political obligation.

In Section C, I shall question the extent to which this explanation of why integrity is valuable provides support for the favoured interpretation. However, for now it is important to note that there is at least one way in which they seem to fit together nicely. The favoured interpretation claims that there are two principles underlying our opposition to checkerboard solutions—the principle that we should not treat people differently in a way that is unjust, and the principle that we should not treat people in a way that cannot be supported by any recognizable principle of justice. Dworkin's account of political obligations appears to support

---

[44] I draw particularly on Alexander & Kress, *supra* note 42, at 778 in offering this reconstruction of an argument that occupies Dworkin for nearly 30 pages in Law's Empire (195–224). I focus only on those aspects of the argument that are relevant to my present concerns.

[45] More than mere consistency is required. *E.g.*, one could not infer (a pervasive set of) non-explicit obligations from a set of three legal rules that bore no relationship to each other.

the former principle. A society that does not respect this principle does not display equal concern for all its members and so does not merit everyone's allegiance. Even if there are principles of fairness that support the differential treatment, those who lose out under the checkerboard solution are being sacrificed to give people an equal share of political influence, and it might be difficult to explain to them why they should give their allegiance to such a society.

This, in turn, suggests that Dworkin is correct in claiming that integrity should characteristically trump justice when these two values conflict. For political obligations to arise, it is not necessary that political decisions always be perfectly just, but it is necessary that such decisions display equal concern for all members of the community, and this would appear to rule out checkerboard solutions (which necessarily treat people differently in a way that is unsupported by any recognizable principle of justice, and so fail to show equal concern for all members of the community). Moreover, if we allowed justice to trump integrity on a regular basis, we would no longer be able to infer non-explicit principles from the explicit rules of our community (since those rules would lack the necessary coherence in principle). This would mean that not only would the law have ceased to show equal concern, but it would also have ceased to show pervasive concern.

There is, however, a well-known objection to this line of reasoning. Dworkin's critics often argue that, where a just outcome cannot be obtained for everyone, it is better to obtain that outcome for as many people as possible, even if this reduces the coherence of the law and does not provide equal treatment for those who are left out. For example, Raz suggests that "we accept the nearest approximation to morally sound solutions that we can obtain, even though by doing so we may reduce the coherence of the law."[46] If this is right, we should be more willing to accept checkerboard solutions (and other breaches of integrity) than Dworkin suggests, where this is necessary to reduce injustice. We might still recognize a pro tanto reason to avoid checkerboard solutions, but we would not regard that reason as characteristically trumping considerations of justice.

However, this objection does not really engage with Dworkin's claim that we must not allow justice *characteristically* to trump integrity, or else our community would cease to express equal and pervasive concern for all its members, and our case for the existence of political obligations would collapse. To determine which side in this debate is correct, it appears that we must weigh up the value of doing justice to as many people as possible against the value of equal and pervasive concern. However, rather than engaging in the difficult task of weighing up those values, I shall explore a different line of thought. I shall argue that the value of equal and pervasive concern does not unequivocally support Dworkin's position, and

---

[46] RAZ, *supra* note 4, at 312–313. The context makes it clear that Raz endorses the view he is ascribing to us. Similarly, Wasserstrom, *supra* note 17, at 267 asserts that, if he were an egalitarian in a libertarian society, he would support legislation that made the community's law more egalitarian, even if this meant that the law was less coherent overall.

that he has therefore failed to establish that integrity should characteristically trump justice when these two values conflict.

While checkerboard solutions treat people differently in a way that we have a pro tanto reason to avoid, so may a refusal to adopt checkerboard solutions. Refraining from adopting checkerboard solutions may disadvantage those people whose moral convictions are not dominant within the community, because their moral position may not be reflected in the law at all.[47] Dworkin seems committed to regarding this as a form of disadvantage, since he claims that the value of fairness supports checkerboard solutions because they ensure that one's moral position is reflected in the law to the extent that one has support within the electorate.[48] This suggests that, whatever one does, one may end up treating people differently in a way that is undesirable. If one upholds a checkerboard solution, one will affirm a right or benefit for some people that one denies (without justification) for others. However, if one refuses to adopt checkerboard solutions, one may give weight to some people's political views but not others' (for example, if law-makers always side with the majority within society, in order to preserve coherence in principle).[49] If we cannot avoid undesirable forms of differential treatment no matter what we do, should we not embrace the form of differential treatment that minimizes instances of injustice (which, we have seen, would involve adopting checkerboard solutions in circumstances in which Dworkin would oppose their adoption)?[50]

(Admittedly, checkerboard solutions not only treat people differently, but do so by reference to something that is not recognizable as a principle of justice. However, if this is the basis on which Dworkin believes that integrity should characteristically prevail over justice, he must explain why a political compromise is acceptable only if it reflects recognizable principles of justice. I consider this issue in Section C.)

I am not claiming that integrity is unimportant. Rather, my point is that integrity safeguards only one aspect of equal treatment, and so—while always a relevant consideration—it may not be as important as Dworkin claims. We have seen that checkerboard solutions can promote equal treatment as well as undermining it. I shall now argue that the sort of community that Dworkin believes is necessary to give rise to political obligations has an equally equivocal relationship to the requirement of equal treatment.

---

[47] Wasserstrom, *supra* note 17, at 267–268.

[48] If one has a different conception of fairness from Dworkin's, the failure of the law to reflect my considered views may not be unfair (especially if I was given an opportunity to participate in the process by which the law was chosen and/or if my views are mistaken). However, the point made in the text poses a problem for Dworkin, given his conception of fairness.

[49] The majority on one issue may be constituted differently from the majority on another issue, but there may be some people who are rarely (if ever) in the majority.

[50] Alternatively, one could embrace whichever form of differential treatment minimizes unfairness, but this would involve accepting checkerboard solutions whenever they produced the fairest distribution of political influence.

To see this, consider a criticism of Dworkin offered by Alexander & Kress.[51] They claim that a reduction in integrity may actually *increase* the extent to which the law displays equal concern for all members of the community. They ask us to imagine a society whose employment laws encourage nepotism. A statute is then passed banning nepotism in private industry (but not in the public sector, because there is insufficient political support for this change).[52] This is a checkerboard solution, because nepotism is still encouraged in the public sector, but is no longer permitted in the private sector, and (we are assuming) there is no recognizable principle of justice that could support the differential treatment involved in permitting nepotism in the public sector but not the private sector. This statute has reduced the integrity of the law, but Alexander & Kress suggest that it has increased the extent to which the law displays equal concern for members of the community, by reducing nepotism (which, by its very nature, is inconsistent with equal concern).

They anticipate the objection that this checkerboard solution has actually made things worse, because there is no longer a coherent set of principles that can be inferred from the existing rules, depriving us of any basis on which to decide novel cases (for example, whether nepotism is permitted by trustees with a discretionary power to distribute trust funds). However, they respond, those who approve of the new statute can at least say that it is based on a new and improved conception of the concern that we owe to each other, a conception with implications for novel cases.[53] This is true, but that conception will not be pervasive—it will be recognized with regard to private industry employment, but not with regard to the public sector. This weakens the case for political obligation, because society is divided into two camps (those who are treated according to correct principles of justice and those who are not) in a way that cannot be justified by reference to any recognizable principle of justice.

This suggests a more complicated picture than either Dworkin or Alexander & Kress acknowledge. In one way, the checkerboard solution reduces the extent to which people are treated differently, by eliminating nepotism in private industry (and so ensuring that all applicants for a job in private industry are treated equally). In another way, the checkerboard solution exacerbates the preferential treatment that exists within society, by treating job applicants in private industry differently from job applicants in the public sector (without there being any recognizable principle of justice that could justify this differential treatment). No doubt, upholding integrity will sometimes result in an overall improvement in terms of reducing (unjustifiable) differential treatment, and so improve the case

---

[51] Alexander & Kress, *supra* note 42, at 779–780. I have changed their example slightly, to avoid a complication they themselves note.

[52] If it strikes one as implausible that such a law could ever be passed, imagine that there were a number of high-profile corporate collapses blamed on the practice of nepotism in private industry, whereas powerful lobby groups supported nepotism in the public sector.

[53] Alexander & Kress, *supra* note 42, at 780.

for political obligation. However, Dworkin must show that this is *characteristically* the case. Presumably, this will depend on a number of contingent facts about the particular legal system being considered, and Dworkin does not even begin to show that it is true of the particular legal systems he has in mind.[54]

If I am right, Dworkin has failed to show that the value of integrity deserves the place of special prominence that he reserves for it. In particular, he has not given us sufficient reason to believe that integrity should characteristically prevail over justice when these two values conflict. This has several significant implications for his broader legal and political theory, of which I shall briefly mention two. First, it threatens to undermine his directions to both legislators and judges. Dworkin claims that legislators should, when making new law, strive to keep the law coherent in principle. He also claims that judges should, when identifying and enforcing the law, seek to view the law as being coherent in principle (167). However, these directions presuppose the pre-eminence of integrity. Coherence in principle should be the primary goal of legislators and judges only if integrity should characteristically trump justice. The fact that Dworkin has failed to establish that integrity should characteristically prevail means that the correctness of his direction to legislators and judges is called into question.

Secondly, Dworkin's failure to show that integrity should characteristically prevail over justice means that his attempt to establish the existence of political obligations is undermined. Dworkin argues that integrity must be valuable because it is necessary for political obligations to arise. However, we can reverse this line of reasoning and argue that—if integrity is not as valuable as Dworkin claims—he has failed to demonstrate the existence of political obligations. Unless integrity should characteristically prevail over justice, we lack sufficient reason to achieve the level of coherence among (and within) explicit legal rules that is required for us to be able to infer non-explicit legal principles to fill in gaps in those rules. Yet, on Dworkin's argument, such coherence is required in order for political obligations to arise. Therefore, Dworkin's failure to show that integrity should characteristically prevail over justice means that he has failed to show that we should achieve the level of coherence among (and within) explicit legal rules that he claims is necessary to give rise to political obligations.

B. How Well Does Integrity Fit Our Political Practices?

Apart from raising concerns about whether Dworkin is right in claiming that integrity should characteristically prevail over other values, my discussion of what is wrong with checkerboard solutions also reveals another problem for

---

[54] Earlier in this section, we saw another way in which checkerboard solutions promote equal concern—they give everybody some input into the content of political decisions. This, too, would have to be weighed against the way in which checkerboard solutions undermine equal concern.

Dworkin's broader theory. That discussion has highlighted that there is not one, but several, principles of integrity. There are at least two factors underlying our attitude towards checkerboard solutions—a concern about differential treatment, and a concern that legal decisions should reflect recognizable principles of justice. If Dworkin is correct in claiming that it is integrity that explains our attitude towards internal compromises, then both of these concerns must reflect aspects of integrity. This in itself poses no problem for Dworkin. There are numerous (correct) principles of justice, and there is no reason why there cannot be several (correct) principles of integrity as well. However, in addition to the two principles that underlie our attitude towards checkerboard solutions, there is at least one more principle of integrity that has little to do with checkerboard solutions. This is the principle that requires coherence between the legal principles that underlie and justify different legal rules, so that they form a single, comprehensive vision of justice. We saw that Dworkin treats this principle as part of the ideal of integrity, and that he recognizes that violation of this principle poses a threat to integrity that is distinct from the threat posed by checkerboard solutions.[55] Indeed, Kress suggests that it is this principle that Dworkin most often refers to when discussing the ideal of integrity.[56] The problem is that, in seeking to show that the ideal of integrity fits with our political practices, Dworkin relies almost exclusively upon his discussion of checkerboard solutions, and this principle of integrity is not relevant to that discussion. Therefore, even if (via his discussion of checkerboard solutions) he has established that the first two principles of integrity fit with our political practices, he has not shown that this third principle of integrity does so.

Dworkin does suggest that, while our legal system often breaches this principle, we regard this as a defect (184). However, more needs to be said to show that a central principle of integrity satisfies one of only two conditions that Dworkin imposes upon its acceptability (namely, the dimension of fit),[57] especially as he concedes that the evidence on this point is equivocal (since our legal system often breaches this principle). This means that Dworkin's defence of integrity is incomplete. He may have shown that *some* principles of integrity fit our political practices, but he has not shown that all do. Nor can he assume that, because some principles of integrity satisfy that requirement, the rest must, too. It is unlikely that *every* correct principle of justice fits our political practices, and there is no reason to assume at the outset that integrity differs in this respect.

[55] Part II, Section C.

[56] K. Kress, *Coherence and Formalism*, 16 HARV. J.L. & PUB. POL'Y 639, 653 (1993). It is also this principle that underlies Dworkin's discussion of the examples at (165).

[57] Even if we regard fit as one aspect of justification (which seems to be Dworkin's preferred position: M. Greenberg, *How Facts Make Law*, 10 LEGAL THEORY 157, 196–197, n.47 (2004)), the failure to show that the third principle of integrity fits our political practices represents a failure to show that it satisfies an important aspect of justification. Dworkin needs either to rectify this failure or else to show that this principle of integrity satisfies other aspects of justification which make up for any lack of fit.

This would not be such a problem for Dworkin if this particular principle of integrity did not play such an important role in his jurisprudential theory. Once we expand our focus beyond checkerboard solutions, Dworkin's legal theory is at least as much concerned with coherence in principle between laws as it is with coherence in principle within laws. The fact that Dworkin fails adequately to explain why we should accept this third principle of integrity should therefore be of substantial concern to him.

Dworkin might seek to avoid this problem by arguing that there is in fact only one principle of integrity (albeit one that can be violated in different ways—for example, via checkerboard solutions or via a lack of coherence between laws). He does claim that "the only basis we might have for opposing checkerboard compromises . . . is the idea of integrity, that the community must respect principles necessary to justify one part of the law in other parts as well" (210). The requirement that the community respect principles necessary to justify one part of the law in other parts as well provides the basis of Dworkin's discussion of coherence in principle between laws, and he appears to be suggesting here that it also provides the basis for opposing checkerboard solutions. However, this suggestion is puzzling. When seeking to achieve integrity between laws, we are seeking to ensure that different laws cohere with each other (and that the principles underlying those laws also cohere with each other). When seeking to eradicate checkerboard solutions, on the other hand, we are seeking to eliminate individual laws that treat different people differently in a way that cannot be supported by any recognizable principle of justice. That there are two distinct sets of principles in play here (one requiring coherence between legal rules and principles, the other requiring that an individual law not discriminate between people in a way that cannot be supported by any recognizable principle of justice) seems obvious. It is further supported by the argument in Part II, Section C that we cannot explain what is wrong with checkerboard solutions on the basis that they both uphold and reject certain principles of justice (something that may be said of *a body of laws* that contains inconsistent legal rules or principles).

C. How Plausible is the Favoured Interpretation?

At the start of this Part, I suggested that—despite being the best interpretation of Dworkin's discussion on offer—the favoured interpretation is not unproblematic. In this section, I shall briefly discuss two difficulties with that interpretation. First, the problem of distinguishing between something that is recognizable as a principle of justice and something that is not remains. We saw in Part II, Section D that it is not clear what counts as a "recognizable principle of justice." I offered a suggestion as to how this phrase could be rendered more precise (in terms of which considerations or reasons satisfy the conceptual constraints on being a *moral* consideration or reason), but I also pointed out that what these conceptual constraints are is disputed. To give more content to the notion of a "recognizable principle of justice," Dworkin would need to take sides in these disputes.

However, in the rest of this section I wish to focus on the *second* problem with the favoured interpretation. Just as Dworkin's argument that integrity fits with our political practices does not apply to the principle of integrity requiring coherence between legal rules and principles (see Section B), his argument that integrity is valuable does not vindicate the principles of integrity that explain what is distinctively wrong with checkerboard solutions. The argument that integrity is valuable because it is necessary to give rise to political obligations may show that coherence between legal rules and principles is important (since this enables us to infer further legal principles, and hence to display pervasive concern for members of the community). However, it does not show that it is important to avoid differential treatment that is unsupported by any recognizable principle of justice.

Admittedly, one of the two principles of integrity violated by checkerboard solutions seems to fit well with Dworkin's argument for political obligations. As mentioned in Section A, treating people differently without adequate justification appears to violate the requirement that the law display equal concern for all members of the community. (Though it could be argued that one may display equal concern even when unjustly treating people differently, if one is sincerely trying to do the right thing by everyone.) However, it is not clear how Dworkin's discussion of political obligations is meant to show that there is something distinctively wrong with differential treatment that is not supported by *recognizable* principles of justice. In other words, it is not clear how Dworkin's attempt to show that integrity is valuable supports the principle of integrity requiring that laws reflect recognizable principles of justice.

Moreover, it is not obvious how one could go about supporting that principle. It *is* obvious why we should want our political decisions to be supported by *correct* principles of justice, but checkerboard solutions are not alone in failing to satisfy this requirement. The distinctive flaw of internal compromises is that the differential treatment that they require is not supported by *recognizable* principles of justice, but why is it so important that our political decisions be supported by such principles?

Dworkin might respond that our attitude towards checkerboard solutions shows that we accept that it is important that our political decisions be supported by recognizable principles of justice. If he is right in claiming that we oppose checkerboard solutions, and that the distinctive feature of such solutions is that they treat people differently in a way that cannot be supported by recognizable principles of justice, does this not show that we oppose political decisions that lack such support? The answer to this question might well be yes, but this does not show that we are *right* to oppose political decisions of this type (or that we are right to regard them as *distinctively* flawed)? To be confident that we *are* right to do so, we need an argument that explains why political decisions must be supported by recognizable principles of justice.

It may be that we cannot display equal concern for all members of our community if we adopt principles that are not *recognizable* as expressing equal concern. In a society marked by moral disagreement, we cannot necessarily expect society to adopt *our* conception of equal concern, but we can at least expect it to adopt a *recognizable* conception. So long as the community adopts a recognizable conception of equal concern, we can feel that we are part of a genuine community, even if we would prefer that it adopt a different conception.[58] However, it is not the case that only recognizable principles of justice reflect a recognizable conception of equal concern. In particular, checkerboard solutions are (at least in some cases) based on principles *of fairness* that are recognizable as expressing equal concern (since they are designed to produce an equal distribution of political influence). It is unclear why this is not enough—why, that is, we need principles *of justice* that we can recognize as expressing equal concern. Provided each side champions recognizable principles of justice,[59] why should it matter if a recognizable principle of fairness requires us to compromise those principles of justice in a way that does not reflect any further, recognizable principle of justice?

It could be argued that there is some sort of category error in resolving a matter of principle (dealing with rights or other moral issues) by reference to something that is not recognizable as a principle of justice. Dworkin defines justice as being concerned with achieving morally defensible outcomes, and so it is principles of justice that must be used to resolve matters of principle. Using something that is not recognizable as a principle of justice reveals a misunderstanding as to the type of solution that is required for such a problem and/or a conceptual misunderstanding of what counts as a principle of justice.

However, this explanation is of little assistance to Dworkin. The requirement that laws should reflect recognizable principles of justice is meant to be a principle of integrity, where integrity is meant to be a political value distinct from justice and fairness. Avoiding category errors or conceptual misunderstandings, on the other hand, would not seem to amount to a political value at all. (The other principle of integrity relevant to checkerboard solutions, on the other hand, does represent a political value, since it prohibits unjust differential treatment.) Moreover, even if the importance of avoiding category errors or conceptual misunderstandings *does* reflect a distinct political value of integrity, it is not clear that such a value should characteristically trump competing considerations of justice or fairness. Obviously, it is desirable to avoid category errors and conceptual misunderstandings, but it is *not* obvious that this is characteristically more important than avoiding or minimizing instances of injustice or unfairness. Therefore, this explanation does not seem well suited to supporting Dworkin's

---

[58] A similar argument is suggested by J. Waldron, *The Rule of Law in Contemporary Liberal Theory*, 2 Ratio Juris 79, 83–84 (1989).

[59] This proviso is necessary so that we can know that they are putting forward views *about justice* (since principles of fairness are meant to govern disagreements *about justice*).

claim that checkerboard solutions are characteristically undesirable all things considered.

To summarize, while the favoured interpretation provides the best account available to Dworkin of what is wrong with checkerboard solutions, it leaves at least two questions unanswered. First, it is not clear what counts as a "recognizable principle of justice." Secondly, it is somewhat mysterious why we should put so much weight on the requirement that differential treatment be supported by a recognizable principle of justice. Until these questions can be answered, there will continue to be nagging doubts that—while there may well be reasons to oppose checkerboard solutions—we cannot elucidate those reasons in the way that Dworkin seeks to, by reference to the value of integrity.[60]

IV. Conclusion

In his discussion of checkerboard solutions, Dworkin identifies (what at least appears to be) a distinctive phenomenon, a phenomenon of which we intuitively disapprove. This chapter has sought to provide an account of what is wrong with checkerboard solutions that is both persuasive in its own right and is consistent with Dworkin's discussion. On the most promising such account, there are two things wrong with checkerboard solutions—they treat people differently in a way that is unjust, and they cannot be supported by reference to any recognizable principle of justice. However, we have also seen that—even on this interpretation—problems remain for anyone seeking to defend Dworkin's broader claims about integrity, the law and political obligations. Dworkin's discussion of checkerboard solutions may establish that there is a distinctive political virtue (integrity) that provides a pro tanto reason to oppose internal compromise, but it does not establish that this pro tanto reason should characteristically prevail over countervailing reasons provided by the values of justice or fairness. In other words, Dworkin may have succeeded in showing that checkerboard solutions are always undesirable, but he has not ruled out the possibility that often they may be the best we can hope for. He therefore has not established that integrity merits the pre-eminent position that he ascribes to it. This, in turn, calls into question his directions to legislators and judges and his account of political obligations. Secondly, his discussion of checkerboard solutions may show that some principles of integrity fit with our political practices and beliefs, but it does not show that all principles of integrity do so. In particular, his discussion of checkerboard solutions does not show that the requirement of coherence in principle *between* laws satisfies the dimension of fit.

---

[60] *See supra* note 17, which points out that a number of commentators have tried to explain our opposition to checkerboard solutions by reference to the values of justice or fairness, not integrity.

As a result, Dworkin is faced with a dilemma. The favoured interpretation of his discussion of checkerboard solutions does not provide the support he needs for some of his further claims about legal and political theory. Therefore, he must either abandon those further claims or find a new way of arguing for them (possibly by suggesting an alternative to the various interpretations of his discussion of checkerboard solutions suggested in this chapter). He cannot both embrace the favoured interpretation of his discussion of checkerboard solutions and treat that discussion as supporting his further claims about law and politics.

On the other hand, someone who does not share Dworkin's further commitments concerning legal and political theory can accept the favoured interpretation without worrying about the above concerns. On this view, checkerboard solutions are always flawed, but in a range of cases they may be the best we can hope for. It is only someone who shares Dworkin's further commitments who must go further and argue that checkerboard solutions are, characteristically, undesirable all things considered (and that there are further principles of integrity that also fit with our political practices). It is only these claims that are unsupported by the favoured interpretation.

Nevertheless, there are two independent concerns about whether, even on the favoured interpretation, Dworkin has provided a satisfactory account of what is wrong with checkerboard solutions. The favoured interpretation makes use of the notion of a "recognizable principle of justice," and it is not entirely clear how to give content to this idea. Moreover, it is not clear how treating people differently in a way that is unjust is made even worse when the differential treatment cannot be supported by a recognizable principle of justice (though it can be supported by a recognizable principle of fairness).

7

Did Dworkin Ever Answer the Crits?

Jeremy Waldron

I.

I am not now, nor ever was, a member of the Critical Legal Studies (CLS) movement. But I want to consider the adequacy of the answer Ronald Dworkin gave almost twenty years ago to an objection (to his conception of law as integrity), which he attributed to CLS though he himself referred to it in more general terms as "internal skepticism."[1] I want to consider the adequacy of his response, not out of any desire to revive the intellectual fortunes of CLS and certainly not as a complaint that Professor Dworkin failed to do justice to CLS criticisms during the brief lifetime of the movement. CLS was never particularly interested in Dworkin, nor he in them.[2] But they had a common interest in what I would like to call "the background elements" of a legal system—the principles and policies that lie in back of the rules and texts that positivists emphasize. Ronald Dworkin and Duncan Kennedy, for example, are both theorists of the legal background. But what they say about it is very different. Dworkin thinks recourse to the background affords the resources necessary for legal decision in cases where the foreground law is disputed or indeterminate. Kennedy thinks the background is so riven with contradiction as to be capable of offering spurious support for everything and determinate support for nothing in legal reasoning.[3] So I am interested in what one might think of as Dworkin's *descriptive optimism*—his view that the background elements (of a legal system like that of the United States) are capable of bearing the weight of determinate argument that he wants to assign to it in his theory of law.

---

[1] R. Dworkin, Law's Empire 266–275 (1986).

[2] *See* A. Altman, *Legal Realism, Critical Legal Studies and Dworkin*, 15 Philosophy and Public Affairs 205, 214–215 (1986) ("For the most part, proponents of CLS and Dworkinians have ignored one another's positions").

[3] *See* D. Kennedy, *Form and Substance in Private Law Adjudication*, 89 Harv. L. Rev. 1685 (1976).

I will argue that, in order to answer the CLS critique, a defender of law as integrity has to place considerable emphasis on what Professor Dworkin regards as the *constructive* side of his argument. Instead of saying that the legal background *is* coherent, Dworkin has to say that it is capable of being made coherent at the hands of a sufficiently resourceful interpreter. Unfortunately the response cannot rest there. Dworkin's constructivism might licence an ingenious and versatile manipulation of existing legal materials: we take the parts of the (often contradictory background) that we like or approve, and we use them to add some sort of doctrinal credibility to the positions we are aiming at. But it is not clear that this fits the justification that Dworkin furnished for his method in *Law's Empire*, for that justification requires a party to argue, not merely that there are legal materials which he can make use of in support of his brief, but that he is using background materials in a way that keeps faith with the network of mutual commitments that makes us the community we are.[4] Unless the Dworkinian advocate can make such an argument, he has nothing with which he can resist the urgings of a pragmatist, to the effect that we should not bother with the background material *at all*, once the foreground has been shown to be indeterminate, but we should make our case directly for whatever is likely to promote the social good. To rebut that pragmatist position—which Dworkin acknowledges has to be rebutted to make room for his conception of law as integrity[5]—it is not enough to show that we *can* make something coherent and attractive out of the legal background. The Dworkinian advocate has to show that we *must* attempt to make something coherent and attractive out of the legal background. And what counts as a good faith attempt has to be responsive to the ideas lying behind that "must." My worry is that the constructivism that Dworkin appeals to, in order to evade the CLS critique, succeeds (if it does) only at the cost of cutting loose of the idea that the community is in some sense already committed to a coherent and principled position which the Dworkinian lawyer has a responsibility to unearth.

So: my aim in this paper is to explore the extent to which Professor Dworkin is put to a hard choice between the agile and discerning constructivism he needs to respond to CLS, on the one hand, and the integrity thesis about the commitments of the community which he invokes to justify the claim that making coherent sense of the existing legal materials, foreground and background, is something we are morally required to do. I think Dworkin really is confronted with a dilemma here, and I am not sure that a way through it can be negotiated. If he hangs on to the integrity position, he makes it harder to respond to the skepticism of CLS. But if he weakens the integrity requirement or loosens its connection to what is to count as an appropriate mode of legal argument, then he leaves himself defenseless against the pragmatist position that—clever though it is—the constructivism of Dworkinian legal argument serves no useful purpose.

[4] Dworkin, Law's Empire, *supra* note 1, at 195–216.
[5] *Id.* at 162–164.

As I said in my opening paragraph, I am not exploring Dworkin's response to internal skepticism in order to revive the moribund fortunes of CLS. The Crits can look after themselves.[6] I am exploring their critique and his response because they highlight a connection between two different aspects of Dworkin's jurisprudence, usually dealt with and criticized—if they are criticized—separately. On the one hand, there is the question of whether his constructive or interpretive method actually delivers the goods for judicial reasoning. On the other hand, there is a philosophical question about the ultimate justification for his insistence that we delve into the legal background rather than give up and resort to an overtly pragmatic approach when foreground law runs out or reveals itself to be indeterminate. The theory of integrity is supposed to give us our answer to the second question: we must persist with the background in order to keep faith with the commitments of our community. But what if the method for delivering the goods in hard cases—creative constructive theory-building—turns out *not* to be a way of keeping faith with our community? What if it makes a mockery of the idea of communal commitments, which law as integrity bows to? Then the two parts of Dworkin's jurisprudence—the clever constructivism and the portentous theory of integrity—sail past each other, and it will be hard to hang on to a sense of the whole. We need to take this prospect very seriously; and if there is an adequate Dworkinian response to the CLS challenge we must ensure that it does not fall at this hurdle.

II.

The key to Dworkin's jurisprudence is and has always been a view about what law involves besides a heap of enacted rules (constitutions, codes, and statutes).[7] Dworkin argues that as well as the enacted rules, which we see in the foreground of legal analysis, a working legal system also comprises background policies and principles, either those associated with particular enactments—as when we say the policy of the Sherman Act is to foster competition—or those that pervade the body of the law as a whole—as when we talk about "the well established policy of English law of imposing a more extensive liability on intentional wrongdoers than on careless defendants,"[8] or as when we invoke the maxim that "[n]o one shall be permitted to profit by his own fraud."[9] Dworkin believes that it is appropriate to

---

[6] I must say, though, that my first-year law students notice at once the connection between Kennedy's work in CLS and Dworkin's jurisprudence. And they do ask me what, if anything, has been written to refute the implicit CLS critique. (They are too young to know that analytic legal philosophers are supposed to disdain and ignore CLS ideas.)

[7] *The Model of Rules I*, in R. Dworkin, Taking Rights Seriously (revised ed., 1977).

[8] *Three Rivers District Council and Others v. Governor and Company of the Bank of England (No 3)* [2003] 2 A.C. 1 (HL), at 162.

[9] *Box v. Lanier*, 112 Tenn. 393, 409, 79 S.W. 1042, 1045 (1903).

invoke these principles and policies in legal argument and indeed that it is inappropriate not to. Not only are they important legal resources to be put to use in hard cases where the foreground law is indeterminate, but they are also capable of standing against foreground law (as the principle last-mentioned above stood against the New York state legislation relating to wills in *Riggs v. Palmer*).[10] Indeed a case may be made that background principles and policies have to be assumed in order to explain why the foreground law has the force it does.[11] Certainly any jurisprudence that neglects these background elements is inadequate.

There is a lot in Professor Dworkin's account of the legal background that I do not want to dispute. In various places, he distinguishes between policies and principles, as different types of background element: he associates "policy" with social goals and "principle" with norms or reasons that command a particular distribution of benefits, freedoms, and responsibilities.[12] I have no quarrel with that, nor with the arguments that Dworkin rests on that distinction. I accept Dworkin's view that background principles (in the narrower sense) are capable of sustaining claims of right.[13] I also see little to quarrel with in what he says about the logical character of the contribution that principles and policies make to legal argument: he talks of the dimension of "weight," which distinguishes their contribution from the contribution made by rules.[14] Finally, I have no quarrel with what Professor Dworkin says about the kind of presence that principles and policies have in a legal system. He argues—convincingly in my view—that their status as law "lies not in a particular decision of some legislature or court, but in a sense of appropriateness developed in the profession and the public over time."[15] (I think, too, that he is right to point up the difficulty this poses for H.L.A. Hart's concept of the rule of recognition.) None of these matters is in dispute between Dworkin and the Crits. In fact, although CLS is certainly less optimistic than Professor Dworkin is about the contribution that these background elements can make to determinate legal reasoning, their criticisms nevertheless presuppose that the legal background is at least as important for jurisprudence as Dworkin claims it is. If anything they are less sympathetic

---

[10] *Riggs v. Palmer*, 22 N.E. 188 (N.Y. 1889).

[11] *See* Dworkin, *The Model of Rules I*, *supra* note 7, at 37.

[12] *See id.* at 22. See also Dworkin, *Hard Cases* in TAKING RIGHTS SERIOUSLY, *supra* note 7, at 82 ff. and DWORKIN, LAW'S EMPIRE, *supra* note 1, at 221–224.

Dworkin notes that "principle" can be used in an inclusive sense to include both principles and policies in these narrower meanings (*The Model of Rules I, op cit.*, at 22), and it is worth noting that there is also a similarly inclusive sense of "policy," at least in judicial discourse, as when it is said, for example, that it is "the general policy of the law that it is preferable that a successful defendant should suffer the injustice of irrecoverable costs than that a claimant with a genuine claim should be prevented from pursuing it" (*Hamilton v. Al Fayed (No. 2)* [2003] Q.B. 1175 (CA) 1178) or that "[t]he policy of the law is to prevent A being judge in his own cause of the value of his life over B's life or his loved one C's life, and then being executioner as well" (*In Re A (Children) (Conjoined Twins: Surgical Separation)* [2001] Fam 147 CA, at 200).

[13] DWORKIN, TAKING RIGHTS SERIOUSLY, *supra* note 7, at 87.

[14] Dworkin, *The Model of Rules I*, *supra* note 7, at 24 ff.   [15] *Id.* at 39–45.

than Dworkin is to the positivist conception that he is attacking,[16] for they believe that a focus on purely foreground elements may radically underestimate various forms of pathology endemic to (say) the modern American legal system.

In his early work, Dworkin imagined that the background elements of a legal system might present themselves as discrete norms, which could be identified and individuated by judges and advocates and spoken about almost in the way that enacted rules are spoken about. Thus we might talk about the principle that no man is to profit from his own fraud, and distinguish it from other principles such as the principle that statutes are not to be given retroactive effect (if a non-retroactive interpretation is possible) or the principle that intentional wrongdoing is worse than equally harmful negligent wrongdoing. Even though background principles are not enacted as texts and even though they have no canonical formulation, still we do sometimes give a principle a verbal formulation and make it the focus of legal argumentation, asking how *it* should be interpreted, and drawing out *its* implications for particular cases. Judges and advocates do this all the time. They make assertions about what the general policy of the law is or what principles pervade it; then they go on to use these assertions as premises for arguing about the disposition of the cases in front of them. This gives the impression of a sort of two-step process involved in the use of background elements in legal argument, analogous to the two-step process that is typically used in arguing about textual rules. In step (1), we *identify* the norm in question—by the recognition and citation of a validly enacted text (in the case of a rule) or by the more diffuse argument used to discern the presence of a policy or principle in the law. Then, in step (2), we argue for a particular disposition of the case in front of us, on the basis of the bearing which we think the rule we have cited or the principle or policy we have identified has on the facts of the case. This is a perfectly lucid model and, as I have said, it is characteristic of much of what lawyers and judges say about principles and policies.

Its disadvantage is the way it assimilates principles and policies to more discrete forms of legal provision, such as statutory rules, as though the identification, individuation, and citation of the former were in the end not much different from the identification, individuation, and citation of the latter.[17] In fact, there are huge differences. It's not just that rules characteristically have a canonical formulation which principles and policies lack; it is also that rules have (as it were) a fixed level of generality, whereas the tendency of principles and policies is always to expand the sphere of their application, something which has to do with their operating more like reasons than like enacted provisions. If there is any limit on the generality of a policy or principle, it is a matter of the esthetics or lucidity of its application to the

---

[16] *See, e.g.* P. Gabel, *Book Review of Taking Rights Seriously*, 91 Harv. L. Rev. 302, 303–311 (1977).

[17] This drew some of Dworkin's early critics to the possibility that discrete principles may be "recognized," within a positivist framework: *see* J. Raz, *Legal Principles and the Limits of Law*, 81 Yale L.J. 823, 843 ff. (1972). See Dworkin's response in Taking Rights Seriously, *supra* note 7, at 68–71.

case with which we are primarily concerned. We state the principle so that its application to the case at hand is patent, rather than a matter of further interpretation. This suggests that the distinction between steps (1) and (2) is somewhat misleading, and that we might do better to think more directly about the relation between the legal background and the instant case.

And that is the model suggested in some parts of *Law's Empire*. The idea there is that in any given case, a judgment for the plaintiff, say, is to be defended by showing that it coheres better with existing legal materials than a judgment for the defendant would. "Coheres better with" is understood as what Professor Dworkin calls a post-interpretive claim. Counsel for the plaintiff offers a justificatory theory which he says makes sense of all or most of the existing legal materials—prior decisions, established doctrine, legislation, and so on—and he shows that that theory would also justify a decision in favor of his client.[18] The defendant offers a contrary case, and counsel for the plaintiff will argue that the theory offered by the defense is either less attractive in itself than the one that he has presented or covers less of the existing materials than his does, or both. Of course, it is unlikely that either of the theories on offer will stand in a justificatory relation to *all* the existing legal materials. Some materials may be simply irrelevant—too far from the issues in question in terms of the concerns they might be thought to embody, even under the most abstract characterization. And some may have to be treated as outliers, relevant but incapable of being reconciled with the theory being put forward. Also, it is unlikely that either theory—plaintiff's or defendant's—will amount to (what anyone regards as) a perfect theory of justice. Even allowing for outliers, both theories will have to accommodate decisions (precedents, enactments) that their proponents might not support if they were setting out their favored account of justice on a blank slate. Still, plaintiff will argue that the theory the defendant invokes to make the existing law look coherent is further from an ideal theory of justice than the theory he (the plaintiff) invokes, and defendant will return the compliment. So they will argue back and forth on this dimension of justice as well as on the dimension of how much of the legal record their rival theories cover.

When we put the matter in this way, the distinction between background and foreground *elements* in a legal system—between principles and rules—is seen as a sort of *façon de parler*. What the existing law really amounts to is nothing more than a mass of decisions—by constitution framers, by legislators, and by thousands of earlier judges. Relying on background elements in current legal argument is not really a matter of introducing a different set of *provisions*, viz. legal principles as opposed to legal rules. It is rather a particular way of working with that existing mass of decisions, though it may also involve self-conscious reference to the recorded

---

[18] I shall leave out of account issues about the compartmentalization of law—see DWORKIN, LAW'S EMPIRE, *supra* note 1, at 250–254—since these do not really affect the criticisms I shall be considering. Everything I say can be qualified with reference to "local priority" or not, as the reader wishes.

efforts of previous decision-makers (earlier judges, for example), to work with the mass of previous decisions that confronted them in just the same sort of way.[19]

So there are these two ways of characterizing Dworkin's approach: (i) his earlier characterization in terms of norms called *principles*, i.e. norms that were comprised in the law just like rules—only in the background of the law rather than in the foreground; and (ii) his later approach which talked of rival *theories* put forward by those who were working with the existing law to justify a current decision. I don't really think they are different, or that any difference between the two really matters. A principle (or a policy) is nothing much more than a theory (or an element of a theory) about what makes sense of the existing law, expressed directly in normative terms.[20] We can say, in the voice of the theorist (or the current advocate) that the best interpretation of the existing law—the theory that covers most of it and makes it look good—is that it does not permit people to profit from their own fraud. Or we can "point to" or "cite" a principle—"No one is to profit from his own fraud"— more or less conscious of the fact that this in effect is something we read into the law when we commit ourselves to the theory just mentioned. The latter characterization will seem particularly appropriate, when the mass of materials we are confronting includes holdings by other judges which interpret the materials that confronted them in just the way that we interpret the materials that confront us: those holdings will enable us to point to something like "authority" for the principles we are relying on.[21] The alternative characterization will be more useful, however, in cases where we have no such authority, but are striking out on a new interpretive path, because we have a theory which we think better explains the existing law (and generates a result for our client) than previous efforts at interpretation do. Dworkin seems happy to move back and forth between these models in *Law's Empire*. Sometimes he says—in line with characterization (ii)—that a judge "must choose between eligible interpretations [theories] by asking which shows the community's structure of institutions and decisions—its public standards as a whole—in a better light."[22] And sometimes he says—in line with characterization (i)—that his method "asks judges to assume . . . that law *is* structured by a coherent set of principles."[23] As I say, I don't think anything much turns on this distinction;[24] I mention it only in order to make it clear that I think the two amount more or less to the same thing, and that the critical points I am going to develop can be applied to Professor Dworkin's jurisprudence in both its phases.

---

[19] This last point turns out to be quite important; see *infra* Section VI, text accompanying notes 56–58.

[20] Thus Dworkin answers the question of what principles the law contains by saying that it contains those principles which belong to the soundest theory of the settled (foreground) law. *See* DWORKIN, TAKING RIGHTS SERIOUSLY, *supra* note 7, at 340 and Altman, *supra*, note 2, at 213.

[21] . . . just as I pointed to "authority" for the various principles I cited, *supra* in notes 8, 9, and 12.

[22] DWORKIN, LAW'S EMPIRE, *supra* note 1, at 256.   [23] *Id.* at 243.

[24] These two ways of approaching the matter are also noted by A. Hunt, *Law's Empire or Legal Imperialism*, in READING DWORKIN CRITICALLY 9, 36–37 (A. Hunt ed., 1992). Hunt thinks the oscillation between them matters much more than I do.

III.

Much of the CLS critique of Dworkin's work is superficial:[25] for example, CLS scholars charge that Dworkin's jurisprudence is "elitist," that he is insufficiently concerned with "the deprived and disadvantaged in society," that he is in denial about the connection between law and politics, that his approach to justice is too abstract, or that he "exhibits a profound antipathy for common consciousness among the citizens."[26] Dworkin himself, however, has identified a line of CLS argument that poses a considerable threat to his enterprise.

The threat presents itself as follows. The law we confront in a modern democracy is not the work of a single author. We do not live in a one party state, nor do we even live in a unitary state. Law-makers of various persuasions coexist at various levels or in the various tributaries of our legal system, and contribute to the growth of the law from their diverse moral and political perspectives. Moreover, we live in a society whose law is the repository of its checkered political history. When one party succeeds another in electoral competition, it does not attempt to wipe the legal slate clean and begin all over again; instead the latest generation of statesmen work incrementally to make such modest changes in the law as their priorities dictate and their political circumstances permit, leaving the remainder—the work of the predecessors—to coexist comfortably or uncomfortably with whatever changes they have managed to make.[27] The law in fact is a patchwork of provisions, the work of a multitude of authors living and dead, with diverse and conflicting political agendas, and diverse and conflicting commitments of principle.

In the midst of this patchwork—in the midst of this mess, we might say— Dworkin's lawyer is supposed to be able to find sufficient coherence to assert credibly that the law is pervaded by principles which favor his client's case and to argue credibly against any similar but opposing claim made on behalf of his opponent. But why should we assume that this is possible? As Dworkin acknowledges, nothing in the way the law was produced guarantees that the lawyer or the judge will succeed in finding a coherent interpretation of it.[28] Or if he can find a coherent interpretation of the patchwork, nothing in the way that the law was produced guarantees that his success precludes similar success for his opponent: nothing guarantees that the law has a shape amenable to a unique coherent justification of principle.[29] Without that guarantee, or at any rate without a reasonable prospect

---

[25] *See also* Altman, *supra* note 2, at 215.

[26] *See* Hunt, *supra* note 24, at 39ff. and A. Hutchinson, *Indiana Dworkin and Law's Empire*, 96 YALE L.J. 637, 600 (1987). *See also* Hutchinson, *The Last Emperor*, in READING DWORKIN CRITICALLY, *supra* note 24, at 66 (common consciousness) and Gabel, *supra* note 16, at 314–315 (on abstraction).

[27] *See* J. Waldron, *The Circumstances of Integrity*, 3 LEGAL THEORY, 1 (1997), reprinted in J. WALDRON, LAW AND DISAGREEMENT (1999).

[28] DWORKIN, LAW'S EMPIRE, *supra* note 1, at 273.   [29] *Id.* at 272.

of a unique coherence result, the Dworkinian style of legal argument is just a recipe for the reproduction of indeterminacy.

The message of Critical Legal Studies is sometimes taken to be that law is systematically biased towards the interests of the ruling class. If that were so, then there might possibly be some hope for Dworkin's jurisprudence: the advocate or judge hoping to dredge up some principled coherence from the law might expect to find in it a more or less coherent version of ruling class ideology. But that has always been a superficial reading of CLS. The most thoughtful CLS scholars have emphasized the contradictory and conflict-ridden aspect of our law. Law, says Roberto Unger, "is the product of real collective conflict, carried on over a long time, among many different wills and imaginations, interests and visions."[30] With this sort of provenance, any given body of legal doctrine is bound to be messy, rich in compromises, exceptions and contradictions.

Warring solutions to similar problems will coexist. Their boundaries of application will remain uncertain. Interests and ideals favored in some domains will be discounted in others for no better reason than the sequence in which certain decisive conflicts took place and the relative influence enjoyed by contending parties of opinion at the time. Intellectual fashions will join with preponderant interests to produce results that neither interests nor fashions alone would have allowed us to predict. Defeated or rejected solutions will remain, incongruously, in the corners of the law as vestiges of past approaches . . .[31]

One would have to be naively optimistic—to the point of some sort of Hegelian faith in the cunning of reason[32]—to believe that these processes yield a single determinate structure of principled reasons.

Indeed the criticism may be drawn even more tightly than that. In any piece of high profile litigation, the parties will represent or say they are representing not only their own interests but competing visions of what law has to offer in society. But given our checkered political history, it is incredible that there will not already be layers in the archeological midden of law to support each of the visions propounded by the rival parties. Plaintiff may be able to find liberal strains in the law, corresponding to the times and the places where liberal principles have predominated in the law-making processes; and defendant will be able to find conservative strains in the law corresponding to the times the law-making processes have been

---

[30] R. Unger, What can Legal Analysis Become? 65 (1996).

[31] *Id.* at 66. By the way, awareness of this incoherence is by no means confined to CLS. *See, e.g.* J. Raz, *The Relevance of Coherence*, in Ethics in the Public Domain: Essays in the Morality of Law and Politics 277, 298–300 (1994) ("[L]aw is the result of the rough-and-tumble of politics, which does not exclude the judiciary from its ambit, and reflects the vagaries of pragmatic compromises and changing fortunes of political forces and the like. . . . [L]aw, therefore, does not form a coherent body of principle of doctrine. . . . [T]here is no reason to expect the law to be coherent. By and large, one would expect it to be coherent in bits—in areas relatively unaffected by continuous political struggles—and incoherent in others.")

[32] *See* J. Waldron, *Dirty Little Secret (Review Essay on Roberto Mangabeira Unger, What Should Legal Analysis Become?)* 98 Columbia L. Rev. 510 (1998).

wrested away from their liberal opponents. All that is there, waiting in the law for the rival parties to come along and raid in their latest forays as litigators.

Duncan Kennedy offers the tightest version of this view.[33] He believes the conflicting tendencies in the law can be resolved into two opposed visions of the individual and society—an individualist vision and an altruist vision—and that these two visions are represented haphazardly in the law that confronts us as the high-water marks of the ascendancy in law-making of first one tendency and then of the other tendency.[34] Hence, what is or appears to be at stake for a given individual engaged in litigation will usually present itself as one or other of these tendencies, and Professor Kennedy's position is that the body of law that any litigation draws upon, and that the parties look to for support for their rival positions, is also riven with the contradictory appearance of both positions. From the advocates' point of view, the result is an uncomfortable awareness that there is enough in the law for his opponent to make an argument of principle every bit as convincing (or as unconvincing) as his own. And from the judge's point of view, there is the sense that his decision might go either way: the judge may be predisposed to approach a case in the individualist mode, but may find himself suddenly, as Kennedy puts it, "shifting modes,"[35] attracted suddenly by the lines of available background argument that might sustain legal argument for the side that represents the altruistic tendency. Either way, whether the judge shifts modes or not, or whatever the direction in which the shift takes place, he will find no difficulty in constructing an argument of exactly the sort, drawing on exactly the sort of elements, that Dworkin recommends. For Kennedy is also a student of the legal background: the only difference is that his more realistic scrutiny of it has not convinced him, as Dworkin is convinced, that it yields to only one compelling argument of principle in difficult cases.[36]

Dworkin, as I said, acknowledges the importance of this objection. He calls it a form of internal skepticism[37]—to be distinguished from external or philosophical

[33] *See* Altman, *supra* note 2, for the view that Kennedy's critique is the most dangerous for Dworkin's enterprise. As a matter of fact, Professor Dworkin barely refers to Kennedy's article: there is one reference, in a slightly different context, in Law's Empire, *supra* note 1, at 438 n.26. (Dworkin's other references to Kennedy in Law's Empire are to a bibliography of CLS that Kennedy co-authored.) Still, Dworkin does acknowledge the substance of Kennedy's position: he says that the story of our legal system told by CLS is a story "of two deeply antagonistic ideologies at war within the law, one drawn, perhaps, from communitarian impulses of altruism and mutual concern and the other from the contradictory ideas of egoism, self-sufficiency, and judgmental moralism." Law's Empire, *supra* note 1, at 272.

[34] Professor Kennedy also believes that these visions are present within each of us, and are not best understood as associated, respectively, with particular parties, classes or factions in society. *See* Kennedy, *Form and Substance, supra* note 3, at 1774–1776; *see also* D. Kennedy, *The Structure of Blackstone's Commentaries*, 205 Buffalo L. Rev., 28, 211–213 (1979).

[35] Kennedy, *Form and Substance, supra* note 3, at 1776.

[36] *See also* D. Kennedy, A Critique of Adjudication (fin de siècle) 34–37 (1977).

[37] Dworkin, Law's Empire, *supra* note 1, at 79, 266–275. For an objection to this equation, *see* P. Schlag, *Missing Pieces: A Cognitive Approach to Law*, 67 Texas L. Rev., 1195, 1198–1200 (1989).

skepticism about the very ideas of value and coherence, which he thinks is a distraction in jurisprudence[38]—and insists that it has to be taken seriously.[39] It is not out of the question, he acknowledges, that the existing law could be so riddled with inconsistency as to be unamenable to the sort of analysis he proposes. After all, we know the foreground law is inconsistent, if not in its direct normative implications,[40] then in the spirit that informs it—in the purposes, principles and policies that must be assumed to make sense of it. The Dworkinian judge "knows that legislative supremacy gives force to some statutes that are inconsistent in principle with others . . . But he assumes that these contradictions are not so pervasive and intractable . . . that his task is impossible." The question now is: can that assumption be defended?

IV.

Dworkin's first pass at the objection is to deny that the extent of contradiction is as great as the CLS scholars make it out to be. "The literature of critical legal studies announces rather than defends these claims [about pervasive contradictions], as if they were self-evident."[41] Pierre Schlag thinks this is just summary dismissal of CLS criticism,[42] but he is wrong and wrong, I suspect, for two reasons. He is wrong, first, because Dworkin does not rest here on a flat denial. Indeed, he goes on to mobilize other arguments, which I will consider in a moment. And Schlag is wrong, secondly, because there may be more to the factual disagreement about the extent of contradiction than meets the eye.

I shall return to the second point in Section VIII. But for the moment, I would like to explore the first point, the one that does not involve Dworkin simply disputing the extent of contradictions. After all, Dworkin is hardly in a position to deny the existence of something like contradiction or incoherence in the law. On the contrary, the background presupposition of his embrace of integrity is that the settled law of any community has had multiple authors—framers, legislators, judges, etc.—with quite radically differing visions of justice. (If there were no conflict between the various views about justice expressed in the enacted law, there would be nothing for the Dworkinian ideal of integrity to do.)[43] So any attempt to rebut internal skepticism simply by saying there are no contradictions, or by saying that whatever contradictions there are, are low-level and unimportant,

---

[38] DWORKIN, LAW'S EMPIRE, *supra* note 1 at 79–86.

[39] Moreover, it is "global" internal skepticism, not just piecemeal. *See id.* at 79. Calling internal skepticism "global," however, doesn't make it the same as "external skepticism"; compare the misapprehension about this in R. J. Lipkin, *Beyond Skepticism, Foundationalism, and the New Fuzziness: The Role of Wide Reflective Equilibrium in Legal Theory,* 75 CORNELL L. REV. 811, 844 (1990).

[40] Foreground inconsistencies are managed by principles such as *lex posterior.*

[41] DWORKIN, LAW'S EMPIRE, *supra* note 1, at 273.   [42] Schlag, *supra* note 37, at 1198.

[43] I argue this at length in Waldron, *The Circumstances of Integrity, supra* note 27.

would undermine the point of his preoccupation with integrity. Of course, opinions about the extent and pervasiveness of such contradictions as there are in the law might vary. And in the end, that's what it may come down to. But my initial suspicion is that Dworkin has not wanted to rely simply on the sort of limp response that H.L.A. Hart gave to the critique of positivism put forward by the Legal Realists—"Well, it's not really as bad as all that."[44] That would make his jurisprudence contingent and precarious, and its applicability to real-world legal systems perhaps unacceptably conditional.

V.

So what else does he say? Dworkin's second response is to argue that this sort of CLS skepticism neglects an important philosophical distinction between *competing* principles (such as autonomy and mutual concern) which may figure in a single view about justice, and *contradictory* principles (such as equality and inequality) which cannot possibly be combined in one coherent conception.[45] Referring to a tort law example he uses in Chapter 7 of *Law's Empire*, Dworkin says there is no contradiction in recognizing both a principle of collective solidarity and a principle of individual fault-based responsibility: "on the contrary, any moral vision would be defective if it wholly disowned either impulse. . . . No general interpretation that denied either one would be plausible; integrity could not be served if either were wholly disavowed."[46] The challenge, he says, is to articulate a principled balance between them in the interpretive theory that we use to justify our particular legal conclusions.

Now, what Dworkin says here is right, as far as it goes. Most moral theories, including theories of justice, do have elements that stand in tension with one another; and it is the mark of moral maturity not to regard this as a logical defect, but rather to see it as an inevitable feature of our coming to terms with the plurality of values and principles.[47] But does pointing this out meet the objection? I fear it does not.

CLS scholars like Kennedy deny that the individualist and altruist elements they discern in the legal background are merely *prima facie* principles or the sort of

---

[44] *See* H. L. A. Hart, *Positivism and the Separation of Law and Morals*, 71 HARV. L. REV. 593, 614–615 (1957). Hart's response to the Realist critique was "to emphasize that the hard core of settled meaning is law in some centrally important sense and that even if there are borderlines, there must first be lines. If this were not so the notion of rules controlling courts' decisions would be senseless as some of the 'Realists'—in their most extreme moods, and, I think, on bad grounds—claimed." *See also* H. L. A. HART, THE CONCEPT OF LAW 136–141 (2d ed. 1994); H. L. A. Hart, *American Jurisprudence through English Eyes: The Nightmare and the Noble Dream*, in his collection, ESSAYS IN JURISPRUDENCE AND PHILOSOPHY 123, 126–132 (1983).

[45] DWORKIN, LAW'S EMPIRE, *supra* note 1, at 269–275.   [46] *Id.* at 269–270.

[47] In this paper, I will not explore the tension between this view of moral pluralism and the more holistic/hedgehog approach that Dworkin defends in other contexts. *See, e.g.* R. DWORKIN, SOVEREIGN VIRTUE (2000).

in-tension ingredients that one would find combined or balanced in a well-worked-out moral theory.[48] What they claim to find in the background of our law are not *rival tendencies* but *incompatible visions* or *incompatible theories* of what we owe to others and to the collective life of our society.[49] Each of these theories or visions already balances egotistical against other-regarding influence. So, for example, on Duncan Kennedy's account, the individualist element in private law is not just a vector, exerting an egoistic influence on the final social solution. It already represents a determination of how self-regarding and other-regarding elements might be balanced. Kennedy observes that "individualism is sharply distinct from pure egotism, or the view that it is impossible and undesirable to set any limits at all to the pursuit of self-interest,"[50] and it is distinct precisely in this point that it already represents an attempt—the individualist attempt—to balance selfish and other-regarding tendencies. Something similar, Kennedy says, is true of what he calls altruism:

[T]he altruist is unwilling to carry his premise of solidarity to the extreme of making everyone responsible for the welfare of everyone else. The altruist believes in the necessity and desirability of a sphere of autonomy or liberty or freedom or privacy within which one is free to ignore both the plights of others and the consequences of one's own acts for their welfare.[51]

Once again, the altruism one finds in the legal background is not just a solidaristic or communitarian tendency; it is already a view about how such a tendency should be balanced against the egotistical tendencies that compete with it. Each of the rival views about justice in society that Kennedy claims to discern in the background is already a view about how competing principles such as autonomy and mutual concern should be ranked and weighed within a single conception. In that sense, each does *contradict* the other's weighting and ranking.

Dworkin ought to have no difficulty seeing this. After all, the presupposition of his concern with integrity is that the authorship of enacted law reflects a diverse

---

[48] And similarly, CLS scholars argue that each of us is psychologically torn, not just between rival tendencies of self-regarding and other-regarding impulses—which would after all be a very, very weak claim and obviously true—but between rival visions of the relation between self and society. *See* Kennedy, *The Structure of Blackstone's Commentaries, supra* note 34.

[49] I should emphasize that it is not being asserted that these are fully worked-out and systematic theories. There was a period, Kennedy says, when individualism did present itself as a systematic body of theory: he is referring to the heyday of *laissez-faire* (Kennedy, *Form and Substance, supra* note 3, at 1729–1731). But with the disintegration of classical *laissez-faire*, both individualism and altruism present themselves as fairly unsystematic bodies of theory. But still there is an important distinction—which Dworkin's response elides—between an unsystematic theory (which unsystematically balances various rival tendencies) and a *prima facie* principle or tendency (which would be the thing to be balanced—systematically or unsystematically—with other tendencies).

Admittedly, Kennedy's formulations are not always consistent on this. The formulation most useful to Dworkin would be the following: "[M]odern individualism presents itself not as a deductive system, but as a pole, or tendency or vector or bias, in the debate with altruism over the legitimacy of the system of rules that emerged in the late nineteenth century." *Id.* at 1732. Still, in context, Kennedy's reference is to haphazard and intuitive balancing exercises that contradict one another, rather than to confrontation among the tendencies as between which balancing is required.

[50] *Id.* at 1714–1715.   [51] *Id.* at 1718.

array of views *about justice*, not merely a diverse array of impulses (some selfish, some communitarian) which would later have to be organized into a single theory of justice by the Dworkinian interpreter.[52] It is not a case of one statute's having been passed by an autonomy faction and another statute's having been enacted by the party of mutual concern, and of its never having occurred to anyone except the judge (now faced with the two statutes together) that a suitably complex position could accommodate both principles.

I have not said anything so far about Kennedy's even *more* skeptical claim, that (whether we regard individualism and altruism as competing balances or as competing principles to be balanced) no metaprinciple of balance can be defended as objectively correct. Kennedy says:

[I]t is futile to imagine that moral and practical conflict will yield to analysis in terms of higher level concepts. The meaning of contradiction at the level of abstraction is that there is no metasystem that would, if only we could find it, key us into one mode or the other as circumstances "required." . . . [W]e cannot "balance" individualist and altruist values . . . except in the tautological sense that we can, as a matter of fact, decide if we have to. The imagery of balancing presupposes exactly the kind of more abstract unit of measurement that the sense of contradiction excludes.[53]

This claim is supposed to cut off an approach that the Dworkinian lawyer might take in the face of what we have said so far. Instead of saying that he is trying to balance conflicting tendencies whose presence in the law does not reflect earlier attempts to balance them, the Dworkinian lawyer could say that he is purporting to replace the existing—and admittedly contradictory—balancings embedded in the law by individualists and altruists, with a *true* balance, one that would be neither individualist nor altruist, but just *correct*. Kennedy wants to pre-empt this by announcing that the idea of a true balance is simply out of the question.

To the extent he considers it, I think Dworkin regards this as an expression of external skepticism about right answers in regard to balancing, and as such he rejects it out of hand.[54] True, it may not be possible for the Dworkinian lawyer to *demonstrate* that the new balancing—with which he proposes to supersede the contradictory balancings embedded in the law by individualists and altruists—is objectively correct. But non-demonstrability is not the same as falsity or futility.

I think this last part of Kennedy's critique is properly dismissed in this way. But whether the dismissal ultimately helps Dworkin is a question we must postpone until after we have examined the merits—in jurisprudence—of the constructivist approach that we are now imagining the Dworkinian lawyer undertaking.

---

[52] DWORKIN, LAW'S EMPIRE, *supra* note 1, at 178; *see also* WALDRON, LAW AND DISAGREEMENT, *supra* note 27, at 193–194.   [53] Kennedy, *Form and Substance, supra* note 3, at 1775.
[54] *Cf.* DWORKIN, LAW'S EMPIRE, *supra*, note 1, at 267.

VI.

According to Professor Dworkin, the CLS or internal skepticism critique labors under another misapprehension. The fact that various elements in our law have conflicting inspirations does not mean that we cannot *construct* a theory that resolves the contradictions into some sort of attractive coherence. After all, Dworkin's judge or lawyer is not simply reporting the provenance of the legal materials he is dealing with: "He tries to impose order over doctrine, not to discover order in the forces that created it."[55] The interpretive task is not to find out the purpose or intention with which past legal decisions were actually made; it is to make something good and coherent of the past decisions whether that good or coherent understanding corresponds to what the decision-makers in the past had in mind or not.

There is a quick version of this Dworkinian response and a longer version. The quick version might go as follows. Dworkin might want to use this point about constructivism to contest Professor Kennedy's assumption that there are elements in the existing legal record which just *are* individualist and that they are contradicted by elements in the existing legal record which just *are* altruist, as though all the elements come to us ready labeled in that way. In fact, Dworkin might want to say, what we face is an array of decisions: say, the enactment of statute S_1, a decision for the plaintiff in case C_1, a decision for the defendant in case C_2, the enactment of statute S_2, and so on. Calling S_1 and C_1 altruistic and S_2 and C_2 individualistic, and asserting therefore that the array of decisions is riddled with contradictions is itself already an interpretation of the materials. Dworkin might protest therefore that Kennedy is rigging the game by helping himself to these characterizations, as though they were part of the preinterpretive specification of the materials.

This is a fair point, as far as it goes, and I shall return to it at the very end of the paper. Some of what Kennedy says about altruism and individualism is that they are characteristics of legal argument, not of legal materials: they are "two opposed attitudes that manifest themselves in debates about the content of private law rules," and "they are helpful in the general task of understanding why judges and legislators have chosen to establish or enact particular private law doctrines."[56] It looks, then, as though a Dworkinian lawyer might resist these characterizations—leaving it open to himself to characterize the various materials in other ways—and thus resist the premise that he is confronted with inherently contradictory materials. This strategy makes particular sense with regard to legislative materials. We should be wary of any attempt to treat particular legislators' purposes as though they were canonical and on a par with the text of the statute they enacted. Dworkin has been a fervent opponent of this mode of

---

[55] *Id.* at 273.   [56] Kennedy, *Form and Substance, supra* note 3, at 1713.

statutory interpretation,[57] and he must be allowed the advantage of that here. So Dworkin's interpreter need not accept that S_1, say, is an altruistic statute; he may want to fit it into his theory in a different way, which is at odds with what its original sponsors thought.

With case law, though, the situation is more complicated and less helpful to Dworkin. I don't think he would (or should) want to associate his constructivist approach to integrity with the claim that all we have to interpret is the actual holding of a case—e.g., appellant loses, plaintiff has to pay $40,000 damages—and that we can ignore the opinion produced by the court explaining that outcome, as though it were the case-law analogue of legislative history. Unless one wants to adopt the position of an extreme legal realist—like Jerome Frank[58]—we will usually regard judicial opinions accompanying decisions as part of the record we are required to interpret and not as extraneous to it. Of course, those opinions are themselves partly interpretive of the materials that *their* authors confronted. The judicial opinion accompanying the decision in case C_3 will be in part an interpretation of the decisions (and the opinions) in cases C_2 and C_1; so the judge in C_4 reading the opinion in C_3 will be reading the opinion of someone who was trying to do just what he is doing (so far as C_1 and C_2 are concerned). What the judge is interpreting is thus in part a set of interpretations. The activity of interpretation is recursive: one interprets the past interpretations of others for they too are part of the community's record. So one interprets not just outcomes but modes of decision, patterns of argument, emergent doctrines, and so on. And for this, it is not inappropriate to say, as Kennedy and others sometimes say, that they *are* individualist or that they *are* altruist. One just has to read them, and it may be very difficult—a Herculean task, in fact—to read the altruism out of the decisions that one wants to reconcile with one's own consistent individualist interpretation or vice versa.

So there is no refuge for the constructivist in this quick gambit. The contradictions among the materials he confronts may be non-negotiable. If this is the case, then Dworkin's constructive interpreter has to adopt a different and less glamorous strategy. He has to pick and choose from among the existing contradictory decisions the ones that his interpretation proposes to fit, and discard the rest. Confronting a given set of legal materials, Dworkin's judge or lawyer will try to construct a coherent theory—or state an appropriate principle or set of principles—that implicates as many of them as possible. Since there *are* contradictions (as opposed to mere tensions) in the materials, no doubt a significant number of them will not be covered by the theory or the principles he proposes. But this doesn't mean he cannot come up with a theory or a set of principles that fits a significant portion of them. (Indeed, if the materials are pervaded by contradiction, as Kennedy asserts, then one would expect Dworkin's interpreter should be able to come up with a theory that fits roughly half.)

---

57 *See* Dworkin, Law's Empire, *supra* note 1, at Ch. 9.
58 J. Frank, Law and the Modern Mind (1970) at 111.

Now, a mischievous interpreter might take a different strategy: he might come up with something purporting to be an interpretive theory, which was as inconsistent as the patchwork of materials it purported to fit. But that would just show bad faith—the bad faith that many opponents of CLS accuse its practitioners of harboring: they *want* to make the law look bad. "Nothing is easier or more pointless," says Dworkin, "than demonstrating that a flawed and contradictory account fits as well as a smoother and more attractive one." But to sustain his internal skepticism, the critic "must show that the flawed and contradictory account is the only one available."[59] The internal skeptic is not entitled to say that the interpretive enterprise is doomed to failure unless he has tried as hard as he can: "[he] must claim to have looked for a less skeptical interpretation and failed."[60]

Actually this last point won't do, so far as the burden of proof is concerned. Internal skepticism is *not* refuted by a showing that a non-contradictory interpretation—a non-contradictory theory or a consistent set of principles—is available. For *of course* one can select a non-contradictory subset from any mass of inconsistent propositions: "p" on this sort of constructivism, would be a consistent interpretation of {p, ~p}, and similarly individualism (or, alternatively, altruism) would be a consistent interpretation—on this constructivist approach—of the law as Professor Kennedy portrays it. After all, it's a matter of basic logic that one can make a case for anything on the basis of contradictory premises. So the onus cannot be on the CLS skeptic to show that *no* case can be made. What must be shown, in order to refute the internal skeptic, is either that only one such coherent interpretation can be constructed or that a credible case can be made that one of the available coherent interpretations of the contradictory materials is better than any of the others.[61] Too often, I think, Dworkin's formulations neglect the forensic adversarial context of legal argument: it is not enough to show that a lawyer can come up with a legal argument; what he comes up with must be capable of refuting and displacing the legal argument that his opponent is likely to come up with as well.[62]

Of course, all this needs to be leavened with some acknowledgment of whatever is legitimate in Dworkin's argument about right answers and demonstrability: there can, he insists, be right answers to legal questions, even though there is no acknowledged method of *demonstrating* that an answer is right.[63] I will assume

---

[59] DWORKIN, LAW'S EMPIRE, *supra* note 1, at 274.   [60] *Id.*

[61] This is seen clearly by M. Strassberg, *Taking Ethics Seriously: Beyond Positivist Jurisprudence in Legal Ethics*, 80 IOWA L. REV. 901, 929 (1995) ("[I]ndividual judges will disagree about whether and how strongly a particular principle is embedded in our law. These interpretive disagreements expose Dworkin to the criticism that judicial decisions relying on such principles are, in fact, a matter of idiosyncratic judicial discretion. Indeed, a cynical view of the law . . . would suggest that institutional support of some kind can be dredged up to support any principle favored by a judge").

[62] I sometimes wonder whether it would have been better for Dworkin to concentrate on an ideal advocate rather than an ideal judge (Hercules), for by the time Hercules comes to write his opinion— sitting as Dworkin imagines him on a single-person bench—there is just the legal argument he is composing; there is no longer a competitor's argument to be refuted.

[63] DWORKIN, TAKING RIGHTS SERIOUSLY, *supra* note 7, at 216.

that this is roughly correct,[64] and that the case for internal skepticism cannot be merely that Dworkin has offered no algorithm for correctness in legal argument.

Still, one is inclined to say: *something* must count as tending to show—or there must be *something* one can do which counts as attempting to show—that the argument one is making is better than any opposing argument one can imagine being made by an opponent in the same case, drawing constructively upon the same array of materials. I mean *something* must count as that, apart from one's consciousness that one's own argument *can* be made or that it just *is* the argument one is making. This is because one is also conscious—confronted as one is, with this mass of contradictory materials—that one's opponent's argument *can* be made as well.

I get the impression that Professor Dworkin is sometimes prepared to say that this is a misplaced demand, analogous to what he regards as the unhelpful demand that for a person who believes that moral propositions are objectively true or false, something must count as trying to show that a given moral proposition is objectively correct, over and above the mere assertion and re-assertion of that proposition.[65] At other times, however, he characterizes the phenomenology differently, in a way that suggests that someone wedded to an interpretive argument *may* sensibly regard himself as having reasons for thinking the argument he is wedded to is correct. The characterization I have in mind is set out, in the first instance, in regard to interpretive claims about literature:

> Someone just converted to a new reading of *Paradise Lost*, trembling with the excitement of discovery, thinks his new reading is *right*, that it is better than the one he has abandoned, that those yet uninitiated have missed something genuine and important, that they do not see the poem for what it really is. He thinks he has been driven by the truth, not that he has chosen one interpretation to wear for the day because he fancies it like a necktie. He thinks he has genuine, good reasons for accepting his new interpretation and that others, who cling to the older view he now thinks wrong, have genuine, good reasons to change their minds.[66]

Now, I have no doubt that *sometimes* legal argument may have this character: trembling with excitement, a jurist comes up with a new interpretation of existing doctrine, a sense of something that others have missed, and of their having good reasons to abandon their old tired reading in favor of one's own. Sometimes it may feel like that (though there would still be philosophical questions about what to infer from such phenomenology). But is this how we expect it to be for most cases? Is this phenomenology—the trembling excitement of discovery—likely to be characteristic of legal work *in the context of materials that are as contradictory as the*

---

[64] But note that, *anyway*, the right answer motif is muted in Law's Empire. I have discussed this further in J. Waldron, *The Rule of Law as a Theater of Debate*, in Dworkin and his Critics (J. Burley ed., 2004)

[65] *See* Dworkin, Law's Empire, *supra* note 1, at 81; R. Dworkin, *Objectivity and Truth: You'd Better Believe It*, 25 Philosophy and Public Affairs 87 (1996).

[66] Dworkin, Law's Empire, *supra* note 1, at 77.

CLS scholars say our existing American law is? For remember: Dworkin is offering the constructive aspect of his argument as a way of finessing the CLS claim about contradictions. Never mind how conflicted the law is, he says, never mind how riddled it is with contradictions; one can always come up with *some* sort of constructive argument for one's position. So the question is—*if* the legal materials are as conflicted (and are known to be as conflicted) as, say, Duncan Kennedy thinks they are[67]—would one expect the process of constructive argument that Dworkin promotes to have the sort of phenomenological flavor of "discovery" and "good genuine reasons" that characterizes our imagined student's new interpretation of *Paradise Lost*? Given the knowledge that anyone faced with a set of contradictions has about the opportunities that inconsistent premises offer for a multitude of arguments in opposite directions, I think this is most unlikely.

We are contemplating the possibility that faced with an array of legal materials as contradiction-ridden as Kennedy and other CLS scholars take them to be, a constructive argument interpreting the law in favor of one side or the other in litigation will be able to satisfy some very modest threshold of "fit." Crudely, it will make sense of roughly half of the materials it considers, and its proponent will be conscious that any remotely competent work done on behalf of the other party will also satisfy that threshold of fit, since it makes sense of the other half of the (conflicting) legal materials under consideration. In these circumstances, should we expect either advocate to make his argument with a burning consciousness that he is *right* about the law and his opponent wrong? Should we expect the judge, who entertains both arguments and understands the condition of the possibility of each of them, to be conscious of a basis for discriminating between them?

Dworkin remains remarkably upbeat, as he faces the prospect of this even rivalry between two equally viable theories purporting to make "sense" of the same mess of contradictory legal decisions. What he says, at least about the judge's situation, is this:

Hard cases arise, for any judge, when his threshold test [of fit] does not discriminate between two or more interpretations of some statute or line of cases. Then he must choose between eligible interpretations by asking which shows the community's structure of institutions and decisions—its public standards as a whole—in a better light from the standpoint of political morality. His own moral and political convictions are now directly engaged.[68]

The idea is that a judge, faced with two arguments that "fit" (in this quixotic sense) an equal quantity of the contradictory legal materials, will resolve the issue between them by considering which is superior on the merits, that is, on grounds of justice or other substantial values. And that will be the tie-breaker.[69]

---

[67] Of course, they may not be. But then Dworkin is thrown back on the position we discussed at the end of Section IV: saying (Hart-style) to the skeptics: it is not really as bad as all that.

[68] DWORKIN, LAW'S EMPIRE, *supra* note 1, at 255–256.

[69] *See also* DWORKIN, TAKING RIGHTS SERIOUSLY, *supra* note 7, at 340–341.

To understand what this position amounts to, we need to recall that on the CLS account the legal materials are not just contradictory in some technical sense. They are contradictory as between the main views about justice (and other substantial values) already held by diverse factions in society, and also as between the main values that are likely to be at stake in any piece of litigation to which it is supposed that law as integrity should be applied. We need to remember, too, that this is the hypothesis that Dworkin is supposed to be responding to, and in connection with which the passage just quoted above is supposed finally to refute the internal skeptic's critique.

Let me put it very schematically: suppose Kennedy is right and there are two recognizable moral positions, *Ind* (for individualism) and *Alt* (for altruism) in the law—contradicting one another, but spread throughout the settled law in an array of decisions in numbered cases $\{Ind_1, Alt_2, Ind_3, Alt_4, Ind_5, Alt_6, \ldots\}$. And now once again, the old adversaries face off against one another in yet another case— case 7, say. So the two sides set about constructing their arguments, following the constructive method that Dworkin recommends to practitioners of law as integrity. The individualist party cites a subset of the established cases $\{Ind_1, Ind_3, Ind_5\}$ and he puts cases 2, 4, and 6 aside. He is conscious, of course, that his opponent is likely to cite an equally sized subset $\{Alt_2, Alt_4, Alt_6\}$, putting cases 1, 3, and 5 aside. So what does the individualist party propose to clinch his argument? He says that his argument with its support in half the case law is better than his opponent's, because it is committed to *Ind* and because *Ind* is, as he believes, a better moral theory than *Alt*. The reason that clinches the matter on his account—the reason that is supposed to be capable of clinching the matter on Dworkin's account—is simply that in this conflict between two moral views that have come to pervade the law, he has aligned himself with the better one!

I very much doubt whether Dworkin will be embarrassed by this (though I will show shortly that he ought to be). The point of the critique implicit in my schematic example tends to be obscured by the fact that when Dworkin says that the judge's "own moral and political values" are engaged in the choice among rival theories that fit the existing legal materials equally well, we are not reminded that those very values are likely to be implicated on one side of the contradictions that pervade the law (on the CLS account). He sometimes writes as though the contradictory legal materials—leading to the impasse of fit—are one thing, and the values the judge brings to his task are another. I don't mean that Dworkin's argument rests on this misapprehension. He would probably bite the bullet and say that the judge has no choice but to rely on his own views about justice, even when his own views about justice are exactly the views that are represented (and contradicted) in the diverse legal materials facing him. But the possibility is not one that he brings to our attention. More important, he doesn't draw to our attention the fact that the attorneys for the parties[70] are already committed to one side or the other in

---

[70] *See also supra* note 62.

this debate; they are litigating the issue precisely because they are partisans of *Ind* and *Alt* respectively. So the values they appeal to when they try to clinch their argument are, in some sense, question-begging arguments. They assume the very point at issue and they then claim that this assumption breaks the tie between their own argument and that of their opponents!

VII.

An even more serious difficulty with Professor Dworkin's constructivist response to the internal skeptic is the question of its compatibility with the underlying argument for integrity in *Law's Empire*.

Briefly: Dworkin's judge (and hence Dworkinian attorneys) are supposed to be preoccupied with the interpretation of the existing legal materials because, like all of us, they have an obligation rooted in political morality to keep faith with the commitments of their community. This, according to Dworkin, is why it is worth persisting in trying to make sense of the existing legal record, tainted as it is with contradiction (if the skeptics are right). Absent that sense of obligation, the sensible thing to do in legal practice would be to abandon wrestling with the messy array of existing law and simply settle (and argue) cases pragmatically on the basis of what will be best for a just and prosperous future. But if the skeptic is right, if the legal materials are as contradictory as he says they are, then there is no coherent record to keep faith with, and therefore no ground for the integrity-based case against pragmatism to stand on. There may be clever moves—constructivist moves—that a Dworkinian lawyer can make which look impressive and which, at a stretch, have the feel of interpreting even the messy record that the internal skeptic postulates. But those moves do not and cannot engage the sort of integrity values that the interpretive exercise is ultimately answerable to. In other words, they have no point or at least they don't have the sort of point that integrity is supposed to give them. Quite the contrary: these constructivist moves in the face of contradictory materials make a mockery of the communitarian values underpinning integrity. That, in the end, is the seriousness of the challenge posed by internal skepticism: the challenge is not merely that Dworkin is giving Hercules an impossible task; it is that the task given to Hercules *makes no sense*, if the legal world is as the internal skeptic says it is.

There are several phases in this argument. The first is Professor Dworkin's own acknowledgment that in the end his own jurisprudence stands or falls with the refutation of pragmatism. He phrases the point in terms of legal rights—that is, rights which are generated by legal principles (or rights which are the upshot of successful interpretive theories).

The pragmatist thinks judges should always do the best they can for the future, in the circumstances, unchecked by any need to respect or secure consistency in principle with what other officials have done or will do. . . . [Pragmatism] rejects what other conceptions

of law accept: that people can have distinctly legal rights as trumps over what would otherwise be the best future properly understood. . . . I do not say this in any triumphant way.
The fact that a true pragmatist rejects the idea of legal rights is not a decisive argument
against that conception. For it is not self-evident that the idea of legal rights is attractive.
Or even sane.[71]

Indeed, as Dworkin goes on to say, it is quite easy to make the idea of legal rights
seem foolish. If a judge is convinced that the doctrine in a line of cases has proved
itself unjust, why should he accept the argument that a party has a legal right that
the injustice be perpetuated? Maybe if the party can show that he would suffer
more on account of his reliance on the injustice than his opponent would gain
were it corrected, or maybe if it can be shown that society is better off with this
doctrine as a basis for social predictability—maybe *then* there are reasons for
accepting his argument. But those arguments are themselves pragmatic and they
don't affect the underlying point that it seems foolish to worry away at difficult
precedents, tangled doctrine, or obscure legislation to find out what the law really
says, when one suspects it will be unjust and when it is clear anyway that no one
is really relying on any particular interpretation and that interpretive argument
contributes nothing to predictability. Dworkin is adamant in *Law's Empire* that
conventionalism, as a theory of law, falls at this hurdle—conventionalism cannot
withstand the pragmatist challenge[72]—and he cannot consistently confront law
as integrity with a lower bar than this.

So a jurisprudence of integrity must be capable of explaining *why* we ought to
refuse the pragmatist invitation to decide cases simply in a way that is best for the
future. A jurisprudence of integrity must explain why it is not foolish to worry
away at difficult precedents, tangled doctrine, or obscure legislation in a quest for
a solution (to the case in front of us) which is consistent with what our community has already committed itself to. *And the account of legal argument that it gives
must connect with that explanation.*

Now, Dworkin's answer to the pragmatist challenge has to do with the conditions for political legitimacy. Decisions by judges and other legal officials will be
enforced, and there is a question about the legitimacy of their enforcement and
the obligation that citizens have to defer to them—particularly those on the losing side in the decisions. Professor Dworkin pursues a long and interesting argument suggesting that legitimacy depends on the extent to which the obligation to
accept legal outcomes can be presented as a form of associative or communal
obligation.[73] Associative obligation, he says, can be sustained only among the
members of a community "who share a general and diffuse sense of members'
special rights and responsibilities from or toward one another."[74] Delving into
the legal record for principles or attempting to produce an interpretive theory

---

[71] DWORKIN, LAW'S EMPIRE, *supra* note 1, 160–162. (I have reversed the order of the first two sentences in this excerpt. That does not affect the sense.)   [72] *Id.* Ch. 4.
[73] *Id.* at 186–216.   [74] *Id.* at 199.

which gives an attractive and coherent account of what has been done among us already in the name of our association—both of these are ways of trying to show what that "diffuse sense of members' special rights and responsibilities" is. And connecting those principles or that theory with the decision one is arguing for in a particular case is a way of showing that parties in the case have an associative obligation to abide by that decision, because they are already in a sense committed to it.

Dworkin argues that such a strategy has a huge legitimacy-advantage over the pragmatist approach. In aiming to make society better for the future, the pragmatist naturally commands the support of those who accept his vision of social justice and the general good. But it is hard to see why anyone with a different or opposed vision of social justice or the general good should accept the decisions of a pragmatist official. Integrity, however, makes a different sort of claim—one rooted ultimately in reciprocity. Even when we disagree with one another about justice or the general good, we can see that some among us have been benefitted by decisions applying principles of a certain sort, and we can appreciate the fairness of allowing others to be benefitted by those principles, even when we disagree with them, because we think that their consistent and open-ended application across a diverse array of cases helps to establish us as a community of principle.

So: this is the case that Dworkin needs in order to make sense of modes of legal argumentation that grapple—in this non-pragmatic way—with the obscure implications of the set of decisions our community has already committed itself to. Such arguments present our association with one another as a community of principle and they use that as a basis for saying that a decision, now, that flows from the principles we have unearthed has legitimacy even for those who would be inclined in the abstract to oppose it. To claim this legitimacy advantage, we have to be willing to view the existing record of our community in a certain light—"to see and enforce it as coherent."[75] A judge who accepts integrity must be prepared to treat the parties who come before him in this spirit: "They are entitled, in principle, to have their acts and affairs judged in accordance with the best view of what the legal standards of the community required or permitted at the time they acted, and integrity demands that these standards be seen as coherent, as the state speaking with a single voice."[76] And it is in this spirit that Professor Dworkin undertakes the enterprise which we have been discussing in Sections II through VI.

Let us return now to the internal skepticism of CLS and to the constructivism that Dworkin uses to respond to it. The internal skeptic denies that it is possible to view the record of a community like ours as one in which a certain set of coherent principles have consistently determined legal outcomes. The record of our community, he says, does not disclose any consistent "sense of members' special rights and responsibilities from or toward one another," diffuse or otherwise. The internal skeptic denies therefore that any resolution of an instant case can made

---

[75] *Id.* at 167.   [76] *Id.* at 218.

legitimate by showing that it flows from such a set of coherent principles. The record of our community, he says, is one of incoherence, in which the principles necessary to sustain some decisions are contradicted by the principles necessary to sustain others. There is nothing, says the internal skeptic, corresponding to Dworkin's description of a consistent set of principles presupposed by all or most of the existing legal materials, from which we could infer legitimate answers to the legal questions that currently confront us. Professor Dworkin may say that "associative obligations can be sustained among people who share a general and diffuse sense of members' special rights and responsibilities from or toward one another, a sense of what sort or level of sacrifice one may be expected to make for another."[77] But Duncan Kennedy's point is precisely that we are conflicted about what we owe one another; we don't share a single conception; we share contradictory ones, if we share anything at all. Again, Dworkin may say that "[l]aw as integrity asks judges to assume, so far as this is possible, that the law is structured by a coherent set of principles . . . and it asks them to enforce these in the fresh cases that come before them, so that each person's situation is fair and just according to the same standards."[78] But the skeptical case is that this is *not* possible, and that this instruction simply cannot be carried out, because the existential assumption fails: law is not structured by a coherent set of principles.

For myself, I find it difficult to see how any form of versatile constructivism can displace or mitigate this verdict. A Dworkinian judge or lawyer might make an *attempt* to establish a record that is consistent *as far as it goes*, in the sense of identifying principles which offer a coherent explanation of *some* of the extant decisions. But the internal skeptic thinks that any such attempt will be easy to discredit. Whatever decisions it explains, it will leave an equal number of decisions unexplained (treated as outliers). So any such interpretation (in Dworkin's own words) will "show the record of the community in an irredeemably bad light, because proposing that interpretation suggests that the community has characteristically dishonored its own principles."[79]

Notice that this is *not* just a matter of there being rival theories available, and no demonstrable way of settling the issue between them. We can accept Professor Dworkin's claim that "people are entitled to a coherent and principled extension of past political decisions even when judges profoundly disagree about what this means"[80] and his view that "consistency in principle [can] be important for its own sake, . . . [even] when it is uncertain and controversial what consistency really requires?"[81] But those maneuvers do not save the position here. For what we face, if the internal skeptic is correct, is not a dispute between two viable interpretations which unfortunately cannot be settled in a demonstrable way; what we face are two rival interpretations, *each of which* is discredited by the fact that it seems to show a very considerable part of the community's record in a very bad light.

---

[77] *Id.* at 199.   [78] *Id.* at 243.   [79] *Id.* at 257.   [80] *Id.* at 134.   [81] *Id.* at 163.

The situation is not saved by a formulation which Dworkin sometimes uses, in which law-as-integrity is understood in terms of an ethic of *trying* to portray the law as coherent, rather than in terms of a duty to uncover the coherence that is actually there. I mean formulations like the following:

We want our officials to treat us as tied together in an association of principle, and we want this for reasons that do not depend on any identity of conviction among these officials, either about fit or about the more substantive principles an interpretation engages. Our reasons endure when judges disagree, at least in detail, about the best interpretation of the community's political order, because each judge still confirms and reinforces the principled character of our association by *striving* in spite of the disagreement, to reach his own opinion instead of turning to the usually simpler task of fresh legislation.[82]

These formulations are quite common in *Law's Empire* and elsewhere. Dworkin says that integrity is upheld "when people in good faith *try* to treat one another in a way appropriate to common membership in a community . . . and to see each other as making *this attempt*, even when they disagree about exactly what integrity requires in particular circumstances."[83] He says that "[w]e gain even through the attempt"[84] and that "[l]aw's empire is defined by attitude, not territory or power or process"[85] and "[l]aw as integrity consists in an approach, in questions rather than answers."[86] But not everything that one does to advance one's own position through legal argument can count as a good faith attempt of this kind. Nor are the conditions for a good faith attempt only subjective—such as that the lawyer is doing the best for integrity that he can, or whatever. The attempt must be something which it makes sense to embark on, and the critical or skeptical case is that, given what participants must know about the pervasively contradictory character of the existing legal materials, picking and choosing from among them those that suit one's purposes can hardly be described as a way of *trying* to display one's allegiance to their underlying coherence.

VIII.

Since the end of Section IV, I have been working on the assumption that the legal background in a society like ours *is* about as riddled with contrary principles as the CLS skeptics say it is. I proceeded on this assumption in order to see whether Professor Dworkin had anything convincing to say in response to their skepticism apart from a flat denial of its factual premise. I think we have concluded that he has not. The distinction between tensions and contradictions does not do the trick and neither does the move to constructivism nor the insistence that non-demonstrability is compatible with objectivity.

---

[82] *Id.* at 264 (emphasis added).   [83] *Id.* at 190 (emphasis added).
[84] DWORKIN, TAKING RIGHTS SERIOUSLY, *supra* note 7, at 338.
[85] DWORKIN, LAW'S EMPIRE, *supra* note 1, at 413.   [86] *Id.* at 239.

That leaves the flat denial. At the end of Section IV, I was inclined to doubt that Dworkin wanted to rest his jurisprudence on this. It sounded flabby and unconvincing, and appeared to make the whole enterprise contingent and precarious. But maybe that was premature, and if we turn around the argument that we have just been developing (in Section VII), we may be able to see why. I said that constructive interpretation by a Dworkinian advocate cannot count as a *bona fide* attempt to keep faith with the commitments of his community if it is known to the advocate that the record of the community is one of pervasive and systematic contradiction. If the advocate knows that roughly half the decisions embody the moral proposition that members of the community have very limited obligations to one another and roughly half of the decisions embody the moral proposition that members of the community have very extensive obligations to one another, he cannot with a straight face pull out just the materials in the latter half and argue on that basis that his opponent has a particular obligation to his client because this is what we—the community—have always been committed to. But suppose his knowledge of the extent and pervasiveness of the contradictions is not so clear. After all, the illustration that we used in Section VI—an array of decisions in numbered cases $\{Ind_1, Alt_2, Ind_3, Alt_4, Ind_5, Alt_6, \ldots\}$—was a ludicrously over-simplified version of the legal record that most advocates are likely to be confronted with. Ludicrously over-simplified, and ludicrously over-clarified: the tens of thousands of extant legal decisions that we find in the law reports and the statute books present a much more equivocal and tangled record than this. Confronted then with real-world legal materials, the Dworkinian advocate will have in the back of his mind the possibility that he will not be able to make a determinate case—or, as I emphasized in Section VI, the possibility that his opponent may be able to make a case as determinate as the one that he makes—but he may think it worth *trying* to see whether he can do any better, for integrity, than that. If it seems to him that the prospect of success here is not out of the question, then there is no reason to say—as I said about the overly simple case—that his attempt just makes a mockery of integrity.

So the factual disagreement between Dworkin and the skeptics may come down to this: Are the contradictions so clear and so pervasive that it is evidently not worth trying to see whether a particular set of principles (or a particular interpretation) fits the existing law? "Not worth trying" is the key predicate in this formulation. It does not mean and it should not be taken to mean that there is no legal argument that we can come up with. If we are prepared to pick and choose, we can always come up with *something*, even if or (as I said earlier on the basis of elementary propositional logic) *especially* if we know the materials are inconsistent. "Not worth trying" must refer to the conditions that would make the attempt important or worthwhile; that is, it must refer to the general idea of integrity. It must not be out of the question that our argument or our principles fit a very significant portion of the legal materials, and it must not be out of the question that this is *not* the case for our opponent's argument. If the constructive strategy that organizes our attempt rests on our having to say, even implicitly, that "the community has characteristically dishonored its own principles,"[87] then it is not an attempt worth making.

I think, in the end, this is where Dworkin should take his stand against the Crits. He should say (and he does say): it is not clear up front that attempts to argue in the mode of law-as-integrity are doomed to failure. If it were clear, we should have no reason to resist the siren charms of pragmatism: forget the existing law; ask instead what's best for the future; and take one's chances on the legitimacy issue. But sometimes legal argument looks promising, and when it does we are obliged to make the attempt (and the theory of integrity explains why). The cruder versions of CLS jurisprudence were easy to discredit: it simply was not so clear that law is systematically biased in favor of one social class as some CLS scholars said it was. Law is more complicated than that. The more sophisticated versions of CLS that I have been considering in this paper are certainly less easy to dismiss, and they deserve as Dworkin says to be taken seriously.[88] But perhaps the least convincing thing about them is the simplicity of their thesis about contradiction: there are these two positions (individualism and altruism) and the existing legal materials divide clearly and evenly between them. So long as we stick with that simple picture, the futility of law-as-integrity is evident. But complicate and muddy it somewhat, with more terms to the contradictions and arrays of less easily legible materials, then the appearance of futility recedes. And at that stage, as Dworkin says,[89] there is nothing to do but try, for nothing else will reveal whether an attempt can succeed while keeping faith with the motivations behind integrity.

The conclusions I have reached are perhaps not quite what Dworkin would want, for two reasons. First, I have insisted that what one is trying to make is a determinate legal argument, and that means one that excludes or promises to exclude the prospect of a similar argument by one's opponent. To repeat: nothing is easier than for a constructive jurisprudence to come up with something that looks like a legal argument. The test is whether there is a reasonable prospect that one can show that *nothing but this argument* will keep faith with the commitments of our community. Secondly, I do think that Dworkin is simply wrong to think that this burden can be discharged by using one's own moral and political convictions to break ties.[90] If the only thing to differentiate plaintiff's argument from defendant's argument, as a matter of law, in plaintiff's eyes is that plaintiff is an altruist and—as the plaintiff thinks—altruism is right (as a theory of justice), then plaintiff is arguing as a pragmatist. He is not arguing in good faith in the mode of law-as-integrity since, *ex hypothesi*, he concedes that the rest of his argument (the legal part) fails to discharge the burden that integrity imposes and what he appeals to as a tie-breaker has no connection with integrity, or nothing that would differentiate the stance of a defender of law-as-integrity from a defender of pragmatism. The moral is that the use of the tie-breaker, too, must satisfy the conditions of integrity. It can't just be wheeled out on an ad hoc basis to rescue an argument that would fail at the bar of integrity without it.

---

[87] *Id.* at 257.   [88] *Id.* at 273–275.   [89] *Id.* at 274.   [90] *Id.* at 256.

8

Associative Obligations and the Obligation to Obey the Law

Stephen Perry

I. Political Obligation

One of the strands woven into the complex fabric of *Law's Empire* (hereinafter LE) is an argument that there exists, under certain conditions, a general moral obligation to obey the law. Whether or not there can ever be such an obligation is an age-old problem in political philosophy, and Dworkin's argument is offered, in part, as a contribution to that particular philosophical tradition. But it is more than that, because the argument also constitutes an integral part of Dworkin's general theory of law. That is why I say it is one strand of a complex fabric; for Dworkin, political and legal philosophy are inextricably connected. For many of the philosophers who have addressed the question of political obligation, as I shall call it, there is no such inevitable connection. Notice, to begin, that no respectable theory of political obligation ever claimed that a person is obligated no matter what to obey the laws of a legal system to which he or she is subject. Every minimally plausible theory sets out certain conditions under which such an obligation is said to arise, and Dworkin's is no exception. Many such theories have, however, regarded these conditions as ones that do not figure in any essential way in the concept of law itself. They assume that law constitutes a system of norms the existence and content of which can be established by, say, looking to certain kinds of social facts, and then asking whether or not a given legal system meets a set of independently specifiable conditions; if these conditions are met, then a general obligation to obey is said to exist. Arguments based on consent are often (although not necessarily) of that form; they look to an independently specifiable condition that asks whether or not everyone who is subject to a legal system has validly consented to obey its laws, whatever they are. The argument from fair play is also of this form; it looks to an independently specifiable set of conditions that asks, first, whether the content of the norms of the system show it to be a mutually beneficial scheme of cooperation, and, secondly, whether or not those subject to the system have "accepted" its benefits.[1] There are, as Dworkin points out, well-known problems with both arguments if they are regarded as the basis of a *general* obligation to obey the law, since it is never the case that everyone subject to any given legal system has validly consented to obey it or has accepted, in the appropriate sense, certain benefits it happens to provide (LE at 192–195).[2] My present point, however, is that these arguments treat the philosophical problem of political obligation as for the most part independent of the philosophical problem about the nature of law.

Dworkin's theory, as I noted, is not like this. Before I say anything about the specifics of his view, however, let me first say a little more about the question of political obligation itself.[3] A general obligation to obey the law exists only if every person who is subject to a given legal system has a moral obligation to obey each and every law of the system *because* it is a law of the system. In saying that one has an obligation to obey the law because it is the law I do not mean that one's reason for action in doing as the law requires must be that the law requires it; for the most part, the law is indifferent to why one complies with the law so long as one does so. To say that one has an obligation to obey the law because it is the law means, rather, that at least one sufficient ground or basis of the obligation is the fact that the law exists. The law need not be the only basis of the obligation. We clearly have independent moral obligations not to assault and murder people, for example. However, if one has a moral obligation to obey the law then the law must be a basis of obligation in addition to one's independent moral obligations. Often, of course, the law modifies (or at least purports to modify) independent moral obligations, or to make them more precise where they are indeterminate, and there would not be much point to law if it was not capable of at least sometimes doing this. But it will not suffice to establish a general moral obligation to obey the law to show that the law has had some effect on one's moral obligations or, more generally, on one's moral situation. It is, as I said, necessary to show that one has an obligation to obey each and every law because it is the law. This challenge must be met not just where the law reproduces independent moral obligations, but also where the law makes moral mistakes, for example mistakes about what justice requires. Theories of political obligation almost always place limits on the extent to which the law can make moral mistakes and still give rise to a general obligation to obey the law, but it is nonetheless no easy matter to show that there is *ever* an obligation to obey an unjust law. And since no legal system is ever perfectly just, a theory of political obligation would not have shown very much if it failed to show

---

[1] *See* H. L. A. Hart, *Are There any Natural Rights?*, 64 Phil. Rev. 185 (1955); J. Rawls, A Theory of Justice 301–308 (2d ed., 1999).

[2] *See* A. J. Simmons, Moral Principles and Political Obligations (1979), especially chs. 3–5.

[3] In this paragraph I draw on material from my article *Law and Obligation*, 50 American Journal of Jurisprudence 263 (2005). For very helpful (albeit skeptical) discussions of political obligation, *see* Simmons, *supra* note 2; L. Green, The Authority of the State (1990), particularly ch. 8; and J. Raz, Ethics in the Public Domain (1994), ch. 14.

that the general obligation to obey is not capable of encompassing at least some unjust laws. Dworkin's theory acknowledges this point. A general obligation to obey the law can, of course, be prima facie and defeasible by other moral considerations; it is possible that an obligation to obey an unjust law can exist, but be overridden by the independent obligations of justice itself. Dworkin's theory acknowledges this point as well.

Here it will be helpful to bring in a distinction that Dworkin draws between the *grounds* and the *force* of law (LE at 108–113). Dworkin does not employ the following formulation, but we can say that the *grounds* of law are the truth conditions of propositions of the form "It is the law (of some specified jurisdiction) that A," where A is a normative proposition that states that some person or group of persons has some normative status, for example that they have an obligation, right, permission, liability, or power. The paradigmatic case is a proposition specifying an obligation, and I will continue to concentrate on that case. (The properly generalized version of the problem of political obligation asks whether the law systematically affects persons' normative status in all the various ways that it claims to do; for present purposes, we can ignore this complication.) For the sake of ease of expression I will from now on omit the reference to a specific jurisdiction, although it should always be understood as present. Suppose the proposition "It is the law that everyone has an obligation to do X" is true.[4] The *force* of law is its normative force, which means its moral force.[5] The concern when we are speaking about force, in other words, is with the truth or falsity of normative propositions such as "Everyone has an obligation to do X" when they figure in true propositions such as "It is the law that everyone has an obligation to do X." To say that a legal system has general normative force is simply to say that it gives rise to a general obligation to obey. Force, as a general concept in legal philosophy, is concerned with the connection between the truth of propositions of the form "It is the law that A" and the truth of "A." For the reasons given in the preceding paragraph, it will not suffice to establish that there is a general obligation to obey the law to show that for all propositions of the form "It is the law that ———," both "It is the law that A" and "A" are true. One must show, in addition, that at least one sufficient basis for the truth of "A" is the truth of "It is the law that A." Stated more precisely, one must show that the various facts, whether social, moral, or both, that serve to establish the truth of "It is the law that A" also serve to establish the truth of "A." A theory of political obligation is a theory about the conditions that

---

[4] "Everyone" can be understood as referring to all persons who are subject to the particular legal system; it does not matter for present purposes what, exactly, that means.

[5] It is of course true that not all normativity is moral, but Dworkin assumes that legal normativity, if it exists at all, is a type of moral normativity. Thus legal obligations (if they exist) are moral obligations, legal permissions (if they exist) are moral permissions, and so on. In my view this assumption is correct, but I cannot discuss the point here. I will limit myself to the observation that it is not an assumption that is in conflict with positivism, although not all positivists accept it. Kelsen and Raz do, but Hart does not.

must obtain in order for this connection to hold in a systematic way for all the laws of a legal system.

This brings me back to the observation that Dworkin's theory of political obligation does not treat the question of whether there is ever a general obligation to obey the law as independent from the philosophical problem about the nature of law. Dworkin says that a theory of law is a theory about the grounds of law, which means that it is a theory about the truth conditions of propositions of the form "It is the law that A." He is not always entirely clear about whether such a theory applies only to the law of particular jurisdictions or whether it is meant to be more general, but I think it is ultimately clear that it is meant to be more general: a theory about the grounds of law is (part of) a theory about the nature of law understood as a general kind of social phenomenon. To say that a theory of law is about the grounds of law is very vague, but I hope the formulation will suffice for present purposes. It is meant to cover, for example, such theoretical views as Dworkin's own theory of law as integrity, Hart's theory of the rule of recognition, and various versions of the social sources thesis. I will say something about the specifics of law as integrity in a moment. The point to be noticed for present purposes, however, is that the theory holds that the grounds of law depend, in part, on considerations having to do with the (potential) force of law. Dworkin does not put the point in the following way, but I believe the essence of his view is this: law as integrity, which is a substantive theory about the grounds of law, presupposes the truth of a particular theory of political obligation, and it does so in such a way that the truth of propositions of the form "It is the law that A" depends, in part and to a limited extent, on whether or not "A" is capable of being made true by that theory of political obligation.[6] This is very abstract, and I will begin to fill in the details of the view later in this section and in section III. But the abstract formulation suffices to show us that, on Dworkin's view, the theory of political obligation does not take the content of law as given and then ask whether or not there is a general obligation to obey; it is, rather, an integral part of the theory of the grounds of law, and therefore itself has an effect on the content of law. This is, as I said, a claim that Dworkin makes about law as integrity. But earlier in *Law's Empire* he makes an even more ambitious, methodological claim, which holds, in effect, that *any* general theory about the grounds of law must presuppose some theory of political

---

[6] Notice that the truth of propositions of the form "It is the law that A" is said to depend in part *not* on the independent truth of the normative proposition "A," in which case we would be dealing with a certain radical kind of natural law theory, but rather on whether or not "A" is capable of being made true by the theory of political obligation. In other words, the truth of "It is the law that A" partly depends on whether or not "A" is capable of being made true by the truth of "It is the law that A." As we shall see, Dworkin's own theory of law as integrity makes this determination holistically, by looking to how "A" fits into the content of the law taken as a whole. There is no vicious or unavoidable circularity here. It should also be emphasized that the truth of propositions of the form "It is the law that A" is said to depend only *partly* on the theory of political obligation. The most important determinant of the truth of such propositions is, of course, social practice, such as facts about what legislatures and courts have done. This is the crucial dimension of "fit" in Dworkin's general theory of interpretation.

obligation in much the same way as his own theory of law as integrity does.[7] Dworkin summarizes the point by saying that "[a] general theory of law . . . proposes a solution to a complex set of simultaneous equations" having to do with both the grounds and the force of law (LE at 110). Different theories of law presuppose different theories of political obligation (or else deny that there can be such a theory). To determine which theory of law is correct we must, therefore, at some point address the general question of political obligation, and this necessarily takes us deep into issues of substantive political morality. This is, I believe, the nerve of Dworkin's general theory of interpretation, understood as a methodology for doing philosophy of law.

I cannot discuss the general theory of interpretation here, except to make the following brief observations. Although the truth conditions of propositions like "It is the law that A" are affected by moral considerations having to do with the capacity of the law to obligate us, they also depend crucially and unavoidably on social facts, and in particular on facts about what legislatures and courts have done. Given that social practice is, necessarily, the starting point of interpretation, I do not think that Dworkin should be understood as saying that propositions of the form "It is the law that A" can never be true unless some theory of political obligation is true (although he is clearly more optimistic on this latter score than most other contemporary theorists). What I believe he is saying, rather, is that the practice of law with which we are familiar *presupposes* that there is a true theory of political obligation. The practice is built on the assumption that certain kinds of social facts serve as a systematic basis or ground for obligations. But this presupposition might be mistaken. It is possible that, as a general moral matter, the truth of a proposition of the form "It is the law that A" can *never* be a sufficient basis for the truth of "A"—i.e., the truth of such a proposition can never be a sufficient basis for the existence of an obligation—in which case law as a general kind of social practice would not make sense; complete skepticism about it would be justified. It is also possible that, whether or not a general theory of political obligation is true, a particular legal system is so unjust or evil that, within that system, the truth of a proposition of the form "It is the law that A" is never, or almost never, a sufficient ground for the truth of "A;" skepticism about the particular legal system would then be justified. In both of these cases, Dworkin need not and should not deny that propositions of the form "It is the law that A" could still be true just by virtue of facts about social practice. In making this acknowledgment, however, we would also have to acknowledge that, in the first case, the general practice was by its own lights a radically defective one, and, in the second case, that we were dealing with a degenerate instance of a legal system. (*Cf.* LE at 101–108.)

There is one more preliminary matter that needs to be mentioned before we consider the specifics of Dworkin's substantive views about political obligation.

---

[7] "In much the same way" is deliberately vague. It is beyond the scope of this paper to explore Dworkin's general methodological claims about legal philosophy in any detail.

Dworkin holds, in keeping with a long and respectable tradition in political philosophy, that the question of whether or not there is a general obligation to obey the law is unavoidably connected to the question of when, if ever, the state is morally legitimate: "A state is legitimate if its constitutional structure and practices are such that its citizens have a general obligation to obey political decisions that purport to impose duties on them" (LE at 191). Given that the state, by means of law, "purports to impose duties," Dworkin is surely right that it is appropriate, and indeed inevitable, to judge its moral legitimacy by reference to the standard of whether or not it succeeds in creating those duties.[8] This is particularly true given that the state claims the authority not just to impose duties but to enforce them by coercive means. As Dworkin notes, there may well be circumstances in which a state is justified in the use of coercion even though there is no duty on the part of those coerced to acquiesce, but these are exceptional (LE at 191). He is also appropriately cautious in describing the relationship between obligation and the justification of coercion: obligation is "close to" a necessary condition for coercion, but it is not sufficient. Although he is sometimes misunderstood in this regard, Dworkin claims no more than the following: "[N]o general policy of upholding the law with steel could be justified if the law were not, in general, a source of genuine obligations" (LE at 191).

This brings me, finally, to Dworkin's particular substantive theory of law as integrity. As the above remarks make clear, Dworkin uses this term to refer both to a theory of law, meaning a theory about the truth conditions of propositions of the form "It is the law that A," and to a related theory of political obligation. Context should generally make clear to which I am referring, although for the most part I shall be focusing on the theory of political obligation. Dworkin's basic approach to the problem of political obligation is interesting and original. He argues that the general obligation to obey the law is an associative obligation, meaning an obligation that arises within certain kinds of limited human associations. The paradigms are friendship and family. Dworkin describes a number of conditions that he maintains are characteristic of associative obligations in general, and then argues that law, when it meets versions of those conditions that are appropriate to its character as a form of human association, likewise gives rise to obligations. I will discuss the general conditions of associative obligation in some detail in the following section, and accordingly will not set them out here. So far as political obligation is concerned, Dworkin's central claim is that it arises when a legal system exhibits the distinct political ideal of integrity. Integrity, which is to be distinguished from the other political ideals of fairness, justice, and procedural due process, "requires government to speak with one voice, to act in a principled and coherent manner towards all its citizens, to extend to everyone the substantive standards of justice or fairness it uses for some" (LE at 165). The content of the law depends, according to Dworkin, on interpretation, and the law should be

---

[8] This is also Raz's view.

interpreted as a whole so as to exhibit integrity, to the extent that this is possible. (This is the upshot of the abstract idea that the truth conditions of propositions of the form "It is the law that A" depend, in part, on whether or not "A" is capable of being made true by the truth of "It is the law that A.") If the content of the law does exhibit integrity, then what would otherwise just be a "bare" community becomes what Dworkin calls a "genuine" political community, and those who belong to it have a general moral obligation to obey the law. This obligation is an associative obligation similar to the obligations that hold between friends and among members of a family.

In the following sections I shall discuss this argument for political obligation in some detail. Here let me just sketch my main conclusions. In Section II I examine Dworkin's general analysis of associative obligations. I conclude that, while there are some difficulties with the analysis, Dworkin has pointed to a genuine and distinct type of obligation that arises within certain kinds of limited relationships among persons. I further suggest that the justification for these obligations, and the reason for their distinctiveness, is that these relationships are ones of intrinsic value. If that is so, then Dworkin's strategy for establishing a general political obligation requires us to show that a genuine political community—one whose law exhibits integrity—has intrinsic value for its members. Properly understood, this is, I believe, precisely Dworkin's argument. In Section III I discuss this idea in more detail and try to show that, despite the obvious differences between personal relationships like friendship and family, on the one hand, and a political community of the kind exemplified by modern states on the other, this line of argument is a promising one. It may well be the only kind of argument for a general political obligation to obey the law that has any chance of success.

II. Associative Obligations

Associative obligations are, very roughly, obligations that arise in connection with certain limited human associations, like friendships and families. Such obligations are, as Dworkin notes, special, which means that they are owed only to certain persons and not universally. Are all special obligations also associative? This is not a question that can be definitively answered before we have in hand an analysis of associative obligations, but as an intuitive matter there does not seem to be any good reason to think that they are. Suppose there is a general moral duty of easy rescue, meaning a duty to assist another person who is in serious danger if one can do so at no great cost to oneself. If you fall into a raging river and I am in a position to throw you a life ring, then it is quite plausible to think that the duty I have in those circumstances is a special one; I owe a duty to you that I do not owe to other people. No doubt there is some formal sense in which the two of us are in association with one another, but this does not look like what people typically have in mind in speaking of associative obligations. Or think of the obligations that arise when we exercise powers of promise or consent. If I promise to read a manuscript of yours, then I come under a special obligation to you to do as I have promised. Again, there is clearly a sense in which we are in association with one another, and yet promissory obligations are often contrasted with, rather than treated as a species of, associative obligations.

What is special, then, about associative obligations? Dworkin, who sometimes uses the term "fraternal" instead of "associative," offers the following general analysis of the concept:

[T]he members of a group must by and large hold certain attitudes about the responsibilities they owe one another if these obligations are to count as genuine fraternal obligations. First, they must regard the group's responsibilities as *special*, holding distinctly within the group, rather than as general duties its members owe equally to persons outside it. Second, they must accept that these responsibilities are *personal*: that they run directly from each member to each other member, not just to the group as a whole in some collective sense. . . . Third, members must see these responsibilities as flowing from a more general responsibility each has of *concern* for the well-being of others in the group; they must treat discrete obligations that arise only under special circumstances, like the obligation to help a friend who is in great financial need, as derivative from and expressing a more general responsibility that is active throughout the association in different ways. . . . Fourth, members must suppose that the group's practices show not only concern but *equal* concern for all members. Fraternal obligations are in that sense conceptually egalitarian. They may be structured, even hierarchical, in the way a family is, but the structure and hierarchy must reflect the group's assumption that its roles and rules are equally in the interests of all, that no one's life is more important than anyone else's. Armies may be fraternal obligations if that condition is met. (LE at 199–201)

Dworkin summarizes the four conditions in the following way: "The responsibilities a true community deploys are special and individualized and display a pervasive mutual concern that fits a plausible conception of equal concern" (201). He adds that "[t]he concern [these conditions] require is an interpretive property of the group's practices of asserting and acknowledging responsibilities—these must be practices that people with the right level of concern would adopt—not a psychological property of some fixed number of the actual members" (LE at 201).

There is much about this analysis that rings true. All four conditions appear to hold for friendship, for example, which is surely a paradigm of a type of human relationship that gives rise to associative obligations. I have some doubts, however, about whether the same can be said of every associative obligation, or at least every example of an associative obligation that Dworkin offers us. Clearly, as already noted, the first condition is a necessary one; associative obligations are special, in the sense that they are owed only to certain persons. The third condition, that associative obligations express a general concern for the other person or persons with whom one is associated, is probably a necessary one as well. But are all associative obligations personal, in the sense defined by Dworkin's second condition? Certainly the obligations that exist in the paradigm cases of friendship and family are personal in this sense. Recall, however, that Dworkin wishes to show that political obligation is a type of associative obligation. If a general political obligation ever exists, it is far from clear that it is personal. In form, at least, it is not. A general obligation to obey the law is usually thought to be owed, if to anyone, to the community or state itself rather than to one's fellow citizens considered one by one. If the obligation is owed to the community it must of course be true that the community is, or is capable of being treated as, a moral agent in some appropriate sense, but this is far from being an obstacle for Dworkin; he insists that a proper understanding of political and legal practice in fact *requires* moral personification of the community. When it comes time to argue that the model of principle, which is Dworkin's preferred model of political community, meets the four stated conditions, he writes with respect to the second condition that the model makes the responsibilities of the relevant community "fully personal" because "it commands that no one be left out, that we are all in politics for better or worse, that no one may be sacrificed, like wounded left on the battlefield, to the crusade for justice overall" (LE at 213). But this is not the sense of the second condition as Dworkin originally defined it. He is not here arguing that the responsibilities in question "run directly from each member to each other member." The idea that the model of principle "commands that no one be left out" sounds, rather, like a restatement of the fourth condition, which holds that the concern expressed by the responsibilities of an associative relationship must be an equal concern.

Turning directly to that fourth condition, what does it mean to say that the concern expressed by the responsibilities of an associative relationship must be an equal concern? Consider friendship. In this context the condition presumably means that the obligations that two friends reciprocally owe to one another must express a more or less equal *level* of concern. This is what Dworkin seems to have in mind when he says that friends ought to have "roughly the same concern" for one another even if they do not share exactly the same understanding of the responsibilities of friendship (LE at 199). In the family context, however, the equality condition seems to mean something different. Dworkin discusses the example of a culture that gives parents the power to choose spouses for their daughters but not for their sons. The culture accepts "in good faith" the equality of the sexes but thinks, mistakenly, that equality of concern requires a paternalism for daughters that it does not require for sons. Dworkin argues that, despite this moral mistake, it is possible that daughters in this culture owe their parents a genuine obligation of obedience, although it is also possible that the obligation might ultimately be overridden by other moral considerations (LE at 204–205). I am not at present concerned with the question of whether or not Dworkin is correct in making this claim. I mean only to point out that the notion of "equal concern" must in this context have a quite different sense from the one it has in the context of friendship. Here, it seems to mean something like the following: the moral powers that one holds over others within an associative relationship may only be exercised in a way that manifests equal concern for all those over whom the powers are held. Dworkin claims, controversially, that children can come under an obligation to obey their parents even if parental power is *not* so exercised, so long as it is exercised in accordance with a conception of equal concern that is plausible and sincerely held. Whether or not this claim is true, "equal concern" does not here refer, as it does in the case of friendship, to an equal level of reciprocal concern that the members of an associative relationship owe to one another. To make this clear, imagine the case of a single parent raising a single child. The parent has an obligation to care for the child, and associated with this obligation is a power to command obedience. The child has an obligation to do as the parent requires. These two obligations—the obligation on the part of the parent to care for the child, and the obligation on the part of the child to obey the parent—are not reciprocal obligations like those that hold between two friends. Both obligations are most plausibly understood as being grounded in the wellbeing of the child alone. It is of course true that the child may eventually come under an obligation to care for the parent in the latter's old age, but this is not an obligation that is reciprocal to the parent's obligation to care for the child when the child is young. This is not because the two obligations cannot exist at the same time. It is because neither obligation is conditioned on the existence—past, present or future—of the other. The parent of a child with a fatal illness has no less a duty to care for the child—and arguably has a greater one—than the parent of a child with a normal life expectancy, and a person close to adulthood who is adopted or becomes a step-child may still come under an obligation to care for his or her new parent in old age.

The main point I was concerned to establish in the last paragraph is that there does not seem to be a single conception of equal concern that informs even the paradigmatic associative relationships of family and friendship. The equality of concern that must hold between friends, which is a form of reciprocity, need not hold between parent and child. (Relations between siblings is a more complicated case, which I do not discuss here.) Nor does there seem to be, in the case of friendship, an analogue to the obligation to exercise parental powers over a number of different children so as to manifest equal concern for each. (We do not, for example, owe the same level of concern to all our different friends, and that is true even within a group of mutual friends; the appropriate level of concern varies with the closeness of the particular friendship.) It does not help to say that there is a more abstract conception of equality underlying the specific conceptions that inform friendship and family, because at a sufficiently abstract level all moral principles, and not just those that underpin associative obligations, are, in Dworkin's phrase, "conceptually egalitarian." None of this calls into question the obligatoriness of true associative obligations, but it suggests, particularly when considered with the point made earlier that some associative obligations might not be personal in character, that the attempt to find a comprehensive set of attributes that hold for all associative relationships is unlikely to succeed. The problem is compounded when one considers the many kinds of social practice that Dworkin regards as being, at least potentially, associative in character: in addition to family, friendship, and political community, he mentions academic colleagueship, union membership, and membership in an army, and he clearly thinks there are others as well. Once we have failed to find common ground even among the paradigm cases, how can we be sure that these apparently quite different kinds of human association are, from a moral point of view, properly grouped together? Relatedly, how can we be sure that *other* features that seem to be essential to the paradigm cases of friendship and family—for example, true emotional bonds of love, affection, or respect—are not essential features of associative obligations in general, thereby ruling out such associations as political community and (I would imagine) academic colleagueship?

Dworkin's response to the above concerns might well be that the four conditions are the basis of an "abstract interpretation of the yet more general practice of associative obligation itself" (LE at 197), and that it is this more general practice that reveals the underlying unity of friendship, family, union membership, and so on. Even if the proffered four conditions fall short as an interpretation of the more general practice—they are, after all, only advanced by Dworkin as a first run at the problem—the very existence of the general practice gives us reason to think, the response would continue, that some satisfactory interpretation can be found. It is, however, far from clear that any such general practice of associative obligation exists, at least in the sense of a practice that self-consciously and reflectively manifests the interpretive attitude. There could only be such a practice if people generally regarded the relevant patterns of behavior *as* a distinct practice, thought the practice had value, and took the requirements of the practice to be sensitive to what its value was taken to be (LE at 47).[9] Even if friendship, family, political community, and so on all exhibit the interpretive attitude within themselves, there does not appear to be a comprehensive practice of associative practices, so to speak, of which that is also true.

There is another kind of objection to Dworkin's account of associative obligations that should be mentioned here. If it has merit it applies even if, contrary to what I have suggested, the four conditions succeed in capturing common features of the paradigm cases of associative relationships. An initial version of the objection runs as follows. Insofar as the analysis based on the four conditions simply identifies certain *attitudes* held by the members of a group about their responsibilities to one another, it is not clear why those attitudes should give rise to, or be taken to be markers of, actual responsibilities within the group, as opposed to mere beliefs about responsibilities. Denise Réaume has argued, for example, that Dworkin's analysis is ultimately no more than a variation on Hart's practice theory of rules, and as such it falls prey to Dworkin's own critique of that theory.[10]

---

[9] I take it that the existence of the interpretive attitude is a psychological or sociological matter. If it were not, there would a danger that the term "interpretive" would simply be a label applied to practices that might, for whatever reason, be capable of being a source of obligation. The general account of interpretation would lose its distinctiveness.

[10] D. Réaume, *Is Integrity a Virtue? Dworkin's Theory of Legal Obligation* 39 U. of Tor. L.J. 380, 402 (1989).

According to Dworkin's critique, the fact that a group treats certain of its practices as obligatory cannot, in and of itself, make them obligatory; something more in the way of normative argument is required.[11] As it stands Réaume's objection skips too quickly over a crucial point, which is that the four conditions are expressly stated by Dworkin to be interpretive properties of a group's practices rather than "psychological propert[ies] of some fixed number of actual members" (LE at 201).[12] The third condition, for example, requires that these practices be ones that "people with the right level of concern would adopt" rather than ones in which some minimum proportion of members actually manifest concern for their fellows (LE at 201).[13] The four conditions together are meant to be an interpretation of what Dworkin takes to be a general practice of associative obligation, and interpretations always have a dimension of justification or value. Dworkin's analysis thus cannot be regarded as a mere variant of Hart's practice theory. That having been said, however, we still run up against the question mentioned in the previous paragraph of whether or not there is, in fact, a general interpretive practice of associative obligation. We also run up against the related problem of what the value associated with such a practice might be. Although Dworkin is not entirely clear about this point, he seems simply to invoke a single general value of community or fraternity. But just as it is not clear that there is, in fact, a general interpretive practice of associative obligation, it is similarly not clear that there is a single value that can be regarded as accompanying such diverse forms of human association as friendship, political community, union membership, and so on. If I am right that the four conditions fail to capture common features of even the paradigmatic instances of associative obligation, then we have at least some reason to doubt the existence of both a general practice and a single value that underlies every instance of such a practice.

In the preceding discussion I have tried to raise some doubts about Dworkin's analysis of associative relationships, but I have not called into question his basic strategy for showing that a general moral obligation to obey the law can exist. He begins, it will be recalled, with the premise that certain limited forms of human

---

[11] R. Dworkin, Taking Rights Seriously (1978), ch. 3.

[12] This does not call into question the point that the existence of the interpretive attitude, and hence the character of a practice as an interpretive practice, is itself a psychological or sociological matter. *See further supra* note 9.

[13] It should, however, be borne in mind that the paradigmatic associative obligations of family and friendship cannot exist unless each friend or family member actually feels certain emotions for, and holds certain attitudes toward, the other person or persons in the relationship. I discuss this point further below. Holding an attitude towards another person is different from holding an attitude about the nature of the duties that you owe to that person, and the four conditions for the most part express attitudes of the latter rather than the former kind. But in the case of the third condition the two types of attitude converge; the mutual concern required by that condition must, in the case of friendship and family, exist in a psychological sense. We must therefore take seriously the possibility mentioned earlier that all associative obligations similarly require actual concern among the relevant persons. This would obviously pose problems for treating political obligation as a type of associative obligation.

association are generally and plausibly regarded as giving rise to obligations, and then argues that political communities are associations of that same kind and therefore they, too, are capable of giving rise to obligations. I believe this strategy is a promising one, but if we are to give effect to it we must characterize associative obligations in a somewhat different way from Dworkin's analysis based on the four conditions. (As I will suggest later, the appropriate characterization turns out to be an important, if perhaps implicit, strand in Dworkin's own discussion of associative obligations.) My approach will be to focus, in the first instance, on the paradigm associative relationship of friendship. Why do friends have obligations towards one another? It seems almost misplaced to ask this question, and it is tempting to answer it by saying that friends have obligations because that's part of what friendship is. So far as it goes this answer is completely correct, but it must be understood as part of a deeper truth. As Aristotle and many others since have observed, friendship has intrinsic value. It may also have instrumental value, of course, but if a relationship between two persons was not intrinsically valuable— and if its intrinsic value did not dominate its instrumental value for each of them—then it would not be friendship. It is partly constitutive of friendship that friends hold certain characteristic attitudes towards one another, the most important of which are affection and respect. But the obligations of friendship— primarily duties of loyalty and mutual assistance—are themselves partly constitutive of the relationship.[14] The attitudes, obviously, evolve over time, and the potential friends must each make choices that permit the friendship to develop. At a certain point, however, they just become friends, and the duties exist. This is not a matter of exercising a power of promise or consent. As Dworkin says, it would be perverse to describe friendship as a matter of *assuming* obligations; the shared history by virtue of which friends come to owe obligations is, on the contrary, "a history of events that *attract* obligations" (LE at 197). This seems exactly right. But the reason this happens is that the relationship of friendship, constituted in part by certain mutual duties, is intrinsically valuable. It might be objected that this is moral bootstrapping. Doesn't it amount to saying that the duties exist because it is good that they exist? Yes, it does. But this kind of bootstrapping is pervasive and unavoidable in morality. Duties are justified either instrumentally or non-instrumentally, but in both cases the existence of the duty turns on its relationship to value. Instrumental duties exist because they promote or contribute to the creation of independently valuable states of affairs, or are likely to do so. Non-instrumental duties exist because they are valuable in themselves, or partly constitutive of a relationship that is valuable in itself. In each case, it is part of the argument for the existence of the duty that it is good that it exists.

Dworkin is of course aware of the relationship between duty and value. One of the two dimensions of interpretation is success in justifying a normative practice— the other is success in fitting the practice—and justifications cannot help but

---

[14] *Cf.* Raz, *supra* note 3, at 337.

invoke value. There is an interesting question about the relationship between associative obligations and interpretive practices in general. Dworkin clearly expresses the view in *Law's Empire* that all associative relationships are either interpretive practices themselves or are formed within broader interpretive practices, but does he also think that all interpretive practices are (potential) associative relationships? It is not entirely clear. Whatever Dworkin's view on this question might have been at the time that he wrote *Law's Empire*, I wish to suggest that associative relationships are a narrower category than interpretive practices generally.[15] Taking friendship as a paradigm, the suggestion is that we can identify a distinctive type of obligation that arises because it is partly constitutive of some form of limited human relationship that possesses intrinsic value. The further suggestion is that Dworkin's strategy for establishing the possibility of political obligation requires one to argue that genuine political community—the term is Dworkin's (LE at 211)—is an intrinsically valuable form of human association. Properly understood, I believe that this is exactly Dworkin's argument. Before defending that conclusion, however, let me say a bit more about associative obligations in general.

Notice, to begin, that this account of associative obligations does not presuppose a general interpretive practice of associative obligation, although it is consistent with the existence of such a practice. The account is, in the first instance, simply a first-order moral claim about the way in which certain kinds of human relationships may give rise to obligations. Whether or not there is a general interpretive practice of associative obligation is not, therefore, a question that needs to be answered definitively for present purposes. I earlier argued that the four conditions that Dworkin advances as characteristic of such a general practice are not found together in every associative relationship. But it is important to emphasize that those conditions are nonetheless likely to figure prominently in most such relationships, although no doubt in different ways and configurations. A further, related point to notice about the account I have offered is that just as it does not require that there be a general interpretive practice of associative obligation, neither does it require that there be a single intrinsic value that all such obligations share. The claim is simply that we can identify certain kinds of obligations that are in an important sense similar to one another, for the reason that they are partly constitutive of relationships that are intrinsically valuable. The account is consistent with the idea that a single value underlies all associative obligations, but it is

---

[15] It is also at least conceivable that associative relationships need not necessarily be, or be formed within the context of, interpretive practices in Dworkin's strong sense. For example, is it only possible for two persons to be friends within a broader interpretive practice of friendship? It is almost impossible to imagine a human world in which most persons did not have ties of respect and affection with others, but the interpretive attitude requires a certain self-consciousness about the general practice of friendship, and, in particular, about what is taken to be its point or value, that might nonetheless be absent from a particular culture. It is at least arguable that so long as individuals hold the appropriate attitudes towards one another an intrinsically valuable relationship, together with its associated duties, comes into being, regardless of whether these or any other persons hold views about the point or value of friendship. I will not, however, pursue this line of thought further here.

probably more plausible to think that we are dealing with a plurality of values; the intrinsic value of friendship would thus be different from the intrinsic value of family, and different again from the intrinsic value, if any, of political community.

As has already been noted, it follows from the account of associative obligation I have offered—that these are obligations that are partly constitutive of some intrinsically valuable form of human relationship—that not all interpretive practices are, either in fact or potentially, associative relationships. There is nothing in Dworkin's general account of interpretation that rules out the possibility that the value or point of some interpretive practices is instrumental, just as nothing rules out the possibility that the value of some is non-instrumental. If the general characterization is right, moreover, then Dworkin casts the net of associative obligation too widely: it seems unlikely, for example, that either union membership or academic colleagueship is an intrinsically valuable form of human relationship. This general account of associative obligation also makes clear that not all special obligations are associative. Earlier I pointed to the example of a general duty of easy rescue that is capable of generating special duties owed to particular individuals. Although I shall not argue the point here, it seems plausible to think that both the general and the special duties are justifiable solely on instrumental, consequentialist grounds. The special duty is thus not an associative one. What about special obligations that arise from the exercise of powers of promise and consent? This is an interesting case. The power to promise is a power deliberately to place oneself under new obligations to others, and the power to consent is, roughly, a power deliberately or knowingly to change one's normative situation in a broader sense. (In addition to consenting to assume an obligation, one can, for example, consent to waive one's rights.) It would be very implausible to think that every relationship that arises from the exercise of such powers is one of intrinsic value—consider commercial contracts, for example—although their exercise can clearly contribute to, or deepen, relationships that have such value independently; the best example is probably the vows of marriage. If the relationships are not intrinsically valuable then neither are the special obligations that constitute them; these obligations are not, or at least are not necessarily, associative obligations. Even if this is true, however, it is quite possible that the powers themselves *are* intrinsically valuable. Joseph Raz, for example, has argued very persuasively that an important justification for such powers, although not the only one, lies in the intrinsic value of being able to create special bonds with others and, more generally, being able to fashion the shape of one's own moral world.[16] (Notice that this is another example of the kind of bootstrapping that I said earlier was unavoidable in morality; these powers exist because it is good that they do so.) If this is correct then there is an important affinity between assumed obligations and associative obligations, even though the former are not necessarily instances of the latter.

[16] J. Raz, *Promises and Obligations*, in Law, Morality, and Society: Essays in Honour of H. L. A. Hart 210, 226–228 (P. M. S. Hacker and J. Raz., eds, 1977); J. Raz, The Morality of Freedom 86–87 (1986).

I will offer, as a final general observation about associative obligations, a pair of related points that were implicit in the discussion of the preceding paragraph. There is no reason why associative obligations cannot coexist with instrumental obligations within a single kind of relationship, and, indeed, no reason why the same obligation cannot be justified on both instrumental and non-instrumental grounds. The second point seems to hold true of families, for example, and possibly the first does as well. If there is love between a parent and a child then the relationship between them is intrinsically valuable, and both the parent's obligation to care for the child and the child's obligation to obey the parent are partly constitutive of that relationship. Both obligations undoubtedly have an important instrumental justification as well, however, since both are necessary to ensure the wellbeing and proper development of the child. The parent–child relationship is one that by its nature is intrinsically valuable but that has, in addition, an important instrumental dimension. It also seems quite possible that certain relationships that do not necessarily have intrinsic value, such as those created by contract, may come to have an element of such value, and thus to give rise to associative obligations that would not otherwise exist, because of the development of trust and respect between the parties. Dworkin gives the interesting example of commercial partnerships (LE at 200). While I do not think that every such partnership necessarily gives rise to associative obligations, it is quite plausible to think that at least some do. It does not follow, of course, that associative obligations that exist within the context of an essentially commercial relationship either are or should be enforceable as a matter of law. Within the legal systems we are generally familiar with the fact that they are not so enforceable, and probably should not be. But that does not mean that they do not exist.

III. Political Obligation and Integrity

It is time to return to the issue of political obligation. As was noted earlier, Dworkin argues that a general obligation to obey the law arises when a legal system possesses the special political virtue of integrity. Integrity, we are told, "requires government to speak with one voice, to act in a principled and coherent manner towards all its citizens, to extend to everyone the substantive standards of justice or fairness it uses for some" (LE at 165). As this characterization makes clear, integrity is a complex ideal which contains a number of different strands. The core idea, however, is easily enough discerned: the state, acting through its various institutions and officials, must always strive to ensure that both its laws and the actions it takes to enforce those laws "express a single and comprehensive vision of justice" (LE at 134). This idea is, in my view, properly treated by Dworkin as central because it is connected in two distinct but related ways to the concept of equality. First, if the state gives effect to a *single* conception of justice, then its various officials will be acting, to put the point deliberately vaguely, in an appropriately similar fashion: litigants can be assured, for example, that their case will be handled in accordance with the same general principles whether they end up in courtroom A or in courtroom B. In that sense government will, in Dworkin's phrase, "be speaking with one voice." But equality in this sense is consistent with great substantive inequality: members of one race, for example, might consistently be treated very differently from members of another race, even though any given individual would be treated exactly the same way in courtroom A as he or she would have been treated in courtroom B. Integrity is connected to substantive equality because it requires not just that the state act in accordance with a single set of logically consistent standards, but that it act in accordance with a single conception of *justice*. In Dworkin's words, the government must "extend to everyone the substantive standards of justice or fairness it uses for some." This is a tricky matter, because integrity is distinct from justice and hence does not require that citizens be treated as justice in fact requires. Dworkin is assuming, I believe, that while true justice necessarily entails equality of concern, equality of concern does not necessarily entail true justice. This is a strong assumption, but it has a great deal of plausibility. Dworkin at times speaks somewhat loosely of integrity as requiring a plausible or coherent conception of equal concern (LE at 213). I think the better way to put the point, however, is to say that integrity requires *actual* equal concern, which will take the form of a plausible or coherent (but perhaps false) conception of justice. Integrity, in other words, is not just a matter of sincerity or plausibility or coherence, but has genuine moral content. That content is provided by the concept of equal concern, which occupies a moral middle ground between simple consistency on the one hand, and true justice, on the other. At any rate this will be my working assumption for present purposes.

When a legal system has integrity, Dworkin suggests, a "bare" political community is transformed into a "genuine" political community, and its members come under a general obligation to obey the law. Integrity, I have suggested, is a matter of true equal concern. Equal concern is, in turn, the bridge between Dworkin's general analysis of associative obligations and his particular argument for political obligation. While I have argued in the preceding section that Dworkin's general analysis, based on the four conditions, cannot be expected to apply to associative obligations across the board, it is nonetheless very plausible to think that the idea of equal concern would play a central role in justifying an associative *political* obligation. The concern in question would be expressed by the state, through its laws and governing actions, towards all its citizens. The state is not, of course, a real person, from which two points immediately follow. First, equal concern *cannot* in this context be a psychological matter; in the case of political obligation, it must be an interpretive property (LE at 201). Secondly, as Dworkin explicitly recognizes, the account requires that the state be morally personified (LE at 167–175). (Recall that it is because political obligation runs between the state and its citizens, rather than between citizens individually, that political obligation cannot be personal in the sense defined by Dworkin.)

Why, then, might integrity make a moral difference of the kind to which Dworkin points? The reason, I wish to suggest, is that when integrity is present, the relationship between each individual citizen and the state—the state being understood as an abstract moral personification of the general political community—becomes, according to Dworkin's argument, one that is intrinsically valuable. He writes that "a political society that accepts integrity as a political virtue thereby becomes a special form of community, special in a way that promotes its moral authority to assume and deploy a monopoly of coercive force" (LE at 188). Dworkin goes on to describe other justifications for integrity that are purely instrumental, such as the fact that it provides protection against partiality, deceit, and corruption. The distinction between the two types of justification suggests that he regards genuine political community as special precisely because it has non-instrumental value. But whether or not I am correct in attributing such a specific view to him, I believe that this idea is the basis of the most compelling philosophical understanding of his argument for political obligation.

In order to defend that claim, however, this interpretation of the argument must be spelled out in greater detail. Why might it be thought that political community, even when it meets certain conditions pertaining to equal concern, could be intrinsically valuable? It may well be the case that simply belonging to or identifying with certain kinds of communities is an intrinsic good for individuals. But the good of belonging or identification seems unlikely to be enough to support an obligation to obey. There are, after all, many kinds of communities other than political ones—for example, ethnic, national, or religious communities—that seem just as likely to provide such a good, and yet it is far from clear that this fact can serve as the basis of an obligation to obey the relevant community's norms.[17] (This is not to deny that there might be other reasons to obey.) The claim must therefore be, I think, that political community is a unique good, and one which is

---

[17] Joseph Raz has argued that the law can have intrinsic value because it is one kind of standard of conduct that a community can have, and "our perception of ourselves, of who we are, depends among other things on our ability to identify with communities we live in, on our ability to belong to these communities in the full sense of the word." J. Raz, *On the Nature of Law*, 82 ARCHIV FÜR RECHTS UND SOZIALPHILOSOPHIE 1, 10 (1996). (Notice that he does not claim that political community is unique in this regard.) But Raz also thinks that there is a voluntary aspect to identification and belonging: "Identification with a community depends on our ability and willingness to accept the standards which these communities endorse as our own. This ability . . . depends [among other things] on one's moral judgement giving basic approval to those standards." *Id.* at 12. Elsewhere he has similarly argued that respect for law, which is an attitude expressing identification with one's political community, can ground an obligation to obey that is, like the obligations of friendship, "semi-voluntary": "Such an attitude, if directed to a community which deserves it, is intrinsically valuable. It is not, however, obligatory. One does not have a moral duty to feel a sense of belonging in a community." Raz, *supra* note 3, at 338. The attitude of respect for law is, in Raz's view, not consent-based but nonetheless semi-voluntary because, like friendship, it grows and develops over time. There are obvious affinities between this view and Dworkin's understanding of political obligation. But Dworkin does not think that there is a voluntary or semi-voluntary aspect to political obligation, and that is why he must make the stronger assumption about the value of political community that is identified in the text.

necessary for individuals to live complete lives or to be completely fulfilled as human or rational beings; there is intrinsic value for such beings in governing themselves *as* a community by means of norms that they create for themselves. Perhaps one might try to fill out this claim by drawing on the enlightenment ideal of self-legislation, which Dworkin mentions in passing in *Law's Empire* but does not elaborate upon (LE at 189). I am not sure whether or not this claim is true, although it has a certain intuitive plausibility. I will not, however, explore the issue in detail here. The main point I want to make for present purposes is that it seems that something like the claim I have identified must hold if political community is ever to have intrinsic value of a kind that does not depend on consent or otherwise have some voluntary aspect. Of course, the argument cannot be that political community fulfills or completes human lives no matter what form it takes, if only for the reason that governments can be thoroughly iniquitous or evil. It is only *genuine* political community that can play this role, and that is where integrity comes in. The basic idea, which again has much intuitive appeal, would appear to be something like this. A political community, morally personified through the state, only has intrinsic value for its citizens when it can be understood as treating each citizen, considered individually, with equal dignity, concern, and respect. It can only have intrinsic value, in other words, when it meets the demands of integrity. A legal system without integrity might still have instrumental value— even a deeply inegalitarian political order might, for example, be morally preferable to social chaos—but it can only make an intrinsically valuable contribution to human flourishing when integrity is present.

Even if it is true that a genuine political community has intrinsic value for its citizens, however, we must still ask why it should be the case that citizens have a general obligation to obey their community's law.[18] Even if the state treats everyone with equal concern, and for that reason makes a certain kind of contribution to human flourishing, why should citizens have an obligation to obey each and every law, including in particular any laws that are unjust? The response to this questions is, I believe, unnervingly straightforward. Political community is in part *constituted* by norms that have been created by, or otherwise have their source in, a certain structure of authority within the relevant society. Norms can be said to

---

[18] Leslie Green raises a related question when he argues that "integrity [in individuals] creates no duty to obey those who display the virtue,"and this does not change in the case of a personified community. L. Green, *Associative Obligations and the State*, in Law and the Community: The End of Individualism? 93, 106 (A. Hutchinson and L. Green, eds., 1989). Green's argument is much more plausible if one assumes, as he at least implicitly does, that integrity cannot confer intrinsic value on a political community. The analogy with integrity in an individual, which Dworkin himself makes, is in fact quite misleading: the integrity of an individual cannot be a source of value for others in the way that the integrity of a political community can, at least conceivably, make that community intrinsically valuable for its citizens. If I am right that the essence of integrity in the political context is a concept of equal concern, then there is no analogue with the virtue of integrity in individuals; integrity in the former sense is a creature of political morality alone. However, even if it is true that political integrity can be a source of value in the way that I have suggested, it does not automatically follow that citizens have a general moral obligation to obey the law.

exist in various ways; there is, for example, a clear sense in which a norm exists simply because the members of a legislature enacted a law. But the argument for political obligation that I am attempting to explicate holds that the relationship between a political community and its citizens is, under certain conditions, intrinsically valuable. It seems to me to be implausible in the extreme to think that this relationship could be morally valuable in that way unless the norms that are partially constitutive of the relationship existed not just in a social or conventional sense, but in the stronger sense of having the normative force that they purport to have. They must, in other words, be *valid* norms, which in this context means morally valid norms,[19] and the obligations they purport to impose must be real obligations. This is moral bootstrapping, but bootstrapping is no more problematic here than it is in the case of friendship. Legal norms (and their attendant obligations) are partially constitutive of the relationship between the state and the citizen in exactly the same way that the obligations of friendship are partially constitutive of friendship. It is in this claim, I believe, that the true power of Dworkin's argument's for political obligation resides. Given the non-instrumental nature of the argument, there is no basis for picking and choosing among laws in the way that attempted instrumental justifications of a general obligation to obey almost invariably permit.[20] It seems to me that not even non-instrumental considerations of a different kind, such as considerations of justice, can negate the obligation, in the sense of justifying the conclusion that it does not exist. (They can defeat or override the obligation, as I will discuss further below, but that is quite a different matter.) We are assuming, it should be recalled, that the state treats all of its citizens with equal concern—since otherwise the law would not have integrity—and we are also assuming that equal concern is a concept that has genuine moral content. If the argument up to this point is correct, then equal concern is the only moral property that the law must have if political community is to have intrinsic value. Political community could not have such value unless the norms that constitute it are morally valid and hence binding. No other moral considerations are relevant to the existence of the obligation, although they may defeat or override it.

The point that other moral considerations may defeat or override the general obligation to obey the law is an absolutely crucial one, since otherwise the conclusion that such an obligation exists will be unacceptable on its face. The point is not, in fact, a controversial one; almost every contemporary theorist who discusses this issue assumes that if there is a general obligation to obey the law, which most deny, it is only prima facie in character. It is perhaps less obvious that the obligation, if it

[19] *See supra* note 3.
[20] *Cf.* Raz *supra* note 3; Green *supra* note 3. Both Raz and Green view the value of law almost entirely in instrumental terms, although Raz thinks that law can also have a non-instrumental dimension: see *supra* note 17. But both cheerfully concede that, precisely because the value of law is (mainly) instrumental, there can be no general obligation to obey. As Raz puts the point, "much of the good that the law can do does not presuppose any obligation to obey." Raz, *supra* note 3, at 328.

exists, need not be particularly strong. It is completely consistent with the argument of the preceding paragraph that the obligation is routinely overridden by considerations of justice, or even by instrumental considerations. A related point is that a general obligation to obey the law need not, by itself, be strong enough to justify the use of coercion by the state. As was noted in section I, Dworkin is careful to note that while obligation is close to a necessary condition for coercion, it is not by itself sufficient (LE at 191). It should be borne in mind in this regard that not all laws are enforceable by coercive means, or even enforceable in any legal sense at all; the laws that govern the relations among different branches of government are only the most obvious example. It is, again, completely consistent with the argument of the preceding paragraph that even if there is a general obligation to obey, the coercive enforcement of any given law can only be justified by reference to instrumental considerations, such as deterrence, or different non-instrumental considerations, such as retribution. Finally, the claim that there is a general non-instrumental obligation to obey the law is completely consistent with the possibility that the obligation to obey many individual laws can *also* be justified on instrumental grounds, such as the need for coordination. As was remarked in section II, there is no reason why an obligation cannot be justified both instrumentally and non-instrumentally.

There is one aspect of Dworkin's discussion of integrity that I have not mentioned up to this point, which is captured by the following passage:

Members of a society of principle accept that their political rights and duties are not exhausted by the particular decisions their political institutions have reached, but depend, more generally, on the scheme of principles those decisions presuppose and endorse. So each member accepts that others have rights and that he has duties flowing from that scheme, even though these have never been formally identified or declared. (LE at 211)

Elsewhere Dworkin goes beyond this claim, arguing that integrity may in fact require the rejection of certain past political decisions as mistakes; despite appearances, those decisions never contributed to the content of the law. The general point that the content of the law may extend beyond past political decisions, or to some extent depart from them altogether, flows from the role that interpretation plays in Dworkin's substantive theory of the grounds of law;[21] it is a consequence of the claim that there is a tradeoff between fit and justification, which are the two dimensions of interpretation, rather than a lexical ordering. It is because interpretation figures in this way in Dworkin's substantive theory that considerations of force can have an effect on the grounds of law. As was noted in section I, within Dworkin's substantive theory the truth of "It is the law that A" depends, in part, on whether or not the normative proposition "A" is capable of being made true by the truth of "It is the law that A." The theory makes this determination holistically, by looking to how "A" fits into the content of the law taken as a whole.[22] The upshot of all this is the following. The answer to the

---

[21] Interpretation plays a separate but related role in Dworkin's arguments about methodology in legal philosophy. See the brief discussion of this issue in section I above.   [22] *See supra* note 6.

question of whether or not there is a general obligation to obey the law of a particular legal system depends on whether or not the content of the law, considered as a whole, has integrity, while the question of what is the content of the law depends, in part, on whether or not law understood as having this content rather than that would have integrity (and hence would give rise to a general obligation to obey). This is complicated but not circular, or at least not viciously so. The only comment that I will make here on the interpretive aspect of Dworkin's theory of the grounds of law is that, while it fits naturally with the claim that the existence of political obligation depends on whether or not the law has integrity, it is logically independent of that claim. One could make the claim that political obligation depends on integrity even if one thought that the content of law was determined solely by social facts. One could make the claim, in other words, as a matter of pure political philosophy, and hence even if one held views about the relationship between political and legal philosophy that were quite different from Dworkin's own.

Dworkin's argument that there is a general obligation to obey the law is, at least in the version I have presented here, obviously controversial. It depends on a number of strong assumptions. One is the claim that the concept of equal concern has independent moral content; another is the claim that political community can have intrinsic value; and yet another is the claim that political community is a unique good which is necessary for human beings to live complete or completely fulfilled lives. Any of these assumptions might be wrong. It is also possible that even if the argument is correct, it does not establish very much of interest because the conditions it requires will rarely, if ever, be met: it may be, for example, that the moral property of equal concern cannot be comprehensively attributed to any existing legal system any more than true justice can. The argument seems to me to be an important one even so, if only because there is no plausible route other than a non-instrumentalist one for establishing the existence of a general obligation to obey the law. Enthusiasts of a predominantly instrumental approach to the value of law have, for the most part, embraced the conclusion that there can be no purely instrumental argument for the existence of such an obligation,[23] and in this I think they are right. They believe that a general obligation to obey the law is a fiction, and in any event could not have any moral significance; whatever the law achieves that is of moral value, they argue, it does so whether there is such an obligation or not. The instrumentalists may be correct. But perhaps it is not entirely irrelevant that so many judges, legislators and ordinary citizens believe

---

[23] *See supra* note 20. John Finnis offers an argument for a general obligation to obey the law that is, I believe, best regarded as combining both instrumental and non-instrumental aspects. *See, e.g.* Finnis, *The Authority of Law in the Predicament of Contemporary Social Theory*, 1 NOTRE DAME J. OF L. ETHICS, & PUB. POL. 115 (1984). Finnis's theory of political obligation is quite different from Dworkin's, in ways that it is not possible to elaborate here. I discuss the details of Finnis's view at some length in Perry, *Law and Obligation, supra* note 3.

that they really do have an obligation to obey the law. If the instrumentalists were right, wouldn't the news have filtered down by now? Perhaps the tenacity of the belief in an obligation to obey the law should give them, and the rest of us, some pause. One of the many merits of Dworkin's argument is that it gives us a way of thinking about the matter that helps to illuminate why that belief is as tenacious as it is.

9

Law's Aims in *Law's Empire*

John Gardner *

I

Does law have a purpose or point? Surely it does. The trickier questions are these: Does law have a *unifying* purpose or point? Does law have a *distinctive* purpose or point? Many think that, inasmuch as law has a unifying purpose—such as "the guidance of conduct"—it is not a distinctive purpose. It is a purpose shared by many things that are not law. And inasmuch as law has more distinctive purposes—such as "being the final public arbiter of disputes" or "monopolizing the use of force"—they are not unifying. Each such purpose is the purpose of some law but not of all law. H.L.A. Hart's book *The Concept of Law* is perhaps the best-known defence of this conjunction of views.[1] Although he accepts that the law has purposes, Hart advances a non-purposive (and more broadly non-functional)[2] account of what legal norms have in common that distinguishes them from other norms.

Ronald Dworkin belongs to a long tradition of writers who hold, by contrast, that law has some purpose that is both unifying and distinctive. His book *Law's Empire* is an unusual contribution to this tradition in that it stands for the view that law must have a unifying-and-distinctive purpose, but it does not commit

* Some of this paper reworks fragments of an earlier and more ambitious (but unpublished) paper co-authored with Elisa Holmes. Thanks to Elisa for, *inter alia*, helping to disentangle the two different projects that got tangled up in the earlier paper. Thanks to Jules Coleman, Scott Hershovitz and Maris Köpcke-Tinturé for demonstrating the need to do so. And thanks to all these people for their many other helpful suggestions, not all of which, alas, have found their way into this final text.

[1] H. L. A. HART, THE CONCEPT OF LAW (1961). On some of law's distinctive but non-unifying purposes, see *id.* at 38–41. On some of law's unifying but non-distinctive purposes, see *id.* at 189–195. See also Hart's postscript to the second edition of THE CONCEPT OF LAW (2d ed., 1994), at 248–249. (Subsequent references are to the first edition unless otherwise indicated.)

[2] Not only is law not distinguished by its purposes; it is also not distinguished by its achievements. For Hart, as for Kelsen, neither intended nor actual effects set legal systems apart from other normative systems. As Green summarizes the Hart-Kelsen view, law is "a modal kind and not a functional kind." L. Green, *The Concept of Law Revisited*, 94 MICH. L. REV. 1687, 1711 (1996).

itself to a final view on what this purpose is.[3] In Chapter 3 of *Law's Empire*, Dworkin provisionally attributes a purpose to law in order to "organize[ ] further argument about law's character."[4] Even if he has this purpose wrong, he argues, *some* unifying-and-distinctive purpose for law must be relied upon if arguments about the nature of law are to get off the ground. We need "a statement of the central concept of [our] institution that will allow [us] to see our arguments . . . as arguments over rival conceptions of that concept."[5] To furnish such a "conceptual statement"[6] in the case of law, he says, we must find "the most abstract and fundamental point of legal practice."[7] For law is an "interpretive enterprise"[8] and this means that those who are interested in finding out what (else) is true about law have to begin by taking an "interpretive attitude" to their subject. This in turn means starting from the assumption that law "has some point" that sets it apart and brings it together as the particular interpretive enterprise that it is.[9]

Here Dworkin's argument proceeds transcendentally. Unlike many before him, he does not try to show that law must have a unifying-and-distinctive purpose by showing what unifying-and-distinctive purpose law has. Rather, he tries to show that law must have a unifying-and-distinctive purpose by showing that we cannot make sense of law without assuming one. The question of which unifying and distinctive purpose law has can be settled later. Meanwhile we can make do with a provisional proposal that is pencilled in for the sake of argument.

So what purpose does Dworkin provisionally attribute to law for the sake of argument? The following purpose, he says, is "sufficiently abstract and uncontroversial" to do the job:

Our discussions of law by and large assume, I suggest, that the most abstract and fundamental point of legal practice is to guide and constrain the power of government in the following way. Law insists that force [= coercion] not be used or withheld . . . except as licensed or required by individual rights and responsibilities flowing from past political decisions about when collective force is justified.[10]

Dworkin's Suggested Purpose, or DSP as I will call it for short, is complex and intriguing. But is it plausible? I think not. At any rate, it is far from uncontroversial. As many have pointed out, a legal system might still exist, and if it did would still have a purpose or point, in a society of angels. Since the *ex hypothesi* perfect population of such a society will be guided by the *ex hypothesi* perfect laws and policies of their *ex hypothesi* perfect government, coercion by that government will not be needed, and will not be used, to get them to fall into line with law. Nor, therefore, will law be called upon to regulate government coercion. Yet there will

---

[3] R. M. DWORKIN, LAW'S EMPIRE (1986) [hereinafter "LE"].   [4] LE, 93.   [5] LE, 92.
[6] LE, 92.
[7] LE, 93. For present purposes I assume that nothing turns, for Dworkin, on the distinction between "law" and "legal practice."   [8] LE, 90.
[9] LE, 47.
[10] LE, 93. The square-bracketed insertion reflects what Dworkin says a few lines later, and is added here to reduce the volume of quotation.

still be co-ordination problems to which angelic law may provide the best solutions (what side of the road to drive angelic vehicles on, what frequencies to allocate to angelic cellphones, etc.). So angelic law may still exist and, if it does, it will still have a purpose—even though there is no coercion by angelic governments for it to "guide and constrain."[11]

There are several things one can learn from this exotic thought-experiment. The most important lesson is this: That the licensing of government coercion in ordinary human legal systems, even when successful, is a consequence of a deeper failure. As Hart captures the point, the resort to legal coercion is a *"pis aller,"* a "secondary provision[ ] for a breakdown in case the primary intended peremptory reasons are not accepted as such."[12] Whatever other purposes law may have, it clearly has the purpose of providing law-subjects, including the government, with normative guidance; that is to say, of subjecting their conduct to the governance of norms. If only law were fully to succeed in this purpose, if only all law-subjects were to use legal norms as they are supposed to be used, by being guided by them *qua* norms, there would be no need, and no case, for the government to coerce people into conformity with those same norms. So there would be no need for law to regulate government coercion. If that much is true, then DSP, even if it is a distinctively legal purpose, is not a unifying one. It is a purpose of law only on those occasions when law has failed to achieve its more unifying (albeit less distinctive) purpose of providing normative guidance for use by its subjects.

II

Although I have just made my own sympathies clear, my interest here is not in developing this critique of DSP.[13] I am interested, rather, in an aspect of DSP that the critique, as it stands, leaves unchallenged. Possibly law's purpose, even in a society of angels, is not merely to provide its subjects (including the government) with normative guidance. Possibly law's purpose, more specifically, is to provide its subjects with *justified* normative guidance. This view has been defended at length by John Finnis in *Natural Law and Natural Rights*. To Finnis, the "society of angels" thought-experiment[14] tends to suggest, not that law lacks a unifying-and-distinctive purpose, but that law has a unifying-and-distinctive purpose quite

---

[11] Aristotle, Nicomachean Ethics 1179b30–1180b28; Hart, The Concept of Law, *supra* note 1, at 195; J. Raz, Practical Reason and Norms 159 (1975); J. Finnis, Natural Law and Natural Rights 266–267 (1980).

[12] Hart, *Commands and Authoritative Legal Reasons* in his Essays on Bentham 254 (1982).

[13] One way to attempt a rescue of DSP might be to argue, with Kelsen, that there *are* no legal norms except those that regulate the coercive conduct of state officials. In Kelsen's words: "Law is the primary norm which stipulates the sanction." *See* General Theory of Law and State 63 (1949). This view of Kelsen's has not, however, survived Hart's critique of it in The Concept of Law, *supra* note 1, at 35–41.

[14] Or "world of saints", as Finnis prefers: Natural Law and Natural Rights, *supra* note 11, at 269.

different from DSP. The purpose is that of providing co-ordination of conduct for the common good.[15] This purpose is in two respects more distinctive than that of merely providing normative guidance to law-subjects. In the first place, according to Finnis, law aims to provide normative guidance to law-subjects that works in a distinctive way, namely by co-ordinating their conduct. In the second place, law aims to provide normative guidance that lives up to a certain standard: it aims to serve the common good. This second specification is the one that we are concerned with here. It entails an important feature that Finnis's suggested purpose shares with Dworkin's. For Finnis and Dworkin alike, law aims to guide its subjects properly, soundly, upstandingly, well. Law aims to be justified in the guidance that it gives to those whom it aims to guide, such that what they do, when they are guided by the law and make no mistakes about the law, will itself be justified.

One should be careful not to trivialize this thesis. In all norm-governed pursuits, questions of justification arise that are, so to speak, internal to the pursuit. They are simply questions of whether the norms are being adhered to. In a game of *Monopoly*, for example, I land on "Chance" and draw the "Go Directly to Jail" card. The "banker" refuses to pay me the "salary" I ususally get for passing "Go." Is this refusal justified? The answer depends on the rules of *Monopoly*. Barring exceptional circumstances (e.g. we are playing for the last space in the lifeboat, or the "banker" is a cheat), the act of denying me the "salary" has no significance outside the game, and there is no relevant extra-ludic standard of assessment. In law, we are sometimes temporarily interested in justification conceived in this purely internal way. On some occasions and for some purposes, we merely want to know whether what we are doing is justified by the legal system's own rules, however quirky and technical. We want to know, for example, what deadline the law sets for serving a notice to quit following a breach of lease, because we want to know what the legal consequences will be of our postponing service of the notice until after rent negotiations are complete. This is a superficially game-like question. As a lawyer, one may sometimes be tempted to think of it on the model of *Monopoly*. But law, as Finnis rightly emphasizes, is not a game.[16] Everything done by law affects someone, or potentially affects someone, in a morally significant way. Thus a question of legal justification always invites, and never eclipses, a *further* question of justification. The law sets, let us suppose, a 14-day deadline for serving a notice to quit following breach of a lease. But in one's relations with one's tenants, should one use this legal deadline rather than some other? This is not a question about what is justified under the legal norm. *Ex hypothesi*, a deadline of 14 days from breach of lease is justified under the legal norm. Rather, it is a further question about whether one is *morally* justified in relying on the legal norm as a justification for one's action. Law, on the view I am associating with Dworkin and Finnis, aims to live up to

---

[15] Finnis, Natural Law and Natural Rights, *supra* note 11, *e.g.* at 334–336.
[16] *Id.* at 305.

this standard: to be something that its users are morally justified in using. In Finnis's terms, law can be "fully understood only by understanding [its] point, that is to say [its] objective,"[17] which is to make a distinctive kind of contribution to "practical reasonableness" (this expression being substituted only because "the term 'moral' is of somewhat uncertain connotation").[18]

No doubt Dworkin would resist this (Finnis-influenced)[19] conceptualization of the contrast between law and game-playing. Dworkin treats the moral questions inevitably raised by law as bearing (mainly) on the correct interpretation of legal norms, not (or not mainly) on the propriety of their use once correctly interpreted.[20] This is the second component of the "interpretive attitude" that law calls for as an "interpretive enterprise." Law not only "has a point"; law's content—what the law of any given jurisdiction says on any given question—is also "sensitive to its point."[21] Thus, for Dworkin, what one is morally justified in doing in one's relations with one's tenants affects (mainly) whether the law should be understood as setting a 14-day deadline in the first place, not (or not mainly) whether one is justified in using the legal deadline once the law is so understood. It follows that in the legal domain, according to Dworkin, there is normally no such thing as justification "internal to the pursuit" where this implies leaving the question of moral justification open in determining what the applicable legal norms are.

I will return to this issue later. For the time being, we need only note that Dworkin's famous view about the determination of legal content (the second component of his "interpretive attitude") does not drive any wedge between him and Finnis on the question of law's purpose or point (the first component). Finnis and Dworkin alike suggest that law has a justificatory purpose. Moreover, for both of them it is a morally justificatory purpose. Theirs is not the easy-to-accept thesis that law is a normative pursuit and hence cannot but provide standards of justification of *some* kind. Theirs is the more substantial and contentious thesis that law aims to provide standards of *moral* justification, and hence to be *morally* justified in the norms it provides. This thesis leaves open whether the aim in question is to be served by interpreting laws morally, or by not following immoral laws, or perhaps sometimes by interpreting laws morally and sometimes by not following immoral laws. This disagreement can be bracketed for now. Our interest for the time being is only in the Finnis-Dworkin "plateau"[22] of agreement, which seems to extend to the following thesis, if no further:

(α) Law aims to be morally justified.

In formulating (α) I have chosen "aims" rather than "has the purpose" or "has the aim," not only to save words, but also to avoid giving the impression that, for either Finnis or Dworkin, (α) fully captures law's unifying-and-distinctive

---

[17] *Id.* at 3.   [18] *Id.* at 15.   [19] *Id. e.g.* at 354–362.   [20] LE, 47–48.
[21] LE, 47.   [22] LE, 93.

purpose. For both of them (α) captures no more than one (unifying but not distinctive) aspect of law's unifying-and-distinctive purpose.[23]

III

Is Dworkin committed to (α)? (α) is entailed by DSP, which is Dworkin's own "conceptual statement" about law. But recall that DSP is only mooted provisionally by Dworkin, as a working assumption to help us "organize[ ] further argument about law's character." Does (α) represent an equally provisional aspect of Dworkin's thought? Does he align himself with (α) only for the sake of argument? Or would (α) also be entailed by every other suggested unifying-and-distinctive purpose for law that Dworkin would be prepared to entertain as an alternative to DSP?

There is much in *Law's Empire* to suggest that the answer is yes. Chapters four to seven of the book are devoted to exploring the question: Which moral ideal is the proper moral ideal for law (through its practitioners and officials) to aim at? Dworkin famously answers: "integrity."[24] His defence of this answer is conducted on the footing that, while the choice of integrity as the proper moral ideal to be aimed at is not itself conceptually determined—"law as integrity" is but one possible "conception" of law—nevertheless, it is part of the concept of law that law aims at *some* moral ideal. Since it is (in turn) part of the concept of a moral ideal that whatever aims at a moral ideal aims to be, at the very least, morally justified, it seems that, for Dworkin, any acceptable conception of law is one that paints law as aiming to be, at the very least, morally justified. So, in these subsequent chapters of *Law's Empire*, (α) seems to be endorsed by Dworkin and not just mooted for the sake of argument.

Yet there are also conspicuous themes in Dworkin's work that seem to militate against his endorsing (α). In the following three sections I will consider three of these themes.

IV

In recent work, Dworkin has expressed scepticism about the personification of law. His scepticism is expressed in the context of a critique of Joseph Raz's work on the nature of law. What can Raz mean, asks Dworkin, when he says (as he often does) that "law claims legitimate authority"? Dworkin answers:

[23] This opens up the possibility that thesis (α) is also endorsed by Hart in THE CONCEPT OF LAW, *supra* note 1, at 186–188. But Hart keeps his options open on this point, and in the postscript to the second edition of THE CONCEPT OF LAW, *supra* note 1, at 248–249, he explicitly disclaims any attachment to (α). Law is not a game, but the difference, for Hart, does not lie in law's aim. It lies, *inter alia*, in law's claim. *See* Section IV below on aims and claims.

[24] LE, 244. Hercules, the ideal judge "follows law as integrity."

This type of personification is often used in philosophy as a shorthand way of stating the meaning or content of a class of propositions. A philosopher might say, for example, that morality claims to impose categorical requirements, or that physics claims to reveal the deep structure of the physical universe. He means that no proposition is a true proposition of morality unless it accurately reports categorical (rather than only hypothetical) requirements or that no proposition is a true proposition of physics unless it correctly reports physical structure. If we read Raz's personification in this familiar way, we take him to mean that no proposition of law is true unless it successfully reports an exercise of legitimate authority. But that would imply not that morality cannot be a test for law, as Raz claims, but that it *must* be a test for law because, as he recognizes, no exercise of authority is legitimate "if the moral or normative conditions for one's directives being authoritative are absent."

It is difficult to find a sensible alternative reading of Raz's personification. He sometimes suggests that when he says "law" claims legitimate authority he means that legal officials claim that authority; legal officials do this when they insist that they have a "right" to impose obligations on citizens and that these citizens "owe them allegiance" and "ought to obey the law." It is one thing to suppose that legal officials often make such claims; it is quite another to suppose that unless they make such claims, there is necessarily no law. In fact many officials do not. Oliver Wendell Holmes, for example, thought the very idea of moral obligation a confusion. He did not suppose that legal enactments replace the ordinary reasons people have for acting with some overriding obligation-imposing directive, but rather that these enactments add new reasons to ordinary ones by making the cost of acting in certain ways more expensive. Whether a community has law does not depend on how many of its legal officials share Holmes' views. So we cannot make sense of Raz's crucial personification by supposing it to refer to the actual beliefs or attitudes of officials.[25]

If sound, these criticisms tell against an important thesis that Raz implicitly defends as a rival to (α). This rival thesis is entailed by the thesis that law claims legitimate authority. It says:

(β) Law claims to be morally justified.

Dworkin's criticisms of Raz on authority tell against (β) because (β) can be true only if law is the kind of thing that can make claims, and in the quoted passage Dworkin denies that law is that kind of thing. But should he deny it?

One may readily agree with Dworkin, as Raz does, that it takes a human being to make a claim. Raz makes tolerably clear that, for these purposes, the relevant human beings are legal officials.[26] Legal officials, he argues, are those who make the claim mentioned in (β). Yet at the same time Raz's attribution of the claim to law itself is not elliptical. It is not shorthand for "legal officials claim that law is morally justified." That is because legal officials, according to Raz, make the claim mentioned in (β) *on law's behalf.* And that in turn is because it is part of the concept of a legal official that, when someone acts as a legal official, she acts on law's behalf. So if (β) is sound, then someone who does not claim moral justification for

---

[25] Dworkin, *Thirty Years On*, 115 Harv. L. Rev. 1655, 1666–1667 (2002).
[26] J. Raz, Ethics in the Public Domain 215–216 (paperback ed., 1995).

what she does is not, in doing it, acting as a legal official, for (in failing to make the claim that law necessarily makes) she is no longer acting on behalf of the law. That is the most important pay-off of (β), and it holds only if the claim in (β) is understood (non-elliptically) to be law's own claim, and not merely the claim of some human beings.[27] It takes a human being to make a claim but it does not follow that human beings are the only things that make claims. Law makes claims through human beings acting on its behalf.

These remarks about (β) matter for present purposes because they apply, *mutatis mutandis*, to (α) as well. True, law cannot make any claims except through human beings acting on its behalf, i.e. legal officials. But by the same token law cannot have any *aims* except through human beings acting on its behalf. For (α) to be non-elliptically true, there must equally be human beings who, on law's behalf, aim at the law's being morally justified, and who are acting on law's behalf (i.e. count as legal officials) only if they aim at the law's being morally justified.

Inasmuch as (β) is offered by Raz as a rival to (α), there must obviously be some objections to (β) that are not objections to (α). But Dworkin's way of rejecting (β), in the passage just quoted, would also commit him to rejecting (α). Consider what it means to make a claim to moral justification. Minimally, it means acting with the aim that one be taken to be morally justified. Legal officials—those acting on behalf of the law—make a claim to moral justification only if they aim that the law should be taken to be morally justified by those law-subjects to whom it is addressed. This in turn means that they aim *either* that law be morally justified *or* that it be mistaken for something that is morally justified. It is the second possibility—the possibility of a pretence or masquerade on the part of law and legal officials—that distinguishes (β) from (α). Some things that would not count as law according to (α)—because they do not aim to be morally justified—still count as law according to (β)—because they masquerade as having that aim. Raz is careful to point out that, as compared with law that lives up to the standard enunciated in (α), law that merely masquerades as doing so is a less central case of law.[28] Just as the central case or paradigm of anything that has an aim is (*ceteris paribus*) the case in which it succeeds at that aim, so the central case or paradigm of anything that makes a claim is (*ceteris paribus*) the case in which it makes that claim sincerely. So the central case of law, according to Raz's criterion (β), is the case of law that is morally justified. Relative to morally justified law, law that merely aims to be morally justified but does not succeed in that aim is a less central case of law. And relative to law that aims to be morally justified (whether or not it succeeds in that aim), law that merely pretends to have that aim but does not really have it is in turn a less central case of law. It is a highly deviant case of law. Yet the claim that is present in the deviant case is also present in the central case. That is one of the features that, for Raz, brings them all together as cases of law. Although there may be law that does not have the aim mentioned in (α), there is no possible law that does not make the claim mentioned in (β).

---

[27] *Cf.* P. Soper, *Law's Normative Claims* in The Autonomy of Law (R. P. George ed., 1996).
[28] Ethics in the Public Domain, *supra* note 26, at 270.

If we understand Raz's thesis (β) in this way, then Dworkin's proposed counterexample—Justice Holmes' rule-sceptical attitude to law—serves as a counterexample to (β) only if it also serves as a counterexample to (α). If truth be told, it does not really serve as a counterexample to either (β) or (α). Admittedly, in his extrajudicial writings, Holmes peddled the mistaken view that legal rules cannot impose moral obligations on law-subjects but can only give them pruden-tial incentives.[29] But were Holmes' arguments and pronouncements from the bench consistent with this view? Didn't he sometimes use legal rules to help justify his own legal rulings, thereby establishing that legal rules *must* be more than mere incentives? And in the process didn't he sometimes treat himself as *bound* to use legal rules in justifying his legal rulings, thereby confirming that at least some legal rules are rules of obligation? And, even when not, didn't he at least insist that his own legal rulings were morally obligatory, never mind why he made them? Or at any rate didn't he insist that his own legal rulings were morally *justified* even if not morally obligatory? Or at the very least didn't he insist on the moral justification of the very ruling he was just in the process of making? It seems to me that, as a legal official, Holmes could not but insist on the moral justification of the very ruling he was just in the process of making. If he spoke from the bench in a way that suggested that he did not insist on this, then it seems to me that he was not speaking on behalf of the law—i.e. in his official capacity—when he did so. For better or worse, he was replacing his official position with his personal position. But even if you doubt all this, ask yourself: What, in Holmes' judicial decisions, could possibly count as a denial of the *claim* to moral justification that would not equally count as a denial of the *aim* of moral justification? How could anything in Holmes' judicial decisions possibly serve as a counterexample to (β) without equally serving as a counterexample to (α)? For the only relevant difference between (β) and (α) is that (β) allows for the extra possibility of officials who, speaking on behalf of the law, pretend to be acting exactly as they would be acting if only (α) were true.

In invoking Holmes, therefore, Dworkin seems to be distancing himself not only from Raz's thesis that law makes a moral claim, but also from the thesis, appar-ently so central to *Law's Empire*, that law has a moral aim: that law's distinctive-and-unifying purpose is a morally justificatory purpose.[30]

V

Perhaps more importantly, *Law's Empire* itself gives us reason to doubt whether Dworkin accepts, or could accept, (α). Consider Dworkin's statement of the first assumption made by those who take the "interpretive attitude" to law. They

---

[29] O. W. Holmes, *The Path of the Law*, 10 HARVARD LAW REVIEW 457, 461–462 (1897).

[30] *Contrast* LE, 172–175, where Dworkin seems to suggest that the law has a moral voice in which officials, acting as officials, cannot but speak.

assume, he says, "that the practice [of law] does not simply exist but has value, that it serves some interest or purpose or enforces some principle—in short that it has some point—that can be stated independently of just describing the rules that make up the practice."[31] There is some equivocation in this remark. To adopt the interpretive attitude, says Dworkin, we need to assume that law *serves* a purpose. Does this mean that law *has* a purpose? Or does it mean that law *achieves* that purpose? The two claims are not, as they stand, incompatible. Many things have a purpose that they also achieve. But the two claims are incompatible as soon as they are understood as "conceptual statements" about law. That is because purposive agency is agency that leaves open the logical possibility of failure. If it is impossible to classify the actions of a certain agent into the categories "failure" and "success" (because failure is conceptually ruled out) then that agent is not a purposive agent. It does not have any purposes. And if a certain action cannot be classified as a failure or success (because failure is conceptually ruled out) then that action is not an action with a purpose. And if a certain action cannot be classified as a failure or success in its possession of a certain property (because failure to possess that property is conceptually ruled out) then having that property cannot figure among the purposes of that action. Accordingly, if law is such that whatever it does is morally justified—if its being morally justified is part of what it means for it to count as law—then it cannot at the same time aim at (have among its purposes that of) being morally justified.

In short, thesis (α) cannot possibly be true if the following rival thesis about law is true:

(χ) Law is morally justified.

If Dworkin accepts (χ) then he cannot accept (α).[32] Moreover, he cannot accept any "conceptual statement" for law of which (α) is an implication. So he must also abandon DSP, the unifying-and-distinctive purpose that he provisionally attaches to law in Chapter 3 of *Law's Empire*. Since by (χ) there is no logical space for law to fail in the moral justification of state coercion—since law's own moral justification in doing whatever it does is conceptually secure—morally justifying state coercion cannot be an aim or purpose of law. It can of course be an aim or purpose of some people writing about law, such as Dworkin himself. Such law-favourers may aim to morally justify (all) law in order to support the case for (χ). My point is only that law itself (acting through its officials) cannot aim to be morally justified if (χ) is true, whereas law itself (acting through its officials) cannot *but* aim to be morally justified if (α) is true.

Does Dworkin accept (χ), and hence eschew (α)? Some other passages in *Law's Empire* maintain the same equivocation between (χ) and (α) that afflicts

---

[31] LE, 47.

[32] *Contrast* J. Dickson, Evaluation and Legal Theory 106 (2001). Dickson allows Dworkin to endorse both (α) and (χ) together, and seems to see them as natural bedfellows.

Dworkin's statement of the "interpretive attitude" above. Consider the following remarks on Nazi law in Chapter 3:

We need not deny that the Nazi system was an example of law, no matter which interpretation we favour of our own law, because there is an available sense in which it plainly was law. But we have no difficulty in understanding someone who does say that Nazi law was not really law, or was law in a degenerate sense, or was less than fully law. For he is not then using "law" in that sense; he is not making that sort of preinterpretive judgment but a skeptical interpretive judgment that Nazi law lacked features crucial to flourishing legal systems whose rules and procedures do justify coercion.[33]

The words "do justify coercion" at the end of this passage might tempt one to suppose that Dworkin means to commit himself to (χ) rather than (α). By his "conceptual statement" for law (DSP) he meant that whatever counts as law *does* morally justify coercion, not that it has the purpose of doing so. And yet the preceding sentence decisively rules out this reading of the passage as a whole. Dworkin sees morally justified law only as the central case or paradigm of law. This is incompatible with his endorsing (χ). It is compatible with his endorsing (α) or (β). It is also *conducive* to his endorsing either (α) or (β). For as we already mentioned, both of these proposed theses share the implication (explicitly endorsed by both Raz and Finnis) that morally justified law is the central case of law, and hence that Nazi law is degenerate *qua* law. That Dworkin thinks there is an available sense in which Nazi law "plainly" was law suggests that, as between (α) and (β), he actually ought to favour Raz's (β). For there is ample evidence to suggest a mere pretence of moral rectitude on the part of many Nazi officials, such that Nazi law made moral claims that were not matched by genuine moral aims. Be that as it may, the passage as a whole certainly militates against the view that Dworkin accepts (χ). Morally justified law only represents law's central case. So "morally justified law" is not a tautology and "morally unjustified law" is not an oxymoron. Both kinds of law are conceptual possibilities. So perhaps there is, after all, nothing here to cast doubt on Dworkin's allegiance to (α). What seem to be statements endorsing (χ), and hence denying (α), are on closer inspection statements denying (χ).

VI

Yet the problem of reconciling (α) with other themes of *Law's Empire* is not yet over. Consider now Dworkin's statement of the second assumption made by those who take the "interpretive attitude" to law. They assume, he says, "that the requirements of [law]—the behavior it calls for or judgments it warrants—are not

---

[33] LE, 103–104.

necessarily or exclusively what they have always been taken to be but are instead sensitive to its point, so that the strict rules must be understood or applied or extended or modified or qualified or limited by that point."[34] Here we find traces of the same equivocation between (α) and (χ) that ran through Dworkin's statement of the first assumption, quoted above. If (χ) is true then the law's "requirements," the "strict rules," are *already* morally justified and officials need not alter them to make them so. If (α) is true, on the other hand, then there may be "requirements" or "strict rules" of law that are not already morally justified, in which case legal officials, acting on behalf of the law, have the (α)-given aim of transforming them into morally justified requirements or rules. The words "extended or modified or qualified or limited" plainly support the second reading of the passage, and hence tend to confirm Dworkin's allegiance to (α) over (χ). Legal officials have the (α)-given aim of taking morally unjustified legal norms ("strict rules") and changing them (by extension, modification, qualification or limitation) into morally justified legal norms. So there can be morally unjustified legal norms that call for legal officials to change them with the (α)-given aim of making them morally justified. (χ) is false because (α) is true.

The words "understood or applied," on the other hand, can be read consistently with either (α) or (χ). Understanding and applying legal norms might be operations that legal officials perform upon legal norms with the aim of improving them, i.e. with the aim of transfoming them into morally justified norms on the occasions when they are not morally justified as they stand. On this reading of "understood or applied," (χ) remains false, for there can be morally unjustified as well as morally justified legal norms. Yet one may also read the words "understood or applied" consistently with (χ), and hence inconsistently with (α). No legal norm is morally unjustified, and therefore no legal official can possibly have the aim of changing a legal norm from a morally unjustified one to a morally justified one. The challenge for legal officials under the heading of "understanding and applying" the "strict rules" is only to bring out what is already in these rules, i.e. to understand each legal norm as the morally justified norm that it already is, and to apply it accordingly.

Dworkin's account of how judges should go about understanding and applying the law—namely, by "constructively interpreting" it—is usually read in the latter way, as an account according to which the law already means what it should mean (i.e. what it would mean if it were morally justified) and hence only needs to have its meaning brought out, not altered, by judges. This is what I referred to above as "Dworkin's famous view about the determination of legal content." But on closer inspection Dworkin's official characterization of "constructive interpretation" in Chapter 2 of *Law's Empire* leans very strongly in the opposite direction:

Roughly, constructive interpretation is a matter of imposing purpose on an object . . . in order to make of it the best possible example of the form or genre to which it is taken to

---

[34] LE, 47.

belong. It does not follow, even from that rough account, that an interpreter can make of [the object] anything he would have wanted it to be, that a citizen of courtesy who is enthralled by equality, for example, can in good faith claim that courtesy actually requires the sharing of wealth. For the history and shape of a[n] . . . object constrains the available interpretations of it . . . . Creative intepretation, on the constructive view, is a matter of interaction between purpose and object.[35]

This passage has an odd start, when set against other passages in the same chapter. Dworkin suggests that a purpose needs to be *imposed* on an object by a constructive interpreter. If this were true it would compete with the thought that law has a purpose. Perhaps Dworkin only means that the interpreter has to work out what the purpose in question is? Or perhaps Dworkin means that, given that law has among its purposes that of being morally justified, the interpreter still needs to do the work of adjudicating between various different moral ideals for law ("conceptions") to decide which particular laws would be morally justified ones and why? Either way, the word "impose" seems ill-suited to capture how the interpreter is supposed to relate to his or her object.

That constructive interpreters "impose" purpose on the object before them seems, then, to be an infelicity in Dworkin's formulation.[36] That constructive interpreters thereby "make [something] of" the object before them seems, however, to be an accurate statement of what Dworkin has in mind. There is always an object of interpretation and the aim of the constructive interpreter is to improve it, transform it into a better object of the same kind. In legal contexts, thanks to the truth of (α), that means a *morally* better object, a legal norm that comes closer to conforming to the proper moral ideal for law, whatever that ideal may be. In the process, there must of course be some preservation of some aspects of the norm one started with. If there is nothing at all left of that norm then what one did to it cannot count as interpreting it. But there must also be some improvement. If one did not improve the norm one started with, one's interpretation of it was not constructive.

That seems to be the sense in which, according to Dworkin, constructive interpretation is a matter of "interaction between purpose and object." There is some continuity in the object but there is also some improvement, some gravitation towards the ideal that properly pertains to an object of that type. The key Dworkinian contrast seems to be that between constructive interpreters, who aim to give the same object a new and better meaning, and what Raz has called "conserving" interpreters, who aim to retrieve some meaning that the object already has or has had.[37] Both differ from non-interpreting improvers—Dworkin calls them "pragmatists"—who are simply inclined to replace the object outright with a new and better one.

---

[35] LE, 52.

[36] *See also* J. Finnis, *On Reason and Authority in* Law's Empire, 6 LAW AND PHILOSOPHY 357, 359–360 (1987).

[37] J. Raz, *Interpretation without Retrieval* in LAW AND INTERPRETATION (A. Marmor ed., 1996).

If this reading is correct, then "understanding" and "applying" the law, when tackled constructively, are also ways of "extending or modifying or qualifying or limiting" the law. The law is not left as it was by the interpreting judge. This conclusion is crucial to the success of *Law's Empire* if it is to be read as a defence and explication of (α). Throughout the book, Dworkin uses the situation of judges to illustrate the force of (α). But if judges are to have the aim, on behalf of the law, that law be morally justified, there must be possible morally unjustified legal norms for them to have and pursue this aim in respect of—morally unjustified legal norms that they can render morally justified by their improving interpretative interventions.[38]

The most striking implication of this, if true, is that the Dworkin of *Law's Empire* has no significant axe to grind with the legal positivist tradition. In order to continue grinding this axe, the Dworkin of *Law's Empire* turns legal positivists into advocates for "conserving" interpretations of legal norms. He thereby creates an issue between himself and legal positivism, namely the issue of constructive versus conserving interpretation. But none of the major recent writers commonly thought of as legal positivists (Kelsen, Hart, Raz, Coleman) shows any predilection for conserving interpretations of legal norms.[39] The thing they all agree on, what unites them as legal positivists, is that the law is made by legal officials, such that if one wants to know what the law says on a given subject in a given jurisdiction one needs to investigate what those officials did or said, not what they ought to have done or said. The law is made up exclusively of norms that have been announced, practised, invoked, enforced, or otherwise engaged with by human beings acting on law's behalf. We can represent this thesis as:

(δ) In any legal system, the law is made up of norms which are part of the law only because some legal official engaged with them, and such an agent is a legal official only because, by engaging with norms in certain ways, he or she can make them part of the law.[40]

---

[38] *Cf.* Nicos Stavropoulos's claim that Dworkin "need not accept that any legal norms or rules are individuated non-interpretively": *Interpretivist Theories of Law*, STANFORD ENCYCLOPAEDIA OF PHILOSOPHY, <http://plato.stanford.edu/entries/law-interpretivist/>. What does Stavropoulos mean? Perhaps all he means is that each new constructive interpreter comes to the norm as already shaped by some previous constructive interpretation of it. This is false (someone has to be the first judge to read the first constitution, the first statute, etc). But even if it were true it would be trivial. Relative to each act of interpretation there would still surely be a pre-interpretive norm, viz. one that was output by a previous interpreter. Dworkin must accept that *these* pre-interpretive norms exist, or else an act of constructive interpretation has norms neither as inputs nor as outputs, and so is in no sense normative.

[39] Furthermore, Hart and Raz explicitly renounce any such predilection: *see* HART, THE CONCEPT OF LAW, *supra* note 1, at 200–202; Raz, *Why Interpret?*, 9 RATIO JURIS 349, 360–363 (1996).

[40] For a perhaps more familiar formulation of (δ), *see* J. Gardner, *Legal Positivism: 5½ Myths*, 46 AMERICAN JOURNAL OF JURISPRUDENCE 199 (2001).

In Chapter 1 of *Law's Empire* Dworkin promises that he will be arguing against this "plain fact" view of law, as he calls it, the view that "what the law is in no way depends on what it should be."[41] This suggests that he will be arguing against thesis (δ). But the subsequent chapters of the book do not fulfil the promise. Instead they argue, consistently with (δ), that judges should improve the law by constructively interpreting it. It is true that, when the law is improved by constructive interpretation, the re-interpreted norms are part of the law because they are (held by the judge to be) morally justified, or as close to morally justified as they can be made. If the parenthetical words "held by the judge to be" are suppressed in this statement, it sounds like an attack on (δ). It seems to make "what the law is" depend on "what it should be." But the parenthetical words cannot be suppressed. For according to Dworkin's own explicit characterization of constructive interpretation, it is not a constructively interpreted norm's being morally justified that turns it into law. Rather, it is the "plain fact" of an official's doing something to a norm (viz. interpreting it constructively) that turns it into law. Remember that constructive interpretation is an "interaction between purpose and object." There must be a human being—a legal official—who has the purpose in question. There must also be an object—a legal norm—to which the purpose is applied. The law is made by the interaction of the two, by the official's engaging with the norm as its interpreter, with the aim of yielding up a morally improved legal norm. If that is the picture he has in mind, then Dworkin's war with the legal positivist tradition is over. He has no quarrel with (δ). He would have a quarrel with (δ) only if the purpose of law were self-fulfilling, and needed no agent, no constructive interpreter, to carry it out on law's behalf. In that case, as I already explained above, it would be wrong to think of it as law's purpose, for there would be no logical possibility of failure on the part of the law.

Thesis (α), to put it another way, is perfectly compatible with thesis (δ). Indeed, thesis (α) presupposes thesis (δ).[42] Dworkin himself shows why in his more recent critique of Raz, quoted at length above.[43] For law to do things there

---

[41] LE, 7. Strictly speaking, the words "in no way" make this view slightly more restrictive than (δ). Some who endorse (δ), including Hart, understand it to be compatible with there being moral tests of legal validity if (but only if) those moral tests have been engaged with (announced, used, etc.) by legal officials: *see* HART, THE CONCEPT OF LAW, *supra* note 1, at 70–71. Elsewhere on the same page Dworkin places a different restriction on the "plain fact" view. He formulates it as the view that "the law is only a matter of what legal institutions have decided in the past . . . So questions of law can always be answered by looking in the books where the records are kept." Such a view may have been held by Austin and maybe even Bentham but it is rejected by Kelsen, Hart, Raz and Coleman, all of whom recognize the *using* of a norm, as well as the announcing of it, as a possible way of engaging with it so as to make it into law. I am assuming that Dworkin means the "plain fact" view to be one that could be taken by Kelsen, Hart, Raz and Coleman—in other words, that, in spite of his ambiguities, he means it to correspond to (δ).

[42] A point that is accepted and emphasized by Finnis. *See* NATURAL LAW AND NATURAL RIGHTS, *supra* note 11, at 232; also *The Truth in Legal Positivism* in THE AUTONOMY OF LAW, *supra* note 27.

[43] *See supra* text accompanying note 25.

must be human beings who do those things on behalf of law. (α) emphasizes that legal norms are made (and modified) by people, for by (α) legal norms are made (and modified) with a certain aim, viz. that they be morally justified. If there are any legal norms that are not made (or modified) by human beings then they cannot have that or any other aim, so they would count as counterexamples to (α). So if *Law's Empire* is a defence of (α), it should also be read as a defence, albeit a back-handed defence, of thesis (δ), which is the thesis that unites members of the legal positivist tradition.

Of course the converse does not hold. One may be a legal positivist—a (δ)-endorser—who does not endorse (α). Raz is an example. As we saw, he endorses (β) over (α). The difference, recall, is that (β) allows for legal officials who only pretend to aim that the law be morally justified: on law's behalf they make the claim to be morally justified but do not really have the aim. (β) makes conceptual space for such pretence, so that Nazi law is law, and Nazi officials are legal officials, even if many of them are only pretending to aim at moral justification. Of course, while it makes logical space for it, (β) does not make any *moral* space for such pretence. (β) is a thesis about law, not a thesis about the moral duties of legal officials. Morally, as Raz says, judges should aim that the law they make or modify be morally justified.[44] That they should have this aim does not entail that, whenever they speak on behalf of the law, they do have this aim. It does not entail that (α) rather than (β) is true, any more than it entails the opposite. It is an independent problem. Nevertheless it is a problem that one confronts only if one endorses (α) or (β) rather than (χ). For if (χ) is true then there is no logical space for judges to act with the aim that the law they make or modify be morally justified. For all the law they engage with is morally justified already, and their only job is to bring this fact out.

VII

Of the three rival theses about law that we encountered, namely:

(α) Law aims to be morally justified;

(β) Law claims to be morally justified;

(χ) Law is morally justified;

---

[44] Sometimes, on Raz's view, this moral imperative should carry judges beyond interpreting the law to make it morally better. Sometimes they should effect moral improvements to the law in ways that are more radical than mere interpretation would allow. They should sometimes decline to follow the law. *See*, among many discussions spread across Raz's work, THE AUTHORITY OF LAW (1979), ch. 10; ETHICS IN THE PUBLIC DOMAIN, *supra* note 26, ch. 14, and *Incorporation by Law*, 10 LEGAL THEORY 1 (2004).

the first two are legal-positivist theses.[45] They presuppose:

> (δ) In any legal system, the law is made up of norms which are part of the law only because some legal official engaged with them, and such an agent is a legal official only because, by engaging with norms in certain ways, he or she can make them part of the law.

Only (χ) is hard to reconcile with (δ). If law is made by people, then law is vulnerable to moral error, for people are vulnerable to moral error. So if law is incapable of being morally unjustified, as (χ) tells us it is, how can it be made by people? There may be some who think that the value of having norms made by people is such as to justify them morally, no matter how (otherwise) morally abhorrent are the norms that are made. Surely some law, even Nazi law, is at least preferable to chaos? This is a deeply unattractive moral position.[46] At any event, it is not Dworkin's position. Dworkin's position is either that the law is morally justified and hence not made by people (i.e. (χ) is true and therefore (δ) is false) or that law aims to be morally justified and hence is made by people who pursue that aim on behalf of the law (i.e. that (α) is true and therefore (δ) is true). *Law's Empire* leaves us puzzled by suggesting that (α) is true but (δ) is false. This is an impossible conjunction of views. Much of the book suggests that we should hold Dworkin to (α) and accordingly discount his expressed (and widely-advertised) opposition to (δ). That being so, we should be pleased to welcome Dworkin back into the best tradition of thinking about law, which is the legal positivist tradition.

---

[45] Robert Alexy has devoted much energy to showing that (β), which he calls "law's claim to moral correctness" is incompatible with legal positivism. But this is only because he holds legal positivism to the thesis that there is no necessary connection between law and morality. Thesis (β) is clearly inconsistent with this, since it states a necessary connection between law and morality.

[46] A more common position is that the positivity of legal norms—the fact that they are made by people—automatically lends some redeeming value to legal norms even when they are (otherwise) morally abhorrent. I also find this position unattractive. In my view there can be immoral laws that have absolutely no morally redeeming features.

10

How Facts Make Law

*Mark Greenberg**

I. Introduction

Nearly all philosophers of law agree that non-normative, non-evaluative, contingent facts—*descriptive facts*, for short—are among the determinants of the content of the law. In particular, ordinary empirical facts about the behavior and mental states of people such as legislators, judges, other government officials, and voters play a part in determining that content. It is highly controversial, however, whether the relevant descriptive facts, which we can call *law-determining practices*, or *law practices* (or simply *practices*) for short,[1] are the only determinants of legal content, or whether legal content also depends on normative or evaluative facts—*value facts*,[2] for short. In fact, a central—perhaps *the* central—debate in the philosophy of law is a debate over whether value facts are among the determinants of the content of the law (though the debate is not usually characterized in this way).

A central claim of legal positivism is that the content of the law depends only on *social facts*, understood as a proper subset of descriptive facts. As Joseph Raz says, "H. L. A. Hart is heir and torch-bearer of a great tradition in the philosophy of law which . . . regards the existence and content of the law as a matter of social fact

* This chapter was originally published as *How Facts Make Law*, 10 LEGAL THEORY 157 (2004). It is reprinted here with permission from Cambridge University Press. For helpful comments on ancient and recent predecessors of this chapter, I am very grateful to Larry Alexander, Andrea Ashworth, Ruth Chang, Jules Coleman, Martin Davies, Ronald Dworkin, Gil Harman, Scott Hershovitz, Kinch Hoekstra, Harry Litman, Tim Macht, Tom Nagel, Ram Neta, Jim Pryor, Stephen Perry, Joseph Raz, Gideon Rosen, Scott Shapiro, Seana Shiffrin, Ori Simchen, Martin Stone, Enrique Villanueva, and two anonymous referees for *Legal Theory*. Special thanks to Susan Hurley and Nicos Stavropoulos for many valuable discussions. I would also like to thank audiences at the University of Pennsylvania, New York University, UCLA, Yale University, the 2002 Annual Analytic Legal Philosophy Conference, and the 2003 International Congress in Mexico City, where versions of this material were presented. Finally, I owe a great debt to the work of Ronald Dworkin.

[1] For the moment, I will be vague about the nature of law practices. For more precision, *see* Section II.B below.   [2] For some explanation of what I mean by "value facts," *see infra* note 22 .

whose connection with moral or any other values is contingent and precarious."[3] In contemporary philosophy of law, there are two distinct ways of developing this tradition: *hard* and *soft* positivism. Hard positivism denies that value facts may play any role in determining legal content.[4] Soft positivism allows that the relevant social facts may make value facts relevant in a secondary way. For example, the fact that a legislature uses a moral term—"equality," say—in a statute may have the effect of incorporating moral facts—about equality, in this case—into the law.[5] On this soft positivist view, however, it is still the social facts that make the value facts relevant, and the social facts need not incorporate value facts into the law. Hence according to both hard and soft positivism, it is possible for social facts alone to determine what the law is, and even when they make value facts relevant, social facts do the fundamental work in making the law what it is—work that is explanatorily prior to the role of value facts. To put things metaphorically, hard positivism and soft positivism hold that there could still be law if God destroyed all value facts.

Ronald Dworkin is the foremost contemporary advocate of an antipositivist position. According to Dworkin, a legal proposition is true in a given legal system if it is entailed by the set of principles that best justify the practices of the legal system.[6] Since the notion of justification on which Dworkin relies is a normative notion, a consequence of Dworkin's view is that the content of the law depends on value facts.

Understanding and resolving the debate between positivists and antipositivists requires understanding the nature of the relevant determination relation—the relation between determinants of legal content and legal content. The debate, as noted, concerns whether law practices are the sole determinants of legal content. It is difficult to see how one can systematically address the question of whether A facts are the sole determinants of B facts without understanding what kind of determination is at stake. But the positivist/antipositivist debate has so far been conducted with almost no attention to this crucial issue.

A preliminary point is that the determination relation with which we are concerned is primarily a metaphysical, or constitutive, one, and only secondarily an epistemic one: the law-determining practices *make* the content of the law what it is. To put it another way, facts about the content of the law ("legal-content facts") obtain *in virtue of* the law-determining practices. It is only because of this underlying metaphysical relation that we ascertain what the law is by consulting those practices.

A second preliminary point, which should be uncontroversial, is that no legal-content facts are metaphysically basic or ultimate facts about the universe, facts for which there is nothing to say about what makes them the case. Legal-content facts, like facts about the meaning of words or facts about international exchange rates

---

[3] J. RAZ, ETHICS IN THE PUBLIC DOMAIN 210 (1994). Raz also puts the point epistemically: the content of the law "can be identified by reference to social facts alone, without resort to any evaluative argument." *Id.* at 211.

[4] *See, e.g.*, RAZ, *supra* note 3, at ch. 10; J. RAZ, THE AUTHORITY OF LAW ch. 3 (1979).

[5] *See, e.g.*, J. Coleman, *Negative and Positive Positivism*, 11 J. LEGAL STUD. 139 (1982); H. L. A. Hart, *Postscript, in* THE CONCEPT OF LAW (2d ed., 1997).   [6] *See* R. DWORKIN, LAW'S EMPIRE (1986).

(for example that, at a particular time, a U.K. pound is worth 1.45 U.S. dollars), hold in virtue of more basic facts. The important implication for present purposes is that the full story of how the determinants of legal content make the law what it is cannot take any legal content as given. It will not be adequate, for example, to hold that law practices plus some very basic legal-content facts (for example, legal propositions concerning the relevance of law practices to the content of the law) together make the law what it is, for such an account fails to explain what it is in virtue of which the very basic legal-content facts obtain.

Descriptive facts about what people said and did (and thought) in the past are among the more basic facts that determine the content of the law. I claim that the content of the law depends not just on descriptive facts but on value facts as well. Given the plausible assumption that fundamental[7] value facts are necessary rather than contingent, there is, however, a difficulty about expressing my claim in terms of counterfactual theses or theses about metaphysical determination. Even if the value facts are relevant to the content of the law, it is still true that the content of the law could not be different from what it is without the descriptive facts being different (since it is impossible for the value facts, being necessary, to be different from what they are). Necessary truths cannot be a non-redundant element of a supervenience base. Hence both positivists and antipositivists can agree that descriptive facts alone metaphysically determine the content of the law.[8]

In order to express the sense in which the content of the law is claimed to depend on value facts, we therefore need to employ a notion different from and richer than metaphysical determination. We can say that the full metaphysical explanation of the content of the law (of why certain legal propositions are true) must appeal to value facts. I earlier put the point metaphorically by saying that if God destroyed the value facts, the law would have no content. The epistemic corollary is that working out what the law is will require reasoning about value.

As we will see, a full account of what it is in virtue of which legal-content facts obtain has to do more than describe the more basic facts that are the metaphysical determinants of legal content. The relevant determination relation is not bare

---

[7] The point of the qualification "fundamental" is to distinguish basic or pure value facts—that, say, harm is a relevant moral consideration—from applied or mixed value facts—that returning the gun to John tomorrow would be wrong. The fundamental value facts are plausibly metaphysically necessary, while the applied value facts obviously depend on contingent descriptive facts as well as on fundamental value facts. This qualification does not affect the point in the text, since the contingent facts are encompassed in the supervenience base of descriptive facts. That is, if the fundamental value facts supervene on the descriptive facts, the applied value facts will do so as well.

[8] The term "metaphysical determination" is typically used in a way that implies nothing about the order of explanation or about relative ontological basicness. In this sense, that the A facts metaphysically determine the B facts does not imply that the B facts obtain in virtue of the obtaining of the A facts. Positivists and antipositivists can agree not only that descriptive facts alone metaphysically determine the content of the law but also that the obtaining of the relevant descriptive facts is part of the explanation of the obtaining of legal-content facts. In this paper, we will be concerned only with cases in which the putative determinants are more basic than and part of the explanation of the determined facts. For convenience, I will therefore say that the A facts metaphysically determine the B facts only when the B facts obtain at least in part in virtue of the obtaining of the A facts.

metaphysical determination. (As we have just seen, if that were the relevant relation, there would be no debate between the positivists and the antipositivists. Positivists would win the debate trivially, since the descriptive facts alone fix the content of the law.) I argue for a particular understanding of the metaphysical relation (between the determinants and the legal content that they determine), which I call *rational determination*. Rational determination, in contrast to bare metaphysical determination, is necessarily reason-based (in a sense that I elaborate in Section II.B).

A quick way to grasp the basic idea is to consider the case of esthetic facts. Descriptive facts metaphysically determine esthetic facts. A painting is elegant in virtue of facts about the distribution of color over the surface (and the like). But arguably there need not be reasons that explain why the relevant descriptive facts make the painting elegant. We may be able to discover which descriptive facts make paintings elegant (and even the underlying psychological mechanisms), but even if we do, those facts need not provide substantive aesthetic reasons why the painting is elegant (as opposed to causal explanations of our reactions). On this view, it may just be a brute fact that a certain configuration of paint on a surface constitutes or realizes a painting with certain esthetic properties. (As noted below, facts about humor provide an even clearer example.) In contrast, if it is not in principle intelligible why the determinants of legal content—the relevant descriptive facts—make the law have certain content, then it does not have that content.

Rational determination is an interesting and unusual metaphysical relation because it involves the notion of a reason, which may well be best understood as an epistemic notion. If so, we have an epistemic notion playing a role in a metaphysical relation. (Donald Davidson's view of the relation between the determinants of mental content and mental content is plausibly another example of this general phenomenon.)[9] For this reason, I believe that the rational-determination relation is of independent philosophical interest.

My main goal in this chapter, however, is to show that, given the nature of the relevant kind of determination, law practices—understood as descriptive facts about what people have said and done—cannot themselves determine the content of the law. Value facts are needed to determine the legal relevance of different aspects of law practices. I therefore defend an antipositivist position, one that is roughly in the neighborhood of Dworkin's, on the basis of very general philosophical considerations unlike those on which Dworkin himself relies.[10]

We have two domains of facts: a higher-level legal domain and a lower-level descriptive domain. It is, I claim, a general truth that a domain of descriptive facts can rationally determine facts in a dependent, higher-level domain only in combination

---

[9] *See infra* notes 17 and 18.

[10] Dworkin's theory of law depends on a view about the nature of "creative interpretation." In particular, he argues that to interpret a work of art or a social practice is to try to display it as the best that it can be of its kind. *See* DWORKIN, *supra* note 6, at 49–65. Dworkin's central argument for the position that legal interpretation is an instance of this general kind of interpretation is that this position is the best explanation of "theoretical disagreement" in law. *Id.* at 45–96; *see also* R. Dworkin, *Law as Interpretation, in* THE POLITICS OF INTERPRETATION (W. J. T. Mitchell ed., 1983).

with truths about which aspects of the descriptive, lower-level facts are relevant to the higher-level domain and what their relevance is. Without the standards provided by such truths, it is indeterminate which candidate facts in the higher-level domain are most supported by the lower-level facts. There is a further question about the source or nature of the needed truths (about the relevance of the descriptive facts to the higher-level domain). In the legal case, these truths are, I will suggest, truths about value.

The basic argument is general enough to apply to any realm in which a body of descriptive facts is supposed to make it the case *by rational determination* that facts in a certain domain obtain. For example, if the relation between social practices, understood purely descriptively, and social rules is rational determination, the argument implies that social practices cannot themselves determine the content of social rules. (At that point, we reach the further question of the source of the truths needed in the case of social rules; the answer may differ from that in the legal case.) Hence the argument is of interest well beyond the philosophy of law. In this chapter, I will largely confine the discussion to the legal case.

In Section II, I clarify the premises of the argument and explain that they should not be controversial. In Section III, I examine why there is a problem of how legal content is determined. The content of the law is not simply the meanings of the words (and the contents of the mental states) that are uttered in the course of law practices. Something must determine which elements of law practices are relevant and how they combine to determine the content of the law. Next, in Section IV, I argue that law practices themselves cannot determine how they contribute to the content of the law. In Section V, I consider and respond to three related objections. Finally, in Section VI, I examine what the argument has established about the relation between law and value.[11]

II. The Premises

In this section, I set out the two premises of the argument and make a number of clarifications. The second premise will require a great deal more discussion than the first. I take both premises to be relatively uncontroversial in many contemporary legal systems, including those of, for example, the United States and the United Kingdom.

A. Premise 1: Determinate Legal Content

The first premise of the argument is the following:

> (D) In the legal system under consideration, there is a substantial body of determinate legal content.

[11] There are interesting connections between this chapter and G. A. Cohen's recent *Facts and Principles*, 31 Phil. & Pub. Aff. 211 (2003). Cohen's paper came to my attention too late for me to explore the connections here, however.

My use of the term "determinate" (like my use of "determine") is metaphysical, not epistemic. That is, for the law to be determinate on a given issue is not for us to be able to ascertain what the law requires on that issue (or still less for there to be a consensus), but for there to be a fact of the matter as to what the law requires with respect to the issue. Thus, when I say that there is a substantial body of determinate legal content, I mean roughly that there are many true legal propositions (in the particular legal system). What do I mean by "legal propositions"?[12] A legal proposition is a legal standard or requirement. An example might be the proposition that any person who, by means of deceit, intentionally deprives another person of property worth more than a thousand dollars shall be imprisoned for not more than six months. For a legal proposition to be true in a particular legal system is for it to be a true statement of the law of that legal system.[13] D is consistent with the law's being indeterminate to some extent, and it is deliberately vague about how much determinacy there is. I think it is obvious that D is true in the legal systems of many contemporary nations.

B. Premise 2: The Role of Law-determining Practices

The second premise is:

(L) The law-determining practices in part determine the content of the law.

The basic idea behind L is that the law depends on the law practices. L thus rules out, for example, the extreme natural-law position that the law is simply whatever morality requires. I take it, however, that very few contemporary legal theorists would defend this position or any other position that makes law practices irrelevant to the content of the law.

By the term "law practices" (or, more fully, "law-determining practices") I mean to include *at least* constitutions, statutes, executive orders, judicial and administrative decisions, and regulations. Although it is unidiomatic, I will refer to a particular constitution, statute, judicial decision, and so on as *a law practice*. So a practice, in my usage, need not be a habitual or ongoing pattern of action. I need to clarify what I mean by saying that a practice can be, for example, a statute. Lawyers often talk as if a statute (or other law practice) is simply a text. It is of course permissible to use the word "statute" (or "constitution," "judicial decision," etc.) to refer to the corresponding text, and I will occasionally write in this way. But if law practices are to be determinants of the content of the law, the relevant practice must be, for example, the fact that a majority of the members of the legislature voted in a certain way with respect to a text (or alternatively the event of their having done so), not merely the text itself. So as I will generally use the term, "statute" ("constitution," etc.) is shorthand for a collection of facts (or events),[14] not a text.

---

[12] The term is Dworkin's. *See* DWORKIN, *supra* note 6, at 4.

[13] I will usually omit the qualification about a particular legal system.

[14] I will hereinafter ignore the possibility of taking law practices to be composed of events rather than facts.

In general, then, law practices consist of ordinary empirical facts about what people thought, said, and did in various circumstances.[15] For example, law practices potentially include the facts that, in a particular historical context, a legislative committee issued a certain report, various speeches were made in a legislative debate, a bill that would have repealed a statute failed to pass, a concurring judge issued a certain opinion, and an executive official announced a particular view of a statute.[16] Once I have clarified the claim that law practices partially determine the content of the law, I will be able to say something more precise about what counts as a law practice.

When L says that law practices determine (in part) the content of the law, what sense of "determine" is involved? As noted above, a preliminary point is that L's claim is constitutive or metaphysical, not epistemic. That is, it is not a claim that we use law practices to ascertain what the content of the law is, but that such practices make it the case that the content of the law is what it is.

I maintain that the relevant kind of determination is not bare metaphysical determination but what we can call *rational determination*. The A facts rationally determine the B facts just in case the A facts metaphysically determine the B facts *and* the obtaining of the A facts makes intelligible or rationally explains the B facts' obtaining. Thus, L is the conjunction of two doctrines, a *metaphysical-determination doctrine* and a *rational-relation doctrine*. Let me elaborate.

I will make the (uncontroversial, I hope) assumption that there are facts that (1) are ontologically more basic than facts about legal content and (2) metaphysically determine that the content of the law is what it is. The *metaphysical-determination doctrine* is that these more basic facts that determine the content of the law non-redundantly include law practices.

Metaphysical determination can be brute. If the A facts are more basic facts that metaphysically determine the B facts, there is a sense in which the A facts explain the B facts, for the A facts are more basic facts, the obtaining of which entails that the B facts obtain. But there need be no explanation of why the obtaining of particular A facts has the consequence that it does for the B facts. To dramatize the point, even a perfectly rational being may not be able to see why it is that particular A facts make particular B facts obtain.

The metaphysical-determination doctrine is not enough to capture our ordinary understanding (which L attempts to articulate) of the nature of the

---

[15] Hypothetical decisions arguably play a significant role in determining the content of the law, but for purposes of this paper they will largely be ignored. Susan Hurley characterizes hypothetical decisions as hypothetical cases that have a settled resolution. *See* S. L. Hurley, *Coherence, Hypothetical Cases, and Precedent*, 10 OXFORD J. LEGAL STUD. 221 (1990). Another possibility is to include any hypothetical case that has a determinate right answer, even if there is disagreement on its resolution. There would be disagreement about which hypothetical cases had determinate right answers and therefore about which were determinants of legal content.

[16] Nothing turns on how we individuate practices, at least in the first instance. E.g. a legislative committee's issuance of a report could be considered part of the circumstances in which a majority of the legislature voted for a statute or could be considered a separate practice. Once the roles of different elements of law practices are determined, there may be a basis for individuation.

determination relation between the law practices and the content of the law. We also need the *rational-relation doctrine*, which holds that the relation between the determinants of legal content and legal content is reason-based. In the relevant sense, a reason is a consideration that makes the relevant explanandum intelligible.[17] Here is one way to put the point. There are indefinitely many possible mappings, from complete sets of law practices to legal content (to complete sets of legal propositions). As far as the metaphysical-determination doctrine goes, it could simply be arbitrary which mapping is the legally correct one. In other words, the connection between a difference in the practices and a consequent difference in the content of the law could be brute. For example, it is consistent with the truth of the metaphysical-determination doctrine that, say, the deletion of one seemingly unimportant word in one subclause of one minor administrative regulation would result in the elimination of all legal content in the United States—in there being no true legal propositions in the U.S. legal system (though there is no explanation of why it would do so). By contrast, according to the rational-relation doctrine, the correct mapping must be such that there are reasons why law practices have the consequences they do for the content of the law.

To put it metaphorically, the relation between the law practices and the content of the law must be transparent.[18] (For the relation to be opaque would be for it to be the case that any change in law practices could have, so far as we could tell, any effect on the content of the law. The effects on the content of the law could be unfathomable and unpredictable, even if fully determinate.)

It bears emphasis that what must be rationally intelligible is not the content of the law but the relation between, on the one hand, determinants of legal content and, on the other, legal content. L holds *not* that the content of the law must be rational or reasonable but that it must be intelligible that the determinants of legal content make the content of the law what it is. For example, there must be a reason that deleting a particular word from a statutory text would have the impact on the law that it would in fact have.[19]

---

[17] I will not attempt to spell out the relevant notion of a reason more fully here. One possibility is that the best way to do so is in terms of idealized human reasoning ability. For example, the idea might be that practices yield a legal proposition if and only if an ideal reasoner would see that they do. The notion of a reason would hence be an epistemic notion. In that case, L would imply that the metaphysics of law involves an epistemic notion; that is, what the law *is* would depend in part on what an ideal human reasoner would find intelligible.

[18] A useful comparison can be made to certain well-known positions in the philosophy of mind. Donald Davidson's radical interpretation approach to mental and linguistic content presupposes that behavior determines the contents of mental states and the meaning of linguistic expressions in a way that must be intelligible or transparent. D. Davidson, *Radical Interpretation, in* INQUIRIES INTO TRUTH AND INTERPRETATION (1984); and D. Davidson, *Belief and the Basis of Meaning, in* INQUIRIES INTO TRUTH AND INTERPRETATION (1984). Similarly, Saul Kripke's "Kripkenstein" discussion presupposes that we must be able to "read off" the contents of mental states from the determinants of content. S. KRIPKE, WITTGENSTEIN ON RULES AND PRIVATE LANGUAGE 24, 29 (1982). *See infra* note 25.

[19] At this point in the text, I have deleted a paragraph that appeared in the original publication of this chapter. I have also made a few changes in the next few paragraphs.

Another important clarification is that it is no part of rational determination that the reasons in question must be value facts. The reasons that the determining facts must provide are considerations that explain in rational terms why particular facts of the target domain, as opposed to others, obtain. In general, non-normative (and non-evaluative) facts can constitute reasons of the relevant kind. Here is an example from a different domain. Consider the facts that (in a particular economy) the total amount of demand deposits is 2 million units and the total amount of currency in the hands of the public is 1 million units. With the fact that the money supply M1 consists in demand deposits plus currency in the hands of the public, these facts make rationally intelligible that the total amount of M1 (in the economy in question) is 3 million units.

As far as the rational-relation doctrine is concerned, it is an open question whether there are non-normative, non-evaluative facts that could constitute reasons for legal facts—and indeed whether there are value facts that could do so. (My ultimate view, of course, is not that value facts could themselves provide such reasons, but that both descriptive and value facts are needed.) The point is important because otherwise positivists could not accept the rational-relation doctrine. The strategy of my argument is to use the rational-relation doctrine, which, I claim below, most legal theorists implicitly accept, to argue for the controversial conclusion that value facts must be determinants of legal content.

In principle, conceptual truths (that are not value facts) about law could, with law practices, make rationally intelligible the content of the law. For example, it might be claimed that it follows from the concept of law that a validly enacted statute makes true those propositions that are the ordinary meanings of the sentences of the statute. On this view, the fact that a statutory text says that any person who drives at more than sixty-five miles an hour commits an offense, together with certain conceptual truths about law, makes it intelligible that the law requires that one not drive at more than sixty-five miles an hour.

The general point, again, is that it is a matter for argument, not something presupposed by L, what kinds of facts (if any) must supplement law practices in order for the determining facts to provide reasons that explain why particular legal propositions are true. In particular, L does not presuppose that value facts are needed.[20]

Why have I made the qualification that law practices *partially* determine the content of the law? Law practices must determine the content of the law. But, my argument continues, there are many possible ways in which practices could determine the content of the law. (Put another way, there are many functions that map complete sets of law practices to legal content.) Something other than

---

[20] At a later stage of analysis, we might find that there are restrictions on what kind of reasons the determinants of legal content must provide. For example, it might turn out that legal systems have functions and that in order for a legal system to perform its functions properly, the determinants of legal content must provide reasons for action. *See infra* the last paragraph of Section VI.A. L does not presuppose any such restrictions, however.

law practices—X, for short—must help to determine how practices contribute to the content of the law (that is, to determine which mapping is the legally correct one). So a full account of the metaphysics of legal content involves X as well as law practices.

This conclusion can be expressed in two equivalent ways. We could say that practices are the *only* determinants of legal content but that an account of legal content must do more than specify the determinants. This formulation is particularly natural if X consists of necessary truths.[21] (A related advantage is that this way of talking highlights that practices are what typically vary, producing changes in the content of the law.) The second formulation would say that X and law practices are *together* the determinants of the content of the law. Because it is convenient to express this paper's thesis by saying that X plays a role in determining legal content (and because I want to leave open the possibility that X may vary), this formulation seems preferable, and I will adopt it as my official formulation. Accordingly, I will say that law practices are only some of the determinants of the content of the law. (For brevity, however, I will sometimes omit the qualification "partially" and write simply that law practices determine the content of the law.)

C. Law Practices as Descriptive Facts

Let me now return to the question of what counts as a law practice. I have said that law practices consist of ordinary empirical facts about what people have thought, said, and done—including, paradigmatically, facts about what members of constitutional assemblies, legislatures, courts, and administrative agencies have said and done. I want to be clear about the exclusion of two kinds of facts. First, law practices do not include legal-content facts. Secondly, law practices do not include facts about value, for example, facts about what morality requires or permits.[22] The law practices thus consist of non-legal-content descriptive facts. (For convenience, I will generally write simply "descriptive facts" rather than "non-legal-content descriptive facts"; this shorthand does not reflect a presupposition that legal-content facts are value facts.) Let me explain the reasons for the two exclusions.

As I said, I am assuming that the content of the law is not a metaphysically basic aspect of the world but is constituted by more basic facts. The reason for the first exclusion—of legal-content facts—is that law practices are supposed to

---

[21] *See supra* text accompanying notes 7 and 8.

[22] By "facts," I simply mean true propositions. Hence facts about value, or value facts, are true normative or evaluative propositions, such as true propositions about what is right or wrong, good or bad, beautiful or ugly. The fact that people value something or believe something is valuable is *not* a value fact but a descriptive fact about people's attitudes. For example, the fact, if it is one, that accepting bribes is wrong is a value fact; the fact that people value honesty is a descriptive fact. This paper does not attempt to address a skeptic who maintains that there are no true propositions about value. One could use an argument of the same form as mine to argue that there must be value facts—for without them there would not be determinate legal requirements. But a skeptic about value facts would no doubt take such an argument to be a case of the legal tail wagging the value dog.

be the determinants of legal content, not part of the legal content that is to be determined.

Suppose an objector maintained that the law practices that determine legal content are themselves laden with legal content. It is certainly natural to use the term "law practices" in this way. After all, the fact that the legislature passed a bill is legal-content laden: it presupposes legal-content facts about what counts as a legislature and a bill. Since legal-content facts are not basic, however, there must be non-legal-content facts that constitute the legal-content-laden practices. At this point, we will have to appeal to descriptive facts about what people thought, said, and did—the facts that I am calling "law practices." For example, the fact that a legislature did such and such must hold in virtue of complex descriptive facts about people's behavior and perhaps also value facts. (If, in order to account for legal-content-laden practices, we have to appeal not merely to descriptive facts but also to value facts, so much the worse for the positivist thesis that the content of the law depends only on descriptive facts.) The convenience of talking as if law practices consisted in legal-content-laden facts about the behavior of legislatures, courts, and so on should not obscure the fact that there must be more basic facts in virtue of which the legal-content facts obtain. To build legal-content facts into law practices would beg the question at the heart of this paper—the question of the necessary conditions for law practices to determine the content of the law. (For ease of exposition, I will continue to use legal-content-laden characterizations of the law practices, but the law practices should, strictly speaking, be understood to be the underlying descriptive facts in virtue of which the relevant legal-content facts obtain.)

It is uncontroversial that certain kinds of facts are among the supervenience base for legal content: roughly speaking, facts about what constitutional assemblies, legislatures, courts, and administrative agencies did in the past. Of course, as just noted, such characterizations are legal-content laden and are therefore shorthand for non-legal-content characterizations of the law practices. (I do not mean, of course, that it is uncontroversial exactly which facts of these kinds are relevant; I'll return to this point shortly.) There are at least two kinds of controversy, however, about the determinants of legal content.

First, it is controversial whether value facts are among the determinants of content. The reason for the second exclusion—the exclusion of value facts—is that this paper tries to argue from the uncontroversial claim that law practices are determinants of the content of the law to the conclusion that value facts must play a role in determining the content of the law. If law practices were taken to be value-laden, it would no longer be uncontroversial that they are determinants of legal content. (On the other hand, even those theorists who think that value facts are needed to determine the content of the law can accept that descriptive facts also play a role.) Moreover, unless we separate the descriptive facts from the value facts, we cannot evaluate whether the descriptive facts can themselves determine the content of the law. In sum, by understanding law practices to exclude value facts, I ensure that L is uncontroversial and I prepare the way for my argument that descriptive facts alone cannot determine the content of the law.

The second kind of controversy about the determinants of legal content is controversy over precisely which descriptive facts are determinants. I have mentioned some paradigmatic determinants of legal content. But there are other kinds of descriptive facts—for example, facts about customs, about people's moral beliefs, about political history, and about law practices in other countries—that are arguably among the determinants of legal content. Also, somewhat differently, it is controversial which facts about judicial, legislative, or executive behavior are relevant. There can be debate, for example, about the relevance of legislative history, intentions of legislators and of drafters of statutes, legislative findings, judicial obiter dicta, and executive interpretations of statutes. I propose to deal with this second kind of controversy by leaving our understanding of law practices open and non-restrictive.

There are several reasons for this approach. First, my argument is that practices, understood as composed of descriptive facts, cannot themselves determine the content of the law. If I begin with a restrictive understanding of practices, my argument will be open to the reply that I failed to include some of the relevant facts. For this reason, I want to be liberal about which descriptive facts are part of law practices. Secondly, my argument will not depend on exactly which descriptive facts make up law practices. Rather, I will make a general argument that descriptive facts—in particular, facts about what people have done and said and thought—cannot by themselves determine the content of the law. Therefore it will not matter precisely which such facts are included in law practices. Thirdly, my view is ultimately that the question of which facts are part of law practices—like the question of how different aspects of law practices contribute to the content of the law—is dependent on value facts. (Indeed, I will often treat the two questions together as different aspects of the general question of the way in which law practices determine the content of the law.) As we will see, that we cannot in an uncontroversial way specify which are law practices and which are not is one consideration in support of my argument for the necessary role of value. All we need to begin with is some rough idea of law practices, which can be overinclusive.

In sum, let law practices include, in addition to constitutions, statutes, and judicial and administrative decisions, any other non-legal-content descriptive facts that turn out to play a role in determining the content of the law.[23] Which facts these are and what role they play are controversial, so we can begin with a rough and inclusive understanding of law practices. One aspect of figuring out how law practices contribute to the content of the law will be figuring out which

---

[23] This proviso does not make L the tautological claim that the determinants of legal content determine legal content. L says that constitutions, statutes, judicial decisions, and so on are (non-redundantly) among the determinants of content.

facts make a contribution and which do not. But there is no reason to expect a clean line between law practices and other facts.[24]

The exclusion of value facts should not be taken to suggest that law practices are to be understood in solely physical or behavioral terms. To the contrary, as I explain in the next section, I take for granted the mental and linguistic contents involved in law practices. In other words, law practices include the facts about what the actors believe, intend, and so on and about what their words mean.

D. Why L Should Be Uncontroversial

The metaphysical-determination doctrine should be relatively uncontroversial, certainly for those who accept that there are determinate legal requirements. Positivists, Dworkinians, and contemporary natural-law theorists as well as practicing lawyers and judges accept that constitutions, statutes, and judicial and administrative decisions are (non-redundant) determinants of the content of the law. That law practices may also include other descriptive facts to the extent that those facts are determinants of the content of the law obviously cannot make the metaphysical-determination doctrine controversial.

More generally, we began with the premise that there are determinate legal requirements. What makes them *legal* requirements is that they are determined, at least in part, by law practices. Contrast the requirements of morality (or, to take a different kind of example, of a particular club). If law practices did not determine legal content, there could still be moral requirements and officials' whims, but there would be no legal requirements. In order to think differently, one would have to hold a strange view of the metaphysics of law according to which the content of the law is what it is independently of all the facts of what people said and did that make up law practices, and law practices are at best evidence of that content. So I think it should be uncontroversial that law practices are among the determinants of the content of the law.

As to the rational-relation doctrine, it is fundamental to our ordinary understanding of the law and taken for granted by most legal theory, though seldom articulated. The basic idea is that the content of the law is in principle accessible to a rational creature who is aware of the relevant law practices. It is not possible that the truth of a legal proposition could simply be opaque, in the sense that there would be no possibility of seeing its truth to be an intelligible consequence of the law practices. In other words, that the law practices support *these* legal propositions over all others is always a matter of *reasons*—where reasons are considerations in principle intelligible to rational creatures. (A corollary is that to the extent

---

[24] One natural understanding of "law practices" is more restrictive than the way I use the term. According to this understanding, law practices are limited to (facts about) what legal institutions and officials do in their official capacities. If we used the term "law practices" in this natural way, we would need, in addition to the category of law practices, a category of other descriptive facts that play a role in determining the content of the law.

that the law practices do not provide reasons supporting certain legal propositions over others, the law is indeterminate.)

I will not attempt to defend the rational-relation doctrine fully here but will mention a few considerations. Suppose the A facts metaphysically determine the B facts, but the relation between the A facts and the B facts is opaque. In that case, how could we know about the B facts? One possibility is that we have access to the B facts independently of our knowledge of the A facts. An example might be the relation between the microphysical facts about someone's brain and the facts about that person's conscious experience. Suppose that the microphysical facts metaphysically determine the facts about the person's conscious experience but that the relation is opaque. The opaqueness of the relation does not affect the person's ability to know the facts about his conscious experience, because we do not in general learn about our conscious experience by working it out from the microphysical facts. (Moreover, since we have independent knowledge of conscious experience, we might be able to discover correlations between microphysical facts and conscious experience even if those correlations were not intelligible even in principle.) To take a different kind of example, the microphysical facts may metaphysically determine the facts about the weather, and the relation may be opaque, but again, we do not learn about the weather by working it out from the microphysical facts.

A second possibility is that we do work out the B facts from the A facts but that we have a nonrational, perhaps hardwired, capacity to do so. For example, it is plausible that the facts about what was said and done (on a particular occasion, say) determine whether what was said and done was funny (and to what degree and in what way). And we do work out whether an incident was funny from the facts about what was done and said. It is plausible, however, that the relation between what was said and done and its funniness is not necessarily transparent to all rational creatures; our ability to know what is funny may depend on species-specific tendencies; that is, there may not be reasons that make the humor facts intelligible; it may just be a brute fact that humans find certain things funny.[25]

Law seems different from both of these kinds of cases. First, our only access to the content of the law is through law practices. It is not as if we can find out what the law is directly or through some other route. And the whole enterprise of lawmaking is premised on the assumption that the behavior of legislators, judges, and

---

[25] Compare the issue of how facts about our use of words determine their meaning. Natural languages are a biological creation. Although many philosophers have thought differently (*see supra* note 18), we cannot take for granted that the correct mapping from the use of words to their meaning will be based on reasons. How, it may be objected, would we then be able to work out from their use of words what others mean? The answer may simply be that we have a species-specific, hardwired mechanism that rules out many incorrect mappings that are not ruled out by reasons. In that case, an intelligent creature without that mechanism would not be able to work out what words mean.

other law-makers will have understandable and predictable consequences for the content of the law.

Secondly, we are able to work out what the law is and predict the effect on the law of changes in law practices through *reasons*, not through some non-rational human tendency to have correct law reactions to law practices.

When lawyers, judges, and law professors work out what the law is, they give reasons for their conclusions. Indeed, if we find that we cannot articulate reasons that justify a provisional judgment about what the law is in light of law practices, we reject the judgment. By contrast, it is notoriously difficult to explain why something is or is not funny, and we do not generally hold our judgments about humor responsible to our ability to articulate reasons for them. A related point is that we believe that we could teach any intelligent creature that is sensitive to reasons how to work out what the law is.

It might be objected that although the epistemology of law is reason-based, the metaphysics might not be. It is difficult to see how such an objection could be developed. For present purposes, I will simply point out that when legal practitioners give reasons for their conclusions about what the law is, they believe that they are not merely citing evidence that is contingently connected to the content of the law; rather, they believe that they are giving the reasons that make the law what it is. The point is not that lawyers believe themselves to be infallible. Rather, they believe that when they get things right, the reasons they discover are not merely reasons for believing that the content of the law is a particular way, but the reasons that *make* the content of the law what it is. Although they would never put it this way, lawyers take for granted that the epistemology of law tracks its metaphysics. And the epistemology of law is plainly reason-based.

Legal theorists generally take for granted some version of the claim that the relation between law practices and the content of the law is reason-based. An example is H.L.A. Hart's argument that the vagueness and open texture of legal language have the consequence that the law is indeterminate.[26] If bare metaphysical determination were all that was at issue—if it were not the case that the relation between practice and content were necessarily intelligible—the vagueness of language would in no way support the claim that law was indeterminate. Similarly, when legal realists or Critical Legal Studies theorists argue that the existence of conflicting pronouncements or doctrines in law practices results in underdetermination of the law, their arguments would be beside the point if what was at stake were not rational determination.[27]

In general, the large body of legal theory that has explored the question of whether law practices are capable of rendering the law determinate (and if so, how

---

[26] H. L. A. HART, THE CONCEPT OF LAW ch. 7 (2d ed., 1997).

[27] *See, e.g.*, A. Altman, *Legal Realism, Critical Legal Studies, and Dworkin*, 15 PHIL. & PUB. AFF. 205 (1986); M. Kelman, *Interpretive Construction in the Substantive Criminal Law*, 33 STAN. L. REV. 591 (1981).

determinate) presupposes that law practices determine the content of the law in a reason-based way. If the relation between law practices and the content of the law could be opaque, any set of law practices would be capable, as far as we would be able to judge, of determining any set of legal propositions. (As long as there are as many possible sets of law practices as there are possible sets of legal propositions, there is no barrier to the content of the law's being fixed by the practices, and we would have no warrant to rely on our assessment of other putative prerequisites for practices to determine the content of the law.) In sum, the doctrine that law practices rationally determine the content of the law captures a basic conviction about the law that is shared by law-makers, lawyers, and legal theorists and is supported by the epistemology of law.

Why does it matter to my argument that the relation between law practices and the content of the law is reason-based? This paper explores the necessary conditions for law practices' making the content of the law what it is. The central argument is that descriptive facts cannot determine their own rational significance—what reasons they provide. The argument therefore depends on the claim that the descriptive facts determine the content of the law in a reason-based way. It turns out that value facts are needed to make it *intelligible* that law practices support certain legal propositions over others.[28]

E. The Scope of the Argument

Premises D and L tell us something about the scope of my argument. The argument is sound only for legal systems in which D and L are true. So my conclusions are limited to legal systems in which there are legal requirements that are determined in part by law practices. If there is a legal system in which there are no determinate legal requirements, my argument would not apply to it. Similarly, if there is a legal system in which law practices, understood as (facts about) various people's sayings and doings, do not play a role in determining the content of the law, my argument would not apply to it. For example, perhaps there could be a legal system in which the content of the law is determined exclusively by the content of morality or exclusively by divine will. In this paper, I do not address questions of the necessary conditions for something's counting as a legal system. It might be argued that a substantial body of legal requirements that are determined by practices of various officials or institutions is a necessary condition for the existence of a legal system, but I do not intend to pursue such an argument.

---

[28] Suppose that the relation between law practices and the content of the law were necessarily intelligible only in a way that depends on some human-specific tendency. As long as practices must provide considerations that are *intelligible* (even if only to humans), a version of my argument should still go through.

III. Is There a Distinctively Legal Problem of Content?

We begin with our two premises: that the law has determinate content, and that law practices in part determine that content. Our question is: What conditions must be satisfied in order for law practices to determine legal propositions?

As I said above, since we are interested in problems of the determination of content only to the extent that they are peculiarly legal, we can take for granted the content of sentences and propositional attitudes.[29] So the question is: How can a collection of facts about what various people did and said (including the facts about what they intended, believed, preferred, and hoped, and about what their words meant) determine which legal propositions are true?

At this point, however, it must be asked whether there is a peculiarly legal problem of content. Once we take for granted the relevant mental and linguistic content, it may seem that no problem of legal content remains. Legal content is simply the content of the appropriate mental states and texts. In this section, I consider this possibility and argue that it is not at all plausible. The ordinary mental and linguistic content of utterances and mental states of participants in law practices— *nonlegal content*, for short—does not automatically endow the law with legal content. Something must determine which aspects of law practices are relevant and how together they contribute to the content of the law.

In the next section, I consider the possibility that, given the content of the relevant utterances and attitudes, law practices themselves determine how they contribute to the content of the law and thus can unilaterally determine the content of the law. But before we turn to whether law practices can solve the problem of legal content, we need to see what the problem is—why the nonlegal content of law practices does not provide the content of the law. That is the topic of this section.

In legal discourse, both ordinary and academic, constitutional or statutory provisions and judicial decisions are often conflated with rules or legal propositions. For example, lawyers will sometimes talk interchangeably of a statutory provision and a statutory rule, or of a judicial decision and the rule of that case. In non-philosophical contexts there is generally no harm in this kind of talk. Since our question, however, is how law practices determine the content of the law, it is crucial not to confuse law practices with legal propositions. For example, if one assumed that a statute was the rule or proposition expressed by the words of the statute, one might think that there was no problem of how law practices could

---

[29] There is no practical problem with taking these matters for granted and proceeding without a solution to basic problems concerning how linguistic and mental content are possible. These problems do not concern difficulties we encounter in practice in attributing linguistic and mental content; the difficulty is in saying what it is in virtue of which a linguistic expression or mental state has its content.

determine legal content; or one might think that the only problem was how to combine or amalgamate a large number of rules or propositions.

Although it would beg the question to take legal propositions for granted, we do have the propositions that are the content of the utterances and mental states of participants in law practices. What is wrong with the idea that those propositions constitute legal content, so that law practices, once they are understood to include facts about mental and linguistic content, automatically have legal content?

I will begin with the least serious problems—those concerning the attribution of non-legal content. Although we are normally able to attribute attitudes to people based on what they say and do and to attribute standard meanings to a large number of sentences of a language we speak, there are difficulties in attributing non-legal content to aspects of a putative law practice. Here are a few examples.

First, when I say that we can take for granted mental and linguistic content, I mean that we need not ignore the mental and linguistic content that is available. We should not, however, assume that all of the contents of the mental states of all of the people involved in law practices are available. That would obviously be false. In general, what is available in the standard reports of law practices is not sufficient to attribute much in the way of attitudes to the people who actually performed the actions and made the utterances; the fact that a particular legislator voted for a bill or a certain judge signed an opinion is not in general sufficient to attribute beliefs, intentions, hopes, and so on, to her. Moreover, the law restricts what *evidence* of the intentions and beliefs of legislators and judges is acceptable to determine the content of the law. Even when the intentions of a legislator or judge are relevant to the content of the law, it is not the case that, say, her private letters or diary may be a source of that intention. Something must determine which evidence of legally relevant attitudes is legally acceptable.

Secondly, though many sentences of natural languages have standard meanings, it is notorious that this is not true of some of the sentences uttered by those engaged in making law practices. The point here is *not* that in legal contexts linguistic expressions often have specialized meanings that are not straightforwardly connected to their ordinary meanings. Rather, some of the contorted sentences in the law books have no standard meaning in a natural language.

Thirdly, even when sentences taken alone have standard meanings, collections of those sentences may fail to do so. In other words, the property of having a standard meaning (on a notion of standard meaning appropriate for present purposes) is not closed under conjunction (for example, because context may introduce ambiguity into an otherwise unambiguous sentence).

Setting aside these problems with ascertaining non-legal content, we can turn to the more important question of the bearing of non-legal content on legal content. One problem is that the non-legal content of some elements of law practices has, or arguably has, little or nothing to do with the legal content determined by those practices. Consider sentences in statutory preambles, sentences in presidential speeches at bill-signing ceremonies, and sentences in judicial opinions that are not necessary to the resolution of the issue before the court. Another example is the actual but unexpressed hopes of the members of the legislature as to how the courts would interpret a statute. Countless sentences are written and spoken at different stages of law-practice making by people with myriad attitudes.[30] Something must determine which sentences' and attitudes' contents are relevant.

Another problem is that the contribution of a particular law practice to the content of the law may not be the meaning of any text or the content of any person's mental state. The actual attitudes of appellate judges may be irrelevant; instead the relevant question may be what a hypothetical reasonable person would have intended by the words uttered by the judges or what would be the best, or the narrowest, explanation of the result reached. Another possibility is that aspects of law practices that contribute to non-legal content in one way contribute to legal content in an entirely different way; facts about what was said and done may have peculiarly legal significance. An obvious example is that common words such as "malice" and "fault" are often used in legal discourse in a technical sense. To take a more subtle instance, when a panel of several judges is badly split, it can be a complex and tricky matter to ascertain the relevance to legal content of the meanings of the words of the different judicial opinions.

Similarly, facts about the circumstances in which sayings and doings occurred that have little to do with the non-legal content of the people's attitudes and words may significantly affect the content of the law. For example, in a judicial decision, the fact that an issue is not in controversy arguably prevents the court's statements on that issue from making any contribution to the content of the law.

Even when the content of sentences and mental states is relevant to the content of the law, there can be no mechanical derivation of the content of the law. For example, how are conflicting contents to be combined? In general, there remains the problem of how the non-legal contents associated with different law practices interact with each other (and with other relevant aspects of law practices) to determine the content of the law.

We have surveyed a number of reasons why non-legal content—the meanings of sentences and contents of mental states—does not simply constitute legal content. But this way of thinking about the problem will have an artificial quality for those familiar with legal reasoning. The idea that the non-legal content of law practices constitutes their legal content presupposes roughly the following picture. Associated with each law practice is a text (and perhaps some mental states). Once we have the meanings of the texts and the contents of the mental states, each law practice will be associated with a proposition or set of propositions. Ascertaining the law on a

---

[30] In the case of a judicial decision, for example, the possibly relevant sentences include sentences uttered by the parties to the controversy, by lawyers, and by judges to lawyers and other judges. They include sentences written by judges in orders and judicial opinions. Judicial opinions alone include a large number and variety of sentences: they state facts, give reasons, summarize, make general claims about the content of the law, state holdings; moreover, there are concurring and dissenting as well as majority opinions.

particular issue is just a matter of looking up the propositions that are applicable to the issue. Even if this picture were accurate, we have discussed a number of reasons why non-legal content would not automatically yield legal content. But the problem is worse than these reasons would indicate. As I will now suggest, the whole picture is wrongheaded. Law practices do not determine the content of the law by contributing propositions which then get amalgamated.

Here is the real problem of legal content. There are many different law practices with many different aspects or elements. There is an initial question of which facts are parts of law practices and which are not. Are preambles of bills, legislative findings, legislative committee reports, dissenting opinions, unpublished judicial decisions, customs, the Federalist Papers, and so on to be included in law practices?

In my view, this question is really just part of a second question: Which aspects of, for example, judicial or legislative practices are relevant to the content of the law? Just to suggest the dimensions of the problem, here are some candidates for the relevant elements or aspects of practices. With respect to a judicial decision: the facts of the case, the judgment rendered, the words used by the court in the majority opinion, the reasons given for the outcome, the judges' beliefs, the judges' identities, the level and jurisdiction of the court; with respect to a legislative action: the words of the statute, the legislature's actual intention (if there is such a thing), the purposes that the words of the statute could reasonably be intended to implement, statements by the person who drafted the statute, speeches made during the legislative debate preceding passage, the circumstances in which the legislature acted, subsequent decisions not to repeal the statute.

Fourthly, once we know which elements of practices are relevant, the problem of determining the content of the law is not simply a problem of adding or amalgamating the various relevant aspects of practices. One obvious point is that some elements of practices are far more important than others, and elements of practices matter in different ways. But more fundamentally, as anyone familiar with legal reasoning knows, the content of the law is not determined by any kind of summing procedure, however complicated. For example, judicial decisions, constitutional provisions, and legislative history can affect what contribution a statute makes. It is not that those practices contribute propositions that are conjoined to a proposition contributed by the statute. The statute's correct interpretation may be determined by a potential conflict with a constitutional provision or by the outcome of cases in which courts have interpreted the same or related statutes.

To take a different kind of example, constitutional provisions, statutes, and judicial decisions can have an impact on the contribution of judicial and administrative decisions to the content of the law by affecting our understanding of the proper role of courts and administrative agencies. Or, differently, statutes can have an impact on what judicial decisions mean by making clear what the legislature cares about, thus affecting which differences between cases matter and consequently whether past precedents control the present issue. A final example is that the principle that a series of cases stands for is not the conjunction of the propositions announced in each case.

It is safe to conclude that the law does not automatically acquire content when actions, utterances, and sentences involved in law practices are attributed content. It is a mistake even to think that the issue is how to convert non-legal content into legal content. We need to reject the simplistic picture in which each law practice contributes to the content of the law a discrete proposition (or set of propositions), which is the result of converting the non-legal content of sentences and mental states into legal content. The bearing of non-legal content on the content of the law is not mechanical. Once we root out any idea of a mechanical conversion of non-legal content to legal content, it is clear that something must determine which aspects of law practices are relevant to the content of the law and what role those relevant aspects play in contributing to the content of the law.

IV. Can Law Practices Themselves Determine How they Contribute to the Content of the Law?

In this section, I consider the possibility that law practices can themselves determine how they contribute to the content of the law. I will argue that without standards independent of practices, practices cannot themselves adjudicate between ways in which practices could contribute to the content of the law.

For convenience, let me introduce a term for a candidate way in which practices could contribute to the content of the law. I will call such a way *a model* (short for *a model of the role of law-determining practices in contributing to the content of the law*).[31] The rational-relation doctrine tells us that there are systematic, intelligible connections between practices and the content of the law. It thus guarantees that there are rules that, given any pattern of law practices, yield a total set of legal propositions. A model is such a rule or set of rules.

A model is the counterpart at the metaphysical level of a method of interpretation at the epistemic level. (A model's being correct in a given legal system is what makes the corresponding theory of interpretation true.) Although the term is not ideal, I use "model" rather than "method of interpretation" to signal that my concern is constitutive or metaphysical, not epistemic; that is, the issue is how practices make it the case that the law's content is what it is, not how we can ascertain the law's content from law practices. Because it is more idiomatic, however, I will sometimes write in epistemic terms when discussing models.

(By way of analogy, it may be helpful to compare, on the one hand, the relation between practices and the content of the law with, on the other, the relation between words and the meaning of a sentence or group of sentences. The meaning

---

[31] My thanks to Nicos Stavropoulos for suggesting this term.

of a sentence depends in a systematic, intelligible way on the arrangement of constituent words; analogously, the content of the law—in a given legal system at a given time—depends on the pattern of law practices. A specification of the meanings of individual words and of the compositional rules of the language is a specification of the rules by which the words determine the meaning of the sentence. Analogously, a specification of a model is a specification of the rules by which law practices determine the content of the law. In this sense, a model is the analogue of the meanings of individual words and the compositional rules for the language.)

I will use the term "model" sometimes for a partial model—a rule for the relevance of some aspect of law practices, for example, of legislative findings or of dissenting judicial opinions, to the content of the law—and sometimes for a complete model—all of the rules by which law practices determine the content of the law. The context should make clear whether partial or complete models are in question. The *legally correct* (or, for short, *correct*) model in a particular legal system at a particular time is the way in which practices in that legal system at that time actually contribute to the content of the law (not merely the way in which they are thought to do so). Which model is correct varies from legal system to legal system and from time to time within a legal system, since, as we will see, which model is correct depends in part on law practices.

Models come at different levels of generality. More specific ones include the metaphysical counterparts of theories of constitutional, statutory, and common-law interpretation. Models can also be understood to include very general putative ways in which law practices determine what the law requires. Thus Hart's rule-of-recognition-based theory of law and Dworkin's "law as integrity" theory are accounts of very general models. Very general models give rise to more localized models of the contributions made by specific elements of practices.

Candidate models are candidate ways in which practices contribute to the content of the law. Since the issue of how practices contribute to the content of the law has several components, models have several closely related roles: they determine what counts as a law practice; which aspects of law practices are relevant to the content of the law; and how different relevant aspects combine to determine the content of the law, including how conflicts between relevant aspects are resolved.

The question of what determines how practices contribute to the content of the law can therefore be reformulated as the question of what determines which models are correct. What settles, for example, the question whether the original-intent theory of constitutional interpretation is true?

We can now turn to the main topic of this section: whether law practices can themselves determine which model is correct. Certainly the content of the law, as determined by law practices, concerns, in addition to more familiar subjects of legal regulation, what models are correct. That is, the content of the law includes rules for the bearing of law practices on the content of the law. For example, it is part of the law of the United States that the Constitution is the supreme law, that bills that have a bare majority of both houses of Congress do not contribute to the content of the law unless the president signs them, and that precedents of higher courts are binding on lower courts in the same jurisdiction.

The content of the law cannot itself determine which model is correct, however, for the content of the law depends on which model is correct. If, for example, statutes contributed to the law only the plain meaning of their words, the content of the law would be different from what it would be if the legislators' intentions made a difference. Obviously, which legal propositions are true depends on which model is correct. But as we have just seen, which model is correct depends in part on the legal propositions. The content of the law and the correct model are thus interdependent.

This interdependence threatens to bring indeterminacy. Consider the law practices of a particular legal system at a particular time and ask what the content of the law is. Suppose that if candidate model A were legally correct, a certain set of legal propositions would be true, according to which model A would be correct. And if candidate model B were correct, a different set of legal propositions would be true, according to which model B would be correct. And so on. Without some other standard, each mutually supporting pair of models and set of legal propositions is no more favored than any other pair.[32]

Can law practices determine which model is correct? The prima facie problem is that we cannot appeal to practices to determine which model is correct because which model a set of practices supports itself depends on which model is correct. But let us consider the matter in more depth. If practices are to determine which model is correct, there are two possibilities.

First, a privileged foundational practice (or set of foundational practices) could determine the role of other practices. This possibility encounters the problem of how practices themselves can determine which practices are foundational. For example, the fact that a judicial opinion states that only the rationale necessary to the decision of a case is contributed to the content of the law cannot determine that that is a correct account of the contribution of judicial decisions to the content of the law. Something must determine that the judicial opinion in question is relevant and trumps other conflicting practices. A putatively foundational practice cannot non-question-beggingly provide the reason that it is foundational.

---

[32] This note registers a rather technical qualification and can be skipped without losing the main thread of the argument. A candidate model, given the law practices, may yield a set of legal propositions that lends support to a different, inconsistent model. To the extent that this is the case, we can say that the model is not *in equilibrium* (relative to the law practices). Models that are in equilibrium (or are closer to it) are plausibly favored, other things being equal, over those that are not (or are further from it). There is no reason to expect, however, that there will typically be only one model that is closer to equilibrium than any other model. In fact, indefinitely many models are guaranteed to be in perfect equilibrium (yet yield different sets of legal propositions). For example, any model that includes a rule that practices (and thus the true legal propositions) have no bearing on which model is correct is necessarily in perfect equilibrium. Without some independent standard for what models are eligible, there is no way to rule out such models. Hence the varying degree to which different candidate models are in equilibrium does not ensure a unique correct model and determinate legal content. *See also* the discussion of a coherentist solution in the text below.

Moreover, it is unwarranted to assume that the significance of a putatively foundational practice is simply its nonlegal content. Its significance depends on which model is correct—the very issue the practice is supposed to resolve. In sum, a foundationalist solution is hopeless because it requires some independent factor that determines which practices are foundational (and what their contribution is).

Secondly, if no practices can be assumed to have a privileged status, the remaining possibility is that all law practices together can somehow determine their own role. Such a coherentist solution might at first seem to have more going for it than the foundationalist one. The idea would be, roughly speaking, that the (total) law practices support the model that, when applied to the practices, yields the result that the practices support that very model. If no model is perfectly supported in this way, the one that comes closest is the correct one.

The problem with this suggestion, crudely put, is that without substantive standards that determine the relevance of different aspects of law practices, the (total) law practices will support too many models. For any legal proposition, there will always be a model supported by the practices that yields that proposition. Or to put it another way, the formal requirement that a model be supported by or cohere with law practices is empty without substantive standards that determine what counts as a relevant difference. Suppose a body of judicial decisions seems to support the proposition that a court is to give deference to an administrative agency's interpretation of a statute. It is consistent with those decisions for an agency's interpretation of a statute not to deserve deference when there is a reason for the different treatment. Such a reason could be, for example, that the agency in the earlier cases, but not in the present case, had special responsibility for administration of the relevant statutory scheme. But since the facts of every case are different, if a model can count *any* difference as relevant, there will always be a model that is consistent with all past practices yet denies deference to agency interpretations of statutes.

As I have argued more fully elsewhere, such considerations show that practices cannot determine legal content without standards independent of the practices that determine which differences are relevant and irrelevant.[33] Hence law practices alone cannot yield determinate legal requirements. The point is a specific application of a familiar, more general point that Susan Hurley has developed.[34] Formal requirements such as consistency are meaningful only in the light of substantive standards that limit which factors can provide reasons.

It would be missing the point to suggest that law practices themselves can determine the appropriate standards. Without such standards, a requirement of adherence to practices is empty. In epistemic terms, we cannot derive the standards

---

[33] *See* M. Greenberg & H. Litman, *The Meaning of Original Meaning*, 86 GEO L.J. 569, 614–617 (1998).

[34] *See* S. L. HURLEY, NATURAL REASONS 26, 84–88 (1989). Hurley credits Ramsey's and Davidson's uses of arguments with similar import. *See, e.g.* D. Davidson, *The Structure and Content of Truth*, 87 J. PHIL. 279, 317–320 (1990).

from the practices because the standards are a prerequisite for interpreting the practices.

It may be helpful to notice that the problem has a structure similar to that of two famous philosophical puzzles: Nelson Goodman's problem about *green* and *grue*, and Saul Kripke's problem about *plus* and *quus*.[35] In order for there to be legal requirements, it must be possible for someone to make a mistake in attributing a legal requirement (if just *any* attribution of a legal requirement is correct, the law requires that P and that not P and so does not require anything). One makes a mistake when one attributes a legal requirement that is not the one the law practices yield when interpreted in accordance with the correct model. For any candidate legal requirement, however, there is always a non-standard or "bent" model that yields that requirement. It is therefore open to an interpreter charged with a mistake to claim that in attributing the legal requirement in question, she has not made a mistake in applying one model but is applying a different model.

The proponent of the coherence solution will respond that law practices themselves support certain models. For example, in appealing to practices to decide cases, courts have developed well-established ways of understanding the relevance of those practices to legal content. The problem is that there will always be bent models according to which the judicial decisions (and other practices) support the bent models rather than the purportedly well-established ones. This kind of point shows that there must be factors, not themselves derived from the practices, that favor some models over others.

Here is an example.[36] Suppose that on February 1, 2005, a judge in a state court in the United States must decide whether a woman has a federal constitutional right not to be prevented from obtaining an abortion. Imagine that the judge holds that the woman does not have such a right. It seems that the judge has misread *Roe v. Wade*,[37] the seminal decision of the United States Supreme Court. The judge claims, however, that according to the correct model of how judicial decisions contribute to legal content, when constitutional rights of individuals are at stake and strong considerations of justice support the claims of both sides, such decisions should be understood as establishing a form of "checkerboard" solution. According to such a solution, whether a person has the right in question depends on whether the person is born on an odd- or even-numbered day.[38] Since Jane Roe was born on an odd-numbered day (let us assume), *Roe v. Wade*'s contribution to content is that only women born on odd-numbered days have a constitutional right to an abortion.

---

[35] *See* N. GOODMAN, FACT, FICTION, AND FORECAST 72–81 (3d ed., 1973); S. KRIPKE, WITTGENSTEIN ON RULES AND PRIVATE LANGUAGE 7–32 (1982). These puzzles involve concepts that seem bizarre and gerrymandered. One challenge is to determine what it is that rules such concepts out (at least in particular contexts), for if they are not ruled out, unacceptable results follow.

[36] The example borrows from Dworkin's discussion of a "checkerboard" solution to the abortion controversy. *See* DWORKIN, *supra* note 6, at 178–186. Dworkin cannot be held responsible, however, for my example.   [37] *Roe v. Wade*, 410 U.S. 113 (1973).

[38] *See* DWORKIN, *supra* note 6, at 178–179.

Before discussing the example, it must be emphasized that the point is not that the judge's position should be taken seriously; on the contrary, the example depends on the fact that the judge's position is plainly a non-starter. Since it is evident that the position cannot be taken seriously, there must be factors that rule out models like the one in the example. The example makes the point that these factors must be independent of practices. Since the unacceptable positions that we want to exclude purport to determine what practices mean, the factors that exclude these positions cannot be based on practices. Moreover, there is no way to rule out such positions on a purely logical level, since, as will become evident, it is easy to construct self-supporting, logically consistent systems of such positions. The claim is, then, that our unwillingness to take the judge's position seriously suggests that we must be depending on tacit assumptions independent of law practices in determining which models are acceptable. Let us look at the example to see why practices themselves cannot exclude the judge's model.

The first objection to the judge's position may be that the Supreme Court in *Roe v. Wade* said nothing about the abortion right's depending on birth dates. The judge replies that according to the correct model, the reasons that judges give in their opinions make no or little contribution to the content of the law. A second objection may move to a different level: the practices of the legal system do not support the judge's model. Judicial decisions, for example, do not interpret the contributions made by other decisions in such a checkerboard fashion, nor do they ignore the reasons judges give. The judge, however, claims that according to his model, judicial decisions have all along been using a bent model, according to which the reasons judges give are significant until February 1, 2005, but not afterwards. Similarly, the model specifies no checkerboard contributions to content until that date, then requires them afterwards. All of the judicial decisions so far are logically consistent with the hypothesis that they are using the bent model. Obviously a third-level objection—that the practices do not support models that give dates this sort of significance—can be met with the same sort of response.

In another version of the example, the judge might claim that according to the correct model, in all cases involving the right to abortion, a Supreme Court decision's relevance to content ends, without further action by the Court, as soon as a majority of the current Supreme Court believes that the decision was wrongly decided. Since the judge believes that that is now the situation with regard to *Roe v. Wade*, he claims that *Roe v. Wade* no longer has any bearing on the content of the law. If it is objected that the judge's position is not an accurate account of how judicial decisions interpret past judicial decisions, the judge will claim that judicial decisions have been following his model all along. Since (let us suppose) it has never been the case before that a majority of the Supreme Court has disagreed with a past Supreme Court decision on the right to abortion, the evidence of past decisions supports the judge's model, which treats only abortion rights cases idiosyncratically, as strongly as a more conventional one.

The point should be obvious by now: these sorts of unacceptable models are unacceptable because there are standards independent of practices that determine that some sorts of factors are irrelevant to the contributions made by practices to legal content. The practices themselves cannot be the source of the standards for which models are permissible.

In this section, I have argued that practices themselves cannot determine how practices contribute to the content of the law. Although I will not discuss the point here, it is worth noting that my argument is not limited to the law. For example, the argument shows that without standards independent of the practices, no set of practices can rationally determine rules. What rules a set of practices rationally determines will depend on what aspects of the practices are relevant and how those aspects are relevant. And the practices cannot themselves resolve those issues. Similarly, my argument does not depend on the complexities of contemporary legal systems. My point therefore holds even for extremely simple cases. Even if there were only one law-maker who uttered only simple sentences, and even if it were taken for granted that the law-maker's practices were legally relevant, the precise relevance of those practices would still depend on factors independent of the practices. For example, there would still be an issue of whether the relevant aspect of the practices was the meaning of the words uttered, as opposed to, say, the law-maker's intentions or the narrowest rationale necessary to justify the outcome of the law-maker's decisions.

V. Objections

I want now to consider three closely related objections. First, it may be objected to that in practice there is often no difficulty in knowing which aspects of a practice are relevant or which facts provide reasons. Bent models are not serious candidates. Secondly, it may be objected to that practitioners' beliefs (or other attitudes) about value questions, not value facts, solve the problem of determining how practices contribute to the content of the law. Thirdly, it may be said that in limiting law practices to descriptive facts, I have relied on too thin a conception of law practices. Properly understood, law practices can themselves determine the content of the law.

I replied to a version of the first objection in discussing the example of the abortion-rights decision, but I will make the point in more general terms here. As I have emphasized, the question of the necessary conditions for law practices to determine the content of the law is a metaphysical, not an epistemic, question. The problems that I have raised concerning how law practices determine the content of the law are not practical problems that legal interpreters encounter in trying to discover what the law requires. Hence it is no objection to my argument that legal interpreters do not encounter such problems.

I have argued that there is a gap between law practices and the content of the law that can be bridged only by substantive factors independent of practices. If legal practitioners have no difficulty in crossing this gap—for example, in eliminating bent models from consideration—that must be because they take the necessary factors for granted. With respect to the example of the abortion-rights decision, I argued that practices themselves cannot rule out the judge's bent models. Therefore our unwillingness to take the judge's position seriously is evidence that we are relying on tacit assumptions about what models are acceptable. The lack of difficulty in practice suggests not that substantive constraints are not needed but that they are assumed.

This point leads naturally to the second objection, which holds that it is the assumptions or beliefs of participants in the practice that solve the problem of how practices determine the content of the law. For example, it might be that a consensus or shared understanding among judges or legal officials determines the relevance of practices to the content of the law. *Beliefs* about value, not value facts, do the necessary work.

As an epistemic matter, of course, we rely on our beliefs about value to ascertain what the law is. But that is exactly what we would expect if the content of the law depended on value facts. After all, in working out the truth in any domain, we must depend on our beliefs. That we do so in a given domain in no way suggests that the truth in that domain depends on our beliefs. Notice, moreover, that if the content of the law depended on beliefs about value, then in order to work out what the law was, we would have to rely on our beliefs *about our beliefs* about value. For example, we might ask not whether democratic values favor intentionalist theories of statutory interpretation, but whether there is a consensus among judges that democratic values do so.

The most important point is that facts about what participants believe (understand, intend, and so on) could not do the necessary work because such facts are just more descriptive facts in the same position as the rest of the law practices. As with the facts about the behavior of law-makers, we can ask whether facts about participants' beliefs are relevant to the content of the law, and if so, in what way. Since the content of the law is rationally determined, the answers to these questions must be provided by reasons. As I have argued, the law practices, including facts about participants' beliefs, cannot determine their own relevance.

More generally, the same kind of argument explains why the questions of value on which the content of the law depends must be resolved by substantive standards rather than by value-neutral procedures. In general, there are procedural ways to resolve value questions—flipping a coin and voting are examples. Such procedures are in the same position as other law practices, however. There have to be reasons that determine that a given procedure is the relevant one and what the significance of the procedure is to the content of the law.

The third objection claims that the additional substantive factors are part of law practices themselves. I have already addressed the suggestion that the law practices, conceived as facts about behavior and mental states, determine their own relevance. The present objection is that my conception is too narrow. It somehow fails to do justice to law practices to take them to consist of ordinary empirical facts about what people have done, said, and thought. If the objection is to be more than hand-waving, the objector needs to say what practices consist of beyond such facts and how the enriching factor solves the problem. For example, it would of course be no objection to my argument to claim that the descriptive facts need to be enriched with value facts.

Another unpromising possibility, addressed in Section II.C above, is for the objector to maintain that law practices are legal-content laden. According to this version of the objection, facts about what counts as a legislature, who has authority to make law, what counts as validly enacted, what impact a statute has on the content of the law—in general, legal-content facts concerning the relevance of law practices to legal content—are somehow part of the law practices. As argued, however, unless legal content is to be metaphysically basic, there must be an account of what determines legal content that does not presuppose it. It simply begs the question to take law practices to include legal-content facts.

The objector challenges my conception of the law practices on the ground that it is too restrictive. Here is one line of thought in support of my conception. We normally assume that law practices can be looked up in the law books. But all that can be found in the law books, other than legal-content facts, are facts about what various people—legislators, judges, administrative officials, and so on—did and said and thought. If there is something else to law practices, how do we know about it? To put the point another way, if I tell you all the facts about what the relevant people said and did, believed and intended, you can work out what the law is without knowing any more about the law practices. So if there is an aspect of law practices other than these facts, it does not seem to play a role in determining the content of the law. (It is true that you may have to be skilled at legal reasoning to work out the content of the law, and that skill may include an understanding of the significance of the practices to legal content. But I have already addressed the suggestion that it is participants' understandings, rather than the substantive factors that are the subject of those understandings, that do the necessary work.)

VI. The Need for Substantive Factors Independent of Law Practices

I have argued that law practices cannot themselves determine the content of the law because they cannot unilaterally determine their own contribution to the content of the law. There must be factors, independent of practices, that favor some models over others. In this section, I sketch where this argument leaves us. In particular, I explain the sense in which the argument requires facts about *value*, and the nature of the claimed *connection* between law and value.

A. Value Facts?

In order for practices to yield determinate legal requirements, it has to be the case that there are truths about which models are better than others independently of how much the models are supported by law practices. Since practices must rationally determine the content of the law, truths about which models are better than others cannot simply be brute; there have to be reasons that favor some models over others.

We have seen that law practices cannot determine their own contribution to the content of the law. By contrast, value facts are well suited to determining the relevance of law practices, for value facts include facts about the relevance of descriptive facts. For example, that democracy supports an intentionalist model of statutes is, if true, a value fact. What about the relevance of the value facts themselves? At least in the case of the all-things-considered truth about the relevant values, its relevance is intelligible without further reasons. If the all-things-considered truth about the relevant considerations supports a certain model of the law practices, there can be no serious question of whether that truth is itself relevant, or in what way. The significance for the law of the fact that a certain model is all-things-considered better than others is simply the fact that that model is better than others.

It might be suggested that an appeal to conceptual truth offers a way to avoid the conclusion that the content of the law depends on value facts. The idea would be that the concept of law (or some other legal concept), rather than substantive value facts, determines that some models are better than others. As noted above, conceptual truth is the kind of consideration that could provide reasons of the necessary sort. The question is whether conceptual truth does so in the case of law.

My response begins with two points about what notion of conceptual truth this kind of suggestion can rely on. According to what we can call a *superficialist* notion, conceptual truths are truths about the use of concept-words, truths that are tacitly known by all competent users of those words or are settled by community consensus about the use of the words. Given such a notion of conceptual truth, we should reject the idea that there are conceptual truths that can do the necessary work. Ronald Dworkin famously argued that disputes about the grounds of law are substantive debates, not trivial quarrels over the use of words.[39] Positivists have generally responded by denying that they hold the kind of view Dworkin was attacking. Thus, both sides agree that questions about which models are better than others are not merely verbal questions that can be settled by appeal to consensus criteria for the use of words. And both sides are correct on this point.

When, for example, Justices of the Supreme Court debate whether legislative history is relevant to the content of the law, the dispute cannot be settled by appeal to agreed-on criteria for the use of words. A lawyer or judge who challenges

---

[39] Dworkin, *supra* note 6, at 31–46.

well-established models is not ipso facto mistaken. For example, a lawyer could advance a novel theory according to which New Jersey statutes make no contribution to the content of the law (on the ground, say, that there is a constitutional flaw in New Jersey's legislative process). The claim would not be straightforwardly wrong merely because it goes against the consensus model, though it is likely mistaken on substantive grounds.

Secondly, we have seen that the practices of participants in the legal system cannot be the source of the standards that support some models over others. It follows that if conceptual truth is to be the source of the standards, conceptual truth must not be determined by the practices of participants in the legal system; it must depend on factors independent of our law practices.

The consequence of these two points is that if conceptual truth is to provide the needed standards, it would have to be conceptual truth of a kind that is not determined by consensus about the use of words and is not determined by our law practices. I am sympathetic to such a notion of conceptual truth. Given such a notion, however, it is not clear that an appeal to conceptual truth is a way of avoiding the need for substantive value facts. Instead, the conceptual truths in question may include or depend on value facts, for example, facts about fairness or democracy. At this point, the burden surely rests on a proponent of the conceptual-truth suggestion to offer a position that avoids the two problems that I have just described without collapsing into a dependence on substantive value facts.

A different kind of appeal to conceptual truth is possible. It could be argued not that there are conceptual truths about which models are better than others, but that conceptual truth determines that such issues are determined by a specific internal legal value. This appeal to conceptual truth does not attempt to avoid the need for value facts; it attempts to explain those value facts as internal to the law. I will turn now to the nature of legal value facts. It is worth noting, however, that an appeal to conceptual truth as the source of internal value facts will encounter the same challenge as the appeal to conceptual truth to avoid the need for value facts. Such an appeal requires an account of conceptual truth according to which truths about the concept of law are independent of our law practices yet also independent of genuine value facts.

I have argued that the content of the law depends on substantive value facts. What is the nature of those value facts? The most straightforward possibility is that, other things being equal,[40] models are better to the extent that they are favored by the all-things-considered truth about the applicable considerations— the Truth, for short. In other words, the legally correct standard or value is simply the truth about value. On this view, there is no special legal standard or value. For example, the bearing of legislative history on the content of the law depends on

---

[40] "Other things being equal" because practices also play a role in determining which models are better than others. *See infra* Section VI.B.

considerations of democracy, fairness, welfare, stability—on every consideration that is in fact relevant to the issue.

A second possibility is that, in the special context of the law, the all-things-considered truth about the relevant considerations is that the standard for models is not the general, all-things-considered truth about the relevant considerations but some different standard. For example, it might be that, taking into account all relevant considerations, the Truth is that the legally correct resolution of value questions is the one that maximizes community wealth. According to this second possibility, special legal value facts are genuine value facts; they are the consequence of the application of genuine value facts—Truth—to the specific context of law.[41] On this view, the fact that, say, wealth maximization is the virtue of models, is a genuine value fact. A version of this possibility would allow the special legal value facts to vary from legal system to legal system.

On the first and second possibilities, the content of the law depends on genuine value facts in a way that is inconsistent with both hard and soft positivism. A positivist might try to argue that even if my argument so far is sound, there is a third possibility. According to this possibility, there are substantive standards that within the law do the work of value facts in resolving value questions but are not genuine value facts. We might describe this possibility by saying that legal value facts are *internal* to the law.

The hypothetical positivist's suggestion that legal value facts are internal to the law would have to mean more than that they have no application outside of law. There could be legal value facts that were genuine value facts applicable only in the legal context. In that case, the second possibility would be actual, and the content of the law would depend at base on genuine value facts. The third possibility is supposed to avoid the conclusion that the content of the law depends on genuine value facts. Perhaps the idea would be that legal value facts matter only to those who are trying to participate in the legal system (and only to that extent). (As with the second possibility, a version of the third possibility would allow that the internal legal value can vary from legal system to legal system.)

I do not mean to suggest that the idea of internal legal values is unproblematic or even fully coherent. I therefore do not need to explain exactly what it would mean for there to be internal values. Nor do I need to explain what, other than the Truth, could make it the case that there is a special legal value. I mention the idea only because it seems to have some currency in philosophy-of-law circles. My point is simply that I do not claim in this paper to have ruled out the view that the content of the law depends on internal value facts rather than genuine ones.

I will briefly comment on the problems facing this view. We have already ruled out the possibility that law practices determine their own relevance to legal

---

[41] The position Dworkin calls "conventionalism" could be advanced as a version of possibility two, though that is not exactly the way in which he presents it. *See* DWORKIN, *supra* note 6, at 114–150.

content. Therefore something other than law practices would have to determine the internal value standard—to make it the case that this standard was the relevant one for the law (or for the particular legal system). It is difficult to see what that could be other than the relevant considerations—the Truth. If we appeal to the Truth, however, we have returned to the first or second possibility.

Any account of internal value facts thus faces a challenge of steering between the law practices on the one hand and the Truth on the other. I have already described the way in which an attempt to ground internal legal facts in conceptual truth faces this challenge. But the challenge confronts any account of internal value facts. For example, suppose a theorist appeals to the *function* of law or legal systems to ground internal value facts. On the one hand, as we saw with conceptual truth, if the law's function is going to provide the value facts necessary for practices to determine the content of the law, that function must be determined by something independent of the law practices. On the other hand, if the law's function is determined by the all-things-considered truth about the relevant factors, an appeal to function is not a way of avoiding an appeal to genuine value facts. Until we have an account of internal value facts that meets the challenge, it is difficult to evaluate the potential of an appeal to internal value facts.

An internal-value view faces a more substantive challenge as well. Internal value facts would have to have appropriate consequences for the nature of law. In a normal or properly functioning legal system, the content of the law provides reasons for action of certain kinds for certain agents. Whether the content of the law can provide such reasons may depend on the nature and source of the legal value facts. For example, it is plausible that for a legal system to be functioning properly, the content of the law must provide genuine reasons for action for judges. An internal-value theorist must explain how legal content determined exclusively by law practices and internal value facts can provide genuine, as opposed to merely internal, reasons for action. More generally, we can investigate the nature of legal value facts by asking what role such facts must play in a theory of law.

B. The Role of Value Facts

Let us now turn to the *role* of value facts in determining the content of the law. Since I do not want to beg the question against the possibility of a special legal value (whether internal or not), I use "X" for that property in virtue of which models are better than others. X might be, for example, (the promotion of) wealth maximization, the maintenance of the status quo, security, fairness, or morality. (If there is no special legal value, X is the Truth, in the technical sense explained above.) Note that the fact that a particular model is favored by X may be a descriptive fact (for example, if X is wealth maximization). In that case, the relevant value fact is that X is what the goodness of models consists in.

I will make two clarifications about the role of X and then consider the implications for the relation between law and value. The first point is that X only *helps* to determine which models are correct. X's favoring model A over model B is neither necessary nor sufficient for A to win out over B. As we saw in Section IV, practices play a role in determining which model is better. Hence the model that is best all things considered may not be the same as the model that is ranked highest by X alone. (For simplicity I sometimes omit this qualification.)

In Section IV we discussed the interdependence between models and legal content. We saw that if we hold law practices constant, different candidate models yield different sets of legal propositions. Without X, each mutually supporting pair of model and set of legal propositions is as favored as any other such pair, and indeterminacy threatens. X's independence makes it possible for the interdependence of model and legal content not to lead to global indeterminacy.

In particular, what bearing practices have on the legally correct model depends on which model is most X-justified *in advance of any particular practices*. For X constrains the candidate models of practices and thus makes it possible for practices to determine anything. Practices themselves have something to say about the second-order question of how practices contribute to the content of the law. But X helps to determine what practices have to say on that question. Roughly speaking, the legally correct model is the one that is most X-justified after taking into account practices in the way that it is most X-justified to take them into account.[42] In other words, the legally correct model is the one that is most X-justified, all things considered.

The second point can be brought out with an objection. Suppose it is objected that X need determine only what considerations are *relevant* to the content of the law but need not go further and determine how conflicts between relevant considerations are to be resolved. According to this suggestion, X would eliminate some candidate models as unacceptable but would have nothing to say between models that give weight only to relevant aspects of law practices. The objector grants my argument that without an independent standard of relevance, practices could not determine which models were correct. The objector points out, however, that once we have an independent standard of relevance, practices themselves might be able to determine which models are correct.

---

[42] In many legal systems, the practices, when taken into account in the way that is most X-justified in advance of the practices, will support a model that is not the most X-justified in advance of the practices. And when taken into account in accordance with *that* model, the practices may support yet a different model. The question therefore arises of how important it is for a model to be supported by the practices (taken into account in accordance with that model). (In the terminology of *supra* note 32, the more that a model is supported by the practices, the more the model is in equilibrium.) Since X is the virtue of models, X is what determines how important it is for a model to be supported by the practices. This is why it is fair to say, as I do in the text, that the legally correct model is the one that is most X-justified after taking into account the practices in the way that it is most X-justified to take them into account.

Here is a brief sketch of a reply to the objector. In order for there to be determinate legal requirements, X must do more than determine what considerations are relevant; X must favor some resolutions of conflicts between relevant considerations over others. Otherwise, given the diversity of relevant considerations and the complexity of factual variation, law practices will not yield much in the way of determinate legal requirements. Inconsistent propositions of law (and inconsistent models) will typically have some support from relevant aspects of law practices. Therefore, in order for there to be determinate legal requirements, X must not only help to determine what considerations are relevant but must also help to determine the relative importance of elements of law practices and how such elements interact.

In fact there is a deeper problem with the objection. It assumes that there are discrete issues of what considerations are relevant to the content of the law and how the relevant considerations combine to determine the content of the law. It may be convenient to separate the two kinds of issues for expository purposes, but we should not be misled into thinking that they are resolved separately. It is not the case that there is an initial, all-or-nothing determination of whether a type of consideration is relevant and then an independent, further determination of the relative importance of the relevant considerations. Rather, the reason that a consideration is relevant determines how and under what circumstances it is relevant and how much force it has relative to other considerations.

For example, legislative history's relevance to the content of the law derives, let us suppose, from its connection to the intentions of the democratically elected representatives of the people. Thus, in order to determine how important legislative history is relative to other factors, we need to ask exactly how it is related to the relevant intentions and what the importance of those intentions is. The point is that the contribution to content of some aspect of a law practice and how it interacts with other relevant aspects depend on why the aspect is relevant. If this suggestion—that relevance and relative importance are not independent questions—is right, then in helping to determine the relevance of various considerations, X will necessarily (be helping to) resolve conflicts between relevant considerations.

I have argued that there is a certain kind of connection between law and value. I would like to conclude by saying something about the implications of this connection. Just for the purpose of exploring these implications, I will assume that X is morality. The point of this assumption is to make clear that *even if* morality were the relevant value, the consequences for the relation between law and morality would not be straightforward. As I will show, it would not follow that the content of the law would necessarily be morally good or even that the moral goodness of a candidate legal proposition would count in favor of the proposition's being true.

First, although (by assumption) morality provides legally relevant reasons independent of the content of the law, the legally correct model is not simply whatever model is morally best (or most justified). "Morally best" here means most supported or justified by moral considerations *in advance of consideration of the practices of the legal system.* The legally correct model need not be the morally best one in this sense because, as we have seen, practices also have an impact on which model is legally correct.

Secondly, morally good models do not guarantee morally good legal propositions. Even if the legally correct model was a highly morally justified one, the content of the law might be very morally bad. A democratically elected and unquestionably legitimate legislature could publicly and clearly promulgate extremely unjust statutes, such as a statute ostensibly excluding a racial minority from social welfare benefits. The judicial decisions may rely on highly morally justified models, ones that, among other things, give great weight to such morally relevant features of legislative actions as the clearly expressed intentions of the elected legislators. The most justified model, all things considered, will be a morally good one yet will yield morally bad legal content. In fact, in such a legal system less justified models could yield morally better legal content than more justified models. (In such cases, a judge might sometimes be morally obligated to circumvent the law by relying on the less justified model.)[43]

Although morally justified models do not guarantee morally good legal propositions, it might be suggested that *part* of what makes a model morally justified is that it tends to yield morally good legal requirements.[44] For example, assume that, other things being equal, a legal requirement is morally better the more it treats people fairly. Some models will in general have a greater tendency to yield legal requirements that treat people fairly. According to the suggestion under consideration, that a model has such a tendency would be one factor supporting that model.

Suppose that the suggestion were correct. According to one line of thought, it follows that the content of the law would simply be whatever it would be morally good for it to be (or more generally, whatever it would be most X-justified for it to be). In that case the practices would be irrelevant. This line of thought might therefore be taken to provide a reductio of my argument for the role of value in determining the way in which practices contribute to the content of the law.

The line of thought is not sound, however. First, even if the tendency of a model to yield morally good legal propositions counts in favor of that model, a variety of other moral considerations favor models that make the content of the

---

[43] The relation between a judge's moral obligations and morally justified models raises interesting issues, but space does not permit discussion.

[44] At the extreme, for example, a model could hold that in some circumstances the goodness of a candidate legal proposition tips the balance in favor of that legal proposition and against competing candidates. (A different way to describe such a position would be to say that value not only can help to determine which model is best, thus indirectly favoring some candidate legal propositions over others, but also can favor candidate legal propositions directly. I will not use this terminology.) As I say in the text, such a model may be less supported both by morality and by practices than models that give less weight to content-oriented considerations. I suggest below (*see* the last four paragraphs of this section), that the role that such a model assigns to value facts is outside the role that this paper's arguments support.

law sensitive to relevant aspects of law practices. A model may be morally better, for example, to the extent that it respects the will of the democratically elected representatives of the people, protects expectations, enables planning, provides notice of the law, treats relevantly similar practices similarly, minimizes the opportunity for officials to base their decisions on controversial beliefs, and so on.

Roughly, we have a distinction between content-oriented considerations and practice-oriented considerations. The relative weight accorded by morality to these two kinds of considerations is a question for moral theory that I will not take up here. On any plausible account, however, morality will give substantial weight to practice-oriented considerations. So the morally best model (considered in advance of law practices) will make the law sensitive to relevant aspects of law practices.

Secondly, as we have seen, the legally correct model also depends on the law practices. Apart from the weight that morality gives to practice-oriented considerations, the practices themselves may support models that make the law sensitive to practices. (Contemporary positivists, my primary target in this paper, are likely to be sympathetic to the view that practices support models that make the law sensitive to practices.) For example, although I will not defend the claim here, in the U.S. and U.K. legal systems, practices themselves strongly support models that make the law sensitive to law practices. Practices are thus a second reason that the role of value need not have the consequence that the all-things-considered best model will be one that tends to yield morally good legal propositions. (Also, even a model that has a *tendency* to produce morally good legal propositions may not do so, given the law practices of a particular legal system.)

Thirdly and finally, if we reflect on the argument for value's role in determining the content of the law, we see that it supports only a limited role for value, one that does not involve supplanting law practices or making them irrelevant. Our starting point was that law practices must determine the content of the law and that they must do so by providing reasons that favor some legal propositions over others. The crucial step in the argument was that law practices cannot provide such reasons without value facts that determine the relevance of different aspects of law practices to the content of the law. The argument thus supports the involvement of value facts in determining the content of the law only for a limited role: determining the relevance of law practices to the content of the law.

We can apply this point to the specific question of to what extent a legal proposition's goodness can help to make it true: the goodness (in terms of morality or of value X) of a candidate legal proposition is relevant to the proposition's truth only to the extent that its goodness contributes to making it intelligible that an aspect of a particular law practice has one bearing rather than another on the content of the law. I will call this *the relevance limitation*.

I want to emphasize that the point is only that the argument of this chapter supports no more than such a limited role for value facts; the argument does not show that the role of value facts must be so limited. Whether there is some other or more expansive role for value in determining the content of the law is left open. This chapter's argument for the conclusion that value facts play a role in determining legal content is that value facts are needed in order to determine the relevance of law practices to the legal content. The argument therefore supports only that role for value facts. There might, of course, be a different argument that shows, say, that morality or some other value supplants the law practices (though of course almost no contemporary legal theorist, least of all one of my positivist targets, thinks that there is such an argument).

Let us consider more specifically the implications of the relevance limitation. The limitation does not imply that the goodness of a legal proposition can never be relevant to its truth.[45] The goodness of a legal proposition will be relevant to the extent that it has a bearing on the intelligibility of law practices' supporting that legal proposition over others.

A Dworkinian theory of law provides a helpful example.[46] Consider a model according to which law practices contribute to the content of the law precisely that set of legal propositions that best *justifies* those law practices. Whether this model respects the relevance limitation will depend on the notion of justification involved in the Dworkinian model. Consider a simplistic understanding of justification that has the following implication: the set of propositions that best justify the law practices is that set that results from taking the morally best set of propositions and carving out specific exceptions for the law practices of the legal system—exceptions tailored in such a way as to have no forward-looking consequences. On this understanding of justification, the model would not respect the relevance limitation, because value facts would not determine the significance of the practices; instead, the practices would simply be denied any significance by a kind of gerrymandering.

On a more sophisticated notion of justification, to the extent that a legal proposition is bent or gerrymandered, it will be less good at justifying law practices. (In the extreme case just considered, where a particular law practice is simply treated as an exception without further application, that practice is not *justified* at all by the propositions to which it is an exception.) I think it is plausible, though I will not argue the point here, that, given a proper understanding of justification, the Dworkinian model I have described respects the relevance limitation. (Below I will consider a different model, often attributed to Dworkin, that arguably does not respect that limitation.)

---

[45] It is easy to see that the goodness of a legal proposition could have evidentiary relevance to the content of the law. Suppose that the intention of legislators matters to the content of the law. If there is reason to believe that the legislators would have intended what is morally better (at least other things being equal), the moral goodness of candidate legal propositions will have a bearing on their truth because it will have a bearing on what the legislators intended. The discussion in the text concerns the question of whether the goodness of candidate propositions can have constitutive rather than evidentiary relevance.

[46] I say "a Dworkinian theory" rather than "Dworkin's theory" to avoid questions of Dworkin exegesis. I believe that the position I describe is the best understanding of Dworkin's position. *See also infra* note 47.

The relevance limitation implies that the goodness of a legal proposition is never sufficient to make it true. That value facts are needed to determine the contribution of law practices to the content of the law does not provide a basis for making law practices irrelevant. To put it another way, that a candidate proposition is a good one does not make it intelligible that the law practices, regardless of what they happen to be, support that proposition. It might be tempting to regard a model on which the goodness of a legal proposition can, at least in some circumstances, be sufficient to make it true as the degenerate or limiting case of a model that determines the relevance of law practices to the content of the law. The model determines that in the relevant circumstances, practices have no relevance. But though this description may be formally tidy, the argument that value facts are needed to enable law practices to determine the content of the law provides no support for a model on which value facts can make practices irrelevant. In other words, though we can describe a putative "model" according to which practices provide a reason favoring any particular set of legal propositions (the morally best ones, for example), it does not follow that practices could provide such a reason. What reasons practices provide is a substantive, not a formal, question.

We can apply this point to an intermediate case. Consider a model that includes rules for the contribution of law practices to the content of the law but also includes a rule of the following sort:

> (R) If more than one legal proposition is supported by the (total) law practices (given the other rules of the model) to some threshold level, the legal proposition that is morally best (of those that reach the threshold) is true.[47]

I suggest that R is not supported by this paper's argument for the role of value. In general, that legal proposition A has morally better content than legal proposition B does not ipso facto make it intelligible that law practices support A over B. Adding the hypothesis that law practices provide strong support for both A and B—support above some threshold level—does not change this conclusion. A

---

[47] Dworkin sometimes seems to suggest such a rule. *See, e.g.,* Dworkin, *supra* note 6, at 284–285, 387–388; R. Dworkin, Taking Rights Seriously 340, 342 (1977). And his commentators typically interpret him in this way. *See, e.g.,* L. Alexander & E. Sherwin, The Rule of Rules ch. 8 (2001); J. Finnis, *On Reason and Authority in Law's Empire,* 6 Law & Phil. 357, 372–374 (1987); Raz, *supra* note 3, at 222–223. I think that this is not the best understanding of Dworkin's view (and Dworkin has confirmed as much in conversation). On the best understanding, fit is merely one aspect of justification, there is no threshold level of fit, and how much fit matters relative to other aspects of justification is a substantive question of political morality. (The idea of a threshold of fit that interpretations must meet to be eligible and beyond which substantive moral considerations become relevant should be taken as merely a heuristic or expository device.) *See* R. Dworkin, A Matter of Principle 150–151 (1985); R. Dworkin, *"Natural" Law Revisited,* 34 U. Fla. L. Rev. 165, 170–173 (1982); R. Dworkin, *supra* note 6, at 231, 246–247. A different point is that Dworkin sometimes seems to suggest that there is an aspect of the question of *the extent to which* interpretations fit law practices that is purely formal or at least not normative. *See, e.g.,* Dworkin, Taking Rights Seriously, at 107 (suggesting that how much an interpretation fits is not an issue of political philosophy); *see also* Dworkin, Taking Rights Seriously, at 67–68 (perhaps suggesting that there are aspects of institutional support that do not depend on issues of normative political philosophy).

moral reason for favoring proposition A over proposition B is not itself a reason provided by law practices, since it is independent of law practices. If this argument is right, my argument for the role of value facts does not support a role like that captured by R—one in which there is room for value facts to favor one legal proposition over another independently of law practices. (Again, however, the point is only that this paper's argument does not support such a role for value facts, not that such a role is necessarily illegitimate.)

In sum, even if value X were morality, it would not follow that the most morally justified model would be legally correct, and even a morally justified model would not guarantee morally good legal requirements. It is no part of the role of value argued for in this chapter that the goodness of a proposition ipso facto counts in favor of the proposition's truth. The role of value is in determining the relevance of law practices to the content of the law.

VII. Conclusion

I have argued that law practices, understood in a way that excludes value facts, cannot themselves determine the content of the law. Different models of the contribution of practices to the content of the law would make it the case that different legal propositions were true, and a body of law practices cannot unilaterally determine which model is correct. In order for there to be determinate legal requirements, the content of the law must also depend on facts about value.

What is the role of such value facts? I have suggested that they support some models over others—that is, they help to determine which features of law practices matter and how they matter. It is not that the goodness of a candidate legal proposition counts in favor of its truth. Rather, the role of value is in helping to determine how practices contribute to the content of the law. This chapter does not attempt conclusively to rule out the view that the needed legal value facts are internal to law. I have argued, however, that the proponent of such a view must overcome significant obstacles to explain how internal legal value facts could be independent of both law practices and genuine value facts. The chapter also suggests a way forward: We can ask what the nature and source of legal value facts must be in order for law to have its central features, for example, for a legal system to be able to provide certain kinds of reasons for action.

11

Hartian Positivism and Normative Facts:
How Facts Make Law II

Mark Greenberg

I. Introduction

In *How Facts Make Law* and other recent papers,[1] I argue that a full constitutive account of the content of the law—of *legal facts*—must appeal to normative facts. The project of *HFML* is to defend this position without assuming that legal facts are themselves normative facts. The argument's engine is a requirement that a constitutive account of legal facts must meet. According to this *rational-relation requirement*,[2] it is not enough for a constitutive account of legal facts to specify non-legal facts that modally determine the legal facts. The constitutive determinants of legal facts must provide reasons for the obtaining of the legal facts (in a sense of "reason" that I develop). In *HFML*,[3] I argue that non-normative, contingent *facts—descriptive* facts, for short—do not provide such reasons without normative facts.[4]

In the present paper, I focus on the rational-relation requirement. I deploy it in three related projects. First, I respond to a family of objections that challenge me to explain why normative facts and descriptive facts together are better placed to provide reasons for legal facts than descriptive facts alone.[5] A unifying theme of

---

[1] M. Greenberg, *How Facts Make Law*, *supra* Chapter 10 [hereinafter *HFML*]. *See also* M. Greenberg, *Reasons Without Values?*, *in* 2 SOCIAL, POLITICAL, AND LEGAL PHILOSOPHY (E. Villanueva ed. in press 2006); Mark Greenberg, *On Practices and the Law*, 12 LEGAL THEORY (in press 2006).

[2] In *HFML*, *id.*, I use the term *rational-relation doctrine*. For elaboration, *see infra* text accompanying notes 12–19.   [3] *HFML, supra* note 1.

[4] This paper was written substantially later than *HFML*, and my terminology has shifted slightly. I use the term "normative facts" here in the way that I used "value facts" in *HFML*. Thus, I use the term to include what are sometimes called "evaluative facts" such as facts about what is good or bad. For further explanation of the notion of a normative fact, *see HFML, supra* note 1, note 22. I explain another minor terminological shift in *infra* note 8 and accompanying text.

[5] I am particularly grateful to Gideon Rosen for his written comments on *HFML* for the Exploring Law's Empire conference held at Princeton University in September 2004. In this paper, I

the objections is that explanations have to stop somewhere; descriptive facts, it is suggested, are no worse a stopping place than normative facts. For example, one objection maintains that if we need a reason why descriptive facts have a particular bearing on the legal facts, we need a reason why normative facts do so. Another claims that any account of law will have to rely on some kind of brute fact about law—in particular, one that can serve a bridge principle linking non-legal facts and legal facts. If a Hartian account of legal facts requires a bridge principle linking officials' dispositions and attitudes to legal facts, a normative account of legal facts will require a bridge principle linking normative facts to legal facts.

Rather than considering such objections in the abstract, I consider an interlocutor who uses the objections to defend a Hartian account of law.[6] I choose a Hartian account because it is the most influential version of legal positivism. The second main project of the paper, accordingly, is to use the rational-relation requirement to show why a Hartian account of law fails.

Thirdly, I spell out a consequence of the rational-relation requirement: if an account of what, at the most basic level,[7] determines legal facts is true in *any* possible legal system, it is true in all possible legal systems. For example, if a Hartian account of legal facts is true in any possible legal system, it is true in all possible legal systems. I use this *all-or-nothing result* in my critique of a Hartian account, but the result is of interest in its own right. For example, a familiar strategy for legal positivists is to argue that because Ronald Dworkin's arguments against legal positivism rely on features of the U.S. and U.K. legal systems, those arguments cannot establish conclusions about all possible legal systems; in particular, they cannot rule out the possibility of a Hartian legal system. My all-or-nothing result makes this positivist strategy unavailable.

---

draw especially on his clear and powerful formulation of the objection. *See* G. Rosen, Comments on Mark Greenberg, *How Facts Make Law* (unpublished manuscript, on file with author). Others who have raised versions of the objection include Scott Hershovitz, Tom Nagel, Ram Neta, Ori Simchen, and Enrique Villanueva. I would like to thank Scott Hershovitz, Herb Morris, Ram Neta, Keemin Ngiam, Seana Shiffrin, David Sosa, and Nicos Stavropoulos for comments on a draft. I am indebted to Scott Shapiro for many valuable discussions. I'm especially grateful to Scott Hershovitz for encouraging me to write this paper and for creating this volume.

[6] I say "a Hartian account" rather than "Hart's account" because I try to address the most powerful and plausible version of a position in the neighborhood of Hart's, rather than to be faithful to the details of Hart's own view. I will largely ignore questions of exegesis of Hart.

[7] The point of the qualification "at the most basic level" is to exclude determinants of the legal facts the relevance of which depends on the contingent facts of the legal system—on, to use a term defined in the text two paragraphs below, *the law practices* of the legal system. As I explain in *HFML*, law practices have an impact on the contribution of law practices to the content of the law. But in order to satisfy the rational-relation requirement, there have to be additional determinants of the legal facts, independent of the law practices. *See HFML*, Sections IV–V. These determinants are the ones "at the most basic level." For example, inclusive legal positivists think that normative facts can be constitutive determinants of legal facts because of the dispositions and attitudes of legal officials. According to inclusive legal positivism, therefore, the role of normative facts is not at the most basic level. The ultimate issue in *HFML* and the present paper is whether normative facts must be among the most basic constitutive determinants of the content of the law. *See HFML, supra* note 1. I will usually omit the qualification "at the most basic level."

It is important that the all-or-nothing result does not depend on the ultimate conclusion that a constitutive account of legal facts must appeal to normative facts, but follows immediately from the rational-relation requirement. (After all, my ultimate conclusion obviously implies that a Hartian legal system is not possible.) The rational-relation requirement is a relatively weak premise, which, I claim, most legal theorists implicitly accept. It therefore may be surprising that it rules out an ecumenical position according to which some possible legal systems are Hartian and some are not.

A bit of terminology will be helpful. A *legal fact*[8] is a true legal proposition—a fact about the content of the law. That contracts for the sale of land must be in writing is a legal fact in many legal systems. *Law-determining practices*, or *law practices* for short, are ordinary empirical facts (paradigmatically, facts about the sayings and doings of members of constitutional assemblies, legislatures, courts, and administrative agencies) that are determinants of the content of the law. I call the relevant facts "law-determining practices" rather than "legal decisions" because the term "decisions" tends to suggest judicial decisions in particular.[9]

A *model of the contribution of law practices to the content of the law*—or, for short, *a model*—is a (putative) way in which law practices contribute to the content of the law. A model is thus the metaphysical counterpart of a method of interpretation. For example, a Hartian rule of recognition (understood as constitutive of legal facts rather than as a way of identifying legal facts) is a candidate model. The *correct* model (in a given legal system at a given time) is the way in which law practices actually contribute to the content of the law (in the legal system at that time), not merely the way in which they are taken to do so. Note that correctness is therefore *legal* correctness, not, for example, moral rightness.

In the next section (Section II), I lay out the structure of the argument of *HFML*. In Section III, I give a brief account of why a Hartian account of legal facts fails to satisfy the rational-relation requirement. In Section IV, I show that a Hartian account requires it to be true *in all possible legal systems* that acceptance of a rule of recognition by officials makes that rule the correct model for the legal system. In Section V, I use this result to undermine an appeal to Hartian intuitions. Our reflective understanding of law does not support the Hartian position that acceptance of a

---

[8] In *HFML*, I use the uglier term "legal-content fact." *HFML, supra* note 1, at 226.

[9] For ease of exposition, I use legal-content-laden terms, such as "legislature" and "court" in characterizing law practices. Strictly speaking, however, the law practices should be understood to be the underlying descriptive facts in virtue of which the relevant legal-content facts obtain. Since legal facts are not basic, there must be non-legal facts that constitute the legal-content-laden practices. These more basic facts will include descriptive facts—the facts that I am calling "law practices." For example, the fact that a legislature enacted a statute must hold in virtue of complex descriptive facts about people's attitudes and behavior and perhaps also normative facts. (If, in order to account for legal-content-laden practices, we have to appeal not merely to descriptive facts but also to normative facts, so much the worse for the positivist thesis that the content of the law depends only on descriptive facts.) The convenience of talking as if law practices consisted in legal-content-laden facts about the behavior of legislatures, courts, and so on should not obscure the fact that there must be more basic facts in virtue of which the legal facts obtain. For elaboration of the notion of a law practice, *see HFML, supra* note 1, Section II.C.

rule of recognition by officials makes that rule the correct model for the legal system. Section VI shows that an account that appeals to normative facts does not run into the problems faced by the Hartian account. I conclude in Section VII.

II. The Argument of *How Facts Make Law*

This section sketches the structure of the argument of *HFML*. It will be helpful to present the argument in a slightly different form from that in which it appears in *HFML*.

The position for which I argue in *HFML* can be described as follows: in any legal system that has a certain three features, a full account of what determines[10] the content of the law will make reference to normative facts.

The three features are captured by the following premises:

(1) Every legal fact is determined in part by law practices.

(2) There are many legal facts.[11]

(3) Every legal fact is rationally determined by non-legal facts.

I think that these three premises are true in many contemporary legal systems, including those of the United States and the United Kingdom. Proposition (3) is the crucial one. The notion of rational determination is explained in *HFML*.[12] In brief, a full constitutive account of the legal facts must do more than specify constitutive determinants that modally determine the legal facts; the constitutive determinants must constitute *reasons* why the legal facts obtain. Reasons, in the relevant sense, are considerations that make the explanandum intelligible in rational terms, as opposed to, say, emotional or aesthetic ones.[13] In other words, the relation between the constitutive determinants and the legal facts must be rationally intelligible.[14] This is the rational-relation requirement mentioned in the Introduction.

---

[10] I use "determination" ("determines," "determinants," etc.) for constitutive, rather than modal, determination. (When I mean modal determination, I will be explicit.) Thus, from the fact that the Y facts supervene on the X facts (or the X facts *fix* the Y facts), it does not follow that the X facts are the only constitutive determinants of the Y facts (or even that they are constitutive determinants of the Y facts at all). For more on constitutive and modal determination, *see* M. Greenberg, *A New Map of Theories of Mental Content: Constitutive Accounts and Normative Theories*, 15 PHILOSOPHICAL ISSUES 299 (2005).

[11] The point of this premise is to ensure that the conclusion (6), *see infra* 271, is not merely vacuously true.

[12] *HFML, supra* note 1, 231–234. For elaboration, *see also* Greenberg, *On Practices and the Law, supra* note 1.   [13] *See HFML, supra* note 1, at 227–228, 231–234, 237–240.

[14] *See HFML, supra* note 1, at 231–232. We could dramatize this point by saying that a full constitutive account of legal facts must do more than specify the mapping or function from non-legal facts to legal facts. It has to specify considerations that make it intelligible in rational terms why a particular function is the operative one. But this way of characterizing the rational-relation requirement should not be understood to suggest that there are two fundamentally different kinds of constitutive determinants—first-order determinants that are the arguments of the function and second-order determinants that explain the function from first-order determinants to legal facts. *See infra* text accompanying notes 21–22 and note 57 and accompanying text.

Because of the rational-relation requirement, rational determination contrasts sharply with constitutive determination in general. For in general, it is an open possibility that the best we can do to explain why certain facts of a target domain obtain is to specify the mapping or function from determining facts to target facts. The determining facts need not provide reasons for the target facts. In *HFML*, I use esthetic facts as an example.[15] Arguably, the facts about the arrangement of paint on a canvas need not provide reasons for the esthetic facts that they determine. A small difference in the arrangement of paint might make a clumsy scene elegant, without providing a reason for the difference. In contrast, it cannot be a brute fact that, say, a particular change in the wording of a statute would have a particular impact on the legal facts.

Before completing the summary of the argument's structure, I want to make three clarificatory points about the rational-relation requirement. First, the rational-relation requirement is only a necessary, not a sufficient, condition on the determinants of the legal facts. It is therefore possible that a fact (or sets of facts) could satisfy the rational-relation requirement, but not be a constitutive determinant of the legal facts.

Secondly, I am sometimes asked whether putative or perceived (normative) facts that turn out not to be facts at all could satisfy the rational-relation requirement.[16] We must, of course, distinguish between beliefs (or facts about beliefs) and the propositions that are believed. The present issue is not whether (false) beliefs about normative matters (or the fact that people have those beliefs) could satisfy the rational-relation requirement. That someone has a certain belief, whatever its content, and whether it is true or false, is an ordinary empirical fact, not a putative normative one. In *HFML*, I consider and reject the idea that beliefs about normative matters can substitute for normative facts in a constitutive account of legal facts.[17]

A putative fact that turns out not to be a fact is merely a false proposition. Consider, for example, the proposition that morality requires that commands issued by members of a particular family have a particular impact on the law. Could this false normative proposition provide a reason of the requisite sort? I am inclined to give a negative answer, but it is not necessary to resolve the question. Only facts can be constitutive determinants of facts. For it is the obtaining of a fact or facts that makes it the case that another fact obtains. In the case of a false proposition, there is nothing to do the metaphysical work. Hence, the important point is that even if a false normative proposition could satisfy the rational-relation requirement, it could not be a determinant of a legal fact.

Before turning to the third clarificatory point, I want to note a consequence of the second one. Positivists cannot retreat to a position that concedes that

---

[15] *See HFML, supra* note 1, at 227–228. *See also* Greenberg, *On Practices and the Law, supra* note 1.   [16] Thanks to Seana Shiffrin for pushing me to address this point.
[17] *See HFML, supra* note 1, at 252.

what are taken to be normative facts are needed to satisfy the rational-relation requirement. The imagined positivist strategy would be to maintain that *merely putative* normative facts can provide rational intelligibility, which is consistent with the positivist view that normative facts need not be among the determinants of legal facts. As noted, however, only real facts can be constitutive determinants of anything. Hence, once it is conceded that putative normative facts are needed to satisfy the rational-relation requirement, it follows that (real, not merely putative) normative facts must be among the determinants of the content of the law.

Thirdly, the rational-relation requirement is not a requirement that the legal facts be shown to be good or valuable.[18] I express the requirement by saying that the determining facts must provide reasons for the legal facts, but as noted above, a reason in the relevant sense is a consideration that accounts for an explanandum in rational terms, not a justification. In general, as I explain in *HFML*, non-normative considerations can constitute such reasons.

The point is important because otherwise positivists could not accept the rational-relation requirement. The strategy of the argument is to use the rational-relation requirement, which I claim most legal theorists implicitly accept, to argue for the controversial conclusion that normative facts must be determinants of legal facts. One can accept the rational-relation requirement, while taking it to be an open question whether non-normative facts could themselves provide reasons for the obtaining of legal facts—and indeed whether normative and non-normative facts together could do so.

In *HFML*, I sketch some reasons for believing that (3) is true,[19] at least in the U.S. and U.K. legal systems and perhaps in all legal systems,[20] though I do not attempt anything like a full defense of that position. I also suggest that most legal theorists implicitly take for granted that (3) is true in the legal systems with which they are concerned.

In fact, I am not especially concerned with the question of whether (3) is true in all possible legal systems. Throughout this paper, I will simply assume that (3) is true in the legal systems with which we are concerned, and I will omit any qualification to that effect. Readers who believe that (3) is true only in some legal systems can understand my arguments as applicable only to those legal systems.

In *HFML*,[21] I argue that:

(4) The law practices cannot themselves rationally determine any legal facts.

I will not repeat that argument here. The basic problem with law practices is that there are many possible ways in which they could bear on the legal facts, and they cannot determine their own relevance. For this reason, I sometimes express the rational-relation requirement by saying that there have to be reasons that determine

---

[18] *See HFML, supra* note 1, at 232–233.   [19] *See HFML, supra* note 1, at 237–240.
[20] To be more precise, all those in which the legal facts are determined by law practices.
[21] *See HFML, supra* note 1, Section IV.

the contribution of law practices to the legal facts. This way of putting things should not mislead us into thinking that the rational-relation requirement is a requirement not only that there be reasons for the legal facts, but that there be reasons that explain why those reasons are reasons. That line of thought could suggest that an explanatory regress lurks.[22] But saying that there have to be reasons for the contribution of law practices to the legal facts is just an intuitive way of summarizing why law practices by themselves do not provide reasons for legal facts. What the rational-relation requirement demands is not higher-order reasons, but determining facts that together provide reasons for the legal facts.

From (3) and (4), it follows that:

(5) Something other than the law practices is among the determinants of the legal facts.

The objections that I want to consider in this paper accept (3), (4), and therefore (5). But they deny that I can reach the conclusion:

(6) The legal facts are in part determined by normative facts.

So for purposes of this paper, we can assume (1)–(5).

III. Hartian Dispositions

Hart provides the most influential account of how non-normative facts determine legal facts.[23] In this section, I explore how that account fares with respect to the rational-relation requirement.

The existence of a rule of recognition does the main work in Hart's account. Although Hart would not put the point this way, on Hart's account, a model of how law practices contribute to the content of the law is legally correct in virtue of the existence of a rule of recognition specifying that model. Hart's account of what makes it the case that a rule of recognition exists is an application of his "practice theory" of rules.

According to the practice theory, a "social rule" is constituted by certain attitudes and dispositions.[24] We can call these dispositions and attitudes *Hartian dispositions*, and, following Hart's terminology, we can say that people who have such dispositions for a particular rule *accept* that rule.[25] The notion of Hartian

---

[22] I discuss below the idea that if normative facts are needed to explain the relevance of law practices, an infinite regress is generated. *See infra* Section VI, especially note 57.

[23] H. L. A. HART, THE CONCEPT OF LAW (2d ed. 1994).

[24] We can avoid the issue of what proportion of the people in a community need to have the appropriate attitudes and dispositions because my criticisms of the Hartian approach will not depend on that issue. When discussing examples, I therefore assume that all or the great majority of the relevant people—in particular, the officials of a legal system—have the attitudes and dispositions.

[25] Because it avoids grammatical awkwardness, I will often use the "Hartian dispositions" terminology rather than talking of "acceptance" of a rule.

dispositions is relative to some rule, so we can talk of Hartian dispositions *for* a given rule, or acceptance *of* a given rule. Given a rule R, for people to have Hartian dispositions for R is for them to regularly act in accordance with R, to regard R as the standard by which to guide their future conduct, to be disposed to criticize or apply other kinds of social pressure to others who fail to follow R (or threaten to do so), and to regard such criticism as justified.[26] (For convenience, I will sometimes use the term "social rule," but I prefer "Hartian dispositions" because using the term "social rule" may lead us to slip into thinking that we have established the existence of something more explanatorily substantial than the specified set of dispositions and attitudes.)

Now, the canonical form of a Hartian social rule is that one is to Φ, where Φing is taking certain action under certain circumstances. For example, Hart mentions the social rule that one is to take off one's hat in church.[27] By contrast, a typical formulation of a rule of recognition specifies what counts as law. Hart gives the example of a rule of recognition that specifies that "what the Queen in Parliament enacts is law."[28] If we took such formulations of rules of recognition seriously, rules of recognition would not fit into Hart's practice theory of rules. For that theory has nothing to say about rules that do not specify a course of action.

Hart simply proceeds on the assumption that the Hartian dispositions for a rule of recognition are what they would be if the rule were specified in terms of what standards an official *is to apply* in dealing with matters that come before her in her official capacity, rather than in terms of what *is* law.[29] That assumption is necessary for the practice theory of rules to yield Hart's account of law. (One way to put the point is to say that the rule of recognition described as "what the Queen in Parliament enacts is law" is more properly stated as "what the Queen in Parliament enacts is to be applied in deciding matters that come before an official." As long as we are aware of the point, however, there will be no harm in following Hart in informally formulating rules of recognition as specifications of what standards are law.)

For example, consider R1, according to which the plain meaning of whatever Rex pronounces is law (and if what Rex pronounces lacks a plain meaning, it has no effect on the law). On Hart's account, for R1 to exist is for the officials to decide

---

[26] *See* HART, *supra* note 23, at 55–61, 255. Let us ignore any difficulties about the indeterminacy of the rule for which officials have Hartian dispositions. If there are any such difficulties, they are problems for the Hartian, not for me. For present purposes, I propose to give the Hartian the strongest possible case by simply assuming that people's Hartian dispositions uniquely determine, in the way that Hart suggested, a particular rule.   [27] *Id.* at 55–57, 109.

[28] *Id.* at 107.

[29] *Id.* at 100–110. In his account of what constitutes a rule of recognition in a contemporary legal system, Hart attributes a limited role to citizens who are not officials. *Id.* at 60–61. As it does not affect the substance of the argument, I will omit reference to citizens in what follows. Thanks to Scott Shapiro for help in formulating the assumption described in the text.

cases according to the plain meaning of whatever Rex pronounces, to criticize other officials if they fail to decide cases in that way, and so on. In other words, for R1 to exist is, roughly speaking, for the officials to treat R1 as the correct model.

Suppose that the officials of a legal system accept R1. And suppose that Rex has made only one pronouncement on the subject of foie gras, a pronouncement the plain meaning of which is that the production of foie gras is prohibited. A Hartian will now claim that the officials' acceptance of R1 plus the fact of Rex's pronouncement make it a legal fact that the production of foie gras is prohibited.

It will be important in what follows that, on Hart's account, what makes something a legal rule (other than the rule of recognition) is not that people have Hartian dispositions for that rule. In our example, the law prohibits the production of foie gras even if people lack Hartian dispositions for the rule that one is not to produce foie gras. On Hart's account, what makes a standard law is not that it is accepted, but that it is identified by an accepted rule.[30]

Given (3) (the rational determination premise), the non-legal facts have to make rationally intelligible the obtaining of the legal fact that the law prohibits the production of foie gras. It may be claimed that the officials' Hartian dispositions and Rex's pronouncement together satisfy this requirement. Is this claim correct?

The facts about the officials' Hartian dispositions are part of the law practices—they are just more of the ordinary empirical facts about the attitudes and behavior of various people that determine the content of the law. But by (4), law practices cannot themselves rationally determine the legal facts. As I argue in *HFML*,[31] the problem is that ordinary empirical facts cannot determine their own relevance to the legal facts.

Without repeating the arguments for (4), I will say very briefly why Hartian dispositions in particular seem inadequate to satisfy the rational-relation requirement. Officials have Hartian dispositions for a rule that requires them to apply certain standards. The Hartian needs this fact to explain why the standards are law. The problem is that it is not clear why we should think that Hartian dispositions for a rule have this significance. As a general matter—outside the legal arena—a case has not been made that Hartian dispositions have explanatory potency. For example, Hartian dispositions for a rule do not in general make the rule binding on anyone or provide *any* reason for acting in accordance with the rule.[32] There are practices or organizations in which there are Hartian dispositions for rules requiring people to haze new recruits, to sell children into sexual slavery, and to use violence to extract "protection money" from shops. It does not follow that these rules obtain or are binding on anyone in any non-trivial sense.

---

[30] *See* HART, *supra* note 23, at 100–110, 256. Hart also suggest that, in addition to the rule of recognition, "certain important legal rules" are social rules. *Id.* at 256.

[31] *HFML, supra* note 1, at 178–185.

[32] For fuller discussion of essentially this point, see Greenberg, *On Practices and the Law, supra* note 1.

The Hartian will likely respond that what is at issue is not whether the rule of recognition is morally or all-things-considered binding or even whether there are any (non-legal) reasons to act in accordance with it. Rather, the issue is simply whether the rule is *legally* authoritative. According to this line of argument, Hartian dispositions for a rule of recognition make it legally authoritative not because of some general truth about Hartian dispositions, but because of some truth specific to the legal case.

Consider, for example, Joseph Raz's account of "why it is true that parliamentary legislation is binding on the courts:"

> The answer is that this is so because of the practice of the courts which follow a rule to that effect and because the rules practised by the courts of a legal system are rules of that system according to the doctrine of identity.[33]

Raz sees that the practice of the courts—their Hartian dispositions—by itself is not an explanation. The "doctrine of identity"—a special truth about how things are with law—is needed to complete the account. In the next two sections, we will turn to the possibility that the Hartian could appeal to a truth specific to the legal case.

It might be thought that there is an alternative to an appeal to a truth specific to the legal case. A Hartian could argue that there is a realm that is broader than and encompasses the legal domain in which acceptance of a rule of recognition has the impact that the Hartian claims it has in the legal domain. One suggestion would be that the relevant realm includes anything that is socially constructed. But this suggestion is a non-starter. What makes something a celebration, a book, a kitchen, or a fashion statement is not the acceptance of a rule of recognition.

A somewhat more promising suggestion would be that we should consider rules of practices (including organizations, games, and so on). Notice, first, that the Hartian cannot claim that ordinary legal rules are an instance of Hartian social rules. As noted above, by the Hartian's own account, the existence of a social rule S is constituted by Hartian dispositions for S, *not* by officials having Hartian dispositions for a rule of recognition requiring officials to apply S. The Hartian needs not a domain of Hartian social rules, but a domain in which acceptance of a rule of recognition by officials charged with applying primary standards makes the standards it specifies rules of the practice (regardless of whether there are Hartian dispositions for those standards).[34] Call a domain that has this feature *Hartian*. Many familiar social practices, such as etiquette, are obviously not Hartian since they have no equivalent to legal officials, let alone to the acceptance by officials of a rule of recognition.

---

[33] J. Raz, The Authority of Law 68 (1979).

[34] Hart maintains that in order for a legal system to exist, it is also necessary that the primary rules specified in the rule of recognition must generally be obeyed. But there need be no Hartian dispositions for those rules. *See* Hart, *supra* note 23, at 116–117, 256.

There has been no serious attempt to pursue this approach to defending the Hartian account of law. Rather than pursuing it here, I will simply register a few comments about the task facing the Hartian who would take this route. First, there is no obvious reason why an attempt to show that there is a domain of practices that is Hartian would fare any better than an attempt to show directly that law is Hartian. (Indeed, Hart himself does not seem to recognize the possibility of practices outside the legal domain in which acceptance of a rule of recognition makes the standards it specifies rules of the practice.) Secondly, even if it were shown that there is a Hartian domain, it would require further work to establish both that law is a member of that domain, and that a legal norm is an instance of a rule of a practice.

Finally, it would not be sufficient for the positivist to show that there are *some* practices that are Hartian. As a preliminary matter, note that it is consistent with my argument that there be some such instances. In the legal domain, constitutive determination is rational determination. That is the source of the rational-relation requirement. But it may be that in the case of some practices, the rules are not rationally determined.[35] In such cases, there will be no requirement that the practices make the rules rationally intelligible. The correct model can be determined arbitrarily, so it can be determined by Hartian dispositions, by normative facts, or in any other way.

The Hartian seeks a non-legal truth that will help to explain the claimed role of Hartian dispositions. If some practices are Hartian and some are not, that may well be because they are members of a domain in which the determination of correctness can be arbitrary. In that case, however, the practices that happen to be Hartian are no evidence of an explanatory truth that could help the Hartian. (This is not to say that the Hartian needs an absolutely general truth. It might be enough if there were an explanatorily significant class of practices—one that forms a social kind—that is Hartian.)

In sum, the approach of identifying a Hartian domain, developing an account of it, and showing that that account can explain the legal case seems more daunting (and less developed) than the more direct approach of appealing to a specifically legal truth. In this paper, at any rate, I focus on the latter approach.

I close this section with a preliminary indication of why an account that appeals to normative facts in addition to law practices is not vulnerable to the problems that we have identified with respect to the Hartian account. We should begin by saying something about the kind of normative facts that are at issue. The relevant normative facts are facts about the bearing of law practices on our legal obligations (or on other aspects of the legal facts). An example might be that fairness supports a statute's contributing its plain meaning to the

---

[35] *See HFML, supra* note 1, at 229.

content of the law. Or that democratic reasons cut against a judicial decision's being able to create a standard that goes beyond what is necessary for resolution of the dispute before the court.

We noted that Hartian dispositions are just more law practices, and thus subject to the arguments of *HFML* regarding why law practices cannot themselves provide reasons for the legal facts. Unlike Hartian dispositions, normative facts are not part of the law practices.[36] More substantively, the normative facts in question seem to be just the sort of fact that, with law practices, could explain in rational terms the obtaining of particular legal facts. Suppose fairness and democracy favor plain meaning over all other models of the bearing of statutes on the content of the law. On the face of it, that normative fact is the kind of thing that could supplement facts about statutory language to yield an explanation of legal facts. I will have more to say about this point in Section V below.

At this stage, we have reason to think that normative facts and law practices together are not in the same position as law practices alone with respect to the rational-relation requirement. It is therefore not open to an objector simply to insist that if law practices cannot satisfy the explanatory demand, neither can normative facts and law practices together. In the next two sections, after developing the Hartian's position, we will take a closer look at strategies a Hartian might pursue to argue that the Hartian account can satisfy the rational-relation requirement.

IV. Hartian Bridge Principles

We mentioned in the previous section the possibility that there are fundamental truths about law that enable the Hartian to meet the rational-relation requirement. For the Hartian positivist, the natural candidate for such a truth is something along the following lines:

> (7) For any rule R (that specifies that standards with certain features are law),[37] officials' Hartian dispositions for R make it the case that a legal system's law practices contribute to the content of the law in accordance with R and only in accordance with R (and if officials do not have Hartian dispositions for any such rule, then there are no legal facts).

Proposition (7) is in effect a bridge principle, one that takes us from ordinary empirical facts—law practices—to legal facts. (7), along with facts about Hartian dispositions and other law practices of a legal system, is supposed to make rationally intelligible the legal facts of the system.

Before we examine whether (7) (or some similar bridge principle) can play the role it is introduced to play, we need to become clearer about (7)'s scope. Is it a claim about all possible legal systems or merely about some legal systems?

---

[36] *See HFML, supra* note 1, at 235–236.

[37] On the proper formulation of rules of recognition, see *supra* text accompanying notes 27–29.

Let us use the term *Hartian legal system* for a legal system in which Hartian dispositions for a rule of recognition make that rule the correct model for the legal system (and in which that is the only way in which the correct model can be determined). It is tempting for the Hartian to rest on the claim that a Hartian legal system is at least *possible*.[38] I want to raise the stakes by arguing that a bridge principle, such as (7), has to be true in *all* possible legal systems in order for it to be true of any legal system. If I am correct, it is not an option to retreat to the mere possibility of a Hartian legal system—it's all or nothing.

A. Hartianism: All or Nothing

Suppose that there are some possible legal systems in which (7) is false. The question at issue in this subsection is whether there can be any legal system in which (7) is true. Suppose, for purposes of *reductio*, that there is such a system, which we can call H (for Hartian).

In H, the correct model is the rule of recognition for which the officials have Hartian dispositions. Call this model M. According to the rational-relation requirement, the determinants of the legal facts have to provide reasons for the legal facts. So the determinants have to provide reasons that explain why M is the correct model in H. There has to be more to those reasons than the facts about the Hartian dispositions of the legal officials. By our initial assumption, there are legal systems in which Hartian dispositions for a rule do not make that rule the correct model. In other words, there are legal systems in which, even if the officials accepted M, it would not be the correct model. Therefore, if the correctness of M in H is not to be arbitrary, there has to be a reason why the Hartian dispositions are operative in H, but not in those other legal systems—i.e. why H is Hartian.

If it is not to be a brute fact about H that it is Hartian, H must have some property X in virtue of which it is Hartian.[39] It follows that (7) is not true in

---

[38] Rosen says: "One need not go all the way with Hart to think that it lies in the very nature of legal systems that *one way* for a legal system to be in place is for Hart's conditions to be satisfied." Rosen, *supra* note 5, at 6. This remark need not be understood to suggest that some legal systems could be Hartian and others not. The remark seems to recognize that it would have to be a general truth about law—"in the very nature of legal systems"—that Hartian dispositions for a rule of recognition can make a model correct. Perhaps the possibility Rosen has in mind is that Hartian dispositions for a rule are sufficient to make that rule the correct model in any possible legal system, but if officials do not have Hartian dispositions for any rule of recognition, there are other ways for a model to be correct. This possibility is consistent with there being a (disjunctive) principle about how legal facts are determined that is true in all possible legal systems.

[39] Could it simply be a brute fact *about a particular legal system* (as opposed to about the law or all possible legal systems) that it is Hartian, i.e. that there are no other facts about the legal system in virtue of which the system's being Hartian can be explained? The rational-relation requirement rules out the possibility of a brute fact about a particular legal system. Accepting the possibility of such a fact is tantamount to accepting that it can be arbitrary which model is correct. Notice that if it could be a brute fact that a particular legal system was Hartian, two legal systems could be identical in every respect, except that one was Hartian and one was not. Two such legal systems would be empirically indistinguishable; they would not differ even in the participants' dispositions, beliefs, and utterances.

H. Hartian dispositions for a rule R are not sufficient to make it the case that R is the correct model in H. Part of the explanation is that H has property X. The supposition that (7) was true in H, but not in all possible legal systems has led to a contradiction. Hence (7) is true in all possible legal systems or in none.

The foregoing argument does not exclude the possibility that in some legal systems, acceptance of a rule makes it the correct model, while in other legal systems it does not.[40] It is just that there will have to be some property, X, in virtue of which a given legal system falls in the former category. The full constitutive account of the legal facts in legal systems in the former category will not be the Hartian account because it will have to make reference to X. (And if the account is to be a positivist one, X will have to be a non-normative property.)

Moreover, the revised account—the one that makes reference to X—will be true in all possible legal systems. For if it were not, then there could be a legal system with property X, but in which Hartian dispositions for a given rule fail to make that rule the correct model for the legal system. But in that case, X is not the property that makes Hartian dispositions operative, after all.

The point generalizes to any account of what, independent of the law practices, determines the correct model of the contribution of law practices to the content of the law. A full constitutive account of the legal facts in a particular legal system A must specify some principle P that is independent of the law practices of A and that, with those law practices, explains the legal facts.[41] Suppose there is a legal system B in which P is not true. In B, the legal facts can be different from those of A in a way that is not explained by differences in the law practices. For example, identical law practices would yield different legal facts in A and B. We have a violation of the rational-relation requirement.

Different models can of course be correct in different legal systems. If a principle Q (about the relevance of law practices to the content of the law) is true in A, but not in B, then that principle cannot be the whole story about what, independent of law practices, determines the correct model. In order to satisfy the rational-relation requirement, a constitutive account of the legal facts of A would have to explain why Q is true in A. In other words, we will need a conditional principle whose antecedent includes the condition that the legal system has the critical property that makes Q applicable. The rational-relation requirement ensures that there will be such a property. But the revised principle will be true even in legal systems that do not possess that property. In sum, principles about the relevance of law practices to the content of the law that are not themselves derived from law practices must be true in all possible legal systems.

Hence the participants in two systems would not be distinguished even by their beliefs about whether their own system was Hartian. It would thus be utterly mysterious what made one system Hartian and not another.

[40] Another possibility is the one described in *supra* note 38 that Hartian dispositions are always sufficient to determine legal facts, but that in the absence of such dispositions, there are other alternatives. The argument in the text applies, with appropriate modifications, to that possibility.

[41] *See HFML, supra* note 1, Section IV.

Returning to the Hartian account, we can conclude that, in order to satisfy the rational-relation requirement, the Hartian needs a bridge principle whose scope is all possible legal systems. Since the Hartian holds that (7) is a complete and correct account of legal facts—that there is no property X—we can hereafter take (7) as our candidate bridge principle.[42] The Hartian needs (7) to be true in all possible legal systems. To save words, I will hereinafter understand "(7)" to make the Hartian claim about all possible legal systems.[43]

B. Does the Bridge Principle Enable the Hartian to Satisfy the Rational-relation Requirement?

If (7) could be taken for granted, the Hartian account would satisfy the rational-relation requirement. But taking (7) for granted would blatantly beg the question in favor of Hartian positivists. A main reason for introducing the rational-relation requirement into the debate was precisely in order to make progress in assessing (7) and related propositions. (Indeed, if the Hartian account does not satisfy the rational-relation requirement, we can conclude that (7) cannot be true.)

According to (3), all legal facts must be rationally determined by *non-legal* facts. Now the Hartian might point out that (7) is not a legal fact in our technical sense—that is, it is not part of the content of the law.[44] Instead it is some kind of basic fact *about* law. Hence, the Hartian might argue that (7) is a non-legal fact, which therefore can be counted among the determinants of the legal facts, and need not itself be rationally intelligible in terms of non-legal determinants. The issue, of course, is not whether (7) escapes the precise formulation that (3) gives to the rational-relation requirement, but whether the reasons for believing in the requirement apply with respect to (7).

The idea that motivates (3) is that all legal facts must be susceptible of being made intelligible in terms of facts that are not part of the legal domain.[45] According to this idea, law is fundamentally not only a human creation, but one that is constructed in such a way that the existence of particular legal facts must always be fundamentally intelligible to rational creatures who know all the facts except those that are specially legal. But if there are brute truths[46] about how the law practices contribute to the content of the law, the requirement of rational

---

[42] A positivist who thinks that some property X needs to be added to the specification of the correct bridge principle can substitute the appropriate bridge principle for (7) throughout. My arguments will generally not be affected by the details of the bridge principle.

[43] In other words, the revised version of (7) is as follows: In all possible legal systems, for any rule R (that specifies that standards with certain features are law), officials' Hartian dispositions for R make it the case that a legal system's law practices contribute to the content of the law in accordance with R and only in accordance with R (and if officials do not have Hartian dispositions for any such rule, then there are no legal facts).   [44] *See supra* text accompanying note 8.

[45] *See* HFML, *supra* note 1, 226–227, 231–232, 237–240 *See also* Greenberg, *Reasons Without Values?, supra* note 1; Greenberg, *On Practices and the Law, supra* note 1.

[46] *See, e.g.,* HFML, *supra* note 1, at 227–228.

intelligibility will be respected in name only. To put the point another way, to allow a bridge principle (from non-legal facts to legal facts) to count as a "non-legal fact" would trivialize the requirement that the relation between the non-legal facts and the legal facts be rationally intelligible. Hence, in (3), the phrase "non-legal facts" should be understood to exclude facts about how non-legal facts contribute to the content of the law, even if those facts are not legal facts in our technical sense.

We therefore find ourselves back to the question of whether (7) is rationally intelligible in light of the non-legal facts, which is really just the original question, addressed quickly back in Section III, of whether Hartian dispositions for a rule of recognition R make it intelligible that the legal facts are determined in accordance with R. Now that we have clarified what the Hartian needs—in particular that what has to be rationally intelligible is that the Hartian bridge principle be true in all possible legal systems—I want to address that question at greater length.

The Hartian is in a difficult position in trying to give reasons why Hartian dispositions for a given rule make it the case that law practices contribute to the content of the law in accordance with that rule. In Section III, we raised and set aside the possibility of reasons that are not specifically legal. The present question concerns reasons specific to law.

First, the Hartian cannot appeal to features of particular legal systems to explain the relevance of law practices to the content of the law. The Hartian needs to explain a truth about all possible legal systems. Secondly, empirical induction is not a promising option. As we will see below, whether Hartian dispositions for a rule make it the correct model in a particular legal system is not a straightforward empirical question. Moreover, we will see that the evidence of our own legal system, if anything, cuts against the Hartian. In the next section, I address the possibility that the Hartian could explain (7) by appealing to our reflective understanding of law.

V. Can the Hartian Explain the Bridge Principle by Appealing to Our Reflective Understanding of Law?

In the absence of non-legal reasons for (7), the Hartian will insist that understanding why (7) is true—i.e. grasping the explanatory relevance of Hartian dispositions—is part of understanding the nature of law, as revealed in our intuitions or convictions about what legal systems are possible. No further explanation is needed or could be given.[47]

The Hartian may add a second point—that any account of legal facts will have to appeal to some such brute fact about law, in particular about the way in which

---

[47] Rosen puts the point this way: "The positivist claim is that someone who fails to see the explanatory force of the sociological facts in this sort of case simply fails to understand *what it is for a law to be the law of a given community.*" Rosen, *supra* note 5, at 6.

non-legal determinants of legal facts relate to legal facts. Hence, it cannot be an objection to the Hartian account that it must appeal to a brute fact about law.

As to this second point, I address it in Section VI below. I show that it is not true that an account of legal facts that appeals to normative facts as well as to law practices has to appeal to a brute fact about law. Normative facts make such a specifically legal bridge principle unnecessary.

As to the first point, I want to examine at some length the claim that understanding law requires understanding the explanatory force of Hartian dispositions. To defend this claim, the Hartian appeals to our intuitions about the nature of law. In addition to relying on an alleged intuition that (7) is true in all possible legal systems, the Hartian may argue that a Hartian legal system seems to be possible. In this way, the Hartian may try to turn to her advantage my all-or-nothing result—that, at the most basic level, principles concerning how law practices determine legal facts have to be true in all possible legal systems. That all-or-nothing result implies that if a Hartian legal system is possible, all possible legal systems are Hartian.

Given this dialectical situation, I think it is fair to offer a thought experiment that tries to elicit the intuition that there could be a legal system in which (7) is false. I do not put much store in our ability to divine what legal systems are possible through the kind of thought experiment I offer. For one thing, the all-or-nothing result should make us cautious about the reliability of our judgments about what legal systems are possible. That result puts our intuitions that different kinds of legal systems are possible in sharp competition with each other.

Hence I do not advance my thought experiment as an affirmative argument that a non-Hartian legal system is possible (and therefore that all legal systems must be non-Hartian). Rather, the point is to counter the Hartian's attempt to rely on intuitions about what legal systems are possible.

Consider rule of recognition R2:

> R2: The plain meaning of whatever the tallest person in the country pronounces is law (and if what the tallest person pronounces lacks a plain meaning, it has no effect on the law).

Imagine a legal system in which at time T1 all legal officials have Hartian dispositions with respect to rule R2. That is, every legal official is disposed to apply the plain meaning of whatever the tallest person in the country pronounces, is disposed to criticize others who fail to do so, takes such criticism to be justified, and so on. Suppose that years go by, and at time T2 a local legal theorist, Themis, proposes that the practices of the officials are, and always have been, mistaken. She points out that the wise king Rex I happened to be both very wise and very tall. And she argues that the practice of treating the tallest person's pronouncements as law is best explained as the result of a confusion about whether Rex I's wisdom or height was the relevant criterion. It seems at least *possible* that Themis is correct that the officials' Hartian dispositions for R2 are mistaken, that it is not legally correct to treat whatever the tallest person pronounces as law.

Whether Themis is correct does not depend on whether the other officials come to agree with her. But, to dramatize the story, we can suppose that they do. At time T3, they come to agree not only about the current situation, but that their Hartian dispositions for R2 were mistaken at T1, and have always been mistaken. Isn't it at least *possible* that they are correct? That is, couldn't there be a legal system in which the officials' Hartian dispositions for a rule could turn out to be incorrect?

It might be objected that I have chosen an implausible or silly rule of recognition. But this objection misses the mark. In order for (7) to play the explanatory role it is supposed to play, the merits of the rule of recognition cannot matter. If it is a brute truth about legal systems that Hartian dispositions for a rule of recognition make it the correct model, then the merits of the rule are irrelevant. If, on the contrary, Hartian dispositions for a given rule are effective in making that rule the correct model only when the rule is sufficiently wise or sensible, then a constitutive account of the legal facts that appealed only to (7) and the law practices would be incomplete. A full account would have to make reference to facts about the wisdom or sensibleness of the rule of recognition. Hence, if (7) is to play the explanatory role it is supposed to play—making normative facts unnecessary—the merits of the rule of recognition must be irrelevant. Therefore, in considering whether there could be a legal system in which (7) is not true, it is fair game to consider situations involving silly or bad rules of recognition. Indeed, we need to consider such situations if we are to separate the work that is being done by acceptance of a rule from the work that is being done by the merits of the rule.

Let it not be objected that if the officials come to agree with Themis, they must already have had a disposition inconsistent with Hartian dispositions for R2. This objection is based on a mistake. From the fact that a person can be convinced that doing X is the wrong thing to do, it does not follow that she was not previously disposed to do X. A person's dispositions can change. And, by hypothesis, that is what has happened here. It is part of the description of the original situation that the officials have Hartian dispositions for R2. The fact that they later decide that their dispositions to follow R2 were mistaken, and consequently come to have new dispositions, is consistent with that description.[48]

We should not get too caught up in the details of an example. The issue is simply whether there could be a legal system in which officials' acceptance of a rule is not the final word on how the content of the law derives from statutes, judicial decisions, and other law practices. In such a legal system, judges and other officials could unambiguously accept a particular rule of recognition, but

---

[48] We can also alter the facts to eliminate any worry of the sort addressed in the last paragraph. We can suppose that none of the legal officials who are convinced by Themis at T3 were legal officials at T1—all of those who were legal officials at T1 have died or retired. Moreover, those who were legal officials at T1 would not have been convinced by Themis that their acceptance of R2 was mistaken. In other words, the legal officials at T1 accepted R2, and were not disposed to reconsider that acceptance.

could nonetheless be mistaken. Remember that I am not using the example to argue that such a legal system is possible, but merely to make the limited point that our intuitions do not rule it out.

Setting thought experiments aside, it is worth noting that support for (7) is not to be found in the evidence of our own legal system. One bit of evidence is that it seems to be coherent for a lawyer to challenge any attitudes and dispositions of officials about the correct model, even ones that are common to all officials and have never been questioned.

Another piece of evidence concerns the way in which our discussions of the relevance of law practices to legal facts actually proceed. When a lawyer, judge, or theorist raises questions about what the correct model is, the ensuing discussions typically make reference to value facts. Advocates of particular positions appeal to normative facts—they give reasons why law practices *should* have one impact rather than another. For example, they claim that their positions are more consonant with democratic values, better protect the rights of minorities, will lead to better states of affairs, are fairer, and so on. Dworkin has made this point very powerfully, and I will not rehearse the evidence here.[49] The relevance of this evidence is as follows. If our legal system were Hartian, then barring a widespread misunderstanding, one would expect that debates over the correct model would be resolved exclusively by appeal to facts about the actual attitudes and dispositions of officials. How law practices *should* affect the legal facts would be irrelevant.

A Hartian cannot respond to this evidence by maintaining that officials in our legal system do not accept a rule of recognition. As (2) states, there are many legal facts in our legal system. According to (7), however, without an accepted rule of recognition, there would be no legal facts.

A Hartian might maintain that the explanation of the relevance of normative facts is that officials in our system accept something like the following rule of recognition: statutes, judicial decisions, and other law practices contribute to the content of the law according to the model that is most supported by the relevant values.[50] In other words, the Hartian could argue that our legal system is not one

---

[49] *See* R. Dworkin, Taking Rights Seriously (1977); R. Dworkin, Law's Empire (1986).

[50] Alternatively, the Hartian might argue that the Hartian dispositions of the officials in our system are for the following rule of recognition: statutes, judicial decisions, and other law practices contribute to the content of the law in the way that *the officials believe* is most supported by the relevant values. But notice that the hypothesis in the text is simpler and better accords with what the officials themselves think and do. The officials do not think that the rule is to take law practices to contribute to the law in the way that *the officials believe* is most supported by the relevant values. They think that the rule is to take the law practices to contribute to the law in the way that *is* most supported by the relevant values. For example, officials who know that they are in the minority with respect to some dispute about the correct model do not automatically concede that they are mistaken, as they would if they believed that the rule of recognition was the one described in this footnote. For discussion of a related point, *see* M. Greenberg & H. Litman, *The Meaning of Original Meaning*, 86 Geo. L.J. 569, 608–609 (1998).

in which values are ultimately doing the work—rather, at the most basic level, dispositions to treat normative facts as relevant is what makes them relevant.[51]

It might be thought that this move by the Hartian leaves us with a stalemate. Against this thought, however, I want to point out an asymmetry between the positions. The positivist position is in tension with what the officials themselves believe. In our legal system, when officials appeal to normative facts, they believe that it is those facts, not other officials' dispositions to be guided by those facts, that ultimately matter.[52] An official who appeals to fairness or democracy does not think that fairness or democracy matters because all or most officials think it does.[53] In contrast, the anti-positivist position is in harmony with what the officials believe. This asymmetry supports the view that our legal system is non-Hartian because, other things being equal, a view that does not have the consequence that the officials are systematically wrong about such a fundamental matter is more plausible than a view that does. Again, the point of this brief discussion is not to argue that our legal system is not Hartian, but merely to refute the claim that (7) is part of our reflective understanding of law, including of our own legal system.

In sum, we have little reason to accept the Hartian's claim that our understanding of law includes an understanding that Hartian dispositions yield legal facts in accordance with (7). If that is right, the Hartian needs to provide reasons why (7) is true for all legal systems, and to do so without appeal to normative facts. We remarked on the dimensions of this task in Section III. We can leave it as a challenge to the Hartian.

VI. Is an Appeal to Normative Facts Subject to Parallel Objections?

I have argued that the Hartian account of the contribution of law practices to legal facts does not fare well with respect to the rational-relation requirement. It remains to address the claim that an account that appeals to normative facts in addition to law practices encounters parallel difficulties.

It might be objected, for example, that in order for an account that appeals to normative facts to be complete, a bridge principle, parallel to the Hartian one, will

---

[51] As readers will have noted, we find ourselves in the vicinity of a familiar debate. *See, e.g.* J. Coleman, *Negative and Positive Positivism, in* RONALD DWORKIN AND CONTEMPORARY JURISPRUDENCE 28 (M. Cohen ed., 1984); R. Dworkin, *Reply to Coleman, in* RONALD DWORKIN AND CONTEMPORARY JURISPRUDENCE 252 (M. Cohen ed., 1984). The rational-relation requirement provides a new perspective on the debate. From this perspective, the issue is whether the practices of officials or the normative facts to which they appeal are the reasons that, at the most basic level, explain the legally correct model.

[52] I think this claim is very plausible, but it is an empirical one, and my basis for it is admittedly unsystematic. I will simply assume that it is true in what follows.   [53] *See supra* note 50.

be required. The idea would be something like the following:

> (8) That a legal system's law practices *should* contribute to the law in accordance with a model M makes it the case that they *do* contribute to the law in accordance with M.

(The bridge principle could be refined by specifying how the term "should" is to be understood. For example, only certain values might be relevant.) Such a bridge principle, the objection continues, is no better off than the Hartian bridge principle (7). The normative theorist must either explain a bridge principle like (8) or rely on a brute fact about law.[54]

We have already suggested the core of a response to this objection, however. In Section III above, in criticizing the Hartian account, we observed that facts about Hartian dispositions were simply more law practices. We noticed that these facts would not provide reasons of the needed sort without a truth about the special relevance of Hartian dispositions in the legal domain. The Hartian bridge principle is just a way of formulating the Hartian's claim about the relevance of Hartian dispositions.

We also suggested in Section III that an account of legal facts that appealed to normative facts does not encounter parallel problems. On the face of it, facts about how law practices should contribute to the content of the law make rationally intelligible how the law practices do contribute to the content of the law. We'll examine this claim further in this section.

To put the point another way, the normative facts in question *are*, or serve the function of, a bridge principle. For they are precisely facts about the relevance of law practices to legal obligations, rights, powers, and so on. Here are a few examples, similar to those mentioned above.

> (9) Fairness requires giving some precedential weight even to incorrectly decided previous court decisions.

> (10) Democratic values cut against legislative history's having any impact on the content of the law.

> (11) All things considered, the relevant values support model M over all other models of the bearing of law practices on the content of the law.

It might be objected that to think that these normative facts could serve as bridge principles, explaining the impact of law practices on the legal facts, is to confuse how things should be with how they are. There is an explanatory gap, the objection claims, between the fact that the law practices *should* have a certain impact on the law and their having that impact on the law.

According to one way of understanding this objection, it makes a logical point. The normative facts, with the law practices, do not logically entail the legal facts. Rational determination does not require logical entailment, however.

---

[54] Rosen makes this objection. Rosen, *supra* note 5, at 6.

The determining facts must both modally entail the legal facts and make the obtaining of the legal facts intelligible in rational terms. Logical entailment may be sufficient for rational intelligibility, but it is not necessary. (The inadequacy of facts about Hartian dispositions was *not* that they do not logically entail legal facts.)

The objection that there is a gap between the normative facts and the correct model should instead be understood as challenging whether normative facts are the right sort of material to combine with law practices to provide reasons for legal facts. For example, it might be claimed that the fact that fairness militates in favor of judicial decisions' contributing to the law in a particular way does not provide a reason that they do contribute to the law in that way.

Because what is at stake in the overall argument is precisely whether the content of the law depends on normative facts, it would be question begging for the objector to assume that there is an explanatory gap between normative facts and the correct model on the ground that the content of the law is independent of normative facts. (Equally, it would be question begging for me to assume that the content of the law depends on normative facts.) The relevant question is not, at this stage, the ultimate one of whether the content of the law is or is not independent of normative facts. (If we had the answer to that question, we would not be engaged in the present discussion.) Rather, it is whether normative facts about the bearing of law practices on legal facts are even the right sort of material to provide, along with law practices, reasons for legal facts. To put it crudely, is the fact that it would be fair or democratic or just for law practices to affect the content of the law in a certain way the right kind of fact to make it rationally intelligible that law practices do affect the content of the law in that way?

If we were trying to explain the occurrence of physical events, we might question whether normative facts were the right sort of material. For such explananda, causal explanations are needed, and normative facts will not feature ineliminably in such explanations. Although it was long thought otherwise, in the physical domain, how it would be good for objects to behave is no explanation of how they do behave.

This platitude about causal explanation tells us little about rational intelligibility. In fact, the platitude is consistent with the claim that facts about how it would be good for objects to behave make it rationally intelligible that they behave in that way. (In fact, it is tempting to speculate that part of the explanation of why people long took for granted teleological explanations of occurrences in the physical world is that people expected that the physical world would be susceptible to being made intelligible in rational terms.) For rational intelligibility is neither necessary nor sufficient for causal explanation. On the one hand, the best we can do to explain the occurrence of physical events may be to cite laws or correlations that cannot be made intelligible in rational terms. And, on the other, a putative causal explanation that makes a phenomenon intelligible may be false.

In contrast, the kind of explanation at issue here is not explanation of the occurrence of events, but constitutive explanation—explanation of what makes it the case that a fact of some target domain obtains. It is not a confusion to think that what significance base facts should have for target facts could make intelligible the significance that they actually have.

Donald Davidson's radical interpretation theory of mind provides a useful analogy.[55] Davidson holds that it counts in favor of an overall attribution of beliefs and desires to a person that it makes the person believe and desire what he or she should believe and desire. The basis for this position is not an empirical hypothesis that humans are likely to believe and desire what they should, but a constitutive thesis. Roughly, the thesis is that the constitutive determinants of one's propositional attitudes must make it intelligible that the person has the beliefs and desires they have.

Davidson's account is, of course, controversial, but what is typically thought to be problematic is (among other things) the constitutive role Davidson gives to rational intelligibility, not the claim that normative facts are the right sort of thing to provide such intelligibility.[56]

An objector might concede that normative facts can, with law practices, provide reasons for the legal facts, but insist that we still need an explanation of the normative facts themselves. If the Hartian bridge principle needs an explanation, it might be suggested, so do normative facts.[57]

---

[55] For citations to Davidson and very brief discussion, *see HFML, supra* note 1, at 232 note 18, 238 note 25.

[56] I do not mean to endorse Davidson's account. *See HFML, supra* note 1, at 238 note 25. Also, it might be objected that Davidson's view in the mental case is not parallel to my view of the determination relation in the legal case. According to this objection, what Davidson holds must be intelligible is the *content* of the subject's mental states, not the relation between determining facts and content facts. On a better understanding of Davidson's view—and on the understanding that is useful for our purposes—the best interpretation of a person makes the person intelligible in light of his or her circumstances and behavior. For example, the attribution of a false belief on a particular issue makes the person more intelligible rather than less if the person's only evidence on the issue is misleading.

[57] Some commentators who have made objections in the general neighborhood of the one described in the text have compared their objections to the point of Lewis Carroll's famous dialogue between Achilles and the Tortoise. *See* Lewis Carroll, *What the Tortoise Said to Achilles*, 4 Mind 278 (1895), reprinted in 104 Mind 691 (1995). On a straightforward interpretation of this comparison, I would stand accused of mistakenly treating normative facts as premises rather than inference rules. In other words, the objector's claim would be that normative facts are analogous to inference rules that allow one to move from law practices to legal facts. But this claim, whatever its merits, would be no objection to my position that normative facts must figure in a full constitutive account of legal facts.

The appeal to Lewis Carroll's dialogue is perhaps more of a loose analogy than a direct application. The idea seems to be that if I make an explanatory demand of the sort that makes it necessary to appeal to normative facts, I open up an infinite regress. But this idea is mistaken.

In the text, I argue that normative facts and law practices together, unlike law practices alone, provide the requisite reasons for the law facts. The type of objection that I want to consider here grants this claim, but maintains that the appeal to normative facts generates a further, higher-order explanatory demand. (And the satisfier of that further demand will generate a still higher-order explanatory demand, and so on.)

The answer to this objection is that the rational-relation requirement applies only to *legal* facts. Specific normative facts about the relevance of law practices to legal facts can be explained as the consequence of applying general normative truths to the circumstances of legal systems.[58] For example, we might explain why fairness requires giving some precedential weight even to incorrectly decided previous court decisions by appealing to more general truths about fairness as well as to non-normative facts about the impact of court decisions on people's lives. Whether or not we can explain general normative truths—ones not specifically concerned with legal systems—is not relevant for present purposes. Again, the rational-relation requirement is that legal facts be rationally intelligible in light of non-legal facts. There is no such requirement with respect to non-legal facts.

Hence, an objector who insists that explanations have to stop somewhere may well be correct. But the important point for present purposes is that explanations do not have to stop with legal facts, or facts about how legal facts are determined. And given the rational-relation requirement, they cannot do so.

Finally, an objector might appeal to a thought experiment, parallel to my thought experiment about the legal system with the height-based rule of recognition, to argue that we have little reason to believe that normative facts have a bearing on the correct model in all possible legal systems. Just as I suggested that we can conceive of a non-Hartian legal system, the objector suggests that we can conceive of a legal system in which normative facts are not relevant to the correct model.

This objection gets the dialectical situation wrong. I appealed to the seeming possibility of a non-Hartian legal system only to answer the Hartian's appeal to intuition in support of a brute truth about law. The normative account of legal content does not rely on a brute truth about law, and thus does not need to appeal

There seem to be two ways to develop the infinite-regress objection. According to the first, if a constitutive account of legal facts appeals to normative facts, it will then have to explain the obtaining of the normative facts. This is the objection that I address in the text.

According to the second version of the objection, if a constitutive account of legal facts appeals to normative facts, it will then have to explain the relevance of those normative facts to the legal facts. As noted above, I sometimes express the intuitive inadequacy of law practices as reasons for legal facts by writing that we need facts that explain the relevance of law practices to legal facts. *See supra* note 14 and text accompanying note 22. Similarly, I sometimes write that we need reasons for the mapping from law practices to the content of the law. In using these formulations, I may have misled readers into thinking that the rational-relation requirement is a requirement not only of reasons for the legal facts, but also of reasons for those reasons. The requirement is only that the constitutive determinants of the legal facts together provide reasons for the legal facts.

A constitutive account appeals to normative facts not to satisfy a second-order explanatory requirement, but simply to meet the first-order explanatory requirement that law practices do not meet themselves. It is tempting to express what is missing from an account that appeals only to law practices by saying that we need facts that explain the relevance of the law practices to the content of the law. But, once again, this is simply a way of expressing the requirement that something must supplement the law practices if the constitutive determinants are to provide reasons for the legal facts. If the law practices and the normative facts together provide the requisite reasons for the legal facts, the rational-relation requirement is satisfied.

[58] For a sketch of this picture of normative facts, *see* Greenberg, *On Practices and the Law, supra* note 1, section IV.

to intuitions about what law is. It has been independently defended on the ground that normative facts are the best candidate for what is needed in addition to law practices to satisfy the rational-relation requirement. As pointed out above, we should be skeptical of the reliability of thought experiments about what sorts of legal systems are possible, especially in light of my all-or-nothing result. I have used the rational-relation requirement to argue against a Hartian account. In the face of this argument, thought experiments get no traction.

VII. Conclusion

In this paper, I have argued that normative facts and law practices together are better placed to satisfy the rational-relation requirement than law practices alone, including facts about officials' Hartian dispositions. Normative facts about the relevance of law practices to legal facts provide reasons why law practices have a particular impact on the law, and facts about Hartian dispositions do not. That law practices should have a particular impact on the content of the law makes rationally intelligible that law practices do have that impact. For instance, that it is fair for judicial decisions to have a certain precedential force is a reason why those decisions in fact have that force. The mere fact that officials are disposed to give decisions a certain precedential force does not by itself constitute such a reason.

Adding a purported truth about law, or bridge principle, to the effect that certain attitudes and dispositions of officials have a certain bearing on which model is legally correct does not help. If the officials' attitudes and dispositions do not provide reasons for the legal facts, the bridge principle is itself just a brute fact about law.

By contrast, normative facts avoid the need to appeal to brute facts about law. With law practices, they provide reasons for the legal facts. That it is fair or democratic for statutes or judicial decisions to have a particular impact on the law, combined with facts about the particular statutes and judicial decisions of a legal system, can explain the legal facts. We can sum up in an intuitive way by saying that normative facts explain the relevance of the law practices to the legal facts. But there is no further requirement to explain why the normative facts explain the relevance of the law practices to the content of the law. Strictly speaking, the rational-relation requirement demands only that the constitutive determinants provide reasons for the legal facts.

Along the way, I argued that the rational-relation requirement yields the relatively immediate result that, at the most basic level, legal systems cannot vary with respect to what determines the relevance of law practices to the content of the law. The most basic principles about the relevance of law practices to legal facts—the ones that do not depend on law practices—must be true in all possible legal systems. One can accept this result even if one rejects other parts of my argument for the conclusion that normative facts must figure in a constitutive account of legal facts.

The result has a variety of implications. It implies, for example, that our convictions about what kinds of legal systems are possible cannot all be correct. It therefore should make us dubious about the reliability of such convictions. I mentioned that the result undermines the familiar claim that because Dworkin's arguments depend on properties of the U.S. and U.K. legal systems, those arguments cannot show that Hartian legal systems are not possible. Of course, the result is a double-edged sword. For example, an argument for the proposition that one legal system is Hartian supports the conclusion that all possible legal systems are Hartian.

Response

Ronald Dworkin

There is not space for a detailed comment on all of the essays in this collection so I concentrate on replying to arguments that challenge the views I have defended and say much less about essays that elaborate and deepen those views. This response is therefore very unbalanced, devoting much space to some authors and little to others, but I hope it is not necessary to say that the imbalance does not reflect any opinion about the relative importance of the essays. The essays with which I mainly agree and therefore comment on little stand on their own, and are each an important contribution to legal theory. I am grateful for all the essays, and grateful particularly to Scott Hershovitz for his exemplary choice of writers and his imaginative editing. Justice Breyer's introduction to this collection is also an important contribution to its themes: I am very grateful for his remarks and welcome them as a brief account of his own constitutional philosophy.[1]

Eisgruber

Professor Eisgruber has made an important contribution to constitutional theory through his clear, illuminating and persuasive writings about the structure of a general theory of constitutional adjudication. I agree with almost everything he says here. I agree with his two-part account of the moral reading thesis, and also with his suggestion that the moral reading, so understood, should not seem either innovative or controversial.[2] I also agree that the moral reading, as we both understand it, does not itself dictate how we should interpret particular constitutional phrases or provisions.[3] I further agree that, as he emphasizes, we must defend any particular interpretation through a more general understanding of the point of removing certain issues from the play of majoritarian politics. Constitutional interpretation is not, as he stresses it is not, a matter of retrieving the psychological state of various historical officials and citizens as they wrote, debated and ratified forms of words. It is rather a matter of making sense of what they did by assigning general purposes that both fit their situation and justify their adopting the language they did.

---

[1] For a fuller statement of the latter, see his book, ACTIVE LIBERTY: INTERPRETING OUR DEMOCRATIC CONSTITUTION (2005).　　　[2] *See* R. DWORKIN, FREEDOM'S LAW 3 (1996).

[3] I emphasized this in FREEDOM'S LAW, at 7ff.

Eisgruber believes, however, that my own concern with the virtue of integrity in legislation as well as adjudication counts against my very broad reading of certain provisions of our own Constitution: in particular the equal protection and due process clauses. He suggests that I would have given more effect to the value of integrity by reading these clauses to enjoin fidelity not to equality and fairness in the abstract but rather to "traditional American principles of equality and fairness." These are different instructions, he believes, because the latter requires respect for the actual practices of American history and so would give history a much more important role than I seem to allow it. I disagree: I think that the latter instruction would not encourage but subvert integrity. Indeed it would provide only what I have called bare consistency which I have argued is very different from integrity.[4]

Integrity requires coherence in moral principle and coherence is especially important in constitution-making when the moral principles in play are fundamental. Integrity commands that the nation speak with one voice on such important matters of principle, and it therefore demands that when its historical practices—of racial segregation, for instance—cannot be seen to be consistent with principles elsewhere recognized, those practices must be abandoned. Respect for settled practices has often been urged as a ground for constitutional decisions: that was the basis of the Supreme Court's decision upholding Georgia's ban on homosexual sodomy in *Bowers v. Hardwick*.[5] But the Court has since declared for integrity over settled practice: it has overruled its *Bowers* decision.[6] Constitution-makers can provide integrity in their constitutional protections only by mandating a moral test that allows the community to identify the principles to which it takes itself to be committed even when it recognizes that it has not kept faith with those principles in the past.

In any case, Eisgruber says, my account of constitutional interpretation remains incomplete because I have not given a basis for the moral reading in a more general theory that explains why a nation should embed certain constraints in a constitutional document that can only be amended by a super-majority with super dedication. I meant to offer such a theory in Chapter 1 of *Freedom's Law*, however. I said that that device creates and protects the right kind of democracy. I distinguished between a majoritarian and what I there called a "constitutional" conception of democracy;[7] I argued for the latter and offered that better conception as part of a justification for the moral reading. So I agree with at least a substantial part of the justification for constitutional protection that Eisgruber himself has advanced, which he summarizes in his present essay in these words: "More specifically, I argue that democracy differs from pure majoritarianism, so

---

[4] *See* R. Dworkin, Law's Empire 219–224 (1988).   [5] 487 U.S. 186 (1986).
[6] *Lawrence v. Texas*, 539 U.S. 558 (2003).
[7] I have called the latter a "partnership" conception of democracy in both earlier and later writing. *See* R. Dworkin, Sovereign Virtue: The Theory and Practice of Equality ch. 10 (2000).

that democracy requires solicitude for the rights and interests of minorities as well as majorities."[8] I hope I am right in supposing that we agree not only on the need for a constitutional justification of the kind he describes but also on at least the general form that such a justification should take.

Fleming

Professor Fleming's study of constitutional interpretation is at once subtle, theoretical and practical. He suggests what he believes to be a better architecture for constitutional theory than he finds in my account of a constitutional or partnership democracy. He believes that my argument makes too much depend on the claim that embedded constitutional rights protect democracy properly conceived: he prefers an account that supposes two distinct goals: protecting both deliberative democracy and deliberative autonomy. His formulation might well have the polemical advantages he claims for it.

I think it important, however, to guard against what I believe to be a mistake in political philosophy that Fleming's formulation might encourage, which is to suppose that there are two values at stake in constitutional adjudication—democracy and autonomy—that might conflict, so that the decision whether to protect substantive "privacy" rights, for instance, could turn on which of these two values is taken to be more important. If I am right, that supposed conflict is illusory. The concept of democracy is an interpretive concept: we need to construct a conception of democracy that sets out a recognizable political value. I believe that no conception of democracy satisfies that test unless it respects what Fleming might regard as a distinct autonomy principle: that no one may submit to the judgment of others in matters that he must, out of self-respect, decide for himself. Of course people disagree about which matters those are. But any conception of democracy that is restricted to process alone and ignores this autonomy dimension fails even to state a *pro tanto* or *prima facie* political value. Process without substance only pretends to be a political value. I agree with Fleming that some of my critics do not make the mistake of confusing democracy with mob rule. But they may make the equally important mistake of confusing democracy with fair elections.

Fleming is right that a great many constitutional scholars, including several who would regard themselves as liberals, have taken up the idea that constitutional interpretation is a matter of retrieving the intentions of statesmen who acted early in our constitutional history. He calls these scholars "broad originalists." The trend he describes may be largely a matter of oscillating intellectual fashion. But it is nevertheless important to consider (as not all these scholars do) why and in what way their historical studies are relevant to contemporary adjudication. The explanation

---

[8] Eisgruber, 20.

must confront a crucial distinction between two kinds of intentions that history may uncover: the semantic intentions of the "framers" who wrote and enacted constitutional provisions—what they intended to *say* in using the words they used—and their expectation intentions—what they hoped or expected would be the impact those words would have on constitutional law in concrete cases.

Chief Justice Roberts insisted on the importance of that distinction in his Senate confirmation hearings,[9] and Professor Eisgruber emphasizes it in his contribution to this volume. I have myself insisted on the decisive importance of semantic originalism: it seems crucial to discover what the framers meant to say because that determines what propositions the Constitution expresses. History is of course at the center of that investigation as Eisgruber says. But expectation originalism is a different matter. If the best interpretive reconstruction of the framers' semantic intention concludes that they laid down abstract moral principles rather than their own understandings of what those principles require in concrete cases, then expectation originalism, whether narrow or broad, is beside the point. I agree that my arguments for that conclusion about semantic intention are rough and might be improved by more careful attention to historical sources, though I also bear in mind Justice Jackson's skepticism on that score. Finally, Fleming's advice to "Do as Dworkin says not as Dworkin does" sounds to me very good advice.

Brown

Professor Brown is much too generous in assigning me credit for the enormous improvement in constitutional theory and law that followed the Supreme Court's decision in the *Brown* case. But she has nevertheless written an elegant and dramatic history of that development and in that way contributed to the intellectual as well as legal history of the period. I hope her own faith can be sustained even if, as many fear, the Supreme Court soon leads lawyers through a period of regression. There must be another renaissance of constitutional law around another corner and her spirit will be necessary to its success.

Hurley

Susan Hurley's characteristically imaginative and brilliant essay makes a very important point: that hypothetical cases play an important role in interpretive legal reasoning. The fact that "it goes without saying" that a particular hypothetical

---

[9] *See* my article, *Judge Roberts on Trial*, 52:16 NEW YORK REVIEW OF BOOKS 14 (October 20, 2005).

case would be settled one way or another sharply limits the eligibility of interpretive claims that fit actual settled cases but do not fit what "goes without saying" in that hypothetical case. She uses this insight to deepen the problem posed for integrity by Kenneth Kress.

She also responds effectively to that problem. Kress pointed out that independent judicial decisions that are made between the time of events that give rise to a legal dispute and the judicial resolution of that dispute may affect what resolution is then appropriate. He fears that this phenomenon might produce retrospective application of new law: the intervening decision may change the law so that the dispute is adjudicated under a different legal structure from the structure in which the parties acted. Hurley points out that this can happen, as a result purely of an intervening decision, only when that intervening decision is mistaken, and she adds that it is hardly surprising that a mistaken decision results in retrospective application of new law. That is what happens in the mistaken decision itself and Kress has only pointed out that the mischief is not confined to that decision but infects even a few later decisions that are, in themselves, correct. It is worth pointing out, however, that this later mischief will be avoided if the intervening decision is *very* mistaken: sufficiently mistaken that it can be labeled a mistake in the sense I described in *Taking Rights Seriously*.[10] Mistakes of that character have no gravitational force in future decisions.

Hershovitz

I am grateful to Professor Hershovitz for a sterling account of the connections between the practice of precedent and the political virtue of integrity. I agree with him that though considerations of fairness, efficiency and certainty may contribute to the justification of *stare decisis*, we cannot understand the character and pervasiveness of that practice without seeing, indeed emphasizing, its connections with integrity. He ends his argument by suggesting that though fairness and efficiency do not figure in the argument for integrity, integrity may nevertheless promote those other political virtues in the long run. That is a useful suggestion to explore. In my response to Dale Smith's essay in this volume I say that I regret a suggestion I made in one passage in *Law's Empire* that fairness conflicts with integrity: I should have said only that we cannot appeal to the ideals of political equality to justify our demand for integrity rather than checkerboard compromise in matters of principle. Hershovitz raises the question, however, whether, even so, integrity contributes to political equality on the right conception in the long run

---

[10] R. Dworkin, Taking Rights Seriously ch. 4 (1976).

because political power is more equal when a majority accepts that what it provides for itself it must provide for all.

Smith

Professor Smith has constructed a very careful and challenging review of my ideas about integrity and his review prompts me to correct an important misstatement in my book, *Law's Empire*. I agree substantially with his conclusions about how to understand my complaint about checkerboard statutes, though I would formulate the principles in play somewhat differently than he does. He identifies two distinct principles of integrity: one condemns checkerboard statutes and the other requires coherence among the different departments of a community's law. He thinks it "obvious" that these are different principles, so that my defense of one has no consequences for the other.[11] I think, on the contrary, that only a single principle is needed. I discuss checkerboard statutes (which are very rare) only to illustrate what I thought to be an obvious way of infringing a general principle of coherence. If law must be coherent over great stretches of doctrine, it must surely be coherent within a single statute; if law need not be coherent across doctrine, then why need it be coherent even within a single statute?

Smith also thinks that the best statement of my view about checkerboard statutes requires a distinction between two distinct charges: first, that such statutes unjustly discriminate and, second, that the discrimination cannot be justified by appealing to any "recognizable" principle of justice. Once again I would prefer a single ideal: integrity requires that the community's law be justifiable through a coherent scheme of principle that provides an eligible interpretation of that law. The idea of justification does indeed presuppose that only some explanations can justify. But an adequate justification of a community's political record also presupposes not just a "recognizable" principle but one that would be recognized as a moral principle there, so that it could make sense to attribute that principle to its law-makers. There might be communities organized around astrological principles whose citizens believe that the oddness or evenness of the year of one's birth carries the moral significance that for many of us is carried by rape or danger to a mother's health. But the fact that that would be "recognizable" as moral in some communities hardly makes it eligible as a justification for us.

Smith believes that I have failed to show why integrity, understood as he describes, should characteristically "trump" other political virtues in legislation and adjudication. He notes, first, a frequent objection to my claim that it should: that a community should not adopt an ideal that entails more discrete instances of injustice. I have frequently replied to that objection. There is no reason to think that requiring judges to seek integrity rather than justice in individual cases will in

[11] Smith, 149.

fact produce more discrete unjust decisions in the long run.[12] Smith mainly focuses on another political virtue, however: fairness. He asks why a checkerboard statute, like a statute forbidding abortion only for women born in odd-numbered years, could not be defended as improving political fairness even though it discriminates among women in a way that cannot be justified by any moral principle. Why should fairness be subordinated to integrity in the way I seem to suppose? I argue that a political community is not legitimate unless it shows equal concern for all its members, and that integrity in the community's laws is essential to that equal concern.[13] But, Smith asks, why is fairness, which is the equal distribution of political power, not also a requirement of equal concern? If it is, why is integrity a more important requirement of equal concern than fairness?

These are important questions, and they call for the correction I mentioned. But I will first say how I have answered them in books and articles other than *Law's Empire*. We must try to understand the various central political virtues, like justice, equality, liberty, political fairness, democracy and integrity, holistically so that our account of each can be seen to be drawn from and reinforced by the others.[14] We can describe the concept of procedural fairness in politics in a very abstract way as I did in *Law's Empire*: fairness, I said, "is a matter of finding political procedures—methods of electing officials and making their decisions responsive to the electorate—that distribute political power in the right way."[15] But we must then establish what "the right way" is. I argue that what political fairness requires is not either equality of impact or equality of influence but rather a structure in which no one is denied vote or voice for impermissible reasons.[16] So, once that strict requirement is satisfied, political power should be distributed with an eye to other values. In matters of policy, like decisions about where roads or airports should be built, for instance, it is desirable that benefits and burdens should be spread across the whole community in proportion to numbers and needs. So a majoritarian decision procedure, in which compromises among interests are facilitated, is appropriate provided that that test of fairness is also met. In matters of principle no such requirement holds, and fairness offers no objection to other decision procedures including properly constructed judicial forums.[17]

[12] *See* my reply to Joseph Raz's version of the objection in DWORKIN AND HIS CRITICS 383 (J. Burley ed., 2004).

[13] I should say that Smith states my argument in what I take to be an odd way. He says that integrity is needed so that law can be pervasive, that is, so that law can be extrapolated from recognized explicit doctrine to cover cases unforeseen in that explicit doctrine. I think this puts the point backwards: we need a legal culture in which law is extrapolated in that way in order to secure integrity and equal concern.

[14] *See* my article, *Hart's Postscript and the Character of Political Philosophy*, 24 OXFORD JOURNAL OF LEGAL STUDIES 1 (2004), reprinted in R. DWORKIN, JUSTICE IN ROBES ch 6. (forthcoming 2006).

[15] LAW'S EMPIRE, *supra* note 4, at 164.

[16] *See* SOVEREIGN VIRTUE, *supra* note 7, at chs 4 and 10. *See also* FREEDOM'S LAW, *supra* note 2, at Introduction.

[17] I introduced the distinction between principle and policy in my earlier book, TAKING RIGHTS SERIOUSLY, and explored the implications of the distinction for political fairness in several chapters of that book.

Smith undertook to study only the arguments of *Law's Empire* and I cite other work, published before and after that book, not to criticize his essay but simply to help in responding to the difficulties he raises. The overall structure and central arguments of *Law's Empire* are drawn from the more general arguments elaborated in that other work. I emphasized in that book that integrity has no application to matters of policy, for instance.[18] But some of my remarks in *Law's Empire* were wrong and misleading. I said:

What is the special defect we find in checkerboard solutions? It cannot be a failure in fairness (in our sense of a fair distribution of political power) because checkerboard laws are by hypothesis fairer than either of the two alternatives. Allowing each of the two groups to choose some part of the law of abortion, in proportion to their numbers, is fairer (in our sense) than the winner-take-all scheme our instincts prefer, which denies many people any influence at all over an issue they think desperately important.[19]

I made these remarks to show that integrity, which condemns checkerboard statutes, is a political virtue distinct from political fairness. I could and should have said only that fairness provides no argument *against* checkerboard statutes. Since nothing in the way in which the checkerboard abortion law I imagined is produced is necessarily unfair, we cannot explain our rejection of such laws by appealing to political fairness. It was unnecessary for me to add the further, mistaken claim that fairness properly understood is advanced by such a statute or that integrity and fairness so understood conflict. My argument for recognizing integrity as a distinct virtue is in no way weakened by withdrawing that claim. I am grateful to Smith for helping me to see and correct this mistake. But once the mistake is corrected, and the argument of *Law's Empire* made fully coherent with my more general arguments in that book and elsewhere, his challenges to integrity are all met.

Waldron

Jeremy Waldron has long been among the most astute legal philosophers. I am grateful for his illuminating discussion here of what some writers have claimed to be an important difference between my "early" and "later" suggestions about the structure of law and legal reasoning. They believe that Hart and other positivists answered my early arguments but have not so far responded effectively to my later ones.[20] I agree with Waldron that the supposed difference between these two stages of my work is largely illusory.

In this essay he resurrects a question I thought dead years ago. There is a radically skeptical tradition in law: it surfaces cyclically. In the 1970s a group of legal

---

[18] Law's Empire, *supra* note 4, at 221.   [19] Law's Empire, *supra* note 4, at 179.
[20] I discuss this claim in ch 8 of my book Justice in Robes, *supra* note 14.

theorists whom Waldron calls "Crits" argued, much in the fashion of the legal "realists" of decades earlier, that American and other mature legal systems are fissured with "contradictions" so that any attempt to discover unifying principles cannot succeed. I believe that judges should seek integrity in law and Waldron asks whether I have ever answered the Crits' claim that this is a pointless search. He cites, as a powerful example of the Crits' argument, Duncan Kennedy's thesis that Anglo-American law exhibits a deep schizophrenia. There are contradictory altruistic and individualistic strains in the law, Kennedy says, just as there are in particular people's individual moral commitments, and these cannot be reconciled by any higher order principle that orders or integrates them. This thesis poses a great danger, Waldron believes, to my claim that a search for integrity in a political community's law is required to carry forward that community's commitment to equal concern. He describes this danger as a dilemma. My thesis that judges can construct successful interpretations of their community's legal practices is plausible only if I suppose that a justifying scheme of principle—say an altruistic scheme—can count as a successful interpretation of a community's law even though it fits at best only half of the legal material it claims to interpret. But if I do weaken my account of interpretation in that way, then I can no longer claim that interpretation is a method of identifying that community commitment of principle.

It is crucial, in assessing this challenge, accurately to describe the kind of contradiction in legal materials that Waldron supposes the Crits to have demonstrated in, say, American law. Kennedy argues that in different stages of American legal history one or the other of his two supposedly contradictory strains, individualism or altruism, was dominant in the American legal culture.[21] As we shall see, it is unclear what that claim means. But in any case no contradiction between what the law permits or requires in different historical stages of a community's culture can pose any difficulty for a contemporary judge seeking integrity within contemporary law. A judge may find integrity across the law that the community now enforces even though that law is strikingly different from what was enforced a century or more earlier. So Waldron must suppose that the Crits have established more than an historical claim: that they have shown contradiction in the American community's contemporary legal practice. But Waldron offers no examples at all of the conflicts he supposes endemic in that practice—perhaps he thinks conflict so apparent that no examples are needed—so we must construct our own example.

A judge must decide whether a defendant who broke a contract may be ordered to perform as agreed or whether he may be held liable only for the economic damages the plaintiff actually suffered in consequence of the breach. The judge distinguishes two justifying schemes. Scheme A, which he calls an "individualist" scheme, emphasizes the rationality of permitting "efficient" breaches of contract, that is,

---

[21] *See* D. Kennedy, *Form and Substance in Private Law Adjudication*, 89 HARV. L. REV. 1685, 1725ff. (1976) [hereinafter, *Kennedy, Form and Substance*].

breaches that improve the economic position of the breaching party without damaging the economic position of the other party. Scheme B, which he calls an "altruistic" scheme, emphasizes instead the moral importance of people keeping their promises. Now distinguish between two kinds of interpretive situation the judge might confront. He might find, first, that both schemes "fit" all the pertinent precedent cases in his jurisdiction in the following sense: a judge guided by either Scheme A or Scheme B would have declared exactly the verdicts, given the facts in each case, that the judges actually declared in all the precedent cases. (Perhaps the plaintiff in each of these cases had originally demanded only economic damages so that a judge guided by Scheme B would have concluded that the plaintiff had waived his right that the contract actually be enforced.) So the judge in the fresh case, in which the plaintiff does demand performance, cannot say that either the "individualistic" or the "altruistic" scheme fits the legal material better than the other. He must find some other way to adjudicate between the two schemes. I shall call this a case of "rival" eligible interpretations.

Or the judge might find, second, that neither Scheme A nor Scheme B fits any more than one half of the pertinent precedent cases in his jurisdiction. The plaintiff had demanded specific performance in all the cases: in half that demand was denied, in half it was sustained, and there were no pertinent differences in the facts of any of these cases that made it distinguishable from the judge's new case. Since a scheme of principle cannot be said to represent a commitment of the community if it was rejected in as many cases as it was accepted, neither scheme provides integrity and the judge must find some other basis for his decision. I shall call this a case of "no" eligible interpretation.

Waldron does not suggest, as I read his essay, that integrity would be a false goal if American law were shot through with rival-eligible-interpretation situations. He is explicit that it is no-eligible-interpretation situations that he had in mind: the schematic structure of conflict he offers as paradigm is explicitly such a case. I agree that if no-eligible-interpretation situations were systemic in American law the pursuit of integrity there would be silly. But as I said, Waldron offers no examples to support his supposition that this situation is pervasive in American law. He apparently relies on Kennedy to support the supposition, but his reliance is very much misplaced because, so far as I can see, Kennedy does not even claim, let alone try to illustrate, an endemic no-eligible-interpretation situation in American law. He does not claim even a single case of such a situation.

Kennedy says that "individualism" and "altruism" are rival ideologies that cannot be combined in a rational overall scheme that combines elements of both. He agrees that most people have elements of each in their moral personalities, but he suggests that this produces not any kind of amalgamation of the two but only a moral schizophrenia within us all. These are very implausible claims and Kennedy's account of the two values does not sustain them. He believes that "liberals" are dominated by "individualism" and "communitarians" by altruism. Contemporary political philosophy shows his mistake. Utilitarianism is the most altruistic of influential political theories: it supposes that people have a basic duty to count the welfare of others as equally important to their own welfare in identifying moral and political principles. But it has provided the impetus for political ideologies, including some forms of economic rationality, that Kennedy counts as "individualistic" instead. More explicitly liberal political theories insist on individual rights to liberty that communitarians reject but also insist on egalitarian goals that communitarians also reject.[22] These various accounts of justice claim to do what Kennedy declares impossible: they offer a principled basis for recognizing both individual rights and shared obligations of economic social justice not as some Procrustean compromise but as flowing from more basic ideals of liberty and equality. Nothing in Kennedy's writings offers to show that the more sophisticated integration of those values fails. Waldron is right that Critical Legal Studies is now, as he puts it, "moribund." That is in good part because its claimed foundations in philosophy proved to be very fragile indeed.

We may put that broad criticism aside now, however, and assume that Kennedy's account of individualism and altruism as two wholly incompatible mind-sets is persuasive. We must then notice that he claims, explicitly and repeatedly, that each of the two ideologies could justify almost all of the law in the sense I indicated earlier: law-makers moved even wholly by one or the other might have produced the very law that we have. Here are representative qualifications of his claim that the ideologies he names clash:

> When we set out to analyze an action, and especially a judicial opinion, it is only rarely possible to make a direct inference from the rhetoric employed to the real motives or ideals that animate the judge. And it is even harder to characterize outcomes than it is personalities or opinions. It will almost always be possible to argue that, if we look hard at its actual effects on significant aspects of the real world, a particular decision will further both altruist and individualist values, or neither. I will therefore avoid talking about "altruistic outcomes" as much as possible.[23]

> Although individualism and altruism can be reduced neither to facts nor to logic, although they cannot be used with any degree of consistency to characterize personalities or opinions or the outcomes of lawsuits, they may nevertheless be helpful to this enterprise.[24]

What enterprise? That is very far from clear, but here is Kennedy's direct answer. "The ultimate goal is to break down the sense that legal argument is autonomous from moral, economic, and political discourse in general."[25] I don't know who ever had that "sense"; I doubt Waldron means to suggest that I do.

So Waldron is wrong to appeal to Kennedy to support his own claim that contemporary American law is shot through with no-eligible-interpretation conflicts. Kennedy argues at most that it is shot through with rival-eligible-interpretation conflicts: that each body of law can be seen as representing the dominance of one

---

[22] *See, e.g.,* J. RAWLS, A THEORY OF JUSTICE (1971), and my book, SOVEREIGN VIRTUE, *supra* note 7. [23] *Kennedy, Form and Substance,* at 1723.
[24] *Kennedy, Form and Substance,* at 1724. [25] *Id.*

or the other of his two ideologies. I would reject that latter claim—it is plainly flawed if, as I believe, Kennedy has failed to state any ideology that could justify any decision at all. But I need not pursue that claim because, as I said, Waldron does not suppose that rival-eligible-conflict would produce the dilemma he poses for integrity.

How might he show that no-eligible-interpretation is pervasive? He accepts that any statement that the law is shot through with contradiction must be the product of—not something antecedent to—interpretation. What interpretive strategy could yield that formidable result? In my illustration I supposed that the no-eligible-interpretation requires showing that Schemes A and B each fit no more that half the interpretive data of past judicial decisions in the sense I described. A law-maker guided by either would impose the verdict of only those past decisions, given the facts the precedents presented, and would reject the verdict of the other half. That seems very unlikely in any jurisdiction with even a weak system of precedent: at least sufficiently unlikely to call for some examples to show that it is nevertheless the case. Any appellate decision holding that specific performance may not be ordered in a certain type of contract case would overrule and remove from the interpretive data set previous cases of that type ordering that remedy.

It may be, however, that Waldron contemplates a less dramatic kind of no-eligible-interpretation conflict. He may have in mind a situation in which only Scheme A fits in that way a settled practice of denying specific performance in contract cases but only Scheme B fits a settled practice of allowing punitive damages in breach of contract cases. That is also very unlikely, however, because contradiction between doctrine in areas of law so closely interconnected would almost certainly also be eroded by the practices of precedent and academic criticism and restatement. Perhaps Waldron has in mind conflict between areas of law much more widely separated: that contract law is inconsistent with Scheme A but tort law is inconsistent with any denial of Scheme A, for instance. But once again that would need careful illustration. It would also require making good a very ambitious claim: that no theory of why tort and contract should differ can justify that doctrinal distinction between the two domains.

Of course I cannot demonstrate that no conflicts of these kinds can be found. I must await actual supposed examples. However, Waldron adopts an entirely differ-ent strategy than I just described: he offers to show that no-eligible-interpretation situations are more common than I suppose not by widening the areas of doctrine that an interpretation is asked to justify but by widening the data set that an inter-pretation must confront within each area. He says that a scheme of principle is not a successful interpretation of a single past judicial decision, even if a law-maker guided by that scheme would have ordered exactly the verdict it imposed on the facts it presented, unless the scheme also fits the reasoning of the judge's opinion that accompanied the decision. Even if all the precedent cases refused to award specific performance as a contract remedy, Scheme A would fit only those decisions accompanied by opinions in which a judge declared principles that the interpreter regarded as "individualistic" principles of economic rationality; it would not fit those other decisions in which the judge cited concern for the situation of people forced to keep their word. This further argument rests on two assumptions: first, that our legal record would be full of no-eligible-interpretation doctrine if an interpretation were required to fit what the judge said as well as what he did and, second, that legal interpretation should include that requirement.

The first assumption is not compelling; certainly not in the absence of any examples offered to confirm it. True, the legal culture changes over time: what was once regarded as the principled basis of some established rule of law gives way to a different and more contemporary basis even though the rule itself is retained. Many ancient common law rules are now thought justified by considerations very different from the reasons why judges originally declared those rules. But Waldron's interpretive strategy would presumably require interpretation to fit only expressions of opinion in the most contemporary decisions enforcing an old rule. The situation is different for old statutes because these do not require any contemporary restatement for their force. A contemporary Congress might disown the principles that inspired Social Security in the New Deal. But Waldron, sensibly, does not insist that his strategy be applied to statutes.

His second assumption is more interesting, however, and we should consider it independently. Waldron says that I would not (and should not) reject the need for an interpretation of judicial decisions to fit opinions as well as verdicts.[26] The "would not" is wrong: I have several times explicitly rejected that requirement,[27] and I have often taken Cardozo's opinion in *MacPherson v. Buick Motor Company*, which rejected it, as a paradigm of legal interpretation.[28] What about the "should not"? Waldron says that if I rejected the requirement that interpretations must fit opinions I would be embracing the legal "realism" of such writers as Jerome Frank. Frank wrote in the era of obsession with Freudian explanations of absolutely everything, and he championed a Freudian explanation of judicial reasoning. But surely one can believe that legal interpretation is not hostage to judicial opinions without also believing that such opinions are only rationalization of Oedipal lusts.

As I tried to explain in *Law's Empire*, we must draw our interpretive strategies in law from our sense of the point of integrity. If we suppose, as I do, that this point is to keep faith with a requirement of equal concern then our strategies must emphasize what we as a community *do* to or for people and give only a secondary and derivative place to the reasons different actors in the legal process offer for what we have decided to do. If Waldron disagrees, then that is the true focus of our present disagreement, and he should offer a reason of political morality why judicial opinions should have a more important role in interpretation than legislators' opinions have. I conclude not that I have answered the Crits but that, as I suspected

---

[26] Waldron, 170.
[27] *See, e.g.*, LAW'S EMPIRE, *supra* note 4, at 247–248, 284–285; TAKING RIGHTS SERIOUSLY, *supra* note 10, at chapter 4. [28] 217 N.Y. 382 (1916).

long ago, there is nothing in what they once said for me to answer. We cannot be sure, before we look, that constructive interpretation can produce integrity in any particular area of the law. But we have no reason to think, in advance, that it cannot.

I should comment on one further aspect of Waldron's argument. He imagines that if I were persuaded that no-eligible-interpretation situations are pervasive in law, I would try to rescue the idea of integrity from that debacle by proposing that judges should choose between rival eligible interpretations by adopting the interpretation that best matches their own moral convictions. He says that that strategy would not provide integrity; rather, it would concede that there was no integrity to find. I agree with his conclusion that no-eligible-interpretation cases imperil integrity, as I said. But one objection he makes to the strategy is odd and would also apply to my claim that judges should prefer the morally better interpretation in rival-eligible-interpretation cases.

He says that judges who choose what they regard as the morally best result are only taking sides between parties who themselves disagree about exactly which result is morally best. I hope it is clear, in spite of some of what Waldron says, that in recommending that judges choose on moral grounds I am not assuming that their choice is right because it matches their own convictions. Of course it does. But a choice is right only when—and then only because—those convictions are themselves right. It is nevertheless true, of course, that in choosing they are taking sides about the issue in controversy. How can they not do that? When the law is unclear the judge must in the end take sides about the very issue that divides the litigants: they disagree about what the law requires. Presumably that fact furnishes no objection to the institution of adjudication. In my view what the law is depends, in some cases, on what morality requires. So in taking sides on the former issue, which he must do, a judge necessarily takes sides on the latter as well.

Perry

Professor Perry's discussion of associative obligations and political obligation clarifies important issues and brings significant problems to light. He supposes that if associative obligations are genuine they must arise from practices that have what he calls intrinsic value and he notes that if that is correct then some of my claims about the range of associative obligations—in particular, my claims that unions and college faculties can be the source of such obligations—must be mistaken. I agree that both friendship and close relations with one's family contribute to the value of a life and that this is also true, for at least some people, of political activity. But I am not persuaded that only practices that can be said to be intrinsically rather than instrumentally valuable can be the source of associative obligations. I believe that such obligations can arise when and because people are joined in certain kinds of relationships—typically relations of collaboration or partnership— even when their lives would lack nothing if they were not.

I agree, of course, that normative conditions must be met in order that associative obligations be genuine. People do not have obligations of family, friendship or political responsibility whenever or just because they or their friends, family or fellow citizens think they do: the conditions of special and equal concern that I described and that Perry reviews must be met. But these may be met without supposing that the practice they structure itself has intrinsic value. Perry suggests that my statement of these conditions needs revision because they are not all met even in all the circumstances in which he and I agree that associative obligations arise. I argue, for instance, that the mutual concern that sponsors genuine associative obligations must be both personal and equal; he doubts that these conditions are met in the case of political obligation.

"A general obligation to obey the law," Perry says, "is usually thought to be owed, if to anyone, to the community or state itself rather than to one's fellow citizens considered one by one."[29] My own view is different, however. I believe that the duty is owed not to the collective entity but to its members as individuals. Of course the duty is enforced by a collective entity: it is that state that prosecutes (or, indeed, waives) the duty. But the state acts, in this instance as well as all others, as the agent of the citizens acting through it. The legislation that establishes particular political obligations in a democracy is the creation of the citizens in the same way and it is a condition of ideal democratic legitimacy, in my view, that what these citizens do collectively can be justified as showing equal concern by each for each.

Perry also doubts that the concern that grounds obligations of family is always equal concern. Consider, he suggests, the obligation a parent owes to a new-born child. Perhaps that child will in due course acquire an obligation to care for his parent, but the parent's immediate obligation is nevertheless independent of any prediction that the child will accept that responsibility. But the needed equality of concern is only a background assumption of the practice, not a condition whose realization can be demonstrated in every moment of the relationship. If a responsible adult makes plain his rejection of any concern for his parents, or for the other members of the family, their associative obligations to him are at least attenuated and, if the rejection is sufficiently decisive, ended.

Gardner

I am thoroughly bewildered by John Gardner's contribution to this volume. He argues throughout that I equivocate between accepting and rejecting a variety of propositions to which he attaches Greek letters, but since I cannot understand what any of those propositions means I suspect that I do not so much equivocate about but ignore them. Gardner's main claim is amusingly mischievous: he claims that a careful reading of my book, *Law's Empire*, shows that I am a legal positivist

---

[29] Perry, 191.

after all. But I do not understand his argument for that arresting claim any more than I understand anything else.

My trouble begins—and perhaps ends—with Gardner's breathtakingly promiscuous personifications of law in all his Greek-letter propositions. He spends much of his essay considering whether I embrace the proposition he labels (α): "Law aims to be morally justified". He notices that I have objected to the argumentative use some legal philosophers make of personification.[30] For example, I do not think that Joseph Raz's statement that the law necessarily claims moral authority can be unpacked without making the resulting statement either plainly false or incompatible with Raz's positivist claims.[31] Gardner labels Raz's statement (β) and defends it, so we should pause over his defense before returning to the mysteries of (α). Gardner says that Raz means only that there is no law in a community unless its legal officials claim moral authority for their decisions. I anticipated this reading of Raz, and said that it cannot seriously be thought that whether or not law exists in a particular community depends on the meta-ethical or moral opinions of its officials. Suppose, I asked, the bulk of a community's officials hold the moral views of Oliver Wendell Holmes? Gardner does not accept this counterexample. He concedes that Holmes' "extrajudicial" writings express the view I describe, and he does not cite any judicial writings in which Holmes states any contradictory view. But he asks a series of questions about Holmes' attitudes, expecting the answer "yes." In fact, the best answer to all these questions, taken to be questions about the historical Holmes, is very probably "no." But only one question counts: since Holmes was deeply skeptical of the very idea of moral authority, he would have denied that his judicial opinions have moral authority.

In any case, to rescue Raz, Gardner would need to claim not only that I am wrong about Holmes but that there would not be law in America if most judges came to hold the meta-ethical opinions I ascribed to Holmes, and the implausibility of that suggestion remains. A group of South African judges met in a clandestine conference with officials of the then illegal African National Congress in Britain in the last years of apartheid: these judges made plain that they did not think the law they administered daily had any moral authority. Would Raz or Gardner think that these judges were not legal officials, or that if a great many other South African judges shared their opinion there was no law there?

Gardner's discussion of Raz's claim is mysterious for a further reason, moreover. He says that although Raz means that legal officials claim moral authority his personification is not to be understood as an elliptical statement exhausted by that fact. Though he agrees with me that "it takes a human being to make a moral claim" he adds that "it does not follow that human beings are the only things that

---

[30] I am guilty, I know, of personifying law and much else in the titles of books and articles. I doubt this non-argumentative and harmless personification has played any part in the spate of argumentative personification now popular, but I apologize if it has. I believe that the personifications that figure in my own arguments can all easily be dissolved.

[31] *See supra* note 14, JUSTICE IN ROBES, chapter 7.

make claims. Law makes claims through human beings acting on its behalf." This statement ruins any proposed redemption of Raz's troublesome personification because it simply invokes the personification all over again. Gardner uses "law" presumably to refer either to a set of social practices or to a set of norms of some kind. How can either have a "behalf"? Is Hegel waiting in the wings? Or is there some further dissolution of that further personification that allows Gardner's claim to make sense? Shall we say that it means only that legal officials claim that *legal* requirements (rather than those of some other institution) have moral authority? Then Gardner's further elaboration of Raz's claim is simply redundant.

So I remain perplexed what anyone could think (β) means who supposes that it is true. I have exactly the same problems with Gardner's (α). What can it mean to say that *law* aims to be morally justified? I have argued, in *Law's Empire* and elsewhere, that the concept of law is an interpretive concept, and that lawyers must therefore identify what the law requires or permits on some matter through a process of interpretation that seeks the best available moral justification of the broad legal practices of their community.[32] Is (α) a baroque way of saying the same thing? If so, then of course I accept it. But I doubt that is what Gardner takes (α) to mean, because he says that (α) is entailed by my suggestion that interpreters might sensibly take the practice they are interpreting to have, as its goal, the appropriate regulation of the use of coercive force by the state. I emphasize, throughout *Law's Empire* and elsewhere, that interpreters who begin in that way may sensibly, and certainly without contradiction, adopt very different, more detailed theories of legal interpretation from my own, including a theory very like legal positivism.[33] Should we understand (α) instead in something of the same way Gardner wants us to understand (β), leaving out the Hegel? Then we would have to say that legal officials all reason about what the law is in the way I recommend, which is undoubtedly false, or that they are not really legal officials unless they reason in the way I recommend, which is tempting but I fear overreaching. I cannot assign any sense to (α) that fits what Gardner says about its implications and that is in the least plausible, so I am not surprised that he makes such heavy weather of deciding whether I believe that proposition or not.

What shall we make of Gardner's further proposition (γ): "Law is morally justified"? Does that statement claim that every true proposition of law is morally justified? If so, it is puzzling why Gardner would spend any space pondering whether I accept (γ). Of course I don't. The mystery deepens when he explains that (γ) and (α) contradict one another. His explanation assumes that (γ) means that law is not just always justified but is necessarily justified, so that the contradiction is like the contradiction some (but not all) theologians find in the proposition that God aims to be moral and necessarily is moral. How can one aim to be what one necessarily is? In fact there is no contradiction here if, as Gardner suggests, (α) includes

---

[32] This is only a very rough summary of my account of legal reasoning. For a recent fuller statement, see the Introduction to my recent book, Justice in Robes, *supra* note 14.

[33] *Id.* at chapter 8.

the proposition that no one is a legal official unless he aims at morally justified law. Then the conjunction would mean that those who are legal officials, because they aim to produce justified law, necessarily do produce justified law, which is not a contradiction though it is of course very silly. So either (α) or (γ) must mean something different from what first appears if they are to be, as Gardner insists they are, incompatible. There may be some sense of (γ) such that it is a genuine interpretive question whether I accept it. But I have no idea what that is. In any case, however, my remarks about Nazis, which Gardner quotes, have nothing to do with (γ).[34] I was explaining how we should understand someone who says that the Nazis had no law: we should understand him as denying that their legal arrangements were such as to justify coercion. The undoubted fact that some people sometimes use the sociological concept of law to carry that moral freight doesn't entail that true propositions of law are always or inevitably morally justified. I believe that reading the entire section of *Law's Empire* from which Gardner takes his quotation makes that plain.[35]

Now we come to the supposedly most consequential of the Greek-letter propositions:

> (δ) In any legal system, the law is made up of norms which are part of the law only because some legal official engaged with them, and such an agent is a legal official only because, by engaging with norms in certain ways, he or she can make them part of the law.

I assume that (δ) is meant to state a version of legal positivism.[36] If (δ) is right, I assume, then the proposition that a plaintiff who cannot prove which manufacturer made the drugs that injured her is entitled to market-share damages from them all is false unless and until some judge so rules, because only then has an official "engaged" with that proposition in an appropriate way.[37] So when a judge does declare that proposition, and does award market-share damages, his decision cannot be seen as applying the law but must be treated as making up new law through his "engagement" and applying it retroactively. That is a familiar view among lawyers who call themselves positivists: it is no doubt Gardner's own view. I have argued against it steadily over three decades, repeating my rejection in a great variety of recent publications some of which Gardner cites. Gardner's claim that I actually embrace that view is therefore indeed "striking."[38]

---

[34] Gardner, 217.

[35] *See also* the Introduction to Justice in Robes *supra* note 14. I there distinguish the sociological concept of law which someone uses when he denies that the Nazis had law from the doctrinal concept which Law's Empire mainly explores.

[36] In any case, the formulation plainly needs tidying in various ways. We need to know more about what "engaging" is and we need to take account of the fact that many people—district attorneys, for instance—are legal officials even though no amount of "engaging" by them makes law. Presumably Gardner has or will remedy these obvious defects and I shall ignore them.

[37] See my description of "Sorenson's Case" in *Hart's Postscript and the Character of Political Philosophy, supra* note 14.   [38] Gardner, 220.

Gardner produces this paradox by ignoring everything I have written about interpretation and law since 1986 and instead pursuing a flatteringly close textual analysis of a few lines in *Law's Empire*. However, he misreads these lines in a way that I and other writers had to correct years ago. He fixes on this passage from that book: "Roughly, constructive interpretation is a matter of imposing purpose on an object . . . Creative interpretation, on the constructive view, is a matter of interaction between purpose and object."[39] That is a general description meant to apply to all examples of what I then took to be constructive interpretation: literary interpretation, for example, as well as the interpretation of a variety of social practices. Gardner apparently assumes that when this description is applied to legal interpretation it means that an interpreter begins with something he takes to be a correct statement of the law as it stands—that is, the "object" in question—and then transforms that statement creatively so as to move the law closer to what it ought to be. He "engages" with the existing law that is, in order to produce new and better law. But everything in *Law's Empire* contradicts that reading. The "object" of legal interpretation is a set of practices that include tentatively *taking* certain propositions of law to be true. Imposing purpose on that set of practices means finding a justification for them that is then used to identify which propositions of law, including those with whom no one has previously "engaged," are *in fact* true.

Gardner's mistake can be readily identified by reading the discussion of "Stages of Interpretation" that figures in the same chapter as the passage to which he devotes such attention.[40] There I contrast the "tentative" assumptions about what the law is that are collected at what I call the "pre-interpretive" stage with judgments about what the law "really" is at the "post-interpretive" stage, judgments that may require concluding that some of the tentative assumptions about the law at the earlier stage were "mistakes," that is, not accurate statements of the law as it actually is. This is a process through which, if I am right, lawyers come to recognize the truth about law, not a process in which they create new law to replace what they acknowledge the law already to be. No doubt arguments can be made in defense of legal positivism, though I agree with Scott Shapiro, Jules Coleman and other positivists that these arguments have yet to be made.[41]

I have so far said nothing about the discussion with which Gardner begins his essay: he says I think that law has a unifying aim which is the aim of regulating a political state's use of coercion. He believes he refutes that proposition by imaging law in a community of angels who obey that law unhesitatingly so that coercion is not only never needed but never even contemplated. Surely, he insists, regulating coercion cannot be the aim of law in such an angelic community. He apparently thinks I believe it is a defining test of law that "it" has the aim of regulating

---

[39] Gardner, 219, quoting Law's Empire, *supra* note 4, at 52.
[40] Law's Empire, *supra* note 4, at 65ff.
[41] *See* Justice in Robes, *supra* note 14, at chapter 8.

coercion so that no set of practices that cannot plausibly be said to serve that aim could count as "law." But I was talking about strategies of legal interpretation and therefore about interpreters. I said that it would be helpful if a view about the "point" of law were sufficiently widely accepted in a community so that, as I put it, interpretive arguments could take place "on the plateau it furnishes" and proceed by contrasting different conceptions of how that point is best understood and achieved.[42] I did not say that amenability to that interpretive strategy is a conceptual necessity so that anyone who rejected it would make a conceptual mistake. On the contrary I conceded that there are "theories that challenge rather than elaborate the connection [my suggestion] assumes between law and the justification of coercion."

I certainly did not say, as Gardner apparently believes I did, that this interpretive strategy would be appropriate everywhere we find anything we might be tempted to call law: it would not be appropriate if angels had to interpret God's law of angelic duties. Gardner's misreading is another example of the serious confusion that has been engendered in legal philosophy by a failure to distinguish between the sociological and doctrinal concepts of law. We have great leeway in deciding whether angelic law (or international law or Nazi law) should be called "law." The sociological concept of law in play in those questions is an indeterminate criterial concept: we can give either answer so long as we make plain what point we mean to make. We must not confuse that concept with the doctrinal concept in play when we ask which interpretive strategies are appropriate to deciding what the law of some community really is.[43] My suggestions about the justification of coercion are claims about the right strategy in communities of the kind lawyers are normally called upon to interpret.

Greenberg

Professor Greenberg's essay is admirable in bringing the concepts and argumentative style of metaphysics to bear on traditional issues of jurisprudence. I applaud him for reminding us that legal philosophy is part of general philosophy, not a special insulated compartment of thought with its own distinct questions and methods. I agree, as he notes, with his conclusion that "value facts are among the determinants of the content of the law."[44] But it is worth distinguishing two forms of that claim: (1) value facts figure in the truth conditions of propositions of law; (2) value facts figure in the justification for any theory about the truth conditions of propositions of law. I emphasize the importance of that distinction for jurisprudence in my recent book, *Justice in Robes*.

---

[42] LAW'S EMPIRE, *supra* note 4, at 93.
[43] *See* JUSTICE IN ROBES, *supra* note 14, Introduction and chapter 8.   [44] Greenberg, 225.

In *How Facts Make Law*, Greenberg argues only for proposition (2), and we should therefore notice that the most influential contemporary versions of legal positivism accept (2) and argue only against (1). They argue, for example, that democracy is better served, or that a political community is more efficient, or that authority is better respected, or that citizens are more likely to be critical of their government, if judges accept that moral or other normative claims are not relevant in deciding what the law requires. In that way these "political" positivists appeal to "value facts" at what we might call the jurisprudential level of analysis to show the irrelevance of such facts at the doctrinal level. It is true that some positivists argue against (1) on what they claim to be purely conceptual grounds that are consistent with rejecting (2) as well. I agree with Greenberg that these arguments are mysterious and in any case fail. But my arguments in *Law's Empire* are meant to support (2) as well as (1).

I should add that I agree with Greenberg's interpretation of my own views about the interaction of the dimensions of fit and justification in legal interpretation.[45] As I have tried to explain elsewhere, these dimensions are best understood as each drawn from a political value. I said in *Law's Empire* and elsewhere that the crude "threshold" account of the interaction of the two dimensions was meant only to illustrate the difference between them.[46] However, I am uncertain that Greenberg has located any metaphysical difficulty in that crude account. If we supposed that two interpretations of the legal record fit that record equally well, and decided between them on moral grounds, we would not be treating the legal record as irrelevant to the content of the law. If the record had been different, the better interpretation might not have been available at all.

---

[45] *See* Greenberg, *supra* Chapter 10, notes 46 and 47, and pages 262–63.
[46] *See* DWORKIN AND HIS CRITICS, *supra* note 12.

Index

Lightning Source UK Ltd.
Milton Keynes UK
UKOW05f1158231116
288336UK00006B/165/P